THE ADOPTED CHILD

THE ADOPTED CHILD

Family Life with Double Parenthood

Christa Hoffmann-Riem

Translated from German by
Mike Brookman

With a foreword by
Anselm Strauss

Transaction Publishers
New Brunswick (U.S.A.) and London (U.K.)

Library of Congress Catalog Number: 89-4609
ISBN: 0-88738-241-X
Printed in the United States of America

Library of Congress Cataloging-in-Publication Data

Hoffmann-Riem, Christa.
   [Adoptierte Kind. English]
   The adopted child : family life with double parenthood / Christa
Hoffmann-Riem ; translated from German by Mike Brookman.
      p. cm.
   Translation of: Das adoptierte Kind.
   Bibliography: p.
   Includes index.
   ISBN 0-88738-241-X
   1. Adoption—Germany (West) 2. Children, Adopted—Germany (West)
I. Title.
HV875.58.G3H6413   1989
362.7"34"0943—dc20   89-4609
                                                                CIP

To Wolfgang, Holger, and Martin

Contents

Foreword

Aside from the general excellence of this book, I enthusiastically recommend it to you. There is something in it for several rather different audiences. Its title should immediately alert those readers (both professional and lay) who are concerned with adoption. They will certainly learn something here about the experiences of adopting parents and adopted children. The action is laid in Germany, for the author is a professor of sociology at the University of Hamburg, and her study is about Germans. Her research, as reported here, has been sufficiently important in Germany—and its import is of such general interest—that the editors of Transaction Books have correctly believed an English translation warranted. (The translation is excellent.) I commend them for this, especially because it takes great effort and sometimes considerable diplomacy for social science books to cross to this side of the ocean.

Aside from its specific information about adoption, Christa Hoffmann-Riem's research is both informative and stimulating with regard to some very subtle aspects of the "normal" nuclear family. There are wonderfully rich data bearing both on adoptive and nonadoptive families in the form of case studies and lengthy quotations taken from the interviews. Because these materials were gathered by a type of interview pioneered in Germany and still relatively unknown in the United States, social scientists interested in qualitative methods of research are likely now for the first time to read about, and later cite, this approach to data as used in Hoffmann-Riem's book.

Not just method and data but also theory is a strong point of her presentation: theory bearing on adoption of course, but also on more general sociological issues such as "normality," identity, stigma, secrecy and disclosure, and the relationships between public and private life. (Her own theoretical perspective is a combination of symbolic interactionism, phenomenology, and ethnomethodology, but she makes wide and catholic use of concepts from other traditions.) Of course, anyone interested in Germans and German society will find her materials revealing and her interpretations of them insightful and wise. What I am suggesting is that American readers might also find quite fascinating both the similarities and differences between our respective countries with regard to family life, adoption, child rearing, and identity.

Now, in the brief space of this foreword I will add a few specific points. One of the book's central topics, carefully discussed and analyzed, concerns the matter of secrecy and disclosure—or in technical vocabulary, "closed and open awareness"—with regard to the children's biological or adoptive origins. Whether a child knows it has been adopted, and at what age it learns or is told, proves to be (just as some adoptive experts have asserted) immensely important; but this is also true for the parents. These consequences are linked with how much the child and its adoptive parents actually know or are told, and in what detail and with what accuracy, about the birth parents.

The author uses a number of sociological concepts, either coined or adopted from the sociological literature, when interpreting these and other phenomena. Two central ones of her own coinage are "as-if normalization" and "own-type normalization." (I leave readers who are curious about these to discover their meanings for themselves.) A more transparently meaningful concept is that of "double parenthood." Because I am especially interested in the varied aspects of work, I paid much attention to Hoffmann-Riem's discussion of several types of what I call "biographical work" that I hadn't thought of, or now am stimulated to think more about. Among these are reconstructive work, accounting work, and integrative work.

The study's central method for data gathering and achieving deep analysis is a combination of the "narrative interview," invented and effectively used by Professor Fritz Schuetze (University of Kassel), *and* a biographical analysis, also worked out in detail by him. The interviewee is asked to tell his or her life story (in this instance, the story of the adoptive experiences), and is asked to talk until the entire narrative is told. Then questions are asked by the interviewer about points that seem conflicting, ambiguous, puzzling, and so on, as well as when a point is judged to need more elaboration. In this particular book, portions of the adoptive stories are reproduced in large numbers as data. These function as they always do—to promote our understanding, give us a sense of being "there," and enhance the credibility of the author's interpretations—but they also provide marvelous windows on the experience of the adoptive parents and their adopted children. The American literature on adoption has many such stories, some presented at much greater length, but certainly few books can have offered commentary on them of such analytic depth or clarity.

Out of the vast literature on adoption Professor Hoffmann-Riem herself especially refers to David Kirk, to whose writings she is greatly indebted. However, as she remarks early,* a lot of other studies on adoption proved to be less helpful for her analysis than theoretical studies from quite other fields. She may have underestimated the theoretical quality of the adoption literature (I doubt it), and she surely was not being denigrating in saying so; but it is a measure of the uniqueness and value of her research that she could say this. What was said about her book by another German colleague, to me, was equally instructive. Reading it taught him how basically conservative his countrymen really are, despite the apparently great changes in German society. You need not agree with his conclusion to understand why some German readers may have found the book fascinating, even if reacting subliminally to this aspect of German society. In closing, and returning again to the book's primary subject matter: Reading about adoption we find very good and grounded reasons for an explicit but stylistically subdued reform thrust of Professor Hoffmann-Riem's presentation concerning the matter of early and well-managed disclosure of adoptive identity to the child. But whether secretive or open toward this highly charged issue, adoptive families certainly do shed considerable light, just as the author claims, on the nature of the nonadoptive or so-called normal family.

Anselm Strauss

*see Appendix, ''Theoretical Background.''

Preface

From its planning stage through to its final publication, this study could not have materialized without the support of many "helping hands." The frank and comprehensive narrative accounts of their adoption histories by 30 adoptive parents provided an invaluable foundation for my research. During the course of data evaluation I was constantly aware of the fact that the detailed disclosure of personal experiences not only opens up analytical opportunities for social researchers, but also binds them to a special responsibility for the future use of the information given in confidence. I hope that the adoptive parents concerned feel that the expectations that accompanied their involvement in the study have been fulfilled. I thank them all most sincerely for their collaboration.

The study began as part of an "Empirical Seminar" at the Institute of Sociology at the University of Hamburg (1978). Through their interviews, transcriptions, and first attempts at analytical evaluation, the students there contributed substantially towards making this project a success. Some of them picked up the thread of the seminar for their own research work and furnished insights into the perspective of other persons involved in the adoption triangle. I was glad to be able to fall back on their findings.

Data evaluation was influenced by the many suggestions made during a variety of discussions. First of all, my special thanks go to the Deutsche Forschungsgemeinschaft (German Society for the Promotion of Research) for giving me the opportunity to familiarize myself with the research style of Anselm Strauss (San Francisco) in the autumn of 1979. By being able to actively take part in his research work I learned to appreciate the art of the case comparison approach and its constant remolding in the light of new aspects. This made it easier to clarify the contours of my own data analysis. I owe a special debt of gratitude to Anselm Strauss for his many years of support for my research activities in the field of adoption.

Discussions with Fritz Schütze and Gerhard Riemann also gave me greater certainty with respect to the course of my own evaluation. Their empirical testing and theoretical elaboration of the narrative interview technique formed a major cornerstone for this study. Without the creation of this new instrument of research by Fritz Schütze, a study of adoptive family life-worlds would not have been possible at all in this form.

The data on adoptive family life acquired with the help of a new methodological approach aroused the interest of David Kirk, the pioneer of a genuinely sociological adoption research who today lives in Canada. His interest in my work confirmed my conviction that it is right to organize data evaluation around the concept of normality. I would like to thank David Kirk for all his encouragement. His adoption research findings over the past three decades "framed" my study to a much greater degree than the text may reveal.

The interest shown in the findings of this study since the German edition was first published extends beyond the field of adoption. The topical relevance of the problems facing adoptive families when coping with the differentness of their familial constellation has increased in conjunction with the proliferating social phenomenon of parenthood without consanguineal kinship ties. The interviews presented in this study document the demands made on parents and children faced by "double parenthood." They provide an orientation, for example, for the structuring of stepparental relationships with their inherent double fatherhood, double motherhood, or both. Furthermore, a greater understanding of the adoptee's sense of genealogy restricts the options open to society when fixing legal regulations for the construction of fragmented parenthood through new reproductive technologies (for example, heterological insemination or surrogate mothering). The adoptive family has a clear message to convey in the process of the losing significance of the nuclear family. It affords an insight into the social construction of a family as well as into the persistent relevance of genealogy.

Thanks to the unwavering interest shown by Irving L. Horowitz this study is now accessible to English-speaking readers. Although tremendous goodwill was shown by all persons involved in publication plans for the English version, its organizational realization turned out to be a complex and time-consuming affair. It illustrated just what overcoming the language barrier means for communicating ideas.

I thank the editors of the "Übergänge" series, Richard Grathoff and Bernhard Waldenfels, for their indispensable advice and intermediary assistance. The Fink-Verlag publishing house, in particular Ferdinand Schöningh, deserves special credit for generously ceding me the English-language publication rights. My special gratitude also goes to Inter Nationes for its financial assistance for the translation. In his capacity as sociologist and translator Mike Brookman had the difficult task of rendering a text ranging from the theoretical to the everyday speech level into English. I thank him for the conscientiousness with which he tackled this transmission of meaning. Very special thanks go to Irving L. Horowitz for sticking to the expectations he pinned on my study despite a number of organizational hold-ups along the way.

1

The Desire for a Child

"We Wanted a Child"

The fact that the Federal Republic of Germany has the world's lowest birth rate could be interpreted as an indication of the fact that the child is becoming less significant for the biographical design of the adult role in this society. Narrative interviews with adoptive parents become particularly interesting against this background, because they document the continuingly high significance of the child in the biographical design.[1] The key statement in almost all adoption histories is: "We wanted a child." No aspect of the later phases of the adoption history is expressed with such linguistic uniformity as the desire of the adoptive parents for a child of their own. The two statements, "We wanted a child" and "We wanted to have a child," virtually represent the syntactic sum total in this respect.

Bearing in mind the consequences of this desire in the case of adoption and the "enactment" required to construct a family, the lack of any apparent need to justify the desire for a child is a particularly striking aspect. The statement stands like a monolith in the narration, complemented in some cases by a temporal specification: "It was clear right from the start of our marriage that. . . ." The narrator is apparently convinced that there is no need for any further clarification of the statement. Only one adoptive mother tries to articulate a biographically consistent classification of the desire for a child, prompted by doubts about whether her orientation framework at that time can still be generally upheld today:

ADOPTIVE MOTHER: Maybe young women don't feel the same way today, but I come from a very intact, a very conservative home, and my parents taught me to believe that the key to a woman's happiness is to have children. And, er, that's the way I felt when I married my husband—I was 21. *I married my husband with the intention of having children.*

1

By taking their stance for granted all other narrators demonstrate their unbroken belief in the naturalness of wanting a child. The socializational internalization of generative behavior seems to be so pronounced that the social constitution of the desire for a child is eclipsed and the reproductive norm assumes the status of an absolute value.[2] My contention is that the desire for a child is not available as a "because-motive"[3] to the persons concerned, at least not without psychoanalytical assistance. The desire for a child as the desire for the reestablishment of the mother–child symbiosis experienced at an early age[4] or as the transformation of penis envy[5]—such constructs have no equivalent in the everyday knowledge of the persons involved.

The Start of Marriage within the Framework of the Pattern of Normality

The marital and motivational history preceding the decision to adopt is divided into sequences. With reference to the aspect of normality the sequences pass through the following stages: pattern of normality, deviation from the pattern of normality, and attempt to reconstruct normality.

Most couples enter into marriage in accordance with the aspect of setting up a family.[6] In line with common practice, however, the realization of the desire for a child is postponed until the phase of establishing a household has been completed. As long as conception is intentionally prevented the married couple experiences itself as in harmony with the institutionally prescribed pattern of the family life cycle. The unquestioned or virtually unquestioned belief in the autonomy of action in the field of reproduction also allows the marriage to seem prospectively congruent with one's own concept of normality. Slight doubts about one's own autonomy in this context occasionally find their expression in narration.

ADOPTIVE FATHER: We already—at the beginning of our marriage we already, er, agreed that if one of us, er, well—if both of us are unable to have children of our own, that we would then decide to go for an adoption, didn't we?

Whereas this case reveals a psychological preparation for the alternative access to the constitution of a family, other narratives reveal the initially unchallenged belief in reproductive autonomy. The following is a drastic example:

ADOPTIVE MOTHER: We saw each other and took to each other straight away, and my husband said: "Come on, let's have a whole bunch of kids together," and, er, I felt pretty much the same way . . .
INTERVIEWER: Hm . . .
ADOPTIVE MOTHER: and I said to myself: "Well, that man and little daughters, that's a really nice idea."

The clarity of the motivational anchorage of the desire for a child is reflected in the lack of any doubt about the autonomy of one's action. This, however, creates a crisis potential for the roughly 10 to 15 percent of those married couples in West Germany who remain involuntarily childless.

The Trajectory of Denormalization

Moving on to the second sequence of the marital and motivational history we find the following statement later on in the interview just cited:

ADOPTIVE MOTHER: And then as time passed by our hopes came to nothing.

The specification of the point of transition from the phase of establishing a household to the realization of a family is the step that subsequently takes the couples further and further away from the pattern of normality. The temporal development of this biographical "denormalization" begins with suspicions that initially are merely confirmed by the passing of time. At a certain level of concern the couple seeks medical help in order to realize the plan that was once regarded as autonomously realizable. The suffering endured during medical procedures,[7] the possible make-or-break factor for biographical designs, is reflected in numerous narratives. A sequence of short and by and large temporally connected sentences ("and then I . . . and then I . . . and then I had to . . . and then the doctor said there's only one possibility left") gives an idea of the extent to which the persons concerned feel rushed,[8] particularly the women affected by sterility, which represents the majority of cases.[9]

I would like to set the despairing utilization of all medical possibilities in relation to theses on the evolutionary history of the family. All speculations concerning the institutionalization process of the family work on the basis of the mother–child dyad as the "irreducible nucleus of all forms of family."[10] Knowledge of the fact that "the same blood pulsates"[11] in the mother and in the child or—as Tyrell calls it—"the archaic discovery of kinship"[12] forms the basis of the interpretive process through which a mother and child are regarded as permanently belonging together. The basic structures of the institutionalization of family were completed at a later stage by extending the idea of genealogical links to siblings and the father–child relationship. Via the socialization-induced acceptance of generative behavior as the cultural superimposition of natural and instinctually motivated targets it became possible to constantly renew the man-made institution of the family.[13]

The constitution of a family in this way led to a situation in which the principle according to which parents live together with their own children, the filiation principle, was taken for granted. The conscious perception of this principle, however, paled into insignificance.[14] My assertion is that the narrative interviews with adoptive parents reveal more about the existence of kinship as the "identity of flesh and blood"[15] than is consciously accessible to parents within the framework of the pattern of normality. I therefore extend my analysis beyond just the 30 sets of adoptive parents surveyed and maintain that the special case of adoption has an indicative function for the normal case. The desire to constitute a family as genealogical bonding only then surfaces emphatically if the realization of this desire is confronted by difficulties. It takes the awareness of the lack of reproductive autonomy and the sense of suffering this causes to reveal the extent to which the biologically constituted family has been institutionalized and is firmly embedded in the biographical concept of the normal adult role.

The Decision to Adopt

Following this indirect access to the normal case via the deviant case I turn to the final sequence of the marital and motivational history, the decision to adopt. After medical confirmation of the improbability or—less frequently—impossibility of becoming birth parents, the trajectory of denormalization reaches a point of transformation. At the end of an eventful sequence of sentences reflecting the despairing utilization of all medical possibilities there is a sudden shift from the feeling of being rushed to a new initiative of action: "And then I'd had enough," "and then we'd had enough." This may be followed in the same breath by: "And then we said to ourselves, OK, let's adopt a child."

Adoption as the Unquestioned Next Step

This breakthrough to the alternative constitution of family is often presented as a "quite short decision" which, once taken, is regarded as just as natural as the original desire for a birth child. Statements such as, "There was no choice but to adopt" ignore the possibility of living without children. In many cases the automaticity ascribed to the decision to adopt does not appear to require any justification.[16] The status passage envisioned in the normal biographical design from the childless couple to the family becomes a distinct possibility, albeit no longer by biological means.

The shift in orientation from the birth child to the adoptive child requires the constitution of a new normality, the legitimacy of which is rooted in the realization of the parental role via a centuries-old substitute. In the light of the experience of the lack of one's own reproductive autonomy this substitute, of which the research subjects have always been aware, assumes a new relevance. Beyond a certain point of necessitated reorientation this socially sanctioned alternative ("there's still the possibility of adoption") moves into an interpretational process that makes the attributes of "artificiality" and "second-best choice" less and less significant. I interpret the described brevity and the unquestioned nature of the decision to adopt repeatedly expressed in the interviews as a step through which the adoptive parents indicate the newly established relative naturalness of the alternative to themselves and to others.

Doubts about the Decision to Adopt: Career as an Equivalent?

Some of the 30 interviews deviate from the pattern of "matter-of-fact" presentations by enabling an insight into the way the married couple tackled the adoption plan. I would like to start by singling out the only contrasting case in which adoption was discussed against the background of a possible equivalent. The linearity of the path towards adoption was interrupted in this case by a subjectively satisfying and socially acknowledged occupational activity on the part of the woman.

The example is worth dealing with in greater detail because it shows signs of a socially constructed alternative to having children. The interviews so far could create the impression that, in view of the apparent necessity of the child for the female adult role, this phenomenon should be interpreted biologically. As shown by the cases of voluntary childlessness, however, the decision to have a child is a contingent act. No matter how strongly it is anchored in the contributions of nature, the desire for a child[17] only leads, as it were, automatically to a child because society is able to renew the desire for a child case by case. The chances that this reproductive guidance will succeed are reduced if a woman's role set already appears to be sufficiently complete to guarantee the self-esteem of the woman in her own eyes or in the eyes of others without the role of mother. The birth of a child is not regarded as essential if it is perceived as a risk to a gratifying occupational activity and if uncertainty exists about whether the role of mother can compensate for the gratification losses.

The birth of a child as a loss and not just as an enrichment is dealt with, for example, in an American study on "career women."[18] The intensity of the desire for a child is also still documented in this group, albeit primarily in the form of a conflict-laden consideration of the matter, and ranging to the view that human beings can "transcend nature."

Let us move from this group of occupationally gratified and successful women back to the adoptive mothers. The occupations stated by the overwhelming majority of the women driven into a crisis by childlessness and, finally, into the decision to adopt are occupations to which they themselves attribute a low gratification level. The marked disparity almost always present between the occupational statuses of husband and wife probably induces a further blockade of occupational interests. The provision of security for the women in the middle or upper middle class via the husband's status (in 23 of the 30 cases) relieves them of any financial need to seek occupational activity. The significance of the child for the biographical design of the female adult role thus becomes unmistakably clear.

The contrasting case relates to one of the women in the sample with a college education. She not only rates her occupational activity as satisfactory herself, but is also regarded by others as completely satisfied by her occupation. The phase of weighing a career and having children is reflected in the following interview disclosure by the adoptive mother in response to the question designed to elicit the initial narration.

ADOPTIVE MOTHER: We've both got jobs we enjoy and that leave us more or less completely satisifed. And after it became clear that we couldn't have any children of our own we again did some soul-searching to find out whether we really wanted children. That's when we realized that if we'd had one of our own, as is usually the case in normal families, we wouldn't have bothered asking whether we want them or not. And although there were a lot of people they all [said]: You don't really need to adopt children, not with your jobs and the whole day so full and [laughing] such a full life . . .
ADOPTIVE FATHER: Right.
ADOPTIVE MOTHER: and you're so fulfilled and have really got, er, plenty to do, inwardly and outwardly.

This narrative passage ends at the point that other married couples reach without elucidating the aspect of occupational activity. At this point the contrasting case also leads on to the already mentioned unquestioned next step: the decision to adopt. The episode of hesitation comes to an end:

ADOPTIVE MOTHER: And then we suddenly, er, realized that that's all nonsense; we wanted children, and we definitely wanted children to be a part of our lives and then we said that, er, we also wanted, that we also really wanted children too, . . .
INTERVIEWER: Hm . . .
ADOPTIVE MOTHER: not just our own, we wanted children in our lives.

The Female as the Driving Force behind the Decision to Adopt

An insight into the marital discussion of the adoption plan is also provided by those interviews that present the finally achieved automaticity of the decision to adopt as the result of negotiation or persuasion. A marked structural uniformity emerges: If adoption assumes differing degrees of relevance for the husband and wife in the marital decision-making process, the wife is the first to consider the substitute of family constitution as a serious alternative to her own biographical design and not just as some distant substitute for others. With two exceptions[19] the wife was found to be what was recurrently referred to as the "driving force" in the adoption history in all the interviews in which the topic of initiating or sharing the responsibility of the decision to adopt was mentioned.

The varying developments of the phases in the case of husband and wife is reflected in varying patterns of narrative presentation with sex-specific differentiation. The husband may incorporate his initial hesitation in a legitimatory history that presents him as in the end fully in favor of the project ("As a rule once a decision has been taken I always identify myself with it completely"). Or the wife presents herself as the person who manages the situation ("I psychologically guided my husband through all the various stages"), as was the case in two interviews that could only be conducted with the wife. The organization of the interviews as a matter for the wife can be interpreted in both cases as evidence of a pattern that emerges in many other narrative passages, namely that adoption is primarily regarded as a matter for the wife right from the very first initiative.

The interviews reflect that the child has a greater significance for the accomplishment of the female than for the male adult role.[20] This can only be partly explained by reference to the evolutionary history of the family, instinctual residues, and the mother-infant symbiosis. Especially the child who is not "one's own flesh and blood" indicates the tremendous significance of institutionalized arrangements for the "normal female biography."[21] The material available does not permit conclusive clarification of any correlation between the extent to which the wife contributes to the management of adoption and her causal role in childlessness in specific instances. A great deal, however, would suggest that the initiative of the female as a means of remedying the childlessness she has caused, and as a means of remedying the deviation from the pattern of normality that she has caused,[22] may be able to reflect the intensity of socially prescribed expectations in a particularly striking manner.

Adoption as the Second-Best Solution and Exceptions to the Rule

The thesis of adoption as the second-best solution is valid in the overwhelming majority of cases surveyed. When applying for adoption at least 27 of the 30 adoptive parent couples covered by the sample assumed that they were involuntarily childless or that they would be unable or unlikely to have more children of their own in the future.[23] Although the cases of family construction and family extension differ insignificantly with regard to the "second-best solution" aspect, the two variants are characterized by varying normality goals. Whereas parents with no children at all strive to acquire the parental role as a key component for the realization of their own plan of biographical normality, those who already have children seek to realize their ideas of family normality on the sound basis of an already acquired parental role. The socializational considerations underlying the decision to adopt in the case of family extension represent comparatively subliminal cultural prescripts in comparison with the more obvious elementary significance of the desire for a child in the case of childlessness.

Two cases illustrate how the adoption of a child can serve to ensure the otherwise jeopardized realization of socialization goals by the birth child. In the first case the interview ran as follows:

ADOPTIVE MOTHER: So then we did our best *not* to turn him into a [spoilt] only
   child . . .
INTERVIEWER: Hm, hm . . .
ADOPTIVE MOTHER: and, er, we gradually, now how old was he? Two? . . . Yes,
   that was roughly when we began saying that's no good, so alone . . . and . . .
   in such an unfavorable position, and even if you don't *want* the child gets too
   much attention.
INTERVIEWER: Hm . . .
ADOPTIVE FATHER: Always this relationship between the three of us.
INTERVIEWER: Hm . . .
ADOPTIVE FATHER: We adults always staring down at this tiny little lad and . . .
   that's bound to overwhelm him. And when we went out for a walk we always
   saw couples with, say, twelve-year-old boys, strolling along with mom and
   dad . . . we said Good heavens, that's not the way we want it, . . .
INTERVIEWER: [Laughter]
ADOPTIVE MOTHER: if we're not careful that's what we'll be like later on, no,
   not if we can help it.

In the second case the reasons given by the adoptive father for opting for adoption differ slightly from those narrated by the adoptive mother:

ADOPTIVE FATHER: Well, in my case the, er, reason was clear, that we . . . only
   had this one son, who was clearly disoriented with regard to adults . . .
INTERVIEWER: Hm . . .
ADOPTIVE FATHER: and was developing into an only child, starting to read at
   the age of two and a half—and doing daft things like that—and, er, that was,
   well, disturbing, and, er, that was supposed to become a family, and that's
   why we wanted—at any rate *I* wanted another child.

Whereas these examples clearly reveal the desired normalizing function of the adoptive child as a substitute for another birth child, we will now examine a few examples that may be able to present the thesis of adoption as a second-best solution in a more differentiated light. All these examples have one thing in common: The substitutive character of adoption is veiled by considerations of adoption's intrinsic value.

The Significance of Social Motives. Under the conditions of autonomous self-presentation in the narrative interview a picture emerges that makes no effort to conceal the instrumentalization of the adoptive child for the adoptive parents' own biographical design. Free of altruistic exaggerations, which are probably also generally alien to birth parents in our society, adoption is utilized from a marriage and egocentric perspective. This function of the child in the personal biographical design does not rule out the possibility that action motivated by self-interest can also be accompanied by "altruistic feelings."[24] It should be emphasized, however, that the applicants primarily require the child in order to realize their concept of family. Against the background of the constraints of self-presentation in the adoption procedure, an aspect to be dealt with at a later stage, I regard the instrumentalization of the adoptive child expressed in the interviews as an indication of how narrative constraints lead to the core of action. Instrumentalization is rarely perceived, let alone regarded as in need of justification, in the case of a birth child, whereas it is particularly manifest in the deviant case. It only reveals itself if it clashes with contrary social norms; adoption as a youth welfare service institution, for example, is based on child-centered orientations.

In the majority of cases the unquestioned legitimacy of adoption as an act of self-interest is reflected in the fact that the central statement, "We wanted a child," is simply transformed, once biological difficulties arise, into: "Well, in that case it will have to be an adoptive child." Only a few examples show how the couples have become aware of and tried to justify the aspect of instrumentalization. Legitimation, for example, may be constructed by admitting the missing autonomy of action:

ADOPTIVE FATHER: OK, we didn't tackle the whole thing with the attitude: "We want to pick up a child in a home and do the child a favor," but . . . definitely, er, egotistically, if that's the right word. I personally feel that that's really the best basis too . . . if you adopt a child, at any rate as a completely normal . . . er, as a completely normal person, who has a family, um, and doesn't have to give priority to any social or moral considerations. . . . And we don't feel that strong anyway.

An even more pronounced equation of self-interest with the interest of the child becomes apparent in the following example:

ADOPTIVE MOTHER: Out of pity . . .
ADOPTIVE FATHER: Right.
ADOPTIVE MOTHER: you really can't adopt a child, and . . .
INTERVIEWER: Hm . . .
ADOPTIVE MOTHER: in our case it's a, um . . .
ADOPTIVE FATHER: You could say, vital interest.
ADOPTIVE MOTHER: Right.

And a little later on:

ADOPTIVE MOTHER: In the end the child is bound to notice if the mother plays
    fairy godmother, . . .
INTERVIEWER: Hm . . .
ADOPTIVE MOTHER: both financially and in other respects.
INTERVIEWER: Hm . . .
ADOPTIVE MOTHER: I don't believe that anything would come of that, and you
    have to make sure that *can't happen.*

This is the most striking example of how social motives are explicitly rejected. The instrumentalization of the child, which the couples become aware of against the background of their own biological limitations, is not subjected to a sublimation that might distinguish the altruistic qualities of the construction of an adoptive family from the qualities of the biologically constituted family. On the contrary, following the conscious realization of the parental self-interest not appreciated as a problem in the "normal case," the self-interest motive is also firmly upheld in the case of the artificially constructed family. Pity appears to be an undesirable category for the establishment of any parent–child relationship, including the special case of adoption.

On the continuum between an explicitly ego-centered and an explicitly child-centered decision to adopt, this example represents one extreme. Those cases in which parents refer to the special circumstances of adoption with the remark, "We then also thought about the children in children's homes," are still close to the range of ego-centered motives. At the other end of the continuum we find those few cases in which couples turned to adoption because of a social conscience, because of "fundamental Christian beliefs," or because of a sense of responsibility towards a hitherto unknown child. The verbal statements in these cases correspond with the taking on of a difficult task at a later stage, such as adopting an older or handicapped child.

Under the aspect of normality the continuum can be characterized as follows: It reflects the shift of emphasis from the construction of normality for oneself (or for the birth child) to the enabling of familial conditions of socialization for a prospective adopted child. Whereas in the one case it is hoped that the child will also benefit from the situation, the more markedly child-centered considerations in the other case are linked with some form of sublimated self-interest on the part of the adoptive parents.

In order to illustrate considerations that focus more markedly on the child's interests I have selected an example that reflects the various stages of dealing with the aspect of instrumentalization. After the husband stated that "the social aspect was very central" in the reasons given by the couple in their joint application for adoption, the wife intervenes to differentiate:

ADOPTIVE MOTHER: Well, maybe I should butt in here, well, um, the most important thing, I suppose, was that I realized the limits to my working life and that this, well, depressed me, the idea that this would carry on and on for years on end . . .

INTERVIEWER: Hm . . .

ADOPTIVE MOTHER: and things in our business developed in such a way that, um, I just didn't feel good, and changing jobs seemed to me to be absolutely meaningless, since sooner or later the situation . . .

INTERVIEWER: Hm . . .

ADOPTIVE MOTHER: would have been the same. I was very unhappy with my situation, but to begin with I didn't really know *why*. As always you can't say I did this and that for this and that reason, there's a whole bunch of reasons, . . .

INTERVIEWER: Hm . . .

ADOPTIVE MOTHER: which aren't that important in themselves, only together. And I had the feeling that we are doing nicely, and I was permanently plagued by a bad conscience.

Following brief flashbacks to the aspect of childlessness in the marriage, which revealed that the couple had decided—after an arduously negotiated consensus—against giving birth to a child because of genetic fears, the interview continues:

ADOPTIVE MOTHER: And then I realized that it would probably be much more meaningful to give a child a home instead of working for a new skirt or a new dress.

INTERVIEWER: Hm . . .

ADOPTIVE MOTHER: And then I had the rather *bizarre* notion that when you *have* a child yourself all you're basically doing is *artificially* setting yourself a task . . .

INTERVIEWER: Hm . . .

ADOPTIVE MOTHER: whereas the alternative is an already existing task, it's *there,* waiting to be fulfilled. Alright, it's pretty abstract, but, um, maybe it gives a rough idea . . .

INTERVIEWER: Yes.

ADOPTIVE MOTHER: of what was going on inside of me, you see? I really felt the need, I wanted to do something *useful*.

In my opinion this "bizarre" notion of a task that already exists and does not have to be set by a birth would seem to represent the minimum of instrumentalization of the child accessible in terms of everyday theory. The instrumental use of the adopted child is not obliterated by this line of reasoning; a little later the narrator herself says:

ADOPTIVE MOTHER: Of course, it's sheer selfishness to look for something you feel is useful. That, too, is . . .

INTERVIEWER: Hm . . .

ADOPTIVE MOTHER: no honorable motive.

The instrumentalization of the adopted child, however, is transformed by the fact that by defining adoption as a task the wife instrumentalizes herself in the interest of the child. The idea of the simultaneity of taking and giving produced here after considerable interpretational work would appear to transcend the instrumentalization of the child in a manner that is probably only possible in the case of the task already waiting to be fulfilled.

Adoption in the Case of Voluntary Childlessness. The intrinsic value of adoption is also emphasized in the two examples in which couples choose to remain childless. These two cases, however, both of which fit in with the pattern of voluntary childlessness currently attracting such journalistic interest, are not clear-cut. In one case the husband takes a pessimistic view of the future and his wife suffers from pregnancy anxieties.

ADOPTIVE FATHER: Yes, that's what I was already saying before, that, on the one hand, we would both like to have children, but that I hardly dare bring children into the world as I take a very pessimistic view of the future. Take overpopulation, just to mention one problem.

ADOPTIVE MOTHER: Hm . . .

ADOPTIVE FATHER: I don't want to get bogged down in details. Well, for one thing the crisis which everybody has heard about, and I can't see the next fifty years, I can't see them at all, and I take a very negative view. OK, that's one thing. On top of that E. didn't necessarily want children of her own.

ADOPTIVE MOTHER: Yes—well, I can well do without having children of my own, and for me pregnancy and all it involves is not necessarily something positive. For some mothers it's a tremendous emotional experience. I'm not sure—I mean—I can't really understand that. And that's where we were a good match, weren't we? For me it was a kind of relief to find such an alternative. Because I'm also very fond of children.

In this case having children would appear to have a motivational anchorage, in which giving birth to a child is rejected for varying reasons, some based on rationalization.[25] The following example represents the most striking contrasting case to all documentations of the otherwise taken-for-granted desire for a child.

ADOPTIVE MOTHER: We never really, we're perhaps a rather abnormal case, we never really spoke about children, did we, to be honest, I suppose we were both or are perhaps in a certain sense not very fond of children, well not in the traditional sense, . . .

INTERVIEWER: Hm . . .

ADOPTIVE MOTHER: what with "do-do" and "da-da."

INTERVIEWER: Hm, hm . . .

ADOPTIVE MOTHER: You know what I mean? In that sense children have never really, and certainly not babies, somehow, interested me . . .

INTERVIEWER: Hm . . .

ADOPTIVE MOTHER: and then it almost . . . a child older than . . . I was more interested in a child if it was older, if it was a partner, but all this fuss and attention, all this care of the brood and what have you . . .

INTERVIEWER: Yes.
ADOPTIVE MOTHER: I've never really in that sense needed it, and . . . my husband also . . . never talked about it.

This solitary example in which parents "can imagine life without children" illustrates how the outside world intervenes as a corrective. Via questions, advice, and the glance at the woman's waistline, the normality of the desire for a child is compounded by the influence of the outside world. First of all, the persons concerned start to become "nervous" about the development of their marriage. The wife is the first to be prompted into turning her thoughts to a child. She soon arrives, however, at the question of whether this has to be a child of her own. She becomes more and more aware of "the misery or distressing situation of children brought up in a home," the result among other things of press reports. Finally, a flashback to her own childhood experiences enables the acceptance of the plausibility of her preoccupation with a child who is not her own.

ADOPTIVE MOTHER: An additional factor in my case is, um, that I also didn't, well, didn't exactly grow up in my parental home myself, but was also cared for by someone else.
INTERVIEWER: Hm . . .
ADOPTIVE MOTHER: You see? So that's why the idea's not so . . . not so remote in my mind, um, it didn't have to be a child of my own in my case, I was loved just as much by people who weren't my parents.

The positive experience associated with this adoptive mother's memories of being "wonderfully cared for" herself by people who were not her biological parents provides the framework for her thoughts on how to establish a parent–child relationship. Whereas having children of her own was initially viewed as an alternative, by the time the couple applies for an adopted child this appears to be the only possibility of constituting a family. In this case the initial voluntary childlessness became involuntary childlessness following an operation.

Adoption also serves to establish normality in this contrasting case. This time the threat to normality is not triggered by the experience of involuntary childlessness, but by the clash between varying definitions of normality for the adult biography. In this case society is apparently able to assert the conception of normality "implanted" in earlier biographical phases in the case of all other interviews. Adoption in this case does not enable the approximation to an already internalized concept of the adult role; rather, the personal conception of marital normality is abandoned and the influence of the dominant norm in the broader social environment confirmed. Due to the wife's relatively low level of education, occupational activity does not offer a particularly satisfactory alternative to the maternal role in this specific case. This loyalty towards the socially binding concept of the adult role does not result from considerations of expediency. An identification with the parental role is established gradually by falling back on personal experience with an artificially constructed parent–child relationship. Whereas, on the one hand, doubts about the "naturalness" of the desire for a child can be questioned in this contrasting case, the case reflects the obligatory character of the parental role also underlying the decision in favor of a substitutive constitution of family in the other cases.

Notes

1. Although the introductory question designed to elicit the initial narration takes the process of adoption placement as its point of departure, almost all interviews also relate to the motivational history. The interviewees referred to the beginning of the chain of events without being prompted to do so by any form of interviewer guidance. The parallelism between the order of narrative sections and the chronology of the events to which they refer also developed in this context via two means of structuring the narrative. In the majority of cases one of the partners interviewed mapped out the chronology right from the outset of the interview by beginning with the marital and motivational history: "Let me tell you about it, in our case it was like this. . . ." In some cases this initial statement was explicitly characterized as a lead-in to the answer to the initial question: "First of all, before. . . ." In other cases interviewees let themselves be guided by the introductory question, but soon discovered that the events described seemed suspended in a vacuum and in need of explanation by reference to the marital and motivational history. Via a flashback ("I must explain a little more on this point; in our case the situation was as follows") the interviewee extended the narration to include the period before the process of adoption placement, thus establishing the plausibility of the described chain of events by specifying the details.
   The centrality of the desire for a child is also reflected in the following studies: Klaus Wahl, Greta Tüllmann, Michael-Sebastian Honig, Lerke Gravenhorst, Familien sind anders! Reinbek 1980, pp. 34ff; and Andrejs Urdze, Maria S. Rerrich, Frauenalltag und Kinderwunsch, Motive von Müttern für oder gegen ein zweites Kind. Frankfurt 1981, e.g., p. 46.
2. Cf. the connection between the establishment of a set of absolute norms and the classification of behavior as "natural" in Arnold Gehlen, Urmensch und Spätkultur. Bonn 1956, p. 117.
3. Alfred Schuetz, Collected Papers, vol. I. The Hague 1971, p. 23.
4. Cf. Nancy Chodorow, The Reproduction of Mothering, Psychoanalysis and the Sociology of Gender. Berkeley, pp. 85–90.
5. Cf. the classic analysis by Helene Deutsch, Psychologie der Frau (original: Psychology of Women, 2 vols., 1944 and 1945), vol. 2. Bern 1945, p. 47. She regards the desire for a child as the overcoming of penis envy, and classifies this phenomenon as a useful achievement in female development. She relativizes the concept of substitute formation. Carol Hagemann-White also orients her analysis towards the thesis of the desire for a child as the transformation of penis envy, emphasizing the aspect that for a woman the child "takes the place

of the penis as a symbol of the sex which woman does not have" (translation: M.B.): Carol Hagemann-White, Frauenbewegung und Psychoanalyse. Basle 1979, pp. 50ff.

6. Cf. the taking for granted of one's own fertility by persons moving into marriage, in David Kirk, Shared Fate. London 1964, p. 5. A detailed analysis of the development from the presumption of parenthood at the beginning of married life to the decision to adopt is presented by Kerry Daly, "Reshaped Parenthood Identity: The Transition to Adoptive Parenthood," in Journal of Contemporary Ethnography, vol. 17, no. 1, 1988, pp. 40–66.

7. Cf. Marshall D. Schechter, "About Adoptive Parents." In E. James Anthony and Therese Benedek, eds., Parenthood—Its Psychology and Psychopathology. Boston 1970, pp. 360f.

8. Cf. the description of deprivation in Kirk (1964), p. 4.

9. In 16 of the 30 cases the woman is said to be infertile; in three cases the man, and in one case both partners. In five other cases various reasons were given for the decision not to have a child, whereas no statement was made on this aspect in five of the interviews.

10. Hartmann Tyrell, Die Familie als "Urinstitution": Neuerliche spekulative Überlegungen zu einer alten Frage. Kölner Zeitschrift für Soziologie und Sozialpsychologie, vol. 30, no. 4, 1978, p. 619.

11. David Schneider, American Kinship—A Cultural Account. Chicago 1980, pp. 23ff.

12. Tyrell (1978), p. 621.

13. Cf. the concept of institutionalization in Peter L. Berger and Thomas Luckmann, The Social Construction of Reality. Harmondsworth 1967, pp. 70–85.

14. In the language of ethnomethodologists this phenomenon would be characterized as "seen but unnoticed", cf. Harold Garfinkel, Passing and the Managed Achievement of Sex Status in an "Intersexed Person," in Harold Garfinkel, Studies in Ethnomethodology. Englewood Cliffs, New Jersey 1967, p. 118.

15. Tyrell (1978), p. 639.

16. A parallel to "Agnes" involuntarily comes to mind here, who describes the development into a woman as, so to speak, automatic in her "accounts." Cf. Garfinkel (1967), pp. 120, 137.

17. Cf. the assumption of a "deep-rooted instinctual background" in Deutsch (1945), pp. 20, 13ff.

18. Cf. Marilyn Fabe and Norma Wikler, Up Against the Clock: Career Women Speak on the Choice to Have Children. New York 1979. Cf. also Thomas Ayck and Inge Stolten, Kinderlos aus Verantwortung, Reinbek 1978, e.g., p. 26.

19. In one case the husband initiated an adoption on behalf of his frequently ill wife following the death of their child just a few days after being born in the hope that a healthy adopted child would have a therapeutic effect on his wife. In the other case the husband encouraged his wife, who suffered from pregnancy anxieties, to choose adoption as an alternative.

20. Schechter (1970), p. 359.

21. René Levy, Der Lebenslauf als Statusbiographie: Die weibliche Normal-biographie in makrosoziologischer Perspektive. Stuttgart 1977.

22. The wife is not described as the "driving force" in any of the three cases in which childlessness is caused by the husband's infertility. The assumption of a link between the approval of an adoption and being the cause of childlessness is hardened by the fact that the percentage share of sterile adoptive fathers in the sample is much lower than the share assumed by gynecologists for the population as a whole (where the cause of childlessness is assumed to be more or less equally attributable to men and women).

23. Helene Deutsch refers in this context to "relative childlessness" (Deutsch, 1945, p. 421). On involuntary childlessness as a reason for adoption, cf. Deutsch (1945), p. 397; Schechter (1970), p. 353. The fact that four of the couples in this study had a birth child later on does not contradict the fact that adoption was initiated in the light of involuntary childlessness.
24. Deutsch (1945), p. 76.
25. As I am unable to carry out a psychoanalytical classification of this text passage it cannot be clarified whether the husband's decision not to have children of his own is interpretable as a rationalization of his wife's pregnancy anxieties.

2

The Adoption Placement Procedure

Following the breakthrough to the decision to adopt a new phase of heteronomy begins. The role of nature is replaced by the role of the social bureaucracy,[1] which initially assesses the general parental suitability of applicants and then—after a process of matching children with adoption applicants—grants or refuses an adoption placement. The evaluation of parental eligibility sets a relationship of dependency in motion between the applicants and the adoption counselor. In some cases subtly, in others more drastically, this relationship makes the applicants realize the discrepancy between their own family construction and the "normal" constitution of a family by birth. In the majority of interviews the conflict potential accompanying this bureaucratic construction of family is reflected in highly emotional and differentiated accounts of the placement procedure. In their reconstruction of the course of events the adoptive parents noticeably demonstrate their emotional management of the situation. The markedly subjective interpretation of the events surrounding placement does not impede the attempt to expose the underlying rules of the placement procedure during the assessment of parental eligibility. Rather, this subjectivity reflects an "explicitly indexical"[2] form of presentation, which has to be sustained to ensure that the recapitulation of the sequence can be assumed to be "factual"—that is, corresponds to the experiential structure of applicants at that time. The regularity structure of the experiences of the adoption applicants discernible in the narrative interviews does not document the regularity of some uncontrolled fantasizing, but the regularity in the cognitive and emotional management of the course of action associated with a bureaucratically mediated construction of family. The reality content of the recapitulation of events can be assumed as long as the narrative scheme[3] is observed—that is, as long as the text reveals that narrative constraints are effective and guide the organization of personal experiences in an explicitly self- or we-related form.

Apart from at the beginning of adoption placement procedure I was not allowed to triangulate the narrative interviews by means of a personal observation of the course of interaction in the Hamburg adoption agency. Furthermore, the inspection of files was refused with reference to the right to anonymity of the individuals concerned.[4] The only figures that could be supplementarily consulted were the data based on meager list entries on all adoption applicants in the year 1976. In addition to the incompleteness of these entries, however, the quality of these figures should be viewed with great caution. Their compilation as a result of interpretational processes[5] (occupation of applicant, occupation of the child's birth mother, sex of child desired by the applicants) makes it impossible to claim even the semblance of objectivity at this stage of research activities.

Nevertheless, despite the inadequacy of the list entries it seemed to make sense to fall back on data covering the entire application year 1976 in order to assess the meaningfulness of the findings of our sample, which was not formed according to aspects of representativity. This approach, however, was only able to provide a vague orientational comparison, especially because applications in our sample were made between 1966 and 1977 (Table 32). The change over the years in the ratio of children available for adoption (slight increase) and adoption applicants (substantial increase, Table 3) is therefore repeatedly taken into account via additional assumptions, for example, when differing selection processes are related to the favorable "market situation" at the end of the 1960s.

The supplementary survey in the Hamburg adoption agency is based on list entries for all applicants during the year 1976.[6] As—in the event of a successful application—the last column in the lists contained the name of the child placed, we combined the applicant data with the list entries for all children available for adoption. Data relating to the following aspects of the cases of family construction or extension were thus made available:

Family status of applicants (Table 9)
Occupation of the male applicant only, or in one case, of a woman living alone
    (Table 10)
Age of the male applicant only (Table 11)
Desired age and sex of the child (Tables 12–14)
Success or failure of applications (Tables 15 and 16)
Time between the submission of the application and the granting of adoption care
    in the case of successful applications (Table 17)
First or second application
Hamburg or external applicants
Age, sex, and birth status of the child placed (Tables 18–22)
Age of the birth mother (Tables 23 and 24), her marital status (Table 25), the

number of her children other than those relinquished for adoption (Table 25), her occupation (Tables 27 and 28), and her nationality (Table 29)
Data on the birth father (Table 30)
Period between the registration of the child as adoptable and adoption care (Table 31)

All data were classified in accordance with the conventionally used social research methods. On the basis of the rating system to determine class membership developed by Gerhard Kleining and Harriett Moore[7] (class self-rating), the data on the occupation of the adoption applicants were considered in such a way as to be able to reconstruct the influence of placement in the status hierarchy as a variable relevant to the process of selection. The construction of the index will not be considered in greater detail here. It is hoped that the use of a routinized technique to determine class membership will make it possible to interpret the orientation expressed in the interviews in a broader albeit less finely meshed framework. It is expected that the extent of the orientation to the hierarchical structure of society, with all its implications for interaction partners, their perspective and meta-perspective of the chances of adoption placement, will again be more clearly assessable against the background of these statistical data.[8]

The supplementary survey covered 357 adoption applicants in the 1976 year of application: 178 (50%) adopted a child from the Hamburg adoption agency, a further 33 from an external institution (altogether, just under 60%, Table 15). The 178 applicants who successfully applied for adoption via the Hamburg adoption agency adopted a total of 188 children, including ten sibling pairs. The narrative interviews will now help throw some light on the background of these figures.

Applicant Expectations and Placement Procedure

Before describing adoption placement procedure as a process of interaction between the applicants for a child and the institution of allocation, let us take a look at the hopes and expectations of prospective parents with respect to their prospective child. As a kind of background stereotype for future placement procedure I would like to identify the ideal type of expectations with respect to the child as it exists at the beginning of the application procedure, still undistorted by the pressures of confrontation with the reality depicted by the social bureaucracy. This initial expectation structure, however, is not openly expressed in the interviews. The reconstruction of relevances by prospective parents can only be indirectly derived via the parental perspective of placement procedure. The reason for this constant structural feature of the narrative interviews will be considered a little later on.

In the majority of interviews the recapitulation of the events associated with placement procedure is a major point of reference. Even ten years after the application for a child the detailed reconstruction of the chain of events by the parents is still marked by the highly emotional involvement experienced at that time, especially the displeasure at the limited scope of autonomous action. Only a few placement cases limit their descriptions of this aspect to just a brief listing of the key events in their chronological order. These brief descriptions always appear to be problem-free and emphasize the outcome of placement procedure, the offer of a child. The six cases in which the child was initially a foster child, or those cases in which the parents asked the agencies to place a child they already knew, can be classed as special cases. Although the area of conflict-laden procedural steps is more limited in these special cases, all cases are characterized by at least one problem, which basically results from the discrepancy between parental action and the perspective of a single social bureaucracy with exclusive decision-making powers in the field of adoption.

The typical narration of the beginning of the procedural history is not marked by the statement "we had this or that child in mind," but by a reference to the institution to which prospective parents turned at some stage following the breakthrough to the decision to adopt. From then on the narration unfolds along the chronology of events—with a number of flashbacks and insertions.[9] With just a few exceptions, the initial expectations with respect to the prospective child can be decoded at two stages in the recapitulation of placement procedure. On the one hand, the adoptive parents relate to a discussion with the adoption counselor or the local social worker, during the course of which questions were asked about their expectations regarding the prospective child. This pattern of action is a central feature of the process of selection. Its outcome has major significance for the assessment of parental eligibility. As the narrators themselves state in their interviews, the expectations articulated by adoption applicants under the pressure of this situation are often marked by initial signs of strategic interaction. Any attempt to draw conclusions about initial expectations here would have to take into account a distortion caused by calculated presentations by the prospective parents designed to ensure procedural success (the same reservations apply to Table 12).

The second positioning of the subject in the interview provides a less vague indication of initial expectations. If the child offered for adoption, for example, differs from the desired child in terms of age or color of skin, the adoption applicants also outline their conflict in the narrative interview.

By means of a detailed flashback they introduce the initial expectations into the narration in an effort to make their initial hesitancy towards the child seem plausible.

The statements on these expectations, which relate to varying contexts, reveal a tendency to emulate as exactly as possible the constitution of family they are unable to realize by birth. The narrative interviews give an idea of the extent to which the hopes of prospective parents center on the young baby, on the still malleable child. Leaving aside the eight cases in which a desire was expressed for an already older child (older than one year), the incorporation of the beginning of the child's life in the adoptive family history and the associated approximation to the circumstances of a biological constitution of family would clearly appear to be highly relevant to the adoption applicants we contacted.

Whereas birth parents can also be certain about the color of the child's skin, adoptive parents appear almost without exception to hope for a white-skinned child. However, apart from a few explicit references to options, such as "no colored child," the subject tends to be excluded from communication in the interviews unless its consideration was initiated by the course of adoption procedure itself (for example, the rejection of the offer of a Chinese child or the request for time to think about the adoption of a dark-skinned child). One attribute of the child birth parents are unable to determine, namely its sex, would also appear to be of secondary importance to adoptive parents, too (see Table 13). Whereas their disinterest in any preference for a certain sex enables adoptive parents to emulate the "natural" circumstances of the constitution of family, they are confronted by similarly stressful imponderabilities as birth parents when it comes to the child's health. The ideal type of parental expectations at any rate is the young, healthy, and white-skinned baby.

This type could already have been deduced from the motivational histories. As long as adoption serves as a substitute for the constitution of family in the case of involuntary childlessness it is fair to assume that prospective parents will design their alternative access to the child in line with the pattern of normality. The parental role they internalized always included the beginning of the child's life as a part of the family history. This is retained as the unquestioned point of orientation even if the biological constitution of family proves impossible. In other words, even though the constitution of a biological family can no longer be taken for granted and the realization of the parental role continues to be a desired goal there is no automatic change in the type of desired child in all its aspects. There is simply a shift from the type "my child" to the type "strange child." Beyond the genealogical difference it retains the attributes associated with the pattern of normality. Child-centered considerations—the altruistic commitment to spare the parentless child a life in a children's home—remain the exception.

The fact that the continuing validity of the pattern of normality is taken for granted explains why one aspect is missing in the narrative interviews: it is not apparently regarded as necessary to mention the initial ideal expectations with respect to the prospective child, because in the chronology of events—between the decision to adopt and the first step towards applying for an adopted child—they have not yet lost their unquestioned power of orientation. It only turns into a subject in need of reflection after its problematic nature becomes clear during adoption procedure. It is then also articulated in the interviews to lend plausibility to the chain of events surrounding the constitution of family.

Major Parameters of the Adoption Placement Procedure

The Mutual Independence of "Supply" and "Demand"

The fact that "supply" and "demand" in the adoption context develop in accordance with their own respective independent structure specificities is one of the reasons for the fundamental conflict potential when matching children and applicant couples. Beyond the knowledge of the institution of adoption, the circumstantial context leading to the plan to relinquish a child for adoption does not have the slightest point of contact with the motivational history of the adoption applicants. Plans of action relating to the child, plans that are characterized by problematic compatibility, unfold in mutual independence.

In this mutual independence supply and demand reveal contrary tendencies. Whereas prospective adoptive parents hope for an approximation to the biologically denied pattern of normality by adopting a young baby, birth mothers often delay the decision to relinquish their child for adoption because they too have internalized and try to maintain the concept of a normal socialization in their own family. The biographical interviews conducted with birth mothers to supplement the survey of adoptive parents make it clear that the relinquishment of a child is very rarely a "smooth" solution.[10] Even though the validity of the norm of a social attachment of mother and child is weakened for these birth mothers— personal experiences of deprivation in the family of origin or in homes reduce its binding nature—the intensity of attachment that still remains makes the relinquishment of the child an ambivalent act.[11] Athough the mother does justice to the norm of an adequate psychological and social care of the child in a family by relinquishing her child, she at the same time contravenes the norm of motherly care for one's own child firmly institutionalized in western society.[12]

Delaying this move is generally accompanied by hopes that the economically and socially unfavorable circumstances for coping with life with a child will improve to such an extent as to enable the birth mother to look after the child for good. The interviews reflect the particular difficulties facing a group of women, most of whom are unmarried or divorced mothers belonging to the lower class, when they try to manage the task of caring for their children on their own. Apart from being entitled to welfare assistance, they lack the resources provided by a favorable family background, school, and occupational socialization.[13] While to begin with the birth mothers often wait for a solution for themselves and for their child within the framework of the pattern of normality, the chances of adoption applicants to adopt a child that corresponds to the ideal type of initial expectations diminish.

The Adoption Agency as the Legally Envisaged Intermediary between Supply and Demand

The difference between ideal and realistic expectations produces a conflict that does not directly take place between the "supplying" birth parents and the "demanding" adoption applicants, but via the social bureaucracy in its legally envisaged role of intermediary. With the intention of protecting the child, the move from the family of origin to the adoptive family has increasingly become a matter subject to government regulations.[14] In line with the changing role of the child in society, adoption gradually ceased to be an "institution designed to provide legal heirs" and was redefined as a "youth welfare institution."[15] The shift in perspectives more or less spans the development between the definition of adoption in the German Civil Code of 1896 ("Annahme an Kindes Statt") and the corresponding definition in the adoption law of 1976 ("Annahme als Kind"). The idea that the child has its own intrinsic value only began to spread in the 20th century. This led to a growing orientation to the needs of the child's personality,[16] a development that found its expression in adoption laws that specified the best interests of the child as the point of reference for a legal regulation of adoptive family structures.[17] Since it was first considered in the German Civil Code of 1896, the "principle of protection"[18] in favor of the child was given more and more priority over the previously observed principle that adoption should be "oriented to the interests of childless couples or individuals in ensuring an heir to their property and their name."[19] In order to create the best possible conditions for the development of the child's personality the status of the institution of adoption was generally upgraded in the new adoption law of 1976. The ties between the adopted child and its family of origin were severed,[20] its status in the adoptive family more emphatically equated with that of a legitimate child,[21] and provisions made for the fundamental indissolubility of parent–child relationships that have not been biologically constituted.[22]

To complement the legal regulations for the adoptive parents specified in the adoption law, an adoption placement law was created that sets out to make the aspect of the best interests of the child a determinant maxim during the course of adoption placement procedure. Adoption placement can only be carried out by state-approved institutions that are known to possess the necessary expertise.[23]

The Adoption Agency as an Administrator of a Given Supply in a Situation of Growing Demand

The conflict with applicants during the placement activities of the adoption agencies is virtually predetermined due to the supply structure. In addition to the fact that it is difficult to meet the requirements of the ideal type of initial expectations because most of the children relinquished for adoption do not correspond to the orientational model of the young (and healthy) baby, the quantity of the adoption supply also jeopardizes the placement of a child at all. Adoption placement today is the allocation of a scarce commodity, culminating more probably than not in failure rather than success.

How dramatically supply and demand have developed over the years depends on the figures selected as a referential basis. Relating to the number of children available for adoption in any one year—regardless of whether they were placed or simply registered for adoption in the year concerned—it becomes clear that up until the time this study was conducted the Federal Republic of Germany experienced no decline in the number of placeable children (Table 3).[24] On the contrary, the number of children already placed for adoption increased steadily: between 1963 and 1978 the number of adoptions by nonrelatives almost doubled (Table 1). This shows that the development of the "adoption supply" does not reflect the general development of the number of births. The almost 45 percent drop in the number of births between 1966 and 1978 (Table 4) was not reflected in the total number of children available for adoption during this period. This means that the percentage share of children relinquished for adoption in the total number of children in Germany must have increased.

The virtual constancy of the "adoption supply" can be partly explained by the fact that the number of children born out of wedlock, traditionally a decisive figure for the recruitment of adopted children,[25] only fell by less than 20 percent between 1966 and 1978. The share of illegitimate births in the total number of births thus increased from the postwar minimum of 4.56 percent in 1966 to almost 7 percent in 1978 (Table 4). It cannot be clarified here whether more children were recruited for adoption from the pool of legitimate or illegitimate children. A great deal would suggest that adoption agencies tend to take a closer look at the legitimate children living in unfavorable circumstances. Both the preference of social welfare institutions for family upbringing rather than upbringing in a children's home,[26] and the realization of the adverse effects of unsuccessful socialization in the family of origin, would appear to have produced a situation in which use is also being made to an increasing degree of adoption as a youth welfare institution for children born in wedlock.[27]

The possibility of terminating parental consent makes it easier for the social administration and the courts to enforce substitute family upbringing in cases where socialization would otherwise be endangered. Apart from the relatively low decline in the number of illegitimate births, a further explanatory factor for this altered recruitment practice by the social bureaucracy is probably the fact that the available supply of children did not decrease despite the drastic decline in the total number of births.

The slight increase on the "supply" side, however, contrasts so markedly with the development on the "demand" side that the increasingly unfavorable ratio between the two repeatedly leads to claims of a less favorable supply situation in absolute and not just relative terms.[28] The number of applicants per annum—irrespective of whether they adopted a child in the year under review or had been waiting for a child since their "assessment"—more than tripled between 1961 and 1978 (Table 3). Even taking into account the fact that this figure is probably exaggeratedly high because of multiple applications,[29] a new stage in the history of adoption in the Federal Republic of Germany cannot be denied. Especially since the beginning of the 1970s there has been a truly explosive trend in the demand for children. The reasons for such a rapid rise in the popularity of adoption undoubtedly merit a special study. The following extremely speculative considerations only provide a few indications of how this phenomenon could be understood.

Even if it is assumed that the number of involuntarily childless couples has probably exceeded the estimate made by doctors on the basis of their experience of 10 percent of the total number of marriages[30]—more recent studies refer to a level between 10 and 15 percent[31]—this biological fact alone is by no means able to explain the extent of the increase in applicants for adoption. A great deal would suggest that the institution of adoption has generally become more acceptable during recent years. The increased media coverage during the 1970s of the problems facing children brought up in children's homes probably contributed towards removing the taboo associated with the substitutive constitution of family. Against the background of problematic lives in these homes, adoption lost its stigma of being nothing more than a second-best solution for childless couples. A generally growing public sensitivity to the distress of children whose lives begin under the burden of physical and psychological deprivation has also probably made adoption more attractive for involuntarily childless couples. This social redefinition of adoption as an instrument in the "best interests of the child" has probably lowered the psychological access barriers without producing a situation in which the motivational histories of the applicants correspond to the idea of child-centeredness in adoption. As clearly documented in the narrative interviews most of the applicants expressed a desire for "the child for us" in continuation of the pattern of normality. The instrumentalization of the child for one's own biographical plan generally represents the point of departure for the decision to adopt, with social motives as secondary factors rather than as a foundation.

A further explantory factor for the growing acceptability of adoption is probably the fact that the declining stigmatization of the illegitimate child has undermined an aspect that has traditionally had adverse effects on the chances of children being adopted. Up until the 1930s there were still attempts to establish the adoptability of children via birth certificates not bearing details of the child's birth status.[32] The sharp increase in the rate of illegitimate births between 1966 and 1978 (Table 4) was accompanied by legal[33] and legitimatory[34] enhancements of the status of the illegitimate child. This probably reduced the significance of the birth status of the adopted child as a factor of orientation for adoption applicants.

Rounding off these speculative considerations it is worth taking a brief look at the extent to which the increased "demand" for adopted children relates to the value of the child in our society in general. My assumption is that the growing interest in the adopted child can be explained by an increased acceptability of the adoptive family, but not by the greater desirability of the institution of the family in general. There are plenty of signs of a growing trend towards voluntary childlessness.[35] Furthermore, the adult female role without the role of mother would appear to be becoming more popular, especially in cases where there is a satisifying occupational alternative. I do not, therefore, wish to link the increased interest in the adopted child with any general change in societal values relating to the family complex, such as the new trend towards inwardness or a new elevation of the importance of family as a means of safeguarding the "quality of life." In my opinion, the growing interest in the adopted child is rooted in the fact that more and more involuntarily childless married couples are venturing to realize their desire for a child through adoption now that the taboo of this institution in public opinion as a youth welfare instrument has been removed.

The growing demand for adopted children also leaves the adoption agency facing a changed problem in its placement activity. Instead of having to recruit suitable adoptive parents in a situation with an inadequate number of applicants, the agencies are confronted by the burden of selection in the face of an overabundant demand. A comparison between the number of children available for adoption each year (regardless of whether they were placed in that year or simply registered) and the number of applicants (regardless of whether they were able to adopt a child in that year or were still waiting for an adoption following their "assessment") shows an about-turn in the ratio of demand and supply around the mid-1960s (Table 3; Tables 1 and 2). The ratio of 1:1 at that time turned into an average of 1:2.55 to 2.85 during the period 1976 to 1978, although the numerical inaccuracies outlined in the tables only allow a rough estimation of the dimension of the ratio shift.

Despite the fact that the chances of successful adoption applications decreased during the course of the 1970s, the situation is nowhere near as hopeless as suggested by the figures forwarded by adoption agencies[36] and literature on this subject.[37] If the number of children still registered as available for adoption at the end of each year is set in relation to the number of still-waiting applicants with an adoption care authorization, the impression is gained that the situation for adoption applicants has deteriorated to the point of zero chance of success (Table 2). Whereas in 1970 two to three applicants were waiting for each child registered for adoption by nonrelatives, four to six applicants were waiting in 1974. In 1978 the supply situation had deteriorated to such an extent that only one out of seven to nine applicants could hope for a placement. These figures, however, are not only problematic because of the multiple applications contained on the demand side (for comments see Table 2). They are also misleading because they fail to show the success rate of the year in question or make it clear that the "degree of scarcity" of adoptable children on December 31st is also connected with the speeding up of the adoption procedure by the youth welfare offices.[38] The more the adoption agencies operate on the basis of the rate of success yet to be achieved, or the rate of potential failure by comparing the small number of children registered for adoption with a huge number of applicants, the more they are themselves likely to encourage a process of multiple applications and thus reinforce the impression of the hopelessness of adoption applications. These officially presented figures would appear to be the prototype of correct calculation with no bearing on the reality of the situation.

Under the burden of the competition between applicants the allocation work of the youth welfare offices is probably made even more difficult by the fact that in their capacity as administrators of supply, the adoption agencies are perceived in the role of a supplier. The applicants are only able to vent the frustration resulting from the deficiencies in the composition and extent of the supply situation to a minimum degree on potential suppliers—heated discussions in the discussion circles for adoptive parents and applicants about the consequences of too many legal abortions reducing the number of placeable children were one of the few channels. This frustration at the discrepancy between ideal and realistic expectations can be expected to be directed against the agency of allocation. Even though the youth welfare offices can exert little influence on the overall supply—for example, they talk to women who consider relinquishing their child[39] or they may try to engineer the replacement of parent consent to adoption—they are nevertheless likely to be viewed in individual cases (as long as a supply exists) as an institution with a potential supply at its disposal. This would mean that the actual lack of autonomy of the "procedural administrator" (youth welfare office) in the determination of the supply is eclipsed in the eyes of the applicants by the aspect of allocational competence. The conflict that results when an attempt is made to match ideal and realistic expectations would then be directed against an interaction partner perceived as having an ability to actively influence the situation.

The Assessment of Adoptive Suitability as the Basis for Matching Supply and Demand

One of the aspects of adoption placement procedure with the greatest conflict potential is the definition of what—depending on the position in the adoption procedure—is described as "suitability for adoption" (in the terminology of the allocational institution) or as "parental eligibility" (in the terminology of the applicants). This "ability," determined during the course of an assessment procedure, comes into conflict with the assumption questioned at most by socialization experts in our society of an "a priori competence of everyman (as a man or as a woman) to lead a marital and family life."[40] As in all probability the idea of one's own parental competence is very closely linked with the internalization of the desire for a child, it seems fair to assume that the assessment of parental suitability is experienced as a hurtful dissociation from the pattern of normality for the constitution of family. The phraseology of the lack of a "natural qualification"[41] of the adoptive parents in comparison with the birth parents used in the legal argumentation probably represents a particularly hurtful blow to those who will feel that this claim of limited parental competence is an additional obstacle to the biologically rooted impossibility or improbability of a pregnancy.

The two-stage selection process begins with the determination of the general suitability of applicants as prospective adoptive parents, the "general parental eligibility." The positive outcome of this step in the procedure finds its expression in the granting of an adoption care authorization. The applicants are then assessed with respect to their suitability as adoptive parents for a specific child in the universe of children available for adoption ("specific parental eligibility"). Irrespective of the criteria available for the evaluation of parental eligibility, legislators have tried via the Adoption Placement Act to ensure that only qualified "experts" are entrusted with the task of adoption placement. These experts have "to assess, in consideration of the child's personality and its special needs, whether adoption applicants are suitable for the adoption of the child." The determination of parental eligibility is based on an ascriptive act by the adoption counselor, the justification of which should be guided by the best interests of the child—in relation to children in general on the one hand ("general eligibility"), and in relation to a specific child on the other ("specific parental eligibility"). The specification of "best interests of the child" as a basis of argumentation gives the adoption counselor a sphere of autonomous decision-making power that is no longer obvious to the applicants. The confirmation of general parental eligibility is potentially an act with no consequences, because general parental eligibility may be deemed inadequate in terms of the interests of the children who happen to be available for adoption. The discrepancy between the ideal type of parental expectations with respect to the child and the reality of the supply situation, together with the act of matching supply and demand via the construction of general and specific parental eligibility, can be expected to accumulate to form a conflict potential that makes harmonious accounts very unlikely in the narrative interviews.

The Confrontation of Applicants with the Adoption Agency's Pattern of Action at the Beginning of Adoption Placement Procedure

The First Information Discussion

In the wake of the growing demand for adopted children, the Hamburg adoption agency decided in the mid-1970s to organize the initial communication situation with adoption applicants on a labor-saving basis. Roughly five married couples,[42] all of which had set forth the reasons for their adoption plan in an informal application, were asked to come along to a "first information discussion" together. During the following I refer to the narrative interviews of seven married couples who applied for a child in or after 1976 and who considered the first information discussion in their recapitulation of the course of events. Even though the number of interviews is small I regard the analysis of the accounts of how initial contact was organized by the placement agency as worthwhile, because the institutional steering of initial communication can provide an insight into the basic feature of adoption placement practice in a situation of overabundant demand. The observations made here will probably remain indicative for the future as long as the adoption agencies see no reason to recruit applicants for a child in view of the ratio of supply to demand. I shall combine the narrative accounts of the beginning of the placement procedure with my own observations after taking part in two such initial information discussions. The adoption agency made it possible for me to gain access to this phase of adoption placement procedure.

The Information about Reality from the Perspective of the Adoption Agency. The first information discussion is the point of intersection of two worlds: the world of private hopes for parenthood and the world of public bureaucratic responsibility for the creation of a parent–child relationship serving the best interests of the child.[43] During the information discussion one of these worlds verbally predominates; the first information discussion is the communication situation created by the procedural administrator to convey his or her perspective of reality.

By outlining a number of facts on adoption placement, "here and now" adoption counselors give the applicants an insight into the constraints on their activities, which—from the perspective of the applicants—are at the same time the constraints of their chances of a successful adoption. The supply of children, for example, is presented in its various attributive dimensions. Particular attention is paid to the age of the child:

ADOPTIVE MOTHER: And then special attention was paid to the aspect of age, you see, and the fact that this and that category . . . and that there are no or hardly any babies. That's something we were told to accept from the start, that, er, it would be difficult to adopt a baby, and that we should already start thinking in terms of a toddler. . . .

During one of the first information meetings I attended the applicants were encouraged to adopt older or handicapped children. The risks associated with the physical and mental development of many children were openly articulated. Apart from information on the "qualitative" character of the supply, statements were also made on the quantitative sitaution. Although I noticed in one of the first information meetings that oblique references to the quantitative aspect of applicants' chances were made only hesitantly and after an explicit inquiry (the 300 applicants assessed in

Hamburg and the 1,200 applicants granted an adoption care authorization by other youth welfare offices were compared with the 140 children placed in the previous year), the narrative interviews do reveal this type of information. The information on the ratio of supply to demand seems to be a frequent feature of the first information discussions, either elicited or spontaneously stated. The response to this quantitative aspect is reflected, for example, in the following narrative passage:

ADOPTIVE MOTHER: About six or seven married couples were sitting there, something like that, well . . . and we were told that as a rule only *one* married couple out of seven, er, the framework we represented in the room, stands a chance of adopting a child, and that really makes you wonder when you first hear that. You look at each other and think: "Just like roulette, isn't it, one, two, three, four, five, six, seven, well, is it worthwhile even trying if only *one* married couple stands a real chance, you see?"

The information on the chances of success is supplemented by the fact that the adoption agency signals the maxim of matching supply and demand right at the start of adoption procedure. The set phrase that regularly crops up in the interviews is: "We are looking for parents for children," followed almost every time by, "not the other way round." Here is the example of an adoptive mother who later employed a variety of strategies to draw attention to her desire to become an adoptive mother and who informs the interviewer about the key content of the agency's maxim:

ADOPTIVE MOTHER: Parents are looked for for children and not the other way round. It's not just a case of picking out a child for us just because we can't have one ourselves. That's not the way it's organized. The children are there, they have no home and have been relinquished for adoption, and now a suitable (parental) home is chosen for them. . . .

Finally, apart from the information on the children and fellow applicants as well as on the maxim of matching children with applicants, the picture of the reality to be expected during the placement procedure is rounded off in the interviews by articulating the course of placement procedure. Application procedure is divided into two phases: the assessment of suitability for adoption (general parental eligibility) and the potential adoption placement (specific parental eligibility). Whereas in Hamburg the adoption agency has sole responsibility for the second phase, the first phase is split between two institutional stages of assessment. The "final discussion" with the adoption counselor, who then decides whether to grant the adoption care authorization or not, is preceded on a decentralized basis by the preparatory activities of social workers in the youth welfare offices of individual city districts. On the basis of application documents and several discussions conducted during visits to the homes of adoption applicants they compile reports accompanied by a recommendation for or against the granting of the authorization for adoption care.

The first information discussion provides applicants with information on the next procedural steps. Whether applicants follow through their adoption plan, and which hopes and fears accompany subsequent stages involved when applicants decide to persevere, depends on how applicants relate the perspective conveyed by the social bureaucracy to their own ideas of a constitution of family; it depends on how they assess the chances of approximating to the pattern or normality.

The Missing Dialogue about Differing Perspectives of Reality. The first information discussion exemplifies how a relationship between the administration and its clientele is structured in line with aspects of efficiency but underrates the conditions of successful communication. The discrepancy in the perspectives of the two interaction partners is so great that there can be no certain assumption of the "congruency of the systems of relevances"[44] required for the initiation of every communication. Even though applicants may be able to appreciate the bureaucratic perspective at a cognitive level during the course of the discussion, adoption applicants wishing to realize the long-planned parental role via a substitute have assigned such central significance to the orientation to the normal case in their relevance structure that the bureaucratic perspective of a reality— marked by a particular supply of children, applicant chances of success, and the maxim of matching supply and demand—is unable to initially penetrate into their own relevance structure. The difficulties of coping with the dominance of the bureaucratic perspective during the first information discussion are reflected in a pretty uniform interpretation in the narrative interviews, where it is claimed that the initial discussion was intended as a "deterrence."

With one exception all seven of the interview passages dealing with the first information discussion were narrated by members of the discussion circle for adoptive parents, from which just under half of our total sample was recruited. Because additional adoptive parents were chosen mainly among those who adopted a child who was already older or who already had an older adopted child, only three couples could be recruited outside of the discussion circle who experienced the new institutional regulation of the beginning of placement procedure during their application period. What is more, only one of these three couples related to the first information discussion when recapitulating its adoption history. The common interpretation of the first information discussion as a deterrence is undoubtedly the result of a common discussion of the problems associated with the initial contact with the adoption agency. Group discussions probably enabled the adoptive parents to become aware of the reasons for a feeling of uneasiness, which might have otherwise remained unclarified. The conflict-laden character of the beginning of adoption procedure, therefore, can be expected to find its expression in the corresponding narrative interviews in much stronger terms than might otherwise be expected.

References to the "deterrence discussion," "nightmare discussion," or "tremendous maneuvers of deterrence by the youth welfare office" indicate just how strongly the adoption applicants experience the bureaucratic perspective of adoption reality as an attack on their own plans. The step expected of them by the social bureaucracy towards acquiring a primarily child-centered orientation represents a threatening challenge for members of society who have anchored the biologically constituted parental role as an integral part of their adult role design as a result of early socialization processes. They are not automatically willing to drop their ideas of familial normality because of this compulsory reorientation to the adopted child. The request by the adoption counselor to mentally prepare for the older, sick, or handicapped child clashes abruptly with the parental ambitions cherished for many years. The maxim of matching supply and demand is also in conflict with the previous expectational structure, because it emphasizes that the adoption agency is looking for "the suitable applicant for the child," not "the child for us." The ratios propagated by the adoption agency turn the other anonymous applicants into potentially superior rivals.

The following example illustrates the demands made on applicants by the first information discussion, during which they are required to reconcile their hopes for constituting a family with the bureaucratically depicted reality of adoption.

ADOPTIVE MOTHER: Well, to begin with, there was a preliminary information discussion. That was the first thing organized by the authorities. The *discussion* made us feel a bit frustrated, didn't it? They started off by giving us a general rundown of the legal situation, of everything which lay ahead for us. It was then said in the next breath how difficult it would be, er, to adopt a child, to go the whole . . . yes, way. . . . I found that everything was presented in a somewhat negative way. . . . Yes, we left, speaking for myself at any rate, pretty . . . not shocked, but so, so depressed . . .
INTERVIEWER: Hm . . .
ADOPTIVE MOTHER: from this discussion.

Following the first information discussion the paralysis felt by many applicants with regard to the realization of one's own adoption plan is connected with the fact that the bureaucratic perspective of procedural reality—although, so far as I can judge, presented in a friendly way—cannot be brought into harmony with one's own conception of family constitution. The structure of adoption procedure at this stage is marked by an asymmetric communication situation, because the informant sets the conditional relevances[45] for the participation of others. Discussion structures are mainly created by the fact that applicants enquire about the information imparted. This distribution of speech interaction means that applicants have to repress the fundamental orientations of their adult role designs throughout the first information discussion. The bureaucratic perspective of procedural reality is conveyed in such a one-sided manner that adoption applicants, left alone with their initial hopes, feel hurt, "frustrated," "depressed," or even "deterred."

The fact that the term discussion is used here to describe a process characterized only superficially by dialogue is reflected in the following critical evaluation by one adoptive father.

ADOPTIVE FATHER: I would like to say something about the initial discussion. Well . . . I, er, I found it symptomatic, er, insofar as . . .
ADOPTIVE MOTHER: That's right.
ADOPTIVE FATHER: it was, er, organized in the form of a group discussion, as already pointed out, and I, er, had the feeling that by doing it that way the authority . . . wanted to show that it was quite progressive. It's progressive nowadays . . .
INTERVIEWER: Hm . . .
ADOPTIVE FATHER: er, to have information discussions in the form of larger circles. . . . But in this respect the whole thing . . . went wrong in my opinion because the social worker responsible didn't really understand the form and possibilities of a group discussion. She, er, the persons in the group were basically frustrated by the way in which the information was presented, as already pointed out. The conversational to-and-fro you need for a normal group discussion, therefore, didn't take place.

The initial discussion represents more than just a one-and-a-half-hour adjustment to the perspective of the procedural administrator. As shown by the key importance of the term "deterrence" for retrospective interpretations, the image of a reality comprising a "supply of children," applicant chances, and the maxim of matching supply and demand—a reality that comes into conflict with one's own parental hopes—is decoded at the relational level. By appealing to the applicants to turn their attention to the older, sick, or handicapped child the adoption counselor tries to initiate a process of redefinition of own objectives, a redefinition that is initially experienced by the prospective adoptive parents as a threat to their identity. In their orientation to the constitution of familial normality their expectations are devalued by the confrontation with the procedurally superior bureaucratic perspective. The degradation of the original perspective of the prospective adoptive parents can be experienced so intensely that degradation is ascribed to the adoption counselor as her style of acting. Here is the example of an adoptive mother who soon rated her own chances as somewhere near zero and who expressed her experience of inferiority and helplessness during the first information discussion with unusually sharp criticism.

ADOPTIVE MOTHER: And then we were also assessed. Maybe I should briefly mention the fact that two years ago . . . we made the application in spring 1976 . . . for adoption, and we were told during the information discussion— there are always several people together, in this case older applicants, that we, er, that we were *really* too old, er, whether we had *considered* it carefully, we were told very directly—they are awfully direct. Well, it's *terrible*, we were all already pretty *strained*. We were told to come along in pairs so that the men see what's happening right from the start. One woman was there *without* her husband, and she was asked: "Do you think you will be able to *tell* your husband what I told you today?"—an insult really, one insult after the other. . . .

Whereas in this particular case the adoption counselor overlooks or ignores the sensitivities of prospective parents to patronizing treatment and thus appears hurtful, it can be generally stated that the significance of the adoption plan in the relevance structure of childless married couples is underestimated during the first information discussion. An event planned "only" to pass on information and marked by the dominance of the bureaucratic perspective poses a threat to applicants, who are at most able to gradually overcome their initial fixation on an approximation to familial normality. Even if one supports the principle that adoption placement procedure should be oriented to the best interests of the child, the question arises whether such an abrupt confrontation with "the other side" is justifiable. In order to clarify this question we shall begin by trying to discover the significance of the first information discussion for the bureaucratic organization of subsequent placement activity.

The Function of Information Policy for Bureaucratic Placement Activity. The feeling of uncertainty experienced by adoption applicants at the beginning of the placement procedure will now be analyzed to discover the possible significance of this feeling in the bureaucratic plan of action. Beyond the possibilities of the narrative interviews with adoptive parents the action goals pursued by the adoption agency can only be hypothetically identified. The underlying objectives for the bureaucratic information policy can only be appraised in a rough functional analysis.

The communication strategies pursued by the adoption counselor would initially appear to be designed to induce applicants to revise their own objectives by depicting the bureaucratic reality of the adoption procedure. Furthermore, the departure from the ideal type of initial expectations probably leads to a lowering of expectations, which in its turn has functional significance for the creation of greater scope for bureaucratic action. The statement, "There are hardly any placeable babies," is probably intended to bring about an adjustment to reality on the part of the applicants, an adjustment that could extend the scope for placing children who do not correspond to the parental ideal type. The maxim of matching supply and demand probably causes applicants to abandon their hopes of an albeit small degree of autonomy in the constitution of their family and take into account the autonomy of the social bureaucracy. The statements on their quantitative prospects probably make them feel that they have only slight chances of being successful. This undermines their original expectations and extends the scope for the professional selection of suitable applicants.

Ensuring sufficient scope for professional action can undoubtedly be rated as a basic requirement for an adoption placement procedure guided by the principle of protecting the interests of the child. Nevertheless, it is fair to ask whether functional alternatives exist for the attainment of this goal, especially in view of the fact that the bureaucratic reference to reality is a construct that has only a very loose factual grounding. Almost 50 percent of adoption applicants in 1976 were able to adopt a child via the Hamburg adoption agency, and a further 9 percent via external adoption institutions (Table 15). 37 percent of the applicants took in a child not older than four months old; over half of the applicants began adoption care with a child younger than one year (Table 33). The bureaucratic reference to "the reality of adoption," therefore, has clearly compensatory features. Against the background of the growing number of applicants, which ties down enormous manpower capacities of the social administration, it develops into an antitype of parental expectations. In doing so it overshoots reality and creates new facts, for example, by triggering multiple applications after emphasizing how slight the chances of success really are. Particularly the fact that it constructs a reality in such a problematic manner suggests that a closer look should be taken at the question of functional alternatives.

To begin with, the first information discussion is an unsatisfactory institution because it burdens applicants with considerable frustration at the very beginning of adoption procedure. Their identity as prospective parents is severely shattered, and their orientation to the pattern of normality degraded, without enabling a redefinition of their own action goals at such short notice. According to the adoptive parents, the suffering they are expected to endure is occasionally legitimated from the bureaucratic perspective as a necessary test of nerves, intended as an introduction to the first stage of selection and conceived in line with the image of the desirable (persevering) adoptive parents. These suppositions cannot be considered in any greater detail within the framework of this study. One thing, however, seems certain: In the name of the best interests of the child applicants are expected to cope with a conflict, triggered by reference to the bureaucratic reference to reality, that cannot be legitimated by the necessary psychological costs of guaranteeing procedural rationality.[46]

The first information discussion is an unsatisfactory institution because it creates a potential for strategic interaction by the applicants detrimental to the rational acts of decision making by the adoption counselor "in the best interests of the child." Via the bureaucratic depiction of reality the applicants are only afforded a superficial insight into the relevances set by the adoption counselor. During the period that follows, therefore, applicants will orient their presentation of self to the values that "count" in the procedure, namely to child-centered orientations; more will be given on this aspect in the analysis of individual case histories during adoption procedure later on in this chapter. The abrupt confrontation of parental expectations with the procedurally dominant perspective of the adoption agency probably produces a situation in which the adoption counselor is unable to gain the understanding of parental value orientations that he or she really needs to be able to take a decision of such importance to the child's future and in the child's interests. The adoption practice described here is an example of how the degree of efficiency of public administration decreases in line with the extent to which the perspective of the persons affected by such decisions is underrated in its significance for a justified course of decision making and in line with the extent to which the orientation towards the satisfaction needs of the persons affected are ignored.[47]

A functional alternative to the first information discussion would be a communication structure that enables a gradual interlinking of perspectives. The necessary scope for action required in professional adoption placement activities would be guaranteed by enabling applicants to gradually learn how to balance out their initial ideal-type expectations regarding the constitution of family with the bureaucratic perspective of procedural reality. The prerequisite for a successful redefinition of own goals by applicants would be the greater acceptability of their initial hopes, which need not then be excluded from communication with the adoption counselor. One adoptive mother formulated the problems associated with an exaggeratedly abrupt degradation of her own perspective as follows:

ADOPTIVE MOTHER: And I find that, that, well, that—that's something I would
    still like to criticize *today,* even though almost three years have passed since:
    that not enough time and attention is given to the adoption applicants, that
    the youth welfare office still organizes *massive* deterrence maneuvers.
INTERVIEWER: Hm . . .

ADOPTIVE MOTHER: And I find that unfair: they still seem to be stuck to the idea that you should turn up with tremendously noble intentions right from the start and that you should be informed about every detail of the situation. And they still take the view there that whoever's unwilling to accept a deprived background and all possible social damage . . .

INTERVIEWER: Hm . . .

ADOPTIVE MOTHER: to accept that, that they're not suited to adopt a child. . . .

A gradual interlinking of perspectives would not only diminish the burden of suffering for applicants. The basis for strategic interaction would also be reduced, thus allowing the adoption counselor to use his or her professional expertise with a greater sense of certainty that his or her action is in the best interests of the child thanks to a deeper insight into the processes of parental learning.

A changing of customary practice could undoubtedly only be achieved by extending bureaucratic staff resources. The shortcomings of the early stages of adoption procedure—the frustration of applicants as well as the long-term consequences of strategic interaction—certainly cannot be blamed on the lack of good will on the part of the adoption counselor.

The Preliminary Decision about Adoptive Suitability by the Local Social Worker

Initial Bureaucratic Selection and Initial Presentation of Self by Applicants

In Hamburg a hierarchy of decision makers decides what constitutes parental eligibility. Via a report on the adoption applications the local social worker provides a basis for the final decision by the adoption counselor on the suitability of applicants as adoptive parents (granting of an adoption care authorization certificate).[48] As indicated by a number of narrative interviews, however, the social worker in the local youth welfare office usually does not begin his or her activity in complete impartiality, but is "put in the picture" beforehand. The file (at least occasionally) is "weighted" by the adoption counselor's assessment of applicant suitability following the first information discussion. This can function as a signal to the social worker, who is in a subordinate position.

The following—most extreme—example of a relatively fast formation of opinion reveals a great deal about a number of the decisive values in the adoption procedure and the varying opportunities of matching these value expectations depending on class membership. During the information discussion an applicant couple belonging to the lower middle class experiences its inferiority with respect to strategies of verbal interaction.

ADOPTIVE MOTHER: And during the first information talk, for example, my husband, er, kept pretty much in the background as we both disliked the whole procedure. And, er, there were two other couples. And the one couple were academics. They spoke up straight away. And, er, they had the biggest mouths, kept on talking the whole time. We didn't get a word in edgeways, so I then, perhaps twice or three times, er, asked some questions myself, something I felt was important. And my husband said hardly anything. . . .

A "very impulsive" discussion with the social worker in this couple's own home prompted the social worker to tell the couple about the discrepancy between the prior assessment by the adoption counselor and her own assessment.

ADOPTIVE FATHER: After I'd talked for an hour or two, very impulsively, she said, shook her head and grinned and said: "Well, it says here in the report that you are very disinterested."

This categorization, which was very hurtful for the adoption applicant, increased his uncertainty during the further course of adoption procedure, to the point of extreme willingness to compromise when an unexpected "offer" was made. Whereas this adoptive father, who invested tremendous effort on behalf of a deprived child later on in the adoption history, raises the question of the fairness of the procedure after suffering from this early classification, a different adoptive father stresses the basic incompatibility of letting the same person lead and assess a discussion, emphasizing the problematic aspects of this selection approach.

ADOPTIVE FATHER: What personally, er, annoyed me a bit afterwards, I must say, was that, that we found out later on that this social worker [adoption counselor] had, er, made a preliminary assessment within the framework of this information discussion of each couple which was there and that was, er, bound to go wrong; and, er, for one thing, er, someone cannot, er, do most of the talking, that's something you will know better than myself, since that's what you study . . .
INTERVIEWER: Yes.
ADOPTIVE FATHER: and, er, at the same time assess the discussion. And, er, in this respect there was on the other hand no form of assessment, since the dialogue was missing. And, er, in my opinion that was the first . . . beginning, that here in the form of selection, in the way the adoptive parents were, er, treated, that the style chosen was not what is might have been.

For the social worker the beginning of the adoption procedure is not only reflected in the selection steering by the adoption counselor. The application documents also bear the marks of the events that have already taken place in the adoption agency. For those applicants who made their applications during more recent years, for example, the experience of the first information discussion finds its expression in the following procedural stages. In a particularly reflected form the following narrative passage establishes a link between the insight into the structures of bureaucratic action gained during the first information discussion and the way in which the applicants present themselves in their application documents, especially in their curriculum vitae.

ADOPTIVE FATHER: And in the light of the basically negative situation [reference to the first information discussion] you naturally ask yourself what should such a, er, curriculum vitae be like so as to be able to pull through such an atmosphere? So we had our doubts, I feel you *should* have doubts when you talk about yourself and when you expect something from other people, who, after all . . . tackle a problem, which could be of, er, decisive personal significance.

In many narrations the curriculum vitae, which in compliance with the request by the adoption counselor should be kept very personal (handwritten), is presented as an event accompanied by sighing and groaning, as "the longest curriculum vitae of my life," as the balancing act between emphasizing certain aspects of one's biography and the assumed criteria of the adoption counselor for procedural success. The uncertainty expressed here, "the doubts," and the tremendous strain of drawing up a curriculum vitae all support the assumption mentioned earlier that the abrupt confrontation with the bureaucratic perspective increases the potential for strategic interaction already latent in the adoption procedure.

The loss of impartiality on the part of the social worker as a result of the prior selection steering corresponds to a partiality on the part of the applicants. They piece together their various documents on their health and material assets as well as their curricula vitae by taking into account the dominant interaction partner in adoption procedure via tentative attempts at role-taking. The application documents are then handed in to the social worker at the local youth welfare office as the first decision-making body.

The Social Worker's Visit to the Home of Adoption Applicants

The fact that the social worker's visit to the home of prospective adoptive parents is not generally recapitulated as a particularly stressful event despite signs of partiality on both sides is probably due to its location. The home of the adoption applicants generally provides a framework that in many respects documents a significant social status and conveys the certainty of a respectable member of society.

Whereas the clientele of social work in many cases experiences a visit to their homes as an intrusion into their own territory—Gerhard Riemann, for example, described a number of experiences of degradation undergone by homeless persons during inspections to check the justifiability of welfare assistance payments[49]—one's own home represents a resource in the case of adoption applicants. Particularly in cases in which the initial stage of the adoption procedure in the adoption agency rooms was experienced as a situation of tremendous uncertainty the territory of one's own home can enable a new autonomy of action. One lower middle class applicant, for example, describes how she heard "that they also look in the closets." When the social worker came along to her home, she took the offensive by asking the social worker to look in the closets. This injunction took the edge off of any possible act of inspection, since it turned the adoption applicant into a subject rather than object of inspection.

In the overwhelming majority of cases the sentiment expressed by the following adoptive father is representative of the response to the home visit:

ADOPTIVE FATHER: She talked to us, but quite . . . *quite normally,* not like a big inspection. . . . It was a quite normal discussion.

The normality of interaction is produced by the interpretation of the situation by both interaction partners. Adoption applicants feel that the objective of this procedural stage is proof of "orderly circumstances" and, to judge by the sample, they generally soon feel certain that they possess the corroborative potential. The unproblematic nature of the fulfillment of these criteria can be reflected in a pretty short narrative consideration of the event.

ADOPTIVE FATHER: A local social worker came along, who then took a look at our domestic circumstances . . .
INTERVIEWER: Hm . . .
ADOPTIVE FATHER: a separate room was there. The circumstances are orderly, well, you know, what they generally inspect. But as we were basically certain about it, it was a good thing really, checking everything so thoroughly. We didn't mind going through the whole thing.

Just as the awareness of one's ability to fulfill the given criteria makes the effort of gathering all the documents for adoption application seem acceptable—in some cases there is even approval of a thorough inspection—the uncertainty about one's own social status can make the exposure of personal circumstances a clear burden for some applicants. Such signs of irritation and annoyance at this status examination can only be found in two interviews with applicants belonging to the lower middle class. In one case the adoptive mother complains:

ADOPTIVE MOTHER: You have to [hesitantly] lay yourself bare. . . .
INTERVIEWER: Hm . . .
ADOPTIVE MOTHER: Somehow, you, you have to expose yourself. . . .

Yet even in these cases of initial reservedness towards individual procedural elements the applicants were soon able to establish a feeling of certainty in their own territory. The social worker is also involved in bringing about a normal discussion; from his or her viewpoint both the financial situation of the adoption applicants and their family situation give no grounds for a more critical examination. Against the background of their usual clientele the adoption applicants generally present a welcome contrast for the visiting social worker. During two group discussions with social workers I discovered that they regard the assessment of an adoption application as one of the more pleasant fields of activity in their professional daily routine. With their occupational, educational, and material resources adoption applicants would also appear to provide a guarantee for the type of family that the social worker classifies as not a burden for future social work. In fact, they embody those values that social workers often miss in their other professional interaction relations. Consequently, misgivings about the adoption of a child are only rarely passed on to the adoption agency. The "normality of the discussion" soon gives applicants the feeling that the social worker is willing to confirm their adoptive suitability. The stage of adoption procedure that takes place on one's home turf is probably a phase marked by a relatively insignificant tendency to engage in strategic interaction.

In the recapitulation of events, efforts to make a good impression are only mentioned in a few cases, primarily by members of the lower middle class. It seems fair to assume that in the other cases the techniques of impression management[50] become less significant as a result of an experienced ability to present a favorable status and territory. As regards the role enactment of the adoption applicants the following example relates to the aspect of requisites, to the domestic environment.

ADOPTIVE FATHER: And we've got it nicely furnished at our place. Of course, that makes a different impression than if we had beer crates or orange crates lying around in the living-room [laughs].

The next example relates to a lower-middle-class applicant couple that had already been refused adoption once before because the husband had not completed his professional training, the couple had not been married long enough (three years) and was too young (both younger than 25). In this case, too, the activities before the expected visit by the social worker initially concentrate on the domestic environment.

ADOPTIVE MOTHER: I then took two days to clean up the place [laughing], since I wanted to make as good an impression as possible.

Although the ascription of parental eligibility here was helped along with housewifely qualities, the biographical peculiarities exposed during the course of the discussion with the social worker were able—in the opinion of the applicants—to reinforce her confirmation of parental eligibility.[51]

ADOPTIVE MOTHER: I can still remember, that she kept on encouraging us to say something about our childhood . . .

ADOPTIVE FATHER: Hm . . .

ADOPTIVE MOTHER: and she, I think, had very, very, slight religious leanings, somehow. And during my youth I went through a girl scout period, organized by the church [laughing], and she was so pleased about that, and then asked me whether we now and again . . . oh yes, and then she saw the guitar.

INTERVIEWER: Hm . . .

ADOPTIVE MOTHER: "Do you play a musical instrument?" I said "Yes, my husband plays guitar, he used to play in a group when he was younger," and I said "Sometimes we sing a bit," ridiculous really. And that then meant . . .

ADOPTIVE FATHER: That then meant family music.

ADOPTIVE MOTHER: [laughing] as if, er, Mr. and Mrs. N. play family music.

ADOPTIVE FATHER: Play music.

ADOPTIVE MOTHER: We were then [classed as] tremendously Christian, and played family music, [amused] we must have really cut a good figure. I found it so strange, well, somehow I felt a bit uneasy. . . .

A number of aspects of the strategic presentation of self in the adoption procedure can be illustrated by referring to this example. The information given during the course of communication with the social worker is not really a "misrepresentation"[52] in the sense that it refers to events that are not "true." Their empirical content is quite correct, but the speech act lacks the element of a construction of reciprocity. The narrator does not "indicate"[53] the content to her interaction partner in the way she sees it herself, but in a filtered form. In the attempt at role-taking on behalf of the more powerful interaction partner in the adoption procedure ("had very, very, slight religious leanings") the information acquires its "strategic significance," which does not comply with the significance in the perspective of the actors "here and now." In the example a past value orientation of action is presented as if it were still of current relevance. Against the background of a previous rejection as adoptive parents the applicant in this case allows herself to be prompted into a presentation of identity that, although contrasting with self-identity, takes the latter into account in one central respect: the desire for a child. Faced by the conflict between self-identity and the presentation of identity—I use the term as applied by Goffman rather than by Krappmann[54]—the applicant, who already feels uncertain because of a refusal once before, opts for the presentation. In her eyes the management of impressions appears to be more likely to create the conditions enabling a future life in harmony with a priority goal of self-identity, namely the role of mother. Admittedly, the price for the discrepancy between self-identity and the presentation of identity is the feeling of uneasiness ("somehow I felt a bit uneasy").

The previous illustration of strategic interaction underlines the problematic nature of determining parental eligibility. The narrative interviews with adoptive parents do not provide a clear indication of the guiding criteria for the assessment by the social worker. Adoption placement guidelines,[55] however, point in the same direction as the assumptions of adoption applicants: The economic and social circumstances—to take up our examples, the nicely furnished and cleaned-up domestic environment, the period as a girl scout, and the playing of family music—as orientation values suggest that parental eligibility cannot be determined as a specific competence in isolation from other factors. Parental eligibility as socializational competence would appear to be embedded in a bundle of status symbols and qualities, which initially relates to the concept of a respectable adult in our society. The fulfillment of generally accepted social values is probably a predeterminative additional quality for parental eligibility. The assumption of an "a priori competence of everyman to lead a marital and family life,"[56] which initially appears to be inoperative in the case of a bureaucratic constitution of family, would again seem to become operative in accordance with respectability of social status.

So far the narrative passages relating to the social worker's visit as an "upstream" stage in the selection process only indicated a number of basic features of adoption procedure as a whole, such as the problem of the strategic presentation of self to ensure parental eligibility. Finally, an example will be considered that presents strategic interaction as a virtually unavoidable reaction by the applicant to the behavior of the social worker in an effort to ensure procedural success and not as a course of action initiated by the weaker interaction partner. Furthermore, the example illustrates the interpretational scope of the procedural administrator, which—without being obvious to the applicants—can determine the fate of the adoption application.

ADOPTIVE MOTHER: I can mention another example. Er, with our first child the social worker kept on asking *again and again*, whether . . .

ADOPTIVE FATHER: *boy or girl.*

ADOPTIVE MOTHER: we would prefer to have a boy or a girl. We *adamantly* refused to answer this question, we couldn't have anyway. It didn't . . .

ADOPTIVE FATHER: matter to us.

ADOPTIVE MOTHER: matter to us really.

INTERVIEWER: Hm . . .

ADOPTIVE MOTHER: In the end, we got the impression that she interpreted that as *indifference*. I mean, it's obvious, you think about how [pleased] you can make the best *impression*.

INTERVIEWER: Hm . . .

ADOPTIVE MOTHER: That's *logical*. And then my husband quite casually said: "Well, a little girl is quite nice really," but really he merely dropped the remark casually.

How the applicants cope with events during the selection phase depends on the numerous pecularities of the communication situation, such as the assessment of one's own communicative abilities during interaction with a certain adoption counselor and the experiences that have accumulated during the course of adoption procedure and that then provide a source of orientational guidance. The following focuses on a particular aspect of the analysis of processes of communication, namely on the question of the interaction resources that applicants bring to bear in the situation. Two types of resources are to be analyzed: (1) the "status-related interaction resources," with which applicants are equipped as already socially defined members of society; and (2) the "child-related interaction resources," which refer to their expectations with respect to the child. With this in mind, an attempt will be made to discover why some applicants move closer to the extreme of an open and egalitarian form of communication, whereas others perceive the disparity of power and the associated barriers to communication.

Applicant Uncertainty and a Tendency to Engage
in Strategic Interaction.

As the procedural administrator does not expose the criteria of selection ("closed awareness context"[67]) the applicant has to assess the words, facial expressions, and gestures of the adoption counselor in a continuous process of interpretation.[68] As a rule, applicants will engage in strategic interaction if they are uncertain about their interaction resources during adoption procedure. Not every uncertainty, however, will lead to strategic interaction. The requirements for a presentation of identity, disguising self-identity and aimed at ensuring procedural success, are:

1. The analytical ability to know how the procedural administrator will assess the applicant's interaction resources in terms of a successful adoption procedure[69] (own acceptability in the meta-perspective)
2. The assumption of a discrepancy between one's own resources and those desired in the procedure (uncertain acceptability in the meta-perspective)
3. The ability to utilize the assumed discrepancy in communication with the procedural administrator in such a way as to reduce it via the presentation of one's own interaction resources (strategic interaction competence[70])

Applicant Uncertainty and the Specification of the Desired Child along
Various Attributive Dimensions

The possibility to engage in the strategic presentation of identity above all presents itself in response to the crucial question asked during the final discussion with the adoption counselor: "What kind of child do you have in mind?" At this stage—contrary to the intention of the persons involved—the symbolism of the commodity character of the child moves into the adoption procedure. Whereas nature provides the indeterminable child—only its biological link is fixed—the question and its constraints of specification obliges applicants to particularize the desired child along various attributive dimensions. During the final discussion the applicant is called upon to simulate an act of choice, which the adoption counselor prestructures along the lines of the "value" concepts of the prospective parents.

The arrangement of the construction of family in this way leads to a clash between two principles: the principle of the intrinsic value of every child (or to put it another way, of the value of the child "in itself") and the parental idea of the value of the child as a child "for us." These two orientations cannot be attributed to just one side respectively during the procedure; a conflict of goals arises for both sides. The adoption counselor verbally expresses her loyalty to the principle of protecting the interests of each child, yet during the actual placement procedure the principle of determining the child's "value" reasserts its significance—which is a service of higher or lower value depending on parental eligibility. On the other hand, in their endeavor to move closer to the pattern of normality, adoption applicants not only come into conflict with the pattern of action declared by the social administration. Their own sense of morality tells them that they should support the humanitarian norms underlying the principle of the intrinsic value of every child. A number of stories relating to the first encounter with the child and to a complicated decision to adopt the child make it particularly clear how strongly these parents feel that "a child is not a commodity." Nevertheless, the parental interests of the adoption applicants initially prevent them from affording so much significance to the principle of every child's intrinsic value as the adoption agency—when matching supply and demand—would like to see. The balancing act performed by applicants between articulating their own desires and making concessions to the assumed expectations of the procedural administrator will now be illustrated.

Just as strategies that move closer to the bureaucratic perspective are rated as more conducive to success, those applicants are assumed to stand the best chance of adoption placement who refrain from insisting on options with respect to the child. Referring to a discussion with the adoption counselor, for example, we find the following in one of the interviews:

ADOPTIVE MOTHER: The only thing which we wanted—I would have liked a girl and my husband a boy, and then I said "80 percent a girl, 80 . . . and 20 percent a boy,'' and then she said ''The more wishes you have the more difficult it is.''

The idea of a possible sanctioning of openly expressed wishes, something discernible in several interviews, would appear to induce applicants right from the start—as opposed to the previous example—to be careful when it comes to stating their options. In many cases applicants simply mark out certain thresholds of tolerance (''up to the age of one''), whereas at the same time, as a counterbalance so to speak, the relinquishment of any express wishes in other fields is thrown into the balance.[71] Here is an example in which the option of a (maximum) age, a central option for almost all applicants, is balanced out a little by refraining from any sex preference.

ADOPTIVE FATHER: That's something we left up to them, whether a boy or a girl.
INTERVIEWER: Hm . . .
ADOPTIVE FATHER: That was something they asked us beforehand . . .
INTERVIEWER: Hm . . .
ADOPTIVE FATHER: and to us it didn't matter. We said that we'd take a child up to the age of one.

During this balancing act between the desired approximation to the pattern of normality and ensuring the success of the adoption procedure by making concessions, the willingness to refrain from a certain sex would appear to function as a calculated contribution to the procedural administrator and his or her scope of action. This does not mean to say that this presentation of identity deviates from the actual orientations of prospective adoptive parents. In comparison with all other concessions, refraining from sex determination is probably least burdened by an ambivalent decision. Assuming the correctness of the claim that the main aim of adoption is to ensure the parental role in the adult role design, this is likely to diminish the significance of the sex of the child.[72] This option is only expressed in isolated (four) cases. (In the supplementary 1976 survey almost 70 percent refrain from stating a sex preference; see Table 13.)

By refraining from any determination of the child's sex the applicants are able to reconstruct the conditions of the pattern of a normal family constitution, which they try to achieve via options in the case of the other parameters of the child—as in the case of age, for example. With the exception of two cases of applicants who were already birth parents and who planned adoption in the interests of the child, all applicants state their desire that the child should not exceed a certain (maximum) age. The prospective parents generally mark out an area still able to fulfill the conditions of a start to socialization, even though they fix different limits. Some want a newborn child (five of the 37 placements), others a child who is still a baby (18), and most applicants hope for a child not older than six months. Even those applicants who decide during the course of adoption procedure to adopt an older child[73] ("up to the age of three") sometimes invest considerable effort to make sure that their limit is taken into consideration. As age is the attributive dimension to which every child, thanks to nature, belongs, it becomes a highly significant option. The clarification of when biological or social parenthood should begin is a crucial decision for adoption applicants. As opposed to the general significance of the dimension of age the significance of other attributes is reduced by the fact that they relate to a contingent case, for example, of the clearly handicapped child, the child of a prostitute, or the dark-skinned child. The constellation of possible unfavorable attributes is sounded out during the final discussion with the adoption counselor to test the scope of parental willingness in terms of the factor of socialization. Depending on the attribute in question, however, there is a varying probability of congruence between the simulation of the act of choice and its reality.

The adaptation of one's own intentions to the assumed intentions of the procedural administrator is often reflected in a "negotiating package" in which the attribute of age—in accordance with its significance in the plan of family constitution—appears on the side of the more clearly specified attributes, balanced perhaps, as in the example just given, by concessions with regard to sex determination. A comparison of the attributes on the "list of desired attributes" gives an idea of the point at which the value of the child "for us" becomes questionable for German adoption applicants during the 1970s. On the list of desired attributes, albeit a long way behind the attribute of age, we find the options on health and the color of the child's skin. Not only the criterion of sex determination is chosen to balance out one's own expectations, but also the willingness to adopt the "child of a prostitute." Even though only a small percentage of the children relinquished for adoption were born of prostitutes (in the 1976 supplementary study 12 percent of the birth mothers were listed under the occupation of prostitute; see Table 27) the "child of a prostitute" appears to be a part of the question repertoire of the final discussion. A child with such a background is only refused in two cases, whereas in a number of other cases the willingness to adopt the child of a prostitute is put to beneficial use in the negotiating situation. The following narrative passage presents an example of a balancing out of insistence on and relinquishment of desired attributes in the dimensions of age, sex, and background, an example that emphasized the factor of undemandingness three times despite the fact that the level of demands is comparatively high.

ADOPTIVE MOTHER: We declared our willingness to adopt any child, it didn't make any difference to us, we would have also taken the child of a prostitute.

... The only qualification we made was that the child should be as young as possible and if possible not older than six months. . . . Otherwise we agreed to everything, but not a handicapped child.

Whereas prospective adoptive parents today are generally able to tolerate the child of a prostitute—in the hope of the social plasticity of its personality—prospective adoptive parents in the Federal Republic of Germany still have problems when it comes to the color of the child's skin.

ADOPTIVE MOTHER: We would have also, er, taken the child of a pro . . . prostitute, that didn't matter to us. We just didn't want a colored child.

The darker color of the child's skin is not only the attribute that most clearly shows a deviation from the pattern of normality. In addition, this attribute has such a high social conflict potential that most applicants are unwilling to risk the project of adoption with such a "handicap" ("That's just something we felt unable to handle"). The following example, however, shows how the shade of color—depending on the deviation from the color that ranks as "normal" in West German society—enables differing levels of tolerance.

ADOPTIVE MOTHER: Right from the start we said that we would also take children from immigrant workers, that's a question that's asked, you see.
INTERVIEWER: Hm . . .
ADOPTIVE MOTHER: We only made the qualification that we would . . . *not* be able to take a full Negroid child . . . you know, completely black. . . .

When determining the child's "value" the child of Negroid origin would appear to get the absolutely lowest rating, a rating that placed such a child beyond the tolerance thresholds of most applicants. It seems to trigger more fears than the older child or the child with physical or mental handicaps. It remains to be seen how the "value" concepts of prospective adoptive parents change as the number of persons living in our society whose skin is a different color increases. Our sample at any rate indicates that for the time being during its planning phase a constitution of family without shared biological roots is mainly limited to children of the same or a similar race.

The narrative interviews provide plenty of indications for the thesis that most applicants would feel that their own acceptability is threatened if their ideal expectations were to be exposed. The willingness to compromise demonstrated in one form or another by almost all couples would suggest that a few additional assets should be added to the resources brought into play in the adoption procedure, assets that can primarily be acquired along the line of parental willingness to also accept a child who deviates from the ideal of the young, healthy, and white-skinned baby. With few exceptions most applicants would appear to present their initially parent-centered decision to adopt in a more child-centered light by taking a more or less small step towards the acceptance of the principle of the intrinsic value of every child. As a result, a further resource is added—for the sake of ensuring the success of adoption procedure—to the resources that already play a part in the procedure. The will to constitute a family in line with aspects of humanity is demonstrated by the parental willingness to also show affection for a child who falls below the relatively high "normality value rating" of the newborn healthy and white-skinned infant.

Testing how great the scope is for options that do not jeopardize the success of adoption procedure is like a project to "determine marginal values." The language of the market, which already sounded through in the comparison of supply and demand, continues when the "value" of the "commodity" is determined. This commodity aspect is not blamed on the individual participants of the adoption procedure; it is caused by the adoption procedure itself as long as prospective adoptive parents are guided by the ideal of a biological constitution of family and as long as they have a certain amount of residual autonomy during the procedure. The sublimation of parental expectations to the point of selfless devotion to any child will remain a model without prospects of realization for the majority of applicants.

Applicant Uncertainty Increased by the Procedural Administrator and the Tendency to Engage in Strategic Interaction

The previously described forms of calculated self-presentation resulted from role-taking attempts for the more powerful person in the interaction relationship. The patterns of action shown by the social bureaucracy during earlier stages of the adoption procedure probably provided points of reference indicating which presentation of identity as prospective parents might stand a chance of improving one's chances of success. Even though the final discussion has key significance in the adoption procedure, communication at this stage would appear to be more relaxed than during the first information discussion. The situation of being able to talk to the adoption counselor in a one-couple-only situation probably gives the applicants the feeling that they are no longer confronted by a strange world, but that they can utilize the possibility of self-presentation. What is more, they have probably already learned a great deal about the possibility of calculated presentations during the preceding course of adoption procedure.

One in four of the narrative interviews, however, contains more than just a brief recapitulation of the questions asked and answers given during the final discussion. The narrative content reveals a great deal about which aspects of the bureaucratic selection procedure applicants regard as the most burdensome, for example:

1. The question strategies of the adoption counselor
2. The fact of being subjected to the assessment by just a single counselor and his or her concept of parental eligibility
3. The feeling of powerlessness when confronted by professional ideas of which child should be placed for adoption

The growing difficulties associated with matching "supply" and "demand" leads to a growing temptation on the part of the procedural administrator to try and gently push applicants in the desired direction of reduced expectations. The calculated presentation of identity as prospective adoptive parents can begin to crumble at any time when faced by irritating questions by the adoption counselor, because the moral position of the applicants with their normal parental interests is weak. Their "value" specifications can easily be devalued in view of the fact that children who are "hard to place" also need parental care. If, for whatever reason, the adoption counselor wishes to question the plausibility of the options specified by the applicants, the fact that he or she seizes on a particular aspect in the best interests of the child will always seem justified. The balancing act between the desired approximation to the pattern of normality and ensuring the success of the adoption procedure, therefore, is extremely prone to disruptions. The following two examples bear out this point. The first example illustrates how the secret desire everybody has for a newborn child can be devalued during the adoption procedure if the applicants have not decided to refrain from expressing such a desire. As this example reflects the entire questioning ritual as well as the uncertainty of the applicants in their situation of dependence, the passage is presented more extensively.

ADOPTIVE FATHER: Then the adoption counselor starts off . . . with a . . . with a kind of shock therapy, you see. "Well, what do you have in mind?" You see? Instead of making the whole thing a bit more relaxed, they, at least that's the way I feel, make it all a bit gray . . .

INTERVIEWER: Hm . . .

ADOPTIVE FATHER: don't they. They say "Well, if you want to adopt a child, well, do you want the child of a prostitute? Do you want, would you also take in a handicapped child? All questions which are understandable, aren't they?

INTERVIEWER: Hm . . .

ADOPTIVE FATHER: OK, and then you come along with your own ideas. You still feel a bit nervous, and you don't want to upset her. You always have the feeling if you say anything wrong they'll put you at the back of the queue. Well, and then they asked these questions. And then we said "Well, we would like to take a *young* child, if possible a baby, and, again if possible, one which has just been born, a clinic adoption." "Yes, do you realize that if the mother has twins you'll have to take the twins?" Such *questions* are asked during this discussion, and then you go back home thinking Christ, if I say something wrong now, you see, then [laughing] the woman's going to be really annoyed. . . .

Whereas doubts are expressed in this case about the applicants as competent planners of a constitution of family oriented to the normal case, the next example provides an insight into the situation of negotiation, but also of coercion,[74] which can arise following a declared willingness to adopt an older child. First of all, the preliminary history, which despite the adoptive mother's criticism of the adoption counselor does contain elements of role-taking.

ADOPTIVE MOTHER: The very first time I called up [in the adoption agency] there was a lady there, and, I mean, they're undoubtedly, you have to see it that way, bombarded by such phone calls, such . . . such incomplete, someone who just spontaneously decided they want to adopt a child.
INTERVIEWER: Hm . . .
ADOPTIVE MOTHER: And now she knew, she didn't know me, just over the phone. "I, we would like to adopt a child." She probably thought to herself "Aha, I wonder what she wants, probably a baby. It has to be fair-haired and blue-eyed," since she . . .
INTERVIEWER: Hm . . .
ADOPTIVE MOTHER: "I see, I see, but if you . . . want a baby, fair-haired, blue-eyed, then you don't need, er, we don't have one" and that was that, bang. And then I happened to tell her that that was not what we wanted. We don't mind if it's . . . slightly deficient or older. "Oh I see," she said, "in that case that's OK." Looking at it from their situation it's understandable. . . . I mean, they . . . are the cases which are most difficult to place.

This couple is finally asked to come along to a discussion in the adoption agency. The adoptive father describes the inquiries about and attempts to influence parental expectations in a quite sarcastic way. The rest of the next section of the narrative interview makes it clear that this couple's own case history forms the background, even though the structure of the verbal presentation is without any special reference to one's own case.

ADOPTIVE FATHER: Then you have to go along to the adoption counselor, and that's when things start, isn't it? . . . Then she says "What do you want then: one or two arms, one or two children, with or without a hare-lip, a Negroid child or what?" Then you are, then they try to sound out the situation: "What are they going to take from what's on offer?"
ADOPTIVE MOTHER: Yes, they play poker, don't they, first of all the worst offers. . . . "Let's see how far they'll go, these parents." And then you're still able . . .

The adoptive father then complains that "this form of inquiry is somehow not motivating" because the agency aims at lowering parental expectations without promising some form of support for the parents who take on difficult tasks. In orientation to his own case he works on the assumption that in many cases specific files provide the background for the process of negotiating.

ADOPTIVE FATHER: If they start speaking about certain criteria, the motivation for the inquiry is frequently some file somewhere, . . .

INTERVIEWER: Hm . . .

ADOPTIVE FATHER: which comes to their mind, undoubtedly, . . .

INTERVIEWER: Hm . . .

ADOPTIVE FATHER: and that's why this inquiry is really a bit . . . discouraging? The way it's organized is not really that positive, a lot of people have confirmed that . . . the fact that the information and the positive presentation of the whole thing is pushed into the background, that this inquiry always has something negative about it. . . . You get a really bad conscience if you say "No, I want it to have two arms at least."

INTERVIEWER: Hm . . .

ADOPTIVE FATHER: "Does it have to have, er, can it have at least a sight defect?" "Well, we don't want it to be blind," like that. And at some stage you move into the situation when you feel as if you can't really turn down any offer. Somehow you feel under tremendous pressure to accept. . . .

The mode of negotiation is finally reflected in the obligation to accept. This transcription extract contains references to the final sphere of autonomy retained by the applicants (two arms; sight defect but not blind). The price to be paid for this residual parental autonomy, however, also becomes clear ("a really bad conscience"). The attributive variants of the hard-to-place older child make even the moral position of the applicants willing to make concessions seem weak if the adoption counselor plays through all possible "devaluations" of the supply of children for adoption within a short space of time to test their acceptability for applicants. The applicants in this case, who were already willing to accept a "slightly deficient" child, are pressured to such a degree into considering an extreme antitype to the normal case that it seems fair to ask whether the concessions made under such communicative coercion can really serve as a sound basis for the evaluation of parental competence.

The extent to which the ascription of parental eligibility is a contingent act that can differ from one adoption counselor to the next is illustrated in the following example of a differing assessment of the same case by two different counselors. In her study on the "professional decisions on the acceptance or rejection of applicants,"[75] Anneke Napp-Peters examined the broad ascriptive spectrum for adoptive suitability. The study clearly shows how individual models of orientation outweigh the occasionally proclaimed stock of shared professional guidelines in this context.[76] The statements by the adoption counselors in the study by Napp-Peters show that the expected motherliness of the prospective adoptive mother is one of the central, albeit highly controversial, aspects of the selection procedure; concern about fatherliness can be viewed as a background aspect. The respective concept of the motherly mother acts as a foreground stereotype that serves as a yardstick for assessment of the applicant's personality structure.

Yet how can an adoption counselor typify a woman not previously met as a motherly personality after simply examining the already completed file and after a single discussion? This question can only be considered in this study with reference to a single case with a "favorable" constellation. In this particular case a change of personnel in the adoption agency enabled an insight into professional behavior that is otherwise inaccessible via an interpretation of the course of the adoption procedure by the persons concerned. In this instance a discussion with a second counselor proved necessary, who then dissociated herself from the first assessment drawn up in a situation described as follows:

ADOPTIVE MOTHER: During this final discussion we came along to someone I . . . I must admit, I didn't take a liking to right from the very first moment, the way it sometimes is, you know, something inside. You meet someone and you've got the feeling there's a wall between you, whether you want it or not and whether you're friendly or not. It was simply there. And she kept on coming back to the fact that I wanted to begin a course in business management in July. The way she presented it, er, this just didn't fit in with her image of a good housewife. She didn't say it directly. She only did that afterwards in the report, that I had no housewifely qualities and didn't fit in that direction at all, that I was more interested in business management, in my job, and other things. All things which never really surfaced during the discussion, where she simply asked me what I was planning to do in the future, and I told her. And I found that a really negative aspect, and she made me out to be an extremely cold and reserved person.

How much the adoptive mother was hurt by this classification is reflected in the structure of the narrative interview, in which she explains how she regarded less emotional forms of communication as appropriate in view of the function of the discussion. It was as if she felt an urge years after the situation to dispute the degradation as not housewifely, cold, and reserved. Two other adoption cases also describe complications relating to the woman's occupational activity. In both cases the applicant couple wanted to split the task of taking care of the child, in one case via half-day jobs for both partners and in the other by giving the husband responsibility for the child in the afternoon while the wife carries out her teaching job at home. In both cases the planned division of labor by the applicants apparently contravened professional adoption placement norms, even though the parental ability to share the workload was credibly presented.

However, the fact that the plan to take up a course in business management, a decision taken in view of the childlessness of marriage, in itself fails to comply with the adoption counselor's concept of the motherly adoptive mother, is the most drastic indication of a retrogressive model of the female role. It is impossible to clarify here how far the concept of the worthy adoptive mother is oriented to the general mother ideal of the adoption counselor or how far it is derived from certain assumptions relating to a successful adoptive mother–child relationship. If the ascription of adoptive suitability is indeed a projection to the requirements of socializational interaction it should not be ignored that, allowing for the significance of emotionality, for a growing number of women occupational activity helps contribute towards ensuring an emotional relationship with the child that is not adversely affected by ambivalence.[77] The potential of occupational activity when it comes to conveying familial environment to the child during later stages of the family cycle is probably also overlooked if a plan by the adoptive mother to attend a course to obtain professional qualifications in an occupation that fails to comply with the stereotype of female occupations is in itself interpreted as a reason to question "maternal eligibility."[78]

The inference made from her interest in business management that the adoptive mother is a "very cold person" was without consequence in this case, because the second adoption counselor annulled the first assessment ("She laughed and found it really amusing"). The experience of helplessness in the face of an identity ascription made by "a somewhat older lady" on the basis of her personal image of an ideal mother, a decision that could have influenced the entire success of the adoption application, sensitized this applicant couple in a special way to the problems involved in the adoption procedure.

ADOPTIVE MOTHER: And that's what I found so negative about it all, you see, the fact that the human aspect was so important, for example, how do I respond to the adoption counselor and how does she respond to me. And the fact that the outcome can be reflected in such a negative way in the report, that's something I don't approve of, er . . .
ADOPTIVE FATHER: Right, you don't know, er, how it could be done differently. But I had the feeling that you're basically . . .
ADOPTIVE MOTHER: at their mercy.
ADOPTIVE FATHER: Right, and that you basically have to put on a show, have to . . .
INTERVIEWER: Hm . . .
ADOPTIVE MOTHER: Right.
ADOPTIVE FATHER: as it were, er, adjust to the woman in charge, er.
ADOPTIVE MOTHER: Have to adjust, hm, hm.

The applicants start searching for strategies to help them make optimal use of the still-remaining scope for self-presentation in accordance with the extent to which they recognize the significance of the presentation of self inherent to the structure of adoption procedure.

ADOPTIVE FATHER: I sometimes had the idea—it may sound a bit heretical now—but you have probably heard of, er, I don't know whether it's done today, but it used to be, that these associations for conscientious objectors offer test, er, lessons so as to, er, simulate and play through the, er, procedure for the recognition of conscientious objection. And, er . . .
INTERVIEWER: Hm . . .
ADOPTIVE FATHER: I had the idea, especially during some of the discussions, that, er, you could probably practice certain things with the help of a corresponding simulation of such discussions and present something which is not really true.

The following narrative passage shows that the applicants then also consistently play along with the game of strategic interaction.

ADOPTIVE FATHER: They wanted to shock us, er, by asking us whether we were willing to take children of prostitutes, er, colored children, and so on. That was designed to give us a proper shock. Well [laughing] *aha,* we had agreed more or less beforehand to react to such shock questions accordingly and say *"yes"*. If you were to honestly ask yourself "Would you take the child of prostitute without hesitation?" you might, er, arrive at a different answer in private or under different circumstances. Under these circumstances, of course, the the question was answered accordingly.

The "costs" of strategic interaction for a well-founded adoption decision cannot be overrated; they only seem relatively insignificant if the connection between initial parental expectations and parent–child bonding is ignored.[79]

As soon as doubts are cast upon the applicant's competence in the field of planning the constitution or extension of a family, the adoption procedure, which is already burdened by a substantial degree of uncertainty, moves into new conflict dimensions. Whereas in the previous example the procedural power of the adoption counselor was reflected in a freedom to carry out a personality typification that did not coincide with the self-typification of the person concerned, a different example illustrates the vulnerabilities that can occur if the applicant's concept of the role of the child in the family is devalued by the procedural superiority of professional action norms on two occasions after she had brought her concept of family extension into play in the belief that this would meet with the understanding of the adoption counselor. She had already considered the problems that might occur for her already older birth child in the case of an adoption of a baby or a toddler—focusing motherly attention on the new member of the family would, in her opinion, have proved too much of a strain for the birth child who was in poor health. She then also justified her desire for an older child in her adoption application by referring to the possibility that the older adopted child and the older birth child would be able to play together.

ADOPTIVE MOTHER: I wrote that playing together would be the best way for the children to get used to each other and that I therefore feel that a child round about the age of five would be a good choice. This was not understood the way I meant it. Only a month had passed, but I thought that they had forgotten about me, when the adoption counselor rang me up one morning and shouted over the phone what on earth I was thinking of, wanting to adopt a child under such circumstances. If I want a playmate for my son, she said, then I should go and have a look in the street. "There are enough children there." "Good God," I said [angry] "All I mean is that they would then be able to get used to one another much better. It's only a thought. It doesn't matter." Other parents state "It has to be fair-haired, it has to be blue-eyed, it has to be tall, it has to be fat, it has to be cheerful, it has to be clean," I said "It can be green-eyed and blue-skinned, I couldn't care less, all I care about is that if I adopt a child now who cannot get on with our son and if there is no chance of them getting on, then it's not right for him."

The adoption counselor then urged this applicant to realize her desire for a playmate for her son via a foster child. The prospective adoptive mother in this case, who had initially openly presented her perspective of family extension, finally beat a retreat and resorted to strategic interaction, to which there is apparently no alternative if the applicant is to stand any chance of success.

ADOPTIVE MOTHER: Afterwards I agreed to everything she said.

This example illustrates the suffering imposed by a selection procedure that—due to its orientation to filtering the overabundant demand—takes no time for the time-consuming communication of the behavioral norms underlying professional action. This particular adoptive mother, who is one of the few primarily child-centered adoption applicants in our study, is again confronted with a guideline of adoption placement practice on a second occasion without any possibility of a communication about reciprocal perspectives of the role of the child in the family. The applicant, who in the meantime had taken in a foster child and given birth to a second child, feels that she and her family would be able to spare yet another child a life without parental care. She decides to apply for an older child. She comments on the placement of a baby against her intention as follows:

ADOPTIVE MOTHER: I didn't find it logical at all. After all, such children always manage to find someone willing to adopt them. In my opinion, an adoption counselor should be flexible to say in such a case "OK, then take an older child." First of all, I've shown that I can manage. But that's where the adoption counselors are just unwilling to budge. And that's that! Every time I rang up I was told "You've already got a little girl [the second birth child] and if we give you an older child now then later on 'Yes, the little girl, the youngest one, she's being spoilt, and the other is being neglected.' '' You can talk like a book, that's the way they see things, so we ended up with a baby.

The second application procedure also leads to a situation in which the scope of action demanded by the procedural administrator is endured and one's own plan dropped. The routine application of professional guidelines, in whatever form they may exist, probably facilitates the already difficult steering function of the adoption counselors. A small number of examples, however, show that under certain circumstances the adoption counselors are capable of role flexibility and grant prospective adoptive parents a certain amount of autonomy in their construction of family. The question is: Which applicants are induced during adoption procedure to agree to everything that the adoption counselor suggests, and which applicants stand a chance of asserting their own conception of the constitution or extension of family? Or, to put it another way: What makes applicants unequal?

Applicant Certainty and No Cause to Engage in Strategic Interaction. There are applicants who very soon notice indications of their own acceptability in the adoption procedure. Some applicants are extremely frank about their desired approximation to the pattern of normality and see no reason to balance out their desires with concessions. Some applicants justify their retention of the ideal type of the young, healthy, and white-skinned baby by honestly admitting their limited capacity to cope with any alternative. The behavior and interpretations of the adoption procedure by the privileged applicants will be illuminated with four case histories.

If the meta-perspective is rated as favorable for a successful adoption application this can find its expression in a verbal form which, via the search for the correct words and a slight delaying of speaking, reflects the effort involved in circumventing the embarrassment of self-praise.

ADOPTIVE FATHER: The adoption counselor in our case *clearly* had the impression that, er, we, er, should quite definitely be considered.

ADOPTIVE FATHER: We came, er, one had . . . we almost had the impression, that they had the impression "Yes, an adopted child must definitely be placed in this family."

The assessment of guaranteed acceptability is reinforced by the experience of cooperativeness on the part of the adoption counselor. In virtually all cases in this category the liberality, straightforwardness, and promptness of the procedure is appreciatively emphasized. Unburdened by the pressure of having to "score points" by demonstrating special socializational competence, the unusually extensive scope for autonomous action is fully utilized in an effort to approximate to the pattern of normality. The positive nature of such a procedure is reflected in the following example:

ADOPTIVE FATHER: Everything took place in line with the prescribed . . . pattern: first of all, a letter stating that we wanted to adopt a child, then an initial discussion to specify our desire for a clinic adoption . . .
INTERVIEWER: Hm . . .
ADOPTIVE FATHER: and that we want a healthy child.

The normality of the options is reflected in the fact that the applicants are able to express them. What is more, the orientation of the applicants to the ideal type of child, which they take for granted, is not shaken by question strategies on the part of the adoption counselor. An inquiry by the interviewer made it clear that it is apparently left to the discretion of the applicants to specify the child they desire along the various attributive dimensions.

INTERVIEWER: Yes, but wasn't a suggestion made to you by the authority . . . that you could also have a sick child or that it's possible or that you must be willing to take a sick child?
ADOPTIVE FATHER: No, quite the opposite. That was presented to us as a possibility, but it was completely left up to us . . .
INTERVIEWER: Hm . . .
ADOPTIVE FATHER: to express our wishes.

Whereas the majority of applicants reduce their own wishes to the tolerance threshold in an effort to signal considerations of humanity in favor of the child in need of parental care, this applicant couple enjoys the privilege of not only being freely able to articulate its own wishes but of also being able to point out the risks that could result for the child from an all too permissive placement practice. The previous narrative passage continues:

ADOPTIVE FATHER: We were even told that we could take a look at the child first, a proper look, and then still say yes or no.
INTERVIEWER: Hm . . .
ADOPTIVE FATHER: Something we almost regarded as unreasonable, to pick out the best of the bunch, as it were, just on the basis of the outward appearance of a [newborn] child. Didn't we?
ADOPTIVE MOTHER: *Yes,* and you could even give it back within some days.
ADOPTIVE FATHER: You could give it back.
ADOPTIVE MOTHER: [Outraged laughing] Yes, that's really *brutal.* . . .

A comparison between cases, a comparison between the special case and the previously considered average case, makes it clear how the two orientations that have always clashed in adoption practice—the principle of parental interests and the principle of protecting the best interests of the child—are strangely distributed. Whereas in the one case the adoption

counselor upholds the principle of protecting the best interests of the child
("parents for children") against the applicants, she lets the principle of
parental interests prevail in the other case and runs the risk of being
accused of neglecting the principle of protecting the child's interests
("That's really brutal"). Whereas the applicants on the one hand are
obliged to reduce their own interests as prospective parents in the interest
of the child in need of parental care, the others enjoy the privilege of being
able to assert their interests in many respects and at the same time to
make an appeal on behalf of the best interests of the child. The rejection
of the possibility of giving the child back can be interpreted as a further
mosaic piece through which the privileged applicant couple (two clinic
adoptions) ensures its approximation to the normal case.

In order to demonstrate the contrast to previously considered calculated
presentations of self by other applicants more clearly, let us take a look at
the following example of a list of desired attributes. It shows how—as the
applicants themselves admit—applicants who approach adoption in a
"quite egotistic" way prepare to carry out their plan in the conviction of
guaranteed acceptability, of not having to concede any lowering of "values." The construction of family in this case is single-mindedly designed
in line with the motto of maximum benefit; adoption is considered as a
means of preventing an only-child situation for the already older birth
child. The prospective adoptive parents, however, do not want the adopted
child to become too much of a rival to their frequently ill "little king"; an
option is therefore chosen for a child of the other sex. The desired child is
also specified exactly along other attributive dimensions.

ADOPTIVE MOTHER: Right from the start we said we want . . . to have a baby,
if possible a clinic placement. And, what is more, I must admit, er, that after
our experiences with him [the birth child], because of his illnesses, er, we
did not feel able to cope with . . .
INTERVIEWER: Hm . . .
ADOPTIVE MOTHER: er, a child damaged by life in a children's home.
INTERVIEWER: Hm . . .
ADOPTIVE MOTHER: I probably would not have had the strength. . . . Another
important aspect: we said right from the start that we didn't want a child
from an asocial background, er, no child from a prostitute, *not,* er, just
because of the social background, but, er, because of the medical side [care
during pregnancy?]. . . . The way we looked at it, er, a prostitute, for
example, keeps on working as long as she can with the help of stimulants,
alcohol, etc., and [the child] is perhaps then already damaged in the womb,
and we didn't want to take such a risk.
INTERVIEWER: Hm . . .
ADOPTIVE MOTHER: Maybe it's unfair, but I honestly wouldn't have had the
strength. . . .

Of the thirty cases this example with its host of options signals most
clearly the claim to an autonomous determination of the cornerstones of

adoption. Aware of their ability to assert their position, the applicants appear to have overcome the feeling that the artificial construction of family is dependent on an allocational institution. Apparently, they do not perceive this institution as an institution obliged to pursue youth welfare principles in its placement of a scarce supply that generally deviates from the type of child desired in their case. The narrative interview does not make it clear whether the reference to the limitations of one's own ability to cope was also articulated in the adoption procedure as a justification for the exclusion of any lowering of "values." The clear rejection of a "half-caste child" in another of the four examples ("we wouldn't feel able to cope") suggests that—once a certain framework is guaranteed—the admission of personal limitations can even become an effective resource. After all, the adoption counselor is also likely to prefer a situation in which the cards are put on the table if the parental eligibility of the applicants is no longer dependent anyway on this or that concession. In a situation with such a guaranteed acceptability, adoption counselors may also be willing to dissociate themselves from norms of professional action, as in one of the cases in which the applicant couple stuck to its option for a girl so as to reestablish a certain familial constellation despite advice to the contrary by the youth welfare office.

Following this look at the contrasting applicant types we shall now try to discover the hidden force that, beyond the course of events documented here, "maneuvers" the adoption applications into the category of the average case on the one hand and into the category of the privileged special case on the other. Regardless of what hidden qualities the applicants may have, all applicants in this "privileged group" belong to the upper (to middle) middle class.[80] The prospective adoptive fathers are successful professionals with a university background, and three have the title of doctor. The certainty derived from the potential of one's own status is reflected in the following narrative passage, in which one of the four couples analyzes its own privileged position.

ADOPTIVE FATHER: In view of the social status we have, upper middle class,
. . .
INTERVIEWER: Hm . . .
ADOPTIVE FATHER: I'd say, educated middle class, er, we had a kind of
    advantage.
ADOPTIVE MOTHER: Yes.
ADOPTIVE FATHER: We were aware of that right from the start: Well, an adopted
    child must be definitely placed in this case, . . .
ADOPTIVE MOTHER: Yes.
ADOPTIVE FATHER: weren't we? I think it's fair to say so. I can very well
    imagine that someone with a different level of education and unable to
    articulate his wishes in such a way with respect to the adopted child finds it
    much more difficult to get a child.

INTERVIEWER: Hm . . .

ADOPTIVE FATHER: Is that the way you see it, too?

ADOPTIVE MOTHER: *Yes, definitely,* and there's another aspect as well . . . that they are also much more easily pushed by the detailed questions on the part of the adoption counselor into . . . forced onto the defensive by the detailed questions asked by the adoption counselor, . . .

INTERVIEWER: Hm . . .

ADOPTIVE MOTHER: because they cannot answer in such a positive way as we can. . . . We at any rate were able to provide a, so to speak, satisfactory solution.

The certainty about the "satisfactory solution" makes strategic concessions superfluous. For the privileged applicants the success of adoption procedure does not appear to be tied to the documentation of a special socializational competence. With the exception of the already older couple, which in its endeavor to continue family life following the loss of a birth child did not expect a very young child anyway, one striking feature in this group is the insistence on the ideal of the very young, healthy, and white-skinned infant. Hence, the following thesis: If applicants possess status-related interaction resources to an above-average extent, they will be relieved of the pressure of having to develop child-centered interaction resources. In other words, if the status-related interaction resources are "acceptable" from the point of view of the procedural administrator, adoption applicants will be able to openly pursue the goal of approximation to the pattern of normality. During the procedure they can be what they are as prospective adoptive parents: The presentation of identity can become the rare extreme case of the presentation of self-identity. The effort required in other cases to avoid saying anything wrong no longer exists; there is a pleasant openness, which not only allows applicants to push through their parental interests but also produces a more humane relational structure.

A few qualifying statements are necessary, however, with regard to this group of applicants. Observations of four of the 30 examples served to construct the category of the privileged applicant. Membership in the upper middle class, however, does not automatically relieve applicants of the pressure to engage in strategic interaction. Some of the examples already presented of applicants belonging to the upper middle class could be further analyzed to discover what made the status-related interaction resources seem less significant ("nonmotherly type," the applicants' anticipation of their own rejection because of their position as teacher).[81] The construction of the privileged applicant category in this study (as shown by the 1976 supplementary study, Table 16) does not mean that upper-middle-class applicants cannot also be excluded from procedural success. A comparison between all eventually successful case histories, however, reveals that the mode of communication during the adoption procedure closely correlates with status-related interaction resources. The pressure to engage in strategic interaction is much greater in the case of the middle and lower middle class than in the case of those few applicants belonging to the "upper middle class," the "educated middle class," who experience an "advantage" and are able to openly strive for a fully adequate substitute for the child nature has denied them. The observation of the varying modes of communication depending on the status-related interaction resources confirms the assumption already developed with regard to the selection phase (local social worker) that parental eligibility is derived as socializational competence from a bundle of status symbols of the repectable adult. If the status symbols suffice to secure an "advantage" in the adoption procedure, the upgrading of one's own negotiating position via the presentation of child-centered orientations becomes superfluous.

Applicant Uncertainty and an Inability to Engage in Strategic Interaction. The thesis of a correlation between status-related and child-related interaction resources could lead to the assumption that the lack of guaranteed acceptability will be balanced out to a growing extent by a lowering of expectations with respect to the child as the negotiating potential declines. This correlation, however, does not appear to exist. This is probably due to the fact that doubts at the beginning of adoption procedure following a move to the meta-perspective are not necessarily connected with an insight into the orientation knowledge of the adoption counselor. The uncertainty of acceptability may be assumed on the grounds of certain indicators without the applicant being able to gain access to the unfamiliar role of the procedural administrator as an action type. Most of the seven interviews with applicants belonging to the lower middle class or lower class only outline vague contours of the presentation of self during the adoption procedure, the placement of the child dating back more than five years in three cases. Only two examples indicate that the strategic interaction competence is probably less pronounced in the lower middle class than in the middle middle class. Allowing for reservations with regard to generalizations I would like to take a brief look at these two examples, because they represent the antithesis to the category of the privileged applicant.

One applicant couple, which much to its own surprise was offered an adopted child soon after the adoption care authorization had been granted, recapitulated the situation of the adoption offer by going back into the history of the procedure. As the child offered already failed to correspond to the type of the desired child because of the color of its skin, the adoption counselor tried to sound out the tolerance of the applicants.

ADOPTIVE FATHER: And then she said "Yes," and, er, whether we had any
    misgivings because we first had ideas, the idea which we explained, er,
    during the first information discussion that we wanted a child which suits us.
    Well, er, that was no good at all, was it. We appreciated that later on. That
    was held against us. [Laughing] And . . . er, somehow that was like running
    against a brick wall.

Despite the naive formulation ("a child which suits us") this is a
reference to exactly the same fact that the upper middle class—as shown
by the examples—expressed as a conceived possibility in a verbally
differentiated presentation of multidimensional options. The difference is
that frank openness is ventured by the couple in the one case in a self-
assessment of guaranteed acceptability, and is tolerated by the interaction
partner, whereas in the other case openness is demonstrated without the
adoption counselor's adequate empathy contributions, and is thus experienced as a faux pas. Due to their role repertoire, members of the upper
middle class will probably tend to be better able to grasp the decision-
making structure of the adoption counselor in analogy to other types of
bureaucratic action[82] and take this into account in the design of their own
applicant activity.[83] Members of the lower middle class, on the other hand,
may be so constrained by uncertainty without being able via role-taking
processes to analytically acquire the guidance for the action they need for
an orientation to the adoption counselor's value system. They may fail to
realize the strategic significance of child-centered concessions in the
procedure because the interaction radius of their own occupational role
does not provide them with the role-taking competence with regard to the
procedural administrator.[84] Their presentation of self may be uncertain yet
honest; the outcome can leave them with no more than marginal chances
of being ascribed parental eligibility. In this particular case the applicants
are finally offered a child who was rejected by a number of other applicants. With a certain embitterment the adoptive parents describe how the
adoption counselor said:

ADOPTION COUNSELOR: Well . . . out of one thousand, er, six hundred adoptive
    parents you're the *only ones* willing to *take in* a colored child.

The next case history of a lower-middle-class couple also gives an idea
of the risks associated with an open presentation of identity. The applicants felt forced onto the defensive as "really too old" right from the
start. In accordance with a problematic calculation designed to ensure a
"natural age difference"[85] the adoption counselor stated that they would
at most be considered for an older child.

ADOPTIVE MOTHER: During this final discussion we were then told "Well, you
    see, you're too old anyway. In your case we can only consider *8 to 10-year-*

old children. Nothing else!" And we said "We don't want that!" We wanted up to four years old at most.

Although the applicants let themselves be "negotiated up" to six years after gaining an insight into the reality of the adoption procedure, this did not alter their suspicion of being among those applicants with no chance of success. The reaction of the adoption counselor to options nevertheless expressed is a signal of rejection.

ADOPTIVE MOTHER: We *already thought at the time,* Christ, she showed such a *dislike towards us* apparently, and found it *crazy* that we did not want children from *prostitutes* and that we also didn't want children from *criminals. . . .*

If the lack of differentiated verbal presentation of the exclusions of certain criteria for the choice of the child in the narrative interview reflects the way in which the options were formulated by the prospective adoptive parents in the adoption procedure, it may be possible to work out the difference in the realization of applicant roles insofar as the options resemble those of the privileged group. It is not clear, however, whether it can be inferred from the brevity of the narrative version that the explanation of the options was also missing in the actual course of events. For this reason I shall only emphasize the exclusion of attributes as a "fact," which was apparently reflected in a further reduction of their acceptability in the case of applicants who had very little chance of success anyway.

The interpretation that the lack of any chance of success in the adoption procedure is triggered by "dislike" indicates that—as opposed to the example of the "educated middle class"—this couple does not perceive the uneven distribution of these chances. As the procedural administrator fails to divulge the criteria for selection (closed awareness context) these applicants respond to their suspicion of unfair treatment by withdrawing into the role of victim: personal dislike spoilt their chances of success in Hamburg. They suffer under their powerlessness, whereas others demonstrate far-reaching autonomy of action, even in the situation of dependence on the social bureaucracy during their efforts to constitute a family. The differentiation of biographical trajectories elaborated by Fritz Schütze in line with the steering shares of the individuals concerned could be applied to this section of the adoption procedure.[86] Whereas some examples in the upper middle class reveal action and steering capacity of applicants ("rising trajectory" towards the desired child), the lower-middle-class case just given shows the loss of capacity of action and the suffering under heteronomous steering in a direction that runs contrary to the desired constitution of family ("falling trajectory," and finally external application).

*The Communication Situation after the Determination of General
Adoptive Suitability*

Even though the ascription of adoptive suitability means that the first
obstacle along the path to the constitution of family has been cleared, the
final outcome of the adoption procedure remains uncertain. The bureaucratic acknowledgement of general parental eligibility can become no more
than a partial outcome of adoption procedure with no consequences at all,
because the adoption counselor can select other applicants as more suitable in the case of each available child. The possibility of arguing along
the lines of the "best interests of the child" gives the procedural administrator autonomous decision-making power that the applicants can no
longer see through. The nervous strain indicated in the narrative interviews
during this phase is caused by the fact that one's own distance from the
desired status passage is incalculable.[87] Parenthood may be within reach—
the news of a child "for us" may arrive at the very next moment—but it
may also never materialize at all.

Just how much power of orientation the biologically determined course
of the constitution of family has for parents-to-be only becomes clear
when this situation is compared with the unstructuredness of prospective
adoptive parenthood. The lack of a definite expectability of parenthood is
apparently made even more difficult to endure for adoption applicants by
the fact that there is generally a lack of institutional norms for the course
of action. During this phase all prospective adoptive parents can do is to
tentatively design their role towards a possible child as well as towards the
procedural administrator.

The orientation to the normal case of family constitution provides only
limited support when preparing for the prospective child, because the
child's developmental stage is unknown. A visit to a baby-care course may
be able to give the adoption applicants a sense of responsible role planning.
Such an attempt at anticipatory socialization for parenthood is unlikely to
be particularly useful, however, if the child eventually offered is at a more
advanced developmental stage. The reverse case is also conceivable. One
applicant couple, for example, declared its willingness to adopt a child
"up to the age of one" and, with this in mind, attended a course dealing
with how to bring up toddlers. The couple was only able to make use of
what they had learnt several months after adopting the baby. The uncertainty about how to anticipate the role of adoptive parents indicates that
this is an additional strain to the already strenuous status passage to
parenthood.[88]

During the preparation of their socializational abilities the adoption
applicants move, on the one hand, into a sphere of action as if the status

passage were about to take place; on the other hand, their activities vis-à-vis the adoption administrator focus on the fact that the event will occur. The design of one's own role in interaction with the adoption agency is characterized by imponderabilities, because it is extremely difficult for the applicant to predict whether a certain course of action will improve or diminish the chances of success. The balancing act of prospective adoptive parents when testing the most promising means of gaining access to the parental role is aggravated by the fact that the adoption agency structures interaction with the applicant at this stage in line with the motto: "We'll get in touch when we've got a child for you." Resigning oneself to the procedurally envisaged role of the waiting applicant, however, leads to conflicts. Expecting a child implies a whole bundle of possible activities through which the parents-to-be can responsibly prepare for the event. Waiting for a child drastically reduces the scope for action conducive to the occurrence of the event, leaving the applicants to more or less drift into the constitution of family. All they can basically do is prepare for the period after the materialization of the event, providing they are lucky enough to be allocated a child.

Furthermore, the pressure to develop activities is probably increased by the fact that the applicants become aware of the competition for the scarce "commodity" child when doubts about the objectivity of the adoption procedure arise. The adoption counselor is required "to assess, in consideration of the child's personality and its special needs, whether adoption applicants are suitable for the adoption of the child" (section 7 of the Adoption Placement Act). This cannot, however, mean the selection of the only possible suitable adoptive parents for a specific child. As assumed as a typical feature of bureaucratic decision-making activities by Niklas Luhmann, "several adequate and several legitimatizable" solutions[89] probably also exist in the field of adoption placement. As the 1976 supplementary survey showed that 44 percent of all applicants in that year adopted a child younger than six months old (Table 33), it seems fair to claim that the candidates are to a considerable extent interchangeable. Accordingly, waiting for a child means refraining from influencing the selection process with the risk of falling behind other "equally" suitable applicants.

The agony of waiting is reflected in the following narrative passage by an adoptive mother who deviated from the procedurally envisaged passivity with carefully dosed intervention. This example is representative of many others.

ADOPTIVE MOTHER: The important thing for me was to have the feeling during this period of waiting that something was happening . . . something was taking place. Well, I couldn't have waited nine months during which nothing happens and all I've got is the small hope that maybe we will get a child sometime. I had to have the feeling. Everyone feels that way.

There are a host of remarks in the interviews showing how impossible it is for prospective adoptive parents to heed the request to simply wait. The desire to do something for the child leads to carefully calculated contravention of the bureaucratic directive. The form and content of this "deviant behavior" reveal a number of regularities. Breaking through the communication network set up by the social bureaucracy to reserve for itself the exclusive right to initiate interaction generally takes place using a relatively unobtrusive medium, the telephone.[90] It allows contact to be established for a short period, a means of drawing the attention of the adoption counselor for a few seconds at least, a moderate inducement of role-taking for one of the applicant couples in the mass of fellow applicants. The telephone is the convenient and at the same time relatively discreet aid when the aim is to risk a balancing act between the bureaucratic request to wait for notification and the orientation of applicants to their own interests.

The following example illustrates just how much diplomatic skill is needed to structure the contact with the procedural administrator over the phone at the content and relationship level of communication[91] in such a way that the result is unobtrusive obtrusiveness.

ADOPTIVE MOTHER: And then nothing happened for another six weeks. And then I thought to myself, now you've got to get in touch and ask. But the word got about that this was frowned on, if people keep on ringing up and preventing the adoption counselor from carrying out her work, since they really are overworked. Nevertheless, you want to know whether your file is somewhere near the top of the pile or among the also-rans down in the cellar. And I must admit I really came up with a lot of ideas on how to keep on making them aware of our case, and I was lucky, without getting on their nerves, to put it plainly. That's something you worry about. You mustn't pester them too much and give them the feeling "For God's sake, she's not going to get a child for a long time. It's just terrible the way she gets on at you."

The balancing act between exerting an influence that is conducive to success and putting on pressure that threatens success is also shown in the next narrative passage, in which—due to an insight into the bureaucratic decision-making structures—intervention is raised to the level of an action postulate for adoption applicants. With reference to applicants who had been patiently waiting a long time, the adoptive father begins:

ADOPTIVE FATHER: And when they explain what happened *then you* get the feeling straight away: "Well, now, I can understand . . .
INTERVIEWER: Hm . . .
ADOPTIVE FATHER: why you had to wait so long," . . .
INTERVIEWER: Hm . . .
ADOPTIVE FATHER: because you're *familiar* with the circumstances there and if you don't *emphatically* and, er, persuasively, er, . . .

INTERVIEWER: Hm . . .
ADOPTIVE MOTHER: Hm . . .
ADOPTIVE FATHER: er, *keep on the ball* there. . . .
ADOPTIVE MOTHER: Well, it's definitely a tightrope walk, you see. You have to make *continual* inquiries. You really have to call up every week and at the same time manage not to . . .
ADOPTIVE FATHER: Not to get on anyone's nerves.
ADOPTIVE MOTHER: *Right.*
INTERVIEWER: Hm . . .
ADOPTIVE MOTHER: Not to be too pushy and [pleased] not to get on their nerves and if possible avoid giving the impression that you are saying "I've got the feeling you *won't do* anything otherwise," you see.
INTERVIEWER: Hm . . .

Two factors combine during the strategy described here. Whereas, on the one hand, the inquiry about how the procedure is coming along is intended as an indication of the seriousness of the adoption plan and thus of the responsibility of parental action, on the other hand there is an element of pressure and of control in the interaction with the procedural administrator. It is hoped that the latter will act as soon as possible in one's own favor. The impatience in the realization of the family plan is not endured for a longer period in any of the cases we surveyed. Impatience is conveyed to the adoption counselor in forms of action that can be attributed to the pattern of the "strategy of being pushy." To judge by the interviews of the eventually successful applicants the strategy of being pushy flourishes in almost all applicant histories once a few weeks have passed after the ascription of general parental eligibility. In some cases interviewees state that they rang up once a month, in others there is reference to weekly phone calls or even—in two examples—to "almost daily" phone calls during a certain phase.

The assessment of recapitulated events during the course of the narration shows that contact over the phone is not, as one might assume in view of the wording of the phone call ("Has anything turned up yet?"), merely intended to discover how procedure is coming along, but that it intends steering the process of selection. Expressions such as "You have to get on their nerves," or "You have to keep on pushing them, otherwise nothing happens" reveal an exercising of power, the little bit of power left to the powerless partner in the adoption procedure.

As opposed to the open admission of the desire to exert pressure, some applicants establish contact with the procedural administrator in a manner that indicates nothing other than a substantial parental sense of responsibility. As shown by a number of examples, the presentation of identity by the applicant who only has the best interests of the child in mind can assume the form of the prospective adoptive mother signaling her full willingness to take on the child immediately by referring to the planned or already effected notice of termination of employment. This can lead to a kind of self-fulfilling prophecy: The assumed proximity to the status passage and the already discernible altruistic orientation to the future role of mother could become a decision-making aid if the adoption counselor has to choose between equally suitable applicants. The concerned question by one applicant whether it is alright to go off on holiday or whether a child is already waiting for her also signals a degree of parental eligibility that could prove binding for the adoption counselor.

The activity that occurs—contrary to the request to patiently wait for notification—to achieve the status passage involves work,[92] work to document one's own parental eligibility and work to influence the orientation knowledge of the adoption counselor. In the face of an overabundant demand for a child, adoption applicants resort to the strategy of being pushy in an attempt to actualize the parental eligibility ascribed to them in the final discussion and to maintain their own acceptability in the perspective of the procedural administrator. They would appear to hope that the documentation of serious interest and of action taken in an anticipated awareness of parenthood will leave a fresh mark in the orientation of the adoption counselor ("Even if the people get annoyed about you, you stay in their memory") and give them a lead in comparison with their chances of success if they were to do and say nothing. The adoption counselor may, for example, have already forgotten her assessment of parental eligibility in this particular case, especially in view of the fact that she is confronted by new applicants every day. The work of drawing attention is an attempt to steer the social bureaucratic construction of family, an attempt that can hardly be legitimated in terms of a rational course of adoption procedure. Two types of work are invested in the procedure; the work on the part of the applicants is unlikely to be synchronized with the professionally defined work of the adoption administrator.

Although the work designed to document one's own parental eligibility is geared to the adoption counselor as a partner of interaction, it also has consequences for all other adoption applicants. Drawing the adoption counselor's attention in this way is also to a certain extent a form of displacement competition. Increasing one's own chances means decreasing the chances of others. The fact that this side of a status passage mediated by the social bureaucracy is not mentioned in any of the 30 interviews may be connected with the power of orientation of the parental role in the adult role design. One's own availability as parents apparently eliminates any thoughts of parental alternatives for the child. As in the case of the biological constitution of family the belief in one's own parental competence prevails. This appears to produce a situation in which the prospective parents perceive their own interests as congruent with those of the child available for adoption. The idea that fellow applicants may possess a superior parental potential would block the primarily parent-centered strategy of being pushy, and give the adoption counselors the autonomy that they officially demand with reference to norms of professional action.

Fellow applicants who drop out of the running are never mentioned in a context that establishes a link between one's own activity and reducing the chances of others. Yet they are mentioned on several occasions when reference is made to applicants who follow the wrong concept, who demonstrate obedience with respect to the adoption counselor's appeal to wait for notification, and who may get no further than the phase of waiting.

ADOPTIVE MOTHER: Persistence is everything. You have to be always friendly but resolute.
INTERVIEWER: I see.
ADOPTIVE FATHER: Even if the people get annoyed about you, you stay in their memory, you see? They think back to you.
INTERVIEWER: Hm . . .
ADOPTIVE FATHER: If someone's particularly persistent you're more likely to give way.
ADOPTIVE MOTHER: [Loudly] The good-natured sheep who keep on thinking "Well, she's sure to get in touch," they never get a child.
INTERVIEWER: Hm . . .
ADOPTIVE MOTHER: Or they have to wait a very long time.

The fact that this strategy would fail if everybody acted in line with the maxim of persistence is ignored. The link established in several interviews between the strategy of being pushy and the success of the adoption procedure seems to be part of the procedure's "logic." The applicants who understand this fact take advantage of the logic and fail to realize that a general pursuance of this approach would cancel out the logic.

ADOPTIVE MOTHER: Well, all I can say is that . . .
INTERVIEWER: Hm . . .
ADOPTIVE MOTHER: you have to be *endlessly* resolute. You must not allow yourself . . .
INTERVIEWER: Hm . . .
ADOPTIVE MOTHER: to be turned away *at all*. I, er, mean, it's obvious. There are more applicants than children, and it's quite obvious: those who make the most effort get the child.

In the following section we will examine whether the link claimed on several occasions by the adoptive parents between the strategy of pestering and a successful adoption application can be confirmed with reference to the available facts and figures. With this aim in view, a closer look will be taken at the time structure reflected in the narrative interviews between the use made of the medium of the telephone and the "notification of an adoption offer." If the existence of the assumed link appears plausible in the light of the observations of the temporal sequence of events in the adoption procedure, the ascription of special parental eligibility would then appear to be the result of a bilateral work process, in which the steering bureaucratic institution is itself steered to a certain extent by its clientele.

The Principle of Chance in Adoption Placement

Adoptive parents are perhaps best able to appreciate the significance of the decision made by the adoption counselor when selecting parents for a child. Role-taking on behalf of the person who "plays fate"[93] often induces adoptive parents in the interviews to emphasize that they "would not like to be in their shoes." The fact that they have experienced the intensity of emotions and the vulnerability of expectations that can be triggered by the bureaucratic combination of the files of the adoptive parents and the prospective adopted child explains their role-taking disinclination.

The assumption is made here that adoption counselors also experience the tremendous significance of their decisions as a strain, particularly at a time of an overabundant demand for the child as a scarce commodity. It cannot be decided here whether counselors have well-founded professional knowledge at their disposal that might make decisions more than just commonsense-based and reduce the subjective strain—doubts about the quality of this knowledge have been frequently expressed.[94]

Even if a certain temporal link between the strategy of being pushy and the success of adoption procedure can be discovered, this observation should not be interpreted as proof of a lack of professional knowledge. To begin with, it can only—in favor of the adoption agency—be interpreted as an indication that there are several legitimate solutions and that, influenced by the strategy of being pushy, the adoption counselor selects a couple from the circle of apparently equally suitable applicants. The intervention over the phone or in a face-to-face contact would then initiate the final reduction of complexity in a multistage process of selection.

In order to clarify the possible temporal link between a strategy of being pushy and the notification of an adoption offer, the applicant cases will initially be differentiated according to their chances of successfully utilizing the possibility of making inquiries. On the basis of the thesis, "the closer the child to the ideal type of the young, healthy, and white-skinned infant, the greater the number of possible legitimatizeable placement solutions," it seems fair to conclude that the significance of the strategy of being pushy will diminish as the distance from the ideal type increases. In other words, once applicants declare their willingness to adopt a child who deviates from the ideal type, they move into a zone in which there is a relative lack of competition and in which—instead of having to be pushy with the adoption counselor to show their interest—the adoption counselor is more likely to show an interest in them.

Not taking into account the seven (of the total of 37) placement cases in which the child was initially a foster child, the parents asked the agency to place a child they already knew, or the child was placed via Terre des Hommes, there are eight cases that—to select just one criterion—clearly departed from the ideal type by expressing their desire for a child who is older than one year. In some of these cases the adoption counselor made an adoption offer after quite a short time, either during or shortly after the final discussion, thus making a strategy of being pushy superfluous.[95]

As for the 22 remaining cases of children placed when they were younger than one year old, there is an indication that the utilization of activities to speed up the procedure increased during the course of the 1970s. Whereas the interviews relating to six placements around 1970 emphasize a more submissive and waiting approach (which, however, did not drag on for too long), references to a preference for making more inquiries are made in interviews relating to placements after 1973, a period when the ratio of children to applicants moved close to a figure of 1:2 (see Table 3). This reference to increased activities by the adoptive parents themselves to speed things up is only missing in four of the cases relating to placements after 1973. These cases were characterized by quite fast notifications of adoption offers and all related to applicants belonging to the upper (to middle) middle class. The strategy of being pushy prevails in the final phase of adoption procedure in all the remaining twelve cases. These twelve cases form the basis for the analysis of the temporal link between applicant intervention and the notification of the adoption offer.

The closer the applicant's last attempt to influence the procedure to the notification of an adoption offer, the greater the probability that the temporal structure of events can be considered a causal connection. Certainty on this aspect is only interpretable in a few cases. If the 12 cases are arranged according to the distance between the last inquiry and the notification of the adoption offer the exact temporal sequence of events remains unclear in half of the cases. The only certain fact is that the placement was eventually successful after the applicants had resorted to the various strategies of drawing attention to their cases. They repeatedly emphasize themselves that the offer was elicited because they maintained the adoption counselor's awareness of their case via their inquiries.

The other six narrative interviews refer to relatively short periods of time—at most one-and-a-half days—between applicant initiative and the

notification of an adoption offer. The "cooperation" between the placement agency and the applicants can take place, for example, as follows:
information about the hopelessness of the application obtained with a
phone call in the morning ("absolutely no children available"), followed
by an offer in the afternoon. Questioners may, however, achieve their
objectives much faster, as shown by a number of cases: the phone call and
the offer can coincide. In these situations the adoption counselor is
probably keen to rule out any suspicions that the applicants influenced the
situation in any way in order to document autonomy of action. For this
reason, it is not clear in the following example which side, the adoption
counselor or the applicant, "steered" the course of events. The applicant's
phone call was immediately followed by a claim by the adoption counselor
that "I was just about to ring you," and then an adoption offer. In at least
two cases it becomes clear that the offer was elicited on an ad hoc basis
during applicant intervention:[96]

ADOPTIVE FATHER: And if I hadn't rang up *that* day—she told us *afterwards:*
   "You would have been the last persons I would have given the child to,"
   [laughing] because we're such pale types and he's darker-skinned.

In no other case is the success of the strategy of being pushy so obvious
as in the case of one applicant who masters the art of drawing attention to
her case with such perfection that she managed to elicit an offer twice
over the phone. The first time the adoption counselor acted as if she was
about to notify this particular applicant about an offer anyway: "Ah, yes,
I would have rung you up anyway." After the placement of the envisaged
child fell through—the birth mother went back on her decision to relinquish the child for adoption—this applicant again resorts to her strategy of
documenting her serious interest. The following narrative passage shows
that there can be no doubt about the ad hoc nature of the decision this
time.

ADOPTIVE MOTHER: I rang up and asked "Well now, what's the situation . . . I
   must be rather abrupt: is there still no child which might suit our family?"
   And the answer was "no," since there is such a workload at the moment and
   a placement for us and for others too was out of the question. And I was just
   about to slam the phone down when I heard her say "Well, wait a moment."
   Just before I was going to hang up. The whole thing was a real coincidence,
   on this particular day the institution where our child came from, where our
   child was, this institution had just got in touch with her. The whole thing's
   ordered alphabetically. And said "Well, we've got a child here and we don't
   know where to place it. It's adoptable and we don't know what to do with
   it." She told me afterwards that she thought to herself during the phone call
   "Could they be considered?" That's why she hesitated and then said: "Well,
   wait a moment. . . ."

The significance for adoptive parent–child bonding of the fact that the relationship resulted from such chance factors cannot be clarified in this study. The applicant mother in the example finishes her description of the application procedure with the words:

ADOPTIVE MOTHER: And that's how our child came about.

The question that arises is who "plays fate" in the case of missing biological bonds. Several interviews indicate that the adoptive parents at any rate do not feel that well-founded professional knowledge was the authority that turned persons who were originally strangers into a family. The tenor of this view is reflected in the words of one adoptive mother who received an adoption offer just a few hours after establishing contact with a new adoption counselor:

ADOPTIVE MOTHER: I just cannot imagine that the whole thing took place on the basis of highly professional considerations.

Instead of believing in the professionally grounded application of the official maxim of adoption placement ("We are looking for parents for children"), these adoptive parents feel that the principle of chance stepped in, prompted by their own intervention.

ADOPTIVE MOTHER: Selected properly? . . . No . . . it was only because we just happened to be there that morning.

The principle of chance—this is also the conclusion in the view taken in the following narrative passage on the act of placement.

ADOPTIVE MOTHER: *One* day we were told "You have *absolutely* no chance; there . . . there aren't any children there."
ADOPTIVE FATHER: Yes, I called up, you see, and . . .
ADOPTIVE MOTHER: Right.
ADOPTIVE FATHER: [I was told] that there was no chance . . . no chance, er, and, er, next day . . .
ADOPTIVE MOTHER: [Pleased] Yes, absolutely no chance . . . and next day . . .
ADOPTIVE FATHER: the next morning she rang me up . . .
ADOPTIVE MOTHER: "We've got a child for you."
ADOPTIVE FATHER: "We've got a child for you." Well, er, . . .
ADOPTIVE MOTHER: [Laughing]
ADOPTIVE FATHER: that's what my wife . . .
ADOPTIVE MOTHER: That's what I mean, where I have my doubts about . . . about selection, you see. [Laughing] It was unbelievable.
ADOPTIVE FATHER: Our file, you see, was put on the top of the pile . . . taken from the bottom and put on the top . . .
ADOPTIVE MOTHER: Hm, yes.
ADOPTIVE FATHER: and [gesticulating] she probably took the child's file from over here and the parental file from over there and must have thought to

herself: let's put them together. [Claps as if putting two files together.] It was just a coincidence that we were . . .
ADOPTIVE MOTHER: Right.
ADOPTIVE FATHER: just happened to be lying on the pile. That's our impression.
ADOPTIVE MOTHER: And, er, it's been confirmed by a lot of other people, hasn't it?

Regardless of what may have preceded the "joining together" of the parental and the child's file, the increased use of the strategy of being pushy as a result of the growing demand for adopted children would appear to lead to a shift in the active part in the adoption procedure. Although applicants may—albeit with doubts[97]—be willing to acknowledge the adoption counselor's initial professional ability to choose between applicants,[98] the impression then gained in many cases is that the applicants themselves initiate the final reduction of procedural complexity. The placement decision then appears to be the ad hoc solution, steered by the clientele, to a bureaucratic process of selection. In view of the difficulties associated with applying professional knowledge when matching parents and children in the social bureaucratic context, the adoption agency would appear to at least partially refer to the "message" of the intervening applicants as an equivalent for the professional weighing up of parent–child combinations, especially because the solution to the placement problem also means the elimination of the strain caused by the applicant's frequent inquiries.

If the institution that plays fate is itself steered into the situation in which it can bring its decision-making power to bear, the solution to the placement problem produces a number of new problems. These relate to both those who have given a helping hand to the "game of fate" as well to those who have let themselves be helped.

First of all, here are a few speculative considerations relating to the adoptive parents in this respect. If they have taken on an active part in shaping the outcome of adoption procedure and fostered the principle of chance via their own contribution, various modes can hypothetically be constructed to come to terms with one's own family construction. One's own contribution could, for example, be interpreted as a parental contribution on behalf of the child, as proof of the intensity of parental effort that finally led to the adoption offer. The strategy of being pushy could then be viewed as a preliminary familial contribution, which could function as part of the basis for the feeling of togetherness to be developed later on in the absence of shared biological roots. However, the other extreme is also conceivable, in which intervention in the course of fate triggers doubts about whether this intervention might not turn out to be a mistake. The forces set free by the principle of chance may exceed the limitations of any progress to such an extent that the applicants finally feel that their construction of family has a weak basis of legitimation, beyond any sound grounding in professional decision-making processes. The narrative interviews themselves do not provide an indication of which strategy is developed to solve the problem of a chance construction of family towards which the adoptive parents made a partial contribution themselves. The news that a child is available for adoption gives the placement procedure a dynamic momentum that temporarily makes other aspects seem more important in narrative reconstruction. For this reason, the possible problems arising from the validity of the principle of chance for the construction of the adoptive family can only be hinted at here. Yet again, however, the alternative case of the constitution of family indicates how relieving it is to possess the certainty of biological ties.

The partial steering of the solution to the placement problem by the clientele of social bureaucracy leaves the adoption agency facing the following question: To what extent is the satisfaction of the applicants achieved in this way compatible with the maxim of acting in the best interests of the child? Or, to use Luhmann's terminology, to what extent is the rationality of the decision oriented exclusively to the best interests of the child reduced by the concession to values of satisfaction on behalf of the applicants?[99] It cannot be clarified in this study whether the social bureaucracy rates the initiation of activities by the applicants as an indicator of adoptive suitability. Some narrative passages make reference to theories of adoption placement that regard the "dynamic" effort of the applicant as a positive factor. If this assumption by the adoptive parents is correct, the justifiability of such a theory of action would have to be clarified. An adoption agency with the interests of the child at heart would have to examine, for example, whether the child's need for empathy and emotionality is more likely to be satisfied by those applicants who push through the realization of their role design despite dependence on a bureaucratic institution, than by those applicants who stick to the prescribed procedure by waiting patiently for notification and perhaps never achieving the ascription of special parental eligibility. The question of the suitability of those applicants who dropped out of the procedure cannot be clarified here. A key problem, however, does emerge: Who in our society has the competence to repeatedly employ the strategic presentation of identity as an eligible applicant for parenthood up to the point of a successful adoption application and who feels obliged to subject themselves to the conformity of procedural rules and regulations? This leads to the aspects considered in the next section.

The Traces of Social Status during Adoption Placement

The adoption stories narrated so far not only expose fundamental processes of structuring the meaning of parenthood and of familial attachment that remain unreflected in the case of a "natural" constitution of family. They also uncover concepts of social hierarchy, which determine whether someone gains access to the role of parent denied by nature by means of a social construction of family. Whereas nature ascribes parenthood independent of status, the curing of childlessness via adoption is entangled in a process of social bureaucratic allocation that bears traces of the social determination of values. The result of this evaluation is not only reflected in whether or not someone attains the desired parenthood. Rather, the question of how the applicant's and child's files are combined reflects differentiations on the basis of the determined values, evaluations of both the applicants as well as of the children. Even the decision relating to the matching of prospective parents and the child is marked by elements of social status evaluation.

Even before the social bureaucracy steps in to play its part, involuntarily childless couples belonging to the lower class would not appear to turn to adoption in order to come nearer to the desired parental role.[100] Whereas roughly 40 percent of the West German population is usually presumed to belong to the lower class,[101] the supplementary survey of list entries in 1976 showed that only 17 percent of the applicants for adoption were members of the lower class (Table 10). It is difficult to say what the reasons are at this stage. In line with Lee Rainwater's findings, one possibility is that consanguinity is so significant in the lower class that any alternatives pale into insignificance in comparison. The possibility for a woman to confirm her self-esteem via pregnancy—her certainty of complying with the will of nature[102]—may produce a situation in which marital childlessness is accompanied by tremendous suffering and a feeling that the problem cannot be solved by any substitute social construction. It is also conceivable that members of the lower class have learned to define their position in the social hierarchy in such a way that they ascribe themselves little chance of success if they decide to turn to the adoption agency. Even if they basically approve of adoption as an alternative, this means that they would anticipate the unfavorable social identity ascribed to them by the social bureaucracy in such a way that they decide not to try for an adoption.[103]

But what happens when members of the lower class do decide to enter into adoption procedure? The insights already gained into the ascription of parental eligibility during the course of this study will help us answer this question. Both the preliminary assessments by the local social worker and the selection work by the adoption counselor revealed that parental eligibility as socializational competence appears to be embedded in a bundle of status symbols of the respectable adult. Furthermore, the study also showed that success in the adoption procedure is almost predetermined if the status-related interaction resources are able to assert their significance (upper to middle middle class); the pressure to engage in strategic interaction is then diminished. If the presentation of status symbols characterizing the respectable adult is experienced as inadequately convincing, the applicants will try with the help of varied interaction strategies to enhance their own acceptability in the meta-perspective and draw the attention of the adoption counselor to their case. Strategic interaction competence, however, is marked by class-specific variance. Although findings are to be interpreted cautiously, two examples of applicants belonging to the lower middle class showed that role-taking ability on behalf of the procedural administrator appears to be limited in accordance with the limitations of one's own interaction radius. The reduction of communicative competence also means the reduction of chances to cleverly employ the strategy of being pushy, without which—as shown by the adoption placement histories of the 1970s—there is a growing risk of failure.

These insights into the selection work of the adoption agency as well as into the practice of strategic interaction on the part of the applicants correspond to the findings of the supplementary survey, according to which there is a significant correlation between success in the adoption procedure and class membership (Table 16). Of course, members of the lower class may also become successful adoption applicants; they account for 13 percent, for example, of the total number of successful applicants in Hamburg in 1976 (Table 34). A comparison between the total number of successful applicants and the total number of clearly unsuccessful applicants,[104] however, indicates that there is a link between the decrease in social status and the decrease in the chances of adoption success (Table 16).

Unfortunately, the experiential structures of those lower-class applicants in this study who achieved their goal despite unfavorable resources could not be clarified, because, apart from one example, the lower class is not represented in the sample (Table 34). This shortcoming was caused by the difficulties in gaining access to research subjects belonging to this social stratum. Members of the lower class do not generally turn to the discussion circles for adoptive parents and make little use of the existing forms of family counseling.[105] The selection of adoptive parents with an already older child was also unable to take this group into account, because it was not covered by the category "friends of friends." In the only lower-class case considered here the applicants were granted an adoption at the end of the 1960s because Catholic parents were sought for a Catholic child.

List entries show that the frequently described over-representation of the middle and upper middle class among adoptive families[106] is not merely the product of the varying application ratios of the different social strata, but is also accentuated by bureaucratic selection practices. Middle-class-specific orientations probably assert their significance more or less behind the backs of the persons involved in the adoption procedure. Guaranteed high income, a nice home, a high level of education, and competence of language would appear to influence the decision-making body towards the assumption that social status is a kind of automatic safeguard for socializational competence. The justifiability of such selection practices cannot be discussed in detail in this study. Social workers are undoubtedly aware of the value of sound financial circumstances. They may also believe that a certain socialization knowledge or the ability to acquire such knowledge or to make use of counseling services will provide a better basis for coping with the greater conflict potential expected in an adoptive family. All this, however, is unlikely to suffice as a legitimation for the practice of incorporating even the acquisition of the parental role in the sometimes drastic and sometimes more subtly discernible process of social privilege, a process that has often been described for so many interaction structures with a dependent character—for example, in school, medical, and social control institutions.

The traces of social privilege, however, are not only discernible in a comparison between successful and unsuccessful applicants. The aspect of success itself reveals a gradation that in its turn reflects certain indications of preference and discrimination. The determination of values by applicants apparently creates cornerstone data for the selection of the child. The question "Who suits which child best?" would appear to be influenced by orientations that do not simply determine matching at the level of the foreseeable development of the child's personality.[107] There are indications that the principle of social ranking is also applied to the children to be placed for adoption and that a certain correspondence develops between the value determination of the parents and of the child.

The clarification of the question of the child's "market value," a highly controversial question in terms of its ethical aspects, begins with the observation that the rating of a child in terms of certain value categories is not a social bureaucratic construction, but is already rooted in the behavioral orientations of the prospective adoptive parents. Even though the applicant options already described, and the weighing up of their list of desired attributes of the child, are partly a product of the style of questioning employed by the adoption counselor, it nevertheless became clear that the ideal type of the young, healthy, and white-skinned infant already shaped parental expectations before adoption procedure began, with only a few exceptions. As long as the aim of the alternative constitution of family is the approximation to the pattern of normality, categories determining the value of the child are always likely to remain effective and, despite all purely humanitarian considerations, to develop a momentum of their own.

In order to examine the hypothesized correspondence between the determination of the value of the child and that of the parents, an index was constructed along the lines of the identifiable value orientations of the applicants during the adoption procedure. The index comprises five attributive dimensions: the child's age, level of physical development, level of mental or psychological development, skin color, and class background (see annex to Table 35). One of the main construction principles for scaling was to fix the point of maximum approximation to normality (zero) in all attributive dimensions. The deviations from the ideal type of child reflected in the same negative scores along individual attributive dimensions were then weighted in such a way that they reflected almost the same concession to a departure from the ideal type in the idealized perspective of the applicant.[108] The elongation of the skin color scale, for example, was calibrated according to how many negative points scored by a darker or dark color of skin are equivalent in the eyes of the applicants to a certain negative scoring along the older child dimension (for example, weighting of the dark color of skin with -6 in orientation to the same weighting of age older than three years).

The impressionistic character of this approach cannot be denied. The "degree of privilegedness," to be more precise "the degree of underprivilegedness," is just a means of roughly determining the value orientations reflected in the narrative interviews in a statistical quantity for each child. To judge by the insights into the process of adoption placement gained so far, an acceptable operationalization of the determination of the child's value can only be represented by taking into account all five value dimensions, and so it seemed appropriate to include quantifying techniques in the evaluation of data to test the hypothesis and to clarify the problematic correlation in terms of ethical values with the help of a number of available means of statistical description.

Here is a brief description of the scaling procedure (see also the annex to Table 35). In line with the fairly differentiated value concepts of applicants with regard to the dimension of age, this scale, with a points rating ranging between 0 (clinic adoption) and -6 (older than three years), served as the point of orientation for the remaining interval calibrations. The dimension of background, which included the arrangements for the relinquishment of the child for adoption, has the least extensive points rating (up to -2), in accordance with the assumption that the condition of the child itself was given priority over any "milieu" values by adoption applicants during the 1970s (see also "Applicant Uncertainty and the Specification of the Desired Child along Various Attributive Dimensions" earlier in the chapter). The lowest points rating in the dimension relating to the level of the child's physical development was fixed at -4 for cases with physical handicaps extremely difficult to overcome. The scale on the child's mental or psychological development was constructed in line with the same principle, although this scale had to be weighted due to interaction effect with the age scale. As there is an increasing probability that developmental deficiencies of a cognitive or psychological nature will not be correctable as the child gets older, a special weighting factor was constructed. It was assessed in such a way that the negative scores remained low wherever there were signs of a problematic development in the case of very young children, falling in the least favorable cases to a rating of -6 for children older than three. On the basis of the racial reservations observed among applicants the skin color scale was graduated so that the Negroid child was fixed at a rating of -6, with a pronounced interval to the child with a slightly dark skin. If the individual scale ratings are added to form a single interval scale, the latter has a possible range of 0 to -24.

The question is whether this index developed on the basis of the assumed determination of values by applicants can help clarify the ascription of special parental eligibility. In other words, we must examine whether the adoption agency shares the orientations underlying the determination of values by applicants and whether there is a tendency to make the organization of the allocation of the child with its "market value" dependent on the status of applicants. In order to clarify this question the index scores were established for each child in the five attributive dimensions and then combined via addition to a single score on the "degree of privilegedness" scale. The scores ranged between -1 and -21. As the determination of the value of applicants by the adoption agency was operationalized in the form of their class membership, the index scores for the children then had to be related to the class membership of their adoptive parents. In line with the social placement of the children in the upper (to middle), the middle, or the lower middle class, the index scores were divided into subgroups, for which the respective average positions on the "degree of privilegedness" scale and the dispersion of index values was calculated. The calculation of the mean produced a score of -3.66 for the upper (to middle) middle class, -6.5 for the middle middle class, and -9.16 for the lower middle class. The standard deviations for the three groups were 2.9, 4.67, and 7.33, respectively.[109]

Due to the sampling technique chosen for this study the graduation discernible here cannot be generalized. Nevertheless, despite the fact that it is impossible to make statistical inferences from the sample to the universe in this context,[110] the findings of the "degree of privilegedness" index deserve a more detailed commentary. Let us again take up the question of the justification of organizing the artificial construction of family within a framework of social privilege. If there are indeed professional orientations that could legitimate a preferential treatment of the upper social classes—for example, because of the greater socializational knowledge to be expected there and its significance for a successful adoptive parent–child relationship—it would only seem fair to infer that such applicants should be able to cope with more stressful and demanding adoptive situations. As shown by our sample, adoption practices refrain from such a balancing of social privileges by socialization abilities, and so it can only be concluded that there is either a lack of any professional justifiability for the privileged treatment of persons belonging to higher social classes or that this preferential treatment takes place—contrary to all professional norms—behind the backs of the persons involved.[111]

Reference to the "Human Side" of Adoption Procedure

As shown in many parts of the previous assessment of the data on adoption placement, the problem of a missing construction of reciprocity is inherent to the construction of family dependent on social bureaucracy. The deviation from the natural constitution of family can easily degenerate into a less humane constitution of family if the bureaucratic perspective of adoption placement asserts its dominance over parental expectations. This final section of the chapter highlights a number of text excerpts[112] that in various forms deal with the human side of the adoption procedure. Although these few examples touch on aspects that are also reflected in other interviews, the emphasis of these remarks is not on their generalizability.

One adoptive couple belonging to the lower middle class, which viewed itself in a marginal position and finally adopted the dark-skinned child rejected by other applicants, complained about the adoption counselor's lack of understanding for their own relevances along the path to a firm legal basis for the constitution of family (the adoption counselor refrained from speeding up the blood test needed for the determination of paternity). The adoptive mother explained that she would like to be given another chance to make her own perspective understandable to the adoption counselor.

ADOPTIVE MOTHER: I will point out our situation to her once again, and then we'll see whether she, er, is a *bit human* or whether she just sits there and . . . er . . .
ADOPTIVE FATHER: Sticks to regulations, right.
ADOPTIVE MOTHER: and *gives herself airs,* you see.

The first feature of this passage is that it interprets the bureaucratic compliance with rules and regulations and the quality of being human as a contrasting combination. Yet the assumption is made that the adoption counselor does have scope for action that extends beyond just "sticking to rules and regulations" and that would allow her to be a "bit human." The adoptive parents, therefore, typify the frame of action open to the procedural administrator in such a way that intersubjectivity could be achieved via role distance to bureaucratic action directives. The lack of humanness thus moves into the category of the subjective accountability.

This withheld humanness triggers so much embitterment on the part of the adoptive parents because the action or failure of the adoption counselor is experienced in a communication situation marked by a discrepancy of power distribution: the adoption counselor "gives herself airs." Empathy is replaced by the assertion of power. The unexpected nature of this drastic demonstration of an asymmetrical relational structure is also taken up in the narrative of a different adoptive mother belonging to the lower middle class. Faced by the consternation of a possible crisis—a child promised her for adoption seemed no longer available because the applicant mother was suddenly taken ill—she develops the following analogy for the presumptuous display of power by the adoption counselor.

ADOPTIVE MOTHER: She sat there like a judge or something,
ADOPTIVE FATHER: Right, right.
ADOPTIVE MOTHER: Like God and simply said "no."

The commonsense management of the critical situation of dependence is also reflected in two interviews with upper (to middle) middle-class applicants. The aspect of humanness, however, is addressed in a different way. The insignificance of humanness in the face of overwhelming bureaucratism is criticized.

ADOPTIVE FATHER: One should perhaps consider the fact that too much emphasis is placed on the bureaucratic situation and that the *really* human aspects of the selection procedure on the case of many, er, of those involved, not all, of course, er, is pushed into the background.

More frequent reference is made, however, to the problems adoptive parents had with the specific type of humanness present in the procedure than with the lack of intersubjectivity, that is, with missing humanness. These problems are experienced very intensely at the time of crisis in two cases when the occupational interests of the applicant adoptive mothers clashed with the adoption counselor's image of the motherly mother. Here are three examples on how this aspect of humanness is addressed in the two interviews.

One adoptive mother describes the problems associated with the arbitrariness of the assessment activity of the procedural administrator and the latter's power to ascribe adoptive suitability on the basis of personal value orientations as follows:

ADOPTIVE MOTHER: And that's what I found so negative about it all, you see, the fact that the human aspect was so important, for example, how do I respond to the adoption counselor and how does she respond to me.

The same adoptive mother comments on the principle of chance in the placement of her child.

ADOPTIVE MOTHER: That all fits in somehow, the fact that everybody's human and that you can only do your job as a human being.

The recapitulation in the final text passage runs along similar lines.

ADOPTIVE FATHER: Well, I don't know, we looked at it this way, that they're only humans too. . . .

A comparison between these cases as well as a comparison between text passages within one and the same case reveal the varying strategies of terminological usage. The ambiguity of the term becomes clear and it is often used in contradictory ways. The examples relate to the problems of humanness that in the end make the course of adoption procedure lack humanness: being all too human moves into focus.[113] The members of the upper (to middle) middle class use their analytical abilities to come to terms with the experience of suffering in this situation of dependence. These considerations go further than drawing a parallel to the role of God; they concentrate on the human being with all its failings and no more than limited ability to do justice to the responsible task of the artificial construction of family.

Notes

1. According to the Adoption Placement Act, which came into force together with the new adoption law on January 1, 1977, only legitimized adoption placement agencies (the community or state (Land) youth welfare offices, the central and regional agencies of the Protestant Church (Diakonisches Werk), of the Catholic Church (Deutscher Caritasverband), and of the workers' welfare association) are allowed to place adoptions; for greater details cf. section 2 of the Adoption Placement Act. In the case of adoption applicants in Hamburg the state adoption agency alone decides on their suitability as adoptive parents and grants an "adoption care authorization" if the assessment is positive. In Hamburg the period of adoption care lasts about one year. The child can then be fully adopted.
2. For an explanation of the concept of explicit indexicality cf. (following the contributions by Bar-Hillel and Garfinkel) Fritz Schütze, "Zur Hervorlockung und Analyse von Erzählungen thematisch relevanter Geschichten im Rahmen

soziologischer Feldforschung—dargestellt an einem Projekt zur Erforschung kommunaler Machtstrukturen," in Arbeitsgruppe Beilefelder Soziologen, Kommunikative Sozialforschung. Munich 1976, pp. 159–260.

3. On the schemes of communication for the presentation of facts, especially the narrative schemes, cf. Werner Kallmeyer and Fritz Schütze, "Zur Konstitution von Kommunikationsschemata der Sachverhaltsdarstellung," in Dirk Wegner, ed., Gesprächsanalyse. Hamburg 1977.

4. In this study I was not yet able to benefit from the improved access to data guaranteed by the amendment to the Code of Social Law in 1981. Since then a special legal disclosure authorization has existed for research purposes.

5. Of the host of ethnomethodological studies dealing with this aspect, cf. Don H. Zimmerman and Melvin Pollner, "The Everyday World as a Phenomenon," in J. D. Douglas, ed., Understanding Everyday Life. Chicago 1970, pp. 88ff, 94ff.

6. As the list entry practice was dropped in the adoption agency after 1976 the year 1976 provided access to the comparatively most up-to-date level of this placement practice. Reference to this applicant year had a further advantage: The cases, successful or not, were concluded before the review period, autumn 1978. During the first few weeks of the year 1978 there were only a very small number of placements (Table 17).

7. Cf. Gerhard Kleining and Harriett Moore, "Soziale Selbsteinstufung," in Kölner Zeitschrift für Soziologie und Sozialpsychologie, vol. 20, no. 3, 1968, pp. 502–552; on the further use of this instrument see also Gerhard Kleining, "Soziale Mobilität in der Bundesrepublik Deutschland," in Kölner Zeitschrift für Soziologie und Sozialpsychologie, vol. 27, no. 1, 1975, pp. 97–121.

8. Gerhard Kleining kindly gave me a list for the determination of the social status of 318 occupations on which his study (Kleining 1975) was based. Deviating from Kleining's classification I formed an upper to middle middle class in order to differentiate the strongly represented middle middle class among adoption applicants. In line with Kleining's ratings, all persons with university education at least were assigned to this category. In his stratification Kleining assumes the following score ranges: upper class 6.30 and above; upper middle class 5.50 to 6.29; middle middle class 4.50 to 5.49; lower middle class 3.50 to 4.49; upper lower class 2.50 to 3.49; lower lower class 1.80 to 2.49; "social outcasts" lower than 1.80. By way of comparison, here are the differences in my supplementary survey in the adoption agency: upper middle class 5.8 to 6.29; upper to middle middle class 5.0 to 5.79; middle middle class 4.50 to 4.99. Because of the difficulty in clearly delimiting the occupational title of "Kaufmann" (= businessman, merchant, clerk) I formed a middle to lower middle class for this undoubtedly heterogeneous occupational group; the remaining classification corresponds to Kleining's own.

9. Cf. William Labov and Joshua Waletzky, "Narrative Analysis: Oral Versions of Personal Experience," in J. H. MacNeish (ed.), Essays on the Verbal and Visual Arts. Proceedings of the 1966 Annual Spring Meeting. Seattle 1967, pp. 12–44; see also Fritz Schütze, "Zur soziologischen und linguistischen Analyse von Erzählungen," in Internationales Jahrbuch für Wissens- und Religionssoziologie, vol. 10, 1976, p. 7.

10. Cf. Monika Witt, Die Erfahrungstrukturen von Müttern, die ein Kind zur Adoption freigegen haben, unpublished thesis, Hamburg 1982; see also the detailed consideration of the situation of birth parents, first of all in the form

of a psychological overview and then with reference to personal documents, in Arthur D. Sorosky, Annette Baran, and Reuben Pannor, The Adoption Triangle. Garden City, New York 1979, pp. 32–61.

11. The fact that 18% of the applications for relinquishment of a child for adoption made in 1976 were withdrawn (Table 5) indicates the conflict-laden nature of this decision. In her study Anneke Napp-Peters pointed out that of the 3,183 child registrations in the adoption agencies covered by the study, 487 (15.3%) were later withdrawn by the birth mothers; cf. Anneke Napp-Peters, Adoption, Das alleinstehende Kind und seine Familien, Geschichte, Rechtsprobleme und Vermittlungspraxis. Neuwied 1978, p. 162.

12. Cf. Tyrell (1978), pp. 619ff; cf. the concept of responsible parenthood ("verantwortete Elternschaft") in Franz-Xaver Kaufmann, "Familie und Modernität," in Kurt Lüscher, Franz Schultheis, Michael Wehrspaun, eds., Die "postmoderne" Familie. Familiale Strategien und Familienpolitik in einer Übergangszeit. Constance 1988, p. 395.

13. Cf. also the consideration of this problem in Napp-Peters (1978), pp. 174ff, 252ff.

14. A detailed account of the historical development of adoption, especially of adoption laws, can be found in Napp-Peters (1978), pp. 16–62.

15. Napp-Peters (1978), pp. 35, 63ff.

16. Cf. Kurt Lüscher, "Die Entwicklung der Rolle des Kindes," in Klaus Hurrelmann, ed., Sozialisation und Lebenslauf. Reinbek 1976, pp. 129–150, in particular pp. 139–145.

17. The 1976 adoption law specifies the best interests of the child as the criterion for the constitution of the adoptive family.

18. Napp-Peters (1978), p. 35.

19. Napp-Peters (1978), p. 35.

20. The new adoption law envisages that the kinship relationship to the birth family should cease to exist following adoption.

21. In accordance with the European Convention on Adoption (1967) the new adoption law of the Federal Republic of Germany introduced the principle of "full adoption"; cf. Klaus Roth-Stielow, Adoptionsgesetz, Adoptionsvermittlungsgesetz. Stuttgart 1976, p. 107.

22. There are only a few exceptions in accordance with the "best interests of the child."

23. In the case of the Hamburg sample the fact that the Adoption Placement Act came into force on January 1, 1977 is not a factor that decisively changed the adoption placement conditions in comparison to earlier dates of application.

24. For information on a different development in the United States, cf. Sorosky, Baran, and Pannor (1979), p. 19; in the Federal Republic of Germany there has also been a clear decline in the number of children available for adoption since the beginning of the 1980s; references to developments in other Western European countries can be found in Napp-Peters (1978), p. 68.

25. On the history of adoption cf. Napp-Peters (1978), pp. 32, 47ff.

26. Cf. Napp-Peters (1978), pp. 51, 63.

27. The Hamburg supplementary survey on the applications for adoptions in 1976 showed 17% of children were born in wedlock (Table 19), whereas the study carried out by Anneke Napp-Peters in 1969 showed only 11% of the children placed were born in wedlock. Cf. Napp-Peters (1978), p. 264.

28. Cf. the remarks by adoptive parents in the narrative interviews and the cited remarks of the adoption counselor a little later on in this chapter.

29. Cf. the commentary on Table 2.
30. Cf. Napp-Peters (1978), p. 69.
31. Lübke and Stauber from the Berlin counseling organization for couples who desire a child work on the basis of an estimate of between 10 and 14%; cf. Joachim Neander, Frei, "aufgeklärt und emanzipiert eilen die Deutschen dem Aussterben entgegen," in Die Welt, no. 76, March 30, 1979. A figure of 10 to 15% involuntarily childless couples is also estimated by the Hamburg gynecologist Leidenberger; cf. "Chance für kinderlose Ehepaare," in Die Welt, no. 240, October 14, 1980. The increase in the number of involuntarily childless couples represents a biological fact whose social parameters are also worth examining (e.g., sterility caused by stress).
32. Cf. Napp-Peters (1978), pp. 48, 44.
33. One example is the 1969 Act on the Legal Situation of Illegitimate Children.
34. Cf. the legitimation of a birth without marriage in parts of the women's movement, e.g., Barbara Franck, "Männer? Ex und hopp!" In Die Zeit, no. 37, September 4, 1981, p. 55.
35. Cf. the problem of a diminishing "unquestionability of having children" among married couples in Hartmann Tyrell, "Familie und gesellschaftliche Differenzierung," in Helge Pross, ed., Familie—wohin? Reinbek 1979, p. 67. The gynecologists expect a ratio of up to 5% voluntarily childless couples. Cf. Joachim Neander (1979), p. 3. See also the consideration of growing voluntary childlessness in the Netherlands in Marie-Louise den Bandt, Sex-Role-Socialization and Voluntary Childlessness in the Netherlands, manuscript for the 17th International Sociological Association in Helsinki 1979; see also the study by Thomas Ayck and Inge Stolten, Kinderlos aus Verantwortung. Reinbek 1978.
36. See the recapitulation of the course of adoption procedure by the adoptive parents further on in this chapter.
37. In its publications on public youth welfare the Federal Statistical Office often maintained this ratio, on which other studies also based their figures, e.g., Napp-Peters (1978), pp. 66–68 (with the conclusion of decreasing adoption figures), p. 101.
38. As the significance of a prompt placement for the development of the child's personality and for the structuring of the adoptive parent–child relationship moved into focus, the adoption agencies were often provided with more staff during the 1970s. According to the supplementary survey, just under 70% of the children relinquished for adoption were placed in the year of application (Table 31). The list entries did not permit a differentiated calculation of how much time passed between the application and adoption care.
39. The problems associated with advising a person whether to relinquish a child for adoption or not cannot be considered in greater detail here. It is difficult to say how far the right of a child to its mother declared by the UN General Assembly is a practical point of reference. For sceptical remarks in this respect cf. Napp-Peters (1978), pp. 59f, 89–93. Also compare the regulations on counseling and supporting parents living alone laid down in youth welfare law in Roth-Stielow (1976), pp. 227f; see also 5. Jugendbericht Budesminister fuer Jugend, Familie und Gesundheit (ed.); Fuenfter Jugendbericht, Bonn 1980, p. 43. The problems arising for the birth mother following the relinquishment of her child are impressively described in Sorosky, Baran, and Pannor (1979), pp. 32–61.

40. Tyrell (1979), p. 42.
41. Spiros Simitis et al., Kindeswohl. Eine interdisziplinäre Untersuchung über seine Verwirklichung in der vormundschaftsgerichtlichen Praxis. Frankfurt 1979, p. 182.
42. Single persons can also apply for a child. Even before the new adoption law there were isolated cases of children being placed with persons living on their own. Applications for adoption by persons in this category, however, have represented the exception so far.
43. I formulate the task of adoption agencies with reference to the wording used in the first sections of the adoption law to define the basis for adoption.
44. Cf. the idealization achieved in commonsense thinking in Alfred Schuetz (1971), pp. 11ff.
45. This term from the field of conversational analysis denotes that a specific type of action is followed by action of a corresponding type (question/answer; greeting/greeting in return). Whoever sets the conditional relevances is in a position to steer the course of interaction. Cf. the application of the concept to institutional–organizational proceedings with the strategic use of conditional relevances in Fritz Schütze, "Strategische Interaktion im Verwaltungsgericht—eine soziolinguistische Analyse zum Kommunikationsverlauf im Verfahren zur Anerkennung als Wehrdienstverweigerer," in Winfried Hassemer, Wolfgang Hoffmann-Riem, and Manfred Weiss, eds., Interaktion vor Gericht. Baden-Baden 1978, pp. 43ff. See also Werner Kallmeyer and Fritz Schütze, "Konversationsanalyse," in Studium der Linguistik, 1979, no. 1, pp. 13ff.
46. On the polarity of administrative efficiency and the satisfaction of the public cf. Niklas Luhmann, Legitimation durch Verfahren. Neuwied 1969, p. 209.
47. In his analysis of administrative behavior Niklas Luhmann gives efficiency aspects priority over the goal of satisfying the public and of guaranteeing a "consensus of persons affected"; cf. Niklas Luhmann, Legitimation durch Verfahren. Neuwied 1969, pp. 207–209. Not only the insight into the experience of suffering on the part of the persons involved prompts me to move away from this position with respect to the field of social administration considered here, but, above all, the dependence of a professionally grounded selection of applicants—the dependence of the rational management of problems—on the knowledge of their relevances. The abrupt confrontation with the procedurally dominant perspective devalues the relevances set by the persons affected and triggers frustration that cannot be expected of the public in order to guarantee an efficient administration, but that reduces efficiency by inducing strategic interaction on the part of the persons affected.
48. For information on the organizational structure of the adoption agency and the division of labor into the family welfare field service and the central office service, cf. Napp-Peters (1978), pp. 146–160.
49. Cf. Gerhard Riemann, Stigma, formelle soziale Kontrolle, das Leben mit den anderen—eine empirische Untersuchung zu drei Gegenstandsbereichen des Alltagswissens von Obdachlosen, unpublished thesis, Bielefeld 1977, pp. 252–257; an extract can be found in Hans-Georg Soeffner, ed., Interpretative Verfahren in den Sozial- und Textwissenschaften. Stuttgart 1979. See also G. Riemann, Eine empirische Erfassung von Alltagswissen: Ein Beispiel aus der Obdachlosenforschung, pp. 127–139, on the aspect of territory p. 134. See also the analysis of territory in its significance for interactions in Erving Goffman, Relations in Public. New York 1971, pp. 28–61.

50. Cf. the consideration of the concept of impression management in Erving Goffman, The Presentation of Self in Everyday Life. Garden City, New York 1959, pp. 208–237.
51. The instruction to the social worker contained in the Hamburg "Working Guide for Adoption Assessment" to probe the childhood of the applicants and include this in a prognosis of parental suitability is reflected in this narrative passage. See also Napp-Peters (1978), pp. 200f.
52. Cf. the category of the presentation of self in Erving Goffman (1959), pp. 58–66.
53. I refer here to the term used by Blumer, with which he tries to describe the interpretational process of the individual with himself as well as with his interaction partners. Cf. Herbert Blumer, Symbolic Interactionism: Prospective and Method. Englewood Cliffs, New Jersey 1969, p. 5.
54. Krappmann deals with the competence of the individual to introduce his identity into interaction as one of the abilities which fosters a person's identity. In his view the presentation of identity means letting self-identity become visible; cf. Lothar Krappmann, Soziologische Dimensionen der Identität. Stuttgart 1969, pp. 168ff. For the clarification of processes in a bureaucratic application procedure I opt for Goffman's concept of presentation, which places greater emphasis on the element of role enactment designed to make a favorable impression; cf. Goffman (1959), pp. 17ff, 208ff.
55. More on this in Napp-Peters (1978), pp. 190ff; a "Working Guide for the Adoption Assessment" used by Hamburg's social workers also points to social status (financial circumstances, living conditions, "social status and social contacts").
56. Tyrell (1979), p. 42.
57. Cf. the use of the term in conversational analysis in the overview in Kallmeyer and Schütze (1976), p. 15.
58. Cf. the legitimating function of the statement of reasons for decisions in Niklas Luhmann (1969), p. 211.
59. I fall back here on the concept used by Alfred Schütz, whose remarks on the various dimensions of time are also considered in another section. Cf. Alfred Schütz and Thomas Luckmann, The Structure of the Life-World. London 1974, p. 27. See also the example of pregnancy as waiting for the passing of biological time in Schütz and Luckmann (1974), pp. 47ff.
60. Cf. the quarterly and annually compiled Hamburg adoption agency statistics. Of the 443 applicants whose applications were accepted for further assessment in 1976, only 12 applicants were rejected ("not suitable as place of adoption care").
61. Despite all the parallels to the conscientious objection procedure, which was repeatedly mentioned by the adoptive parents themselves during the narrative interviews, there is one major difference that also determines the differences in the ratios of rejection: the assessment "limited suitability" to a certain extent replaces the rejection. Cf. the binary decision-making structure in conscientious objection procedures in Schuetze (1978), p. 32.
62. Cf. the quarterly and annually compiled Hamburg adoption agency statistics; in 1976, 999 applications were made, 443 of which were accepted. On the other hand, 568 applications by applicants from the Federal Republic of Germany or, to a smaller extent (18), from abroad were rejected.
63. Cf. Grunow's remarks on the dependence of the client associated with the

monopoly position of public administration: Dieter Grunow, Alltagskontakte mit der Verwaltung, vol. 3 of the series "Bürger und Verwaltung" (edited by Grunow, Hegner, and Kaufmann) Frankfurt 1978, pp. 39f.

64. This monopoly position of the local adoption agency with respect to the granting of the adoption care authorization must be distinguished from its position as supplier when placing a child for adoption. Its monopoly in this respect was broken by section 2, paragraph 2 of the Adoption Placement Act.

65. Concrete examples of the considerable disagreement among adoption counselors on the binding criteria for the assessment of adoptive suitability are presented by Anneke Napp-Peters in her empirical study "Experimentelle Studie beruflicher Entscheidungen über die Annahme oder Ablehnung von Bewerbern." Napp-Peters (1978), pp. 211–250.

66. Grunow characterizes the contact situation in public administration inter alia in terms of the intensity of the subjective and objective need ("Bedürfnis/ Bedarf") to be satisfied by the performance of the administration; cf. Grunow (1978), p. 45.

67. Barney G. Glaser and Anselm L. Strauss, Awareness of Dying. Chicago 1965, p. 11.

68. In his clarification of the elements of strategic interaction, Goffman emphasizes the "assessments" that the players make when calculating their moves; cf. Erving Goffman, Strategic Interaction. Philadelphia 1969, pp. 85–145. The application of the conceptual frame to institutional-cum-organizational procedures with their constraints of action is only hinted at in Goffman (e.g., pp. 132–142). In his analysis of the conscientious objection procedure Fritz Schütze exposed the occurrence of strategic interaction in terms of conversational analysis and emphasized its significance as an instrument of power for the "dominant interactant." Cf. Schuetze (1978), pp. 43ff. The following analysis centers on the scope for strategic interaction perceived by the dependent party in the interaction relationship. The constraints of a factual presentation of events triggered by the dominant interactant can occasionally be taken into account by the available data.

69. Cf. Goffman (1969), p. 136.

70. Cf. Schuetze (1976), p. 16.

71. The following examples of weighing up and rejecting options will be described using the term "balancing." I fall back on the concept used by Anselm Strauss and his fellow researchers, who repeatedly came across the observation when dealing with work processes associated with the pain of a patient, that the treatment of the pain is weighed up with respect to various consequences and that there was a corresponding "juggling" with options; cf. Shizuko Y. Fagerhaugh and Anselm Strauss, Politics of Pain Management: Staff-Patient Interaction. Menlo Park, California 1977, pp. 241ff.

72. The changing sex preference would undoubtedly be worth a separate study. Whereas the preference for a son was probably prevalent under the social pressure to provide a legal heir, there was apparently a marked preference for girls during the first decades of the 20th century in Germany, which is felt to be connected with the uncertainties in the adoptive parental role; cf. Napp-Peters (1978), pp. 76f.

73. Of the total of 37 adoptions only eight applicants declared their willingness right from the start to adopt a child older than one year, two applicants after being encouraged to do so. Four cases cannot be classified because of the

initial foster child status or because the parents themselves asked the agency to place a child they already knew.

74. Cf. the alternatives to negotiation such as persuasion, manipulation, and coercion in Anselm Strauss, Negotiations—Varieties, Contexts, Processes and Social Order. San Francisco 1978, e.g. p. 7.

75. Napp-Peters (1978), pp. 211–250.

76. Cf. Napp-Peters (1978), pp. 248f.

77. Cf. the problem of a limited ability to love during role conflicts of mothers who are "family mothers" only, e.g., in Friedhelm Neidhardt, "System-theoretische Analysen zur Sozialisationsfähigkeit der Familie," in Friedhelm Neidhardt, ed., Frühkindliche Sozialisation. Stuttgart 1975, pp. 182–185; Friedhelm Neidhardt, "Strukturbedingungen und Probleme familialer Sozial-isation," in Dieter Claessens and Petra Milhoffer, eds., Familiensoziologie— ein Reader als Einführung. Frankfurt 1973, pp. 214f.; Zweiter Familienbericht, published by the Federal Minister for Youth, Family Affairs and Health. Bonn 1975, pp. 38f.; Hartmann Tyrell (1979), pp. 62f.; Edward Shorter, The Making of the Modern Family. New York 1975, pp. 269–280.

78. Cf. the problems of familial disintegration and familial overorganization, for example, in René König, "Familiensoziologie," in René König, ed., Hand-buch der Empirischen Sozialforschung. Stuttgart 1969, pp. 267ff.; Tyrell (1979), pp. 32f. See also the growing significance of school socialization, which is viewed in connection with the increasing disintegration of the family and—linked with this fact—the growing incompetence of the family in its preparation for the demand of role games outside of the family, for example, in Manfred Brusten and Klaus Hurrelmann, Abweichendes Verhalten in der Schule. Munich 1973, p. 11. On the rejection of "working mothers" by some adoption counselors, cf. Napp-Peters (1978), pp. 195f.

79. In view of the current educational level of the adoption counselors—profes-sional school, often without any special preparation for dealing with adop-tion—there can be no claims of a psychoanalytically grounded adoption practice able to include the applicants' unconscious expectations with respect to the role of the child. On parental role expectations cf. Horst-Eberhard Richter, Eltern, Kind und Neurose. Stuttgart 1967.

80. To simplify matters reference will often be made in the following to the "upper" rather than the "upper to middle" middle class, cf. the description of the classification indices in footnote 8 of this chapter.

81. The transcription example presented on page xx ("I had the feeling I can't say what I want to here") relates to an applicant couple belonging to the upper middle class, which felt discriminated against in many respects despite its status-related interaction resources (occupation, teacher; already a birth child; in addition, the interaction style of the adoption counselor, displaying her own occupational certainty in the face of doubts by the applicants about their competence). The limited prognostic meaningfulness of class member-ship with respect to the mode of communication should again be emphasized in the light of this case, the most extremely deviating case in this category.

82. For a fundamental consideration of coping with strangeness cf. Schuetz (1971), pp. 7ff, 19ff; Schuetz and Luckmann (1974), pp. 3–8.

83. Dieter Grunow points out the sense of a lack of orientation citizens suffer when they try to determine how binding the norms stated by administrative officials are. There are probably also differing class-specific modes of over-

coming this problem; for a characterization of the interaction situation in line with unclear determination of roles cf. Dieter Grunow (1978), pp. 69–74.

84. Cf. the analysis of narrations in terms of the competences of action in Schuetz (1976), pp. 31f. The problems associated with role-taking resulting from the limitations set by self-identity are considered in Krappmann (1973), p. 143.

85. The "natural age difference" laid down by the Hamburg adoption agency is roughly 35 years. It seems doubtful whether the calculation made in this particular case of a 42-year-old applicant mother ("In your case we can only consider 8-10-year-old children") is in accord with the adoption law stipulation of the best interests of the child. Even if one agrees with the opinion expressed by Roth-Stielow, who relates to the problem of the flexibility limits of adoptive parents who have not grown old with their child by referring to the example of the adoption of minors by applicants older than 50 (Roth-Stielow, 1976, p. 69, Section 7), this practice is nevertheless questionable. The limited flexibility of the 42-year-old woman does not become tolerable from a youth welfare point of view by offering her a 10-year-old child, which with its experience of changing reference persons and stays in homes that can generally be assumed in this group is more likely to overtax the adoptive mother's capacity to cope with the situation.

86. Cf. Fritz Schütze, "Prozess-strukturen des Lebensablaufs," in Joachim Matthes, Arno Pfeifenberger, Manfred Stosberg, eds., Biographie in handlungswissenschaftlicher Perspektive. Nuremberg 1981, pp. 88–92.

87. There are occasional references in the interviews to the fact that the adoption counselor herself drew a parallel between the course of the placement period and the course of a pregnancy—"Feel as if you were in your 3rd month of pregnancy!" Apart from the fact that structuring the period of waiting in this way leads to problems of how to assess the situation when the adoptive mother feels that she is "in her 10th month," this practice seems questionable as it can trigger a more fundamental misguidance of the establishment of an adoptive parent–child bond. David Kirk proved the existence of the strategy of "rejection-of-difference" in the adoption agencies as well as among the adoptive parents, emphasizing their disastrous consequences for adoptive family life; cf. David Kirk, Adoptive Kinship: A Modern Institution in Need of Reform. Toronto 1981, pp. 71–83.

88. On the problems of status passage cf. E. E. Le Masters, "Parenthood as Crisis," in Marvin B. Sussman, ed., Sourcebook in Marriage and the Family. Boston 1963, pp. 194–198. See also Karol Szemkus, "Geburt des ersten Kindes und Übernahme der Elternrolle," in Hans Braun and Ute Leitner, eds., Problem Familie—Familienprobleme. Frankfurt 1976, pp. 51–61.

89. Niklas Luhmann (1969), p. 203.

90. Cf. the importance of contacts with administration by phone in Dieter Grunow (1978), pp. 48, 133.

91. Cf. the use of the terms with respect to the simultaneity of the content and relationship aspects of the message in Paul Watzlawick, Janet H. Beavin, and Don D. Jackson, Pragmatics of Human Communication: A Study of Interactional Patterns, Pathologies and Paradoxes. London 1968, pp. 51–54.

92. "Work" in the conceptual significance used here entails both aspects of instrumental work as well as of "emotional work" in the sense of the term as used by Anselm Strauss. In accordance with the intention of the callers the work is instrumental; the mode of communication, however, is determined by

emotional work; cf. Anselm Strauss et al., Social Organization of Medical Work. Chicago 1985, pp. 129–150.

93. The formulation used repeatedly by the adoptive parents corresponds to the role social work assumes in adoption of "playing God" described by Kirk (1981), p. 85. See also the practice of using the same terms in New Zealand described in Joss Shawyer, Death by Adoption. Auckland 1979, p. 261.

94. Cf. Kirk (1981), pp. 88f; Napp-Peters (1978), pp. 87, 211–250.

95. Table 31 also points out the longer availability of older children for adoption placement. The older the child, the longer the period of time between the registration of the child for adoption and the start of adoption care.

96. The widespread practice of "matching" according to similarity of outward appearance will not be considered in greater detail here. Its problems with regard to the strategies of normalization chosen by the adoptive family, however, are taken into account in Chapters 5 and 6. On the associated misguidance of the parent–child bond towards a denial of the adoptive status, cf. Kirk (1981), pp. 71ff; Napp-Peters (1978), pp. 122–124.

97. These doubts are based, for example, on observations made by Kirk (1981, pp. 90–95) on the visibly limited competence of the adoption agency when evaluating applicants and children and when justifying their selection. For the situation of the West German adoption agencies see the experimental study on placement decisions in Napp-Peters (1978), pp. 211–250; see also the doubts expressed in Michael Hesseler, "Die Institution der Adoption und die Diskussion einer Sozialisationsperspektive," in Soziale Welt, vol. 31, 1980, pp. 242f. More recent developmental psychology studies have also indicated that studies so far do not allow inferences to be derived from the child's mental characteristics during the first two years of its life concerning its future development; see Jerome Kagan, Richard B. Kearsley, and Philip R. Zelazo, Infancy, Its Place in Human Development. Cambridge, Mass. 1980, pp. 143–148. See also the criticism of adoption placement practice from a feminist viewpoint in Shawyer (1979), pp. 256–288.

98. The ascription of general parental eligibility, however, cannot be regarded as such a stage, because hardly any rejections are made at this stage for fear of legal repercussions.

99. Cf. Luhmann (1969), p. 207.

100. An impressive consideration of the "high value of the family and of children" in the lower class can be found in the study by Klaus Wahl, Greta Tüllmann, Michael-Sebastian Honig, and Lerke Gravenhorst, Familien sind anders! Reinbek 1980, pp. 34ff.

101. Cf. Gerhard Kleining, "Soziale Mobilität in der Bundesrepublik Deutschland," in Kölner Zeitschrift für Soziologie und Sozialpsychologie, vol. 27, no. 2, 1975, p. 275.

102. Cf. Lee Rainwater and Carol K. Weinstine, And the Poor get Children, Chicago 1960; Lee Rainwater, Richard P. Coleman, and Gerald Handel, Workingman's Wife, Her Personality, World, and Life Style. New York 1959, pp. 88f.

103. Assumptions in this direction are reinforced, for example, by observations made by Wahl et al. (1980, p. 233) on the uncertainty of members of the lower class when dealing with authorities and their attempts to keep their distance; see also Grunow's concepts (1978, pp. 93ff; willingness to cooperate, realizational motivation, communicative competence), which could probably—as already shown in this study—be applied class-specifically.

104. In order to determine the clearly unsuccessful applicants, those applicants listed in Table 15 in the category "other" were eliminated from the total number of applicants as well as four cases with the adoption of a foster child or the start of a foster child relationship.

105. Cf. Zweiter Familienbericht, published by the Federal Minister for Youth, Family Affairs and Health, Bonn-Bad Godesberg 1975, p. 110; Klaus Wahl, Familienbildung und -beratung in der Bundesrepublik Deutschland, Schriftenreihe des Bundesministers für Jugend, Familie und Gesundheit, vol. 8, Stuttgart 1975, pp. 62–64.

106. Cf. Kirk (1981), pp. 85, 94f; Napp-Peters (1978), p. 291; Gordon Scott Bonham, "Who Adopts: The Relationship of Adoption and Social-Demographic Characteristics of Women," in Journal of Marriage and the Family, vol. 39, no. 2, 1977, p. 303; Cynthia D. Martin, Beating the Adoption Game. La Jolla 1980, p. 84; Hesseler (1980), p. 244.

107. Kirk doubts whether this claim officially made by adoption agencies can at all be realized; Kirk (1981), pp. 93f.

108. This technique was simplified insofar as those few cases in which a desire was expressed for an older child or a child in particular need of parents are treated here as if these applicants orient themselves to the pattern of normality.

109. In order to be able to statistically consider the question of how far class membership has a systematic effect on the degree-of-privilegedness index, an unbalanced one-way analysis of variance was calculated (cf. B. J. Winer, Statistical Principles in Experimental Design. New York 1962, pp. 96ff), which did not, however, lead to a significant result; $F (2.26) = 2.063$; non-significant. In the paired comparison of means, however, a difference was confirmed between lower and upper middle class; $t (13) = 2.240$; $p < 0.025$. It should be pointed out that the required homogeneity of variance required for the t-test only existed in this case with a level of significance of 1%. If $\alpha = 0.05$ is chosen, there are significance variances between the upper and middle middle class; $F (5.8) = 6.387$; $p < 0.05$. On the whole, these findings can probably be interpreted as a statistical corroboration for the probable differing adoption placement practice for members of the upper and lower middle class. No differences could be confirmed, however, between the upper and middle middle class ($t [21] = 1.65$; not significant) and between the middle and lower middle class ($t [18] = 0.99$; not significant).

110. The connection between the class membership of applicants and the age of the child placed for adoption is also shown in Napp-Peters (1978), p. 91; see also the theory of a greater ability of the lower class to cope with strain presented in Hesseler (1980), p. 244.

111. In the report he compiled on unsuccessful adoption relationships for the Hamburg youth welfare office, Michael Jasinsky refers to the "strange logic that older children, often disturbed or handicapped children, are placed with 'undemanding' parents, which is expressed in the reports of the social workers or the staff of the home as a commonsense theory" and which—as Jasinsky shows—"in the final analysis" runs contrary to the interests of these children. Michael Jasinsky, Untersuchung zur Bewährung von Adoptionen, unpublished survey report, June 1980.

112. Three interviews are considered here, the only interviews in which the concept of humanness is explicitly addressed in some form with respect to the

adoption placement process. Within these three interviews, however, a number of terminological usages along similar lines are not taken into account.

113. Grunow (1978, p. 73) describes various strategies of dealing with bureaucracy, including the typification of the interaction partner as "simply" a "human being."

3

The Status Passage from Applicant for a Child to Mother and Father

The final sequence of the bureaucratically mediated constitution of family begins when the adoption counselor matches the universe of placeable children with the universe of adoption applicants to make a specific adoption "offer": "We have a child for you." Adoption applicants experience this announcement as a drastic move out of the phase of waiting and into a phase of renewed autonomy yet including constraints of action. Up to this stage they were obliged to more or less powerlessly accept heteronomous guidance. News of the adoption offer revives their residual autonomy as parents-to-be. The design of family constitution created by bureaucratic allocation must now be ratified by an act of cooptation on the part of the prospective parents. As the number of adoption offers cannot be increased at will the pressure of cooptation reduces the remaining parental autonomy even further.

Most of the interviews contain pretty detailed descriptions of the chain of events beginning with the notification of the adoption offer, continuing to the first face-to-face encounter with the possible adoptee and the decision to take in the child, and culminating in the actual taking in of the child "at home." This narration of the first encounter is missing, however, in those cases in which the future adoptive parents did not meet the child under the perspective of adoption (foster relationship, work in the children's home). Furthermore, in several cases in which a newborn child or at least a very young baby was adopted, the description of the first encounter contains no more than rudimentary details on aspects of place and time as well as minimal information on the child itself ("she had chicken-pox"). These examples of a relative approximation to the normal case would suggest that once the adoption offer has been made, cooptation in such cases was no longer a dispositional act, but that the notification of the offer and cooptation tended to coincide. With the exception of two indistinct cases it seems fair to assume that the lack of the "encounter narrative" or its limited descriptiveness is connected with the intensity of the strain experienced during the initial face-to-face interaction. The significance of the first encounter can be omitted to a substantial degree and subordinated to other events in the reconstruction of the adoption history ("I had no diapers, nothing") if the drama of the initial encounter is not additionally heightened by the undecidedness of the situation. In the majority of interviews, however, an accumulation of burdensome factors was documented. The decision to take in a certain child as an adopted child was even experienced in a number of cases as a "stressful life event." In these cases the meaning of the event "at that time" reconstructed in the narrative clearly reveals the difference between cooptation and birth.

"We Have a Child for You"

The construction of family in the case of adoption is typically ushered in over the phone. The technical medium of communication transports the message from the planning institution to the prospective adoptive parents. For the adoption applicants this means a transition from the phase of uncertain waiting for an as-yet-indeterminate child to a phase of concrete constitution of family.

Irrespective of whether the couple has been waiting a long time or not, the news of a child "for us" is almost always experienced as a sudden event. The following metaphor is representative of the numerous commentaries on the unforeseen sequence of events accompanying the notification that a child is available for adoption:

ADOPTIVE FATHER: It came like a bolt from the blue on the Thursday before Easter.

The element of surprise associated with the notification is only less intense in those few cases in which the adoption counselor had already guided discussions towards a certain child during the examination procedure ("She already had the child in mind"). It is also less pronounced in three of the six cases of a clinic adoption, in which the birth of a child in a few weeks time was announced rather than the immediate availability of a child for adoption. In approximation to the model of the "natural" family, the beginning of parenthood in such cases can already be predicted for a specific child, even though the freedom of the biological parents to reverse their decision to relinquish their child still casts a shadow of uncertainty on this parenthood. In other cases of clinic adoption, on the other hand, the prospective parents are often given absolutely no opportunity to prepare for the status passage:

ADOPTIVE MOTHER: Well, the children you get from the clinic, they come very suddenly, and it's as if, the child is there on the day it's born, and the adoptive parents are informed at short, very short notice that they're now parents and will be getting a baby in four days' time.

The suddenness of the artificial constitution of family documented in so many of the interviews reflects the process of bureaucratic construction in this field, which—in a multidimensional decision-making process—has to match a hardly calculable supply of children with the demand for such children. For adoption as a youth welfare institution the factor of the waiting period cannot be the priority principle of structuring. Whereas in the "normal case" a pregnancy reduces the intensity of the status passage to the parental role and the transition is marked by elements of a realization of continuity,[1] the announcement of a "child for you" could be best described as a social precipitate delivery. The unforeseeability of the announcement intensifies the abruptness of the event; in many cases it is not even certain that the procedure will come to a successful end, let alone when this will be. Yet even in cases marked by a greater degree of predictability the anticipation of the event during the period of waiting is presumably no more than an unsatisfactory mental preparation for the inceptive "moment of truth" of the artificial constitution of family. At the moment of its announcement the news of an adoption offer hits prospective parents "like something out of the blue." The actual experience of the constitution of family within "actual reach"[2] can only be partially anticipated before the event itself.

The Limitations of Notification over the Phone

The announcement of the child as an item of information on the latest stage of the adoption procedure requires a detailed specification that can already be used as a decision-making filter before the child is actually seen. The notification, "We have a child for you—please come take a look at it," is incomplete. The communication situation between the adoption counselor and the applicants that generally precedes the first encounter with the child reveals how much importance is attached to the child's nonvisible dimensions. The basis for cooptation is not just the child's current physical existence, but also its history.

To judge by the organization of the procedure reflected in the narratives, adoption counselors generally avoid any concretization of their "offer" when notifying the prospective parents about the potential adoptee:

ADOPTIVE MOTHER: [Citing what the adoption counselor said] "I've got a file
here on a lovely little boy."

In the case of the bureaucratically organized construction of family it
looks as if the limitations of communicability over the phone are reached
via the "bare" notification of the event. The adoption counselor avoids
succumbing to any temptation to provide more fragments of information
on the child by pointing to the need for a meeting in the adoption agency
as soon as possible. Via this institutionalization of the procedural norms
relating to the location, time, and medium of communication (face-to-
face), the adoption counselor is able to avoid being forced to answer
awkward questions that might develop their own momentum by the prospective parents.[3] Adoption counselors in their capacity as "procedural
administrator" thus retain the ability to present a brief biography of the
child whose file is lying on the desk and at the same time to visually assess
the reactions of the prospective parents.

The following would appear to be an untypical specification of the
adoption offer:

ADOPTIVE FATHER: [Citing what the adoption counselor said] "Well, there's a,
there's a little, but that's strange, . . .
ADOPTIVE MOTHER: [Also citing the adoption counselor] That's a child, I didn't
really have you in mind for this child, . . .
ADOPTIVE FATHER: [Citation] "and that's a child, yes, that's a child, you have
to . . . it's got a Mongolian spot," and, er. . . .

A contextual analysis shows that the untypical specification in this case
was caused by a reversal of the initiation of the action scheme. It was not
the adoption counselor who initiated the discussion about a possible
adoption offer, but the applicant who manages to elicit an ad-hoc offer as
a result of a "strategy of being pushy":

ADOPTIVE FATHER: And then she said to me, after I got hold of her on the
phone, I said "Well, Mrs S., has anything come up?" "Well", she said, "*not*
really turned up, I mean, there *might* be a child, but . . ." I said "What does
that mean, there *might* be a child, is there one or not?" [This interview
continues with the passage just cited above.]

The adoption counselor loses her procedural superiority in this case by
letting herself be maneuvered into an improvization of family constitution
on the basis of a temporal coincidence of an offer and an impromptu
demand. In this as in other cases, the inquiry over the phone about the
latest developments in the adoption procedure is able to produce a "reduction of complexity" in a field in which the current principles of professional
action are not able to meet the requirements of the situation. The principle
of chance, therefore, often overruns the few maxims of bureaucratically

organized constitution of family: "That's a child I never really had in mind for you." The offer hesitantly made in the subjunctive—linguistically identical with the potential existence of a child—obliges the adoption counselor to specify the offer "with reservation." The result is a specification of the offer with a rejection potential untypical for the procedural control of the adoption counselor ("Mongolian spot"—"What? Mongoloid we thought").

The Specification of the Adoption Offer

The discussion in the adoption agency as the legitimate framework for specifying the details of the adoption offer reflects what, according to the current orientation of professional activities in this field, adoptive parents should know about their future child. In the case of biological parents, knowledge of the common genealogical bond makes all further elements of knowledge about the child irrelevant for the assumption of the parental role: The child becomes the child of its parents without their knowledge of the child's specific attributes. The parental role of adoptive parents, on the other hand, is constituted via a set of information and the classification of its relevance for familial attachment. The cooptation decision is dependent on knowing who the child is.

The child's identity cannot be determined independent of social norms. Allowing for all the possible shifts of emphasis in the professional orientation on this point, the definition of the child by the adoption agency can be expected to reflect the societal definition of a child. The text examples demonstrate that the definition of a child is never its definition as a person "in itself": Insofar as information exists on the identity of the parents (not so, for example, in the case of a foundling from the Third World), the child is typified as the child of its biological parents.

Even though the adopted child is on the verge of a new social placement, the general rules of ascribing status to the child apply when the adoption offer is specified: The child's identity and which child is to be coopted is defined through knowledge of its origins.[4] The socially binding character of the "primary" placement—placement based on the principle of filiation—becomes particularly evident wherever the primary placement is initially rated as the indispensable component of the "identification" of the child despite the planned secondary placement in the adoptive family. Irrespective of the considerations underlying the professional specification of the details of the adoption offer,[5] the incorporation of the child's genealogical origins into its definition places an element of the "natural" family of the child at the beginning of the adoptive family history. Adoption procedure, therefore, does not play down the child's already effected primary placement. On the contrary, an awareness is created of the fact that the envisaged allocation of the child to the adoptive family is a redefinition; this underlines the insurmountable structural specificity of the adoptive family.

During their reconstruction of the events surrounding the first encounter with the child, the narrators frequently confine their remarks to the statement that they were told something about the birth parents ("rough details") without mentioning specific details of the primary placement of the adopted child. This is probably due in part to their concern about retaining anonymity; the adoptive parents have read information on the birth parents, including their names, in the adoption file, whereas apart from a typifying description without any possibility of personal identification, the adoptive parents are unknown and wish to remain unknown to the birth parents. Furthermore, the institutional framework of the "social precipitate birth" does not exactly foster the interest of adoptive parents in the child's birth parents. The short space of just a few hours in many cases between the notification of the offer and the first encounter with the child probably induces applicants to focus their attention prospectively on the child and on their own parenthood rather than retrospectively on the birth parents. They will probably tend to forget the information on the birth parents, their relationship to one another, their life situation, their class membership, and so on, if it is not repeated in written form. As the knowledge of the specific structural character of the adoptive family is a key prerequisite for overcoming the associated problems—a claim that will be supported later on—the significance of the permanence of awareness of information on the primary placement of the adopted child should not be underrated.

I will now refer to a few examples illustrating two components of the definition of the child, the description of the child as the child of its parents and as a personality "in itself." The degree to which the interviews relate to the "derived" or "ego-based" identification of the child varies. As expected, narrative passages relating to clinic adoptions planned before the child was born exclusively contain "derived" descriptive elements:

ADOPTIVE MOTHER: The mother had three children, this was her third, and she was about to get a divorce from her husband, and found out that she was going to have another child, and he told her: "That's not mine." And that must have left her *thunderstruck,* and then she didn't want to have it. . . .

The other extreme of the identification of the child purely on the basis of its own ego-based attributes can be found in the example of a foundling from the Third World:

ADOPTIVE MOTHER: And then a child's file was sent to us two days later with a doctor's report, all from Vietnam, in English, originally in Vietnamese with an English translation, with a little photograph enclosed and "If you would like to adopt this child. . . ."

All other descriptions of the adoption offer reconstructed in the interviews contain a mixture of information on the child's derived and ego-based identification. In many cases in which babies were placed the adoptive parents confine their remarks to outlining the processes surrounding the verbal presentation of the child: a girl, two-and-one-half months old. "The parents were described, or the mother, and the previous history" with reference to the file in the adoption agency. The description of the adoption offer was particularly detailed in the only case in which the child was outlined to the adoptive parents in a letter. Referring to the officially enforced transfer to a children's home because of child neglect ("catastrophic state of the child") we find the following passage:

ADOPTIVE FATHER: And in this letter he pointed out that the child had already suffered a great deal, and might be damaged. And what he wrote about the parents, about the birth parents . . .
ADOPTIVE MOTHER: That was incredibly negative.
ADOPTIVE FATHER: The father had such a violent temper.
ADOPTIVE MOTHER: And was pretty crazy, that's what they wrote.
ADOPTIVE FATHER: Crazy. The parents apparently, the husband and the wife, were always arguing, a really hellish situation. And the child was kept in the shed somewhere.

This example of a four-month-old child already indicates that the birth parents are not just integrated into the definition of the child as progenitors and child-bearers but as inadequate socializing agents. The history of children adopted at a much older age reveals the even more conflict-laden biographical involvement with the history of parental action. The more the development of the child beyond the embryonic phase becomes the social history of its personality, the more difficult it becomes to distinguish between the ego-based and derived parts of identification. Apart from age and sex of the child, every biographical fact appears to be part of the interaction history in the case of a child made available for adoption at the age of five and a half years:

ADOPTIVE MOTHER: At the time the child was with its mother. The child was with its mother. The child was never in a home, apart from the eight and a half months it was in hospital. She was battered and then referred to the hospital by the family doctor.
. . . .
ADOPTIVE MOTHER: But the mother wanted to have the child back, you see . . .
INTERVIEWER: Yes.
ADOPTIVE MOTHER: and . . . somehow, I don't know how it came about. It looks as if she did *in fact* go back to her mother, and she was there three weeks, and the whole carry-on started again . . .

INTERVIEWER: Hm . . .

ADOPTIVE MOTHER: and then the youth welfare worker was called in, you see, and . . . the mother probably became frightened of herself. . . . She didn't know how long it would be before she would start hitting the child again, you see.

The example of a girl offered for adoption at the age of four and a half years illustrates how the final sequences of a child's preadoption history may have long since been taken out of the hands of the birth parents. A bureaucratic history had already been superimposed on the primary social placement by the birth parents three years previously before the child was presented to her prospective adoptive parents. Following rough information on the ego-based identification of the child (sex, age, present whereabouts), the description of the child develops in the form of a fluctuating socializational history with reference to parents and parent substitutes. Following an "anonymous report to the authorities," the child was admitted to a home at the age of one suffering from symptoms of retardation; she was placed in a foster family at the age of about two and a half after more than one and a half years in the home; breakdown of the foster relationship had disastrous psychological effects on the child ("in a real mess"), and a second stay in a home for several months began at the age of three and a half.

This is one of the most extreme examples of why the cooptation decision must not only presuppose knowledge about the genealogy of the child if adoption is to be successful. Knowledge about the socializational history is also an indispensable component of an understanding relationship between adoptive parents and the child that begins so far away from the beginning of socialization. In this case the knowledge needed to enable a successful adoption requires a social scientific grounding, which helps overcome the current problems by setting them in relation to the history of their evolution.

The example illustrates the varying significance of socializational knowledge when assuming the biological and the social parental role. The assumption of an "a priori competence of everyman"[6] to bring up children is at the latest rendered invalid when the lack of a shared socializational history necessitates a reconstruction of the past and a comprehension of its relevance for adoptive family life in the present and in the future.

The Decision to See the Child

Whereas in the previous example of an already advanced and, in addition, crisis-laden socialization, the prospective adoptive parents were cautiously informed about the child, most applicants feel under pressure to make a quick decision when the adoption offer is presented. The intensity of this pressure is reflected in the fact that in the majority of cases the specification of the adoption offer by the adoption counselor prompts applicants to drive off immediately to take a look at the child. Yet even though this plan may emerge in a matter of just a few minutes, it may reflect no more than a relative approval of the child. In many cases the assumption of the parental role as the priority goal forms the background against which applicants are willing, in view of the constraints of the "market," to reduce their expectations vis-à-vis the child. The following example serves to illustrate the hierarchy of goals and the reorientation this triggers with respect to the cooptable child:

> ADOPTIVE FATHER: Then Mrs. Keller rang us up: "We have a child for you, could you drop by?" We said "Of course, we'll drop by straight away." And then we drove off, and then she . . . she began by *beating about the bush,* this and that and back and forth, and flicked through the file from the bottom to the top, where the picture of the little girl was. She deliberately *covered up* the picture, so that we couldn't *see* it, and then she started beating about the bush. And then I said to her "Well, now, Mrs. Keller, it's about time you told us what's really wrong with the little girl." After a while we found the situation a bit ridiculous. . . .
>
> INTERVIEWER: Hm . . .
>
> ADOPTIVE FATHER: And . . . "Yes, and this is, you see, a colored child."

After a flashback by the adoption counselor to the desire initially expressed by the applicants for a child "who suits us," the prospective parents start questioning their own conception:

> ADOPTIVE FATHER: We talked it over and then came to the opinion "Why, why have we got these ideas? Really, they're absolutely absurd." And then we thought it over and said "It might just as well . . . right, OK, be a negro or, or . . . or, as far as I'm concerned, a Vietnamese child or . . . or a Turkish child . . .
>
> INTERVIEWER: Hm . . .
>
> ADOPTIVE FATHER: or, or a Pakistani or anyone else," you see?
>
> ADOPTIVE MOTHER: Well, and then we were worried that we might have to wait such a long time . . .
>
> ADOPTIVE FATHER: Right, there was that as well.
>
> ADOPTIVE MOTHER: for a child.
>
> ADOPTIVE FATHER: We had the six years of waiting in mind, which we were told about again and again, and that was nothing for us. And then we said "Let's not be choosy, let's make a quick decision, then things will work out OK."

Whereas in this case the reduction of expectations in favor of the realization of normality for the adult role is actively elaborated by the applicants themselves, the next example shows how the adoption counselor helps engineer the constitution of family via persuasion:

ADOPTIVE MOTHER: Well, after two hours she said "Well, I have a *child* for you." "How old?" "Six." "Oh," we said, *"we don't really want such an old child!"* "OK," she said, "but give it a try."
INTERVIEWER: Oh, I see.
ADOPTIVE MOTHER: *"Take a look at* the child!" So off we went. . . .

These applicants, equipped with few resources (low middle class, older age), are confronted by a child who is hard to place because of its age. Faced by the possibility that even applicants with such unfavorable chances of success might turn down the adoption offer, the adoption counselor tries to avert the risk of failure by encouraging the applicants to "take a look at" the child, a kind of noncommittal "test." This act of persuasion, which was undoubtedly planned in the interest of the child, can be interpreted as reflecting the superior position of the procedural administrator in such a way that the strategy initiated is based on professional experience. As a result of the successful inducement to take a look at the child a cooptation moves within reach. Although the rejection of a child cannot be ruled out following a face-to-face encounter, the noncommittal character of the "commodity test" is difficult to maintain in the case of a child. As also shown by other examples in the sample, the confrontation with the child can develop an unforeseeable momentum for the applicants. The character of the child as a commodity with "no obligation to buy" gradually disappears following the face-to-face encounter with the child as a subject in its own right. More on this aspect later on.

The Phase Preceding the First Encounter

As long as there is no doubt about the common genealogical bond, the adult role is assumed unburdened by doubts about its correctness. During the course of a long process of familial institutionalization the filiative bond has acquired the status of an indisputable foundation for the definition of parental responsibility.[7] The parental role vis-à-vis one's "own" child is not a discretionary obligation[8]—with the exception of the few cases in which a child is temporarily or permanently relinquished due to difficulties in coping with the parental role. The nuclear family has frequently been analyzed in terms of the aspect of its functionality for the recruitment of social offspring. Due to the fact that parental responsibility[9] for a child is firmly laid down in this constellation, many of the costs associated with the artificial construction of family, such as the "psychological costs," and not to mention the administrative costs, do not exist. The high risk of the cooptation of a child experienced by prospective adoptive parents sheds light on the functionality of the principle of filiation.

Members of this society are unfamiliar with the interactional model of treating a strange child as if it were a child of one's own. The certainty sealed by nature in the normal family case that the child is the child of its biological parents forms the frame of psychological management in the case of cooptation, where the openness of the decision is experienced as suffering and the arbitrariness of the parental role with respect to any child is regarded as a potential risk. The doubtfulness about the constitution of family (and, in a less intense form, about the extension of family) via cooptation instead of birth is reflected in extreme tension. During the phase between the notification or specification of the adoption offer and the first encounter with the child, the fears couples have had ever since they became involved in the adoption procedure are intensified yet again. In one interview we find the following:

ADOPTIVE MOTHER: We wandered off, through the snow-covered winter forest, hearts beating like mad . . .
ADOPTIVE FATHER: [agreeing] Hm . . .
ADOPTIVE MOTHER: I . . . oh, that was the hardest thing—up to now—in my life. . . .

In another example an attempt is made to describe the extent of the tension by referring by way of comparison to the "normal yardstick" of birth:

ADOPTIVE MOTHER: You go there, really nervous, I can tell you.
ADOPTIVE FATHER: Yes, you really feel nervous. I reckon you're even a bit more nervous than when a woman has a normal birth.

The deviant case and the normal case can also be more precisely defined by reference to their respective counterparts, therefore, with regard to the complex of nervous tension in expectation of a strange child. The nervousness as a basic experience in the pre-encounter phase can be traced back to three problematic dimensions of coping with the difference between birth and cooptation.

The Indeterminacy of the Child

The first problematic dimension is the indeterminacy of the child. In the case of genealogical attachment the indeterminate nature of the child is reduced by the fact that no matter how the child "turns out," it "belongs" to the family. One's own flesh and blood does not generally trigger thoughts about whether the childs suits the family or not. The indeterminacy of the child is experienced as adequately determinate against the background of the principle of filiation; the forthcoming constitution of family is "in perfect order."

The indeterminacy of the adopted child begins with its physical qualities.

ADOPTIVE MOTHER: You still feel, er, I don't mean to say . . . unsure, er, that
would be going too far, but you, er, don't really know what to expect. . . .
What kind of child are you going to get? If it's, er, if it's your own child you
might also expect certain dispositions.

INTERVIEWER: Hm . . .

ADOPTIVE MOTHER: If, say, you're dark-haired . . .

INTERVIEWER: Hm . . .

ADOPTIVE MOTHER: and your husband is dark-haired, maybe the child will also
be dark-haired.

INTERVIEWER: Hm, hm . . .

ADOPTIVE MOTHER: In our case it's what kind of child are we going to get? A
red-haired one . . .

INTERVIEWER: Hm . . .

ADOPTIVE MOTHER: or a dark-haired one? Are we going to get an absolutely
fair-haired child?

It cannot be ruled out that the prospective adoptive parents also experience the indeterminacy of the child with an eye to possibly disturbing
dispositions. As will be shown later on, the thoughts of a number of
adoptive parents during the course of the adoption history frequently
revolve around the aspect of hereditary traits. It seems reasonable, therefore, to assume that after the specification of the adoption offer prospective
adoptive parents are also plagued by such doubts when they set off to
meet the child of birth parents whose life history has just been outlined.
The interviews, however, with their relatively nonspecific reference to the
birth parents, do not provide any clear indication on this aspect.

Furthermore, the indeterminacy of the child lies in the already completed process of socialization, a process that is not accessible to the
prospective adoptive parents. The biographical description of the child by
the adoption counselor can just about reconstruct the geographical and
temporal coordinates or name the respective persons or institutions that
have taken care of the child. The past experiences of the child as a
sedimentation of personality layers that provide the basis for its developmental potential remain an unknown factor. Fear that the child has suffered
psychological damage, in particular during its stay at the children's home,
often leads to the question of the limitations of one's own parental ability—
"Will we be able to handle the situation?"

The Act of Choosing

The second stressful dimension—which is connected with the first—
relates to the act of choosing by prospective parents. In the normal case
of the constitution of family, the guiding hand of nature removes any

freedom of choice on the part of the parents. Adoption today, however, generally takes place via a two-stage choice process. Following an interpretation of the mutual suitability of applicants and child, the adoption counselor makes a prior selection. The suitability of this selection for familial attachment is then examined in turn by the prospective parents. The freedom of choice for applicants is reduced to the freedom to reject the offer, a decision that, depending on the "market situation," could jeopardize the entire adoption plan. Yet even a freedom of choice created by the possibility of negation guarantees the illusion that the adoptive family is also constituted by the prospective parents themselves, with the social bureaucracy assuming the role of obstetrician.

During the interviews two polar means of overcoming the considerable uncertainty experienced during the phase of the forthcoming selection of a child emerge. On the one hand, the lack of any socially predetermined pattern of development for familial cooptation induces applicants to cling to their decision-making freedom and view this a source of strength for the endurance of a situation that borders on anomie. This "model of autonomy" can be illustrated by reference to the example of one adoptive father who endorses his wife's adoption plan to avoid a single-child constellation for the couple's birth child.

ADOPTIVE FATHER: And when the whole thing got going, I meant to say, I assumed that you could have a look at the child in the home and, if there's no rapport at all, you know, straight away, I thought to myself: "You'll just have to reject it," . . .
INTERVIEWER: Hm . . .
ADOPTIVE FATHER: right, reject this adoption. Regardless of the fact that our adoption counselor dropped hints that we would then never get a child.

This and several other examples show that during the phase of waiting for a strange child the only evaluation criterion that provides some kind of orientation is the belief in a vague "rapport" with the child. The conflict with the lack of clear orientation criteria is also reflected in the following case. As opposed to the example above, however, the "model of autonomy" already probably ceased to be effective during the phase preceding the first encounter, because the pressure on the involuntarily childless couple to adopt the child is much greater than in the case of applicants with an already accomplished parental role.

ADOPTIVE MOTHER: And then we also said [to the adoption counselor] "If we don't take to this child, you never know, you take to some babies too and not to others, do we get . . . are we then put on the waiting list?" Of course, that's really depressing, and "no," she said.

Whereas here—as in many other cases—the model of autonomy is threatened as a result of the adjustment to reality, a few of the applicants construct the situation of choice right from the start as if it were the situation of the final decision. In three examples of a markedly child-centered decision to adopt, the event is associated with the fatefulness of a birth; there is no scope for the rejection of the child in this "model of fate." In one case an already existing family takes in a five-and-a-half-year-old girl without going along to see her beforehand; in another case the young child of a mentally disturbed mother is accepted as the fourth child in the family from the moment of the specification of the adoption offer onwards. Reflecting on the genetic misgivings expressed by others, one adoptive mother says:

ADOPTIVE MOTHER: I can't guarantee either that the child who crawls out of my belly is not suddenly crazy. And I can't say to the doctor "Put it back in. I'll wait for a new one."

In this case the adoptive mother works her way towards normalization by equating the as-yet-unknown and indeterminate child with a child of her own, whose qualities are also indeterminable until birth. By framing it with the "normal case" the arbitrariness of parental responsibility in the case of cooptation is transmuted into the definitiveness of natural parental responsibility.

The attempt to free oneself from the act of choice is reflected in the narrative presented by one woman who, because of her husband's genetic fears, decides not to have a child of her own. In an arduous process of structuring the meaning of her life she brings herself to view the adoption of a strange child as a "task" waiting to be fulfilled.

ADOPTIVE MOTHER: What we were really afraid of, something which tormented me *tremendously,* was the thought: Off I go [to the children's home], I'm shown a child, and what if . . . what if I don't like it.
INTERVIEWER: Hm . . .
ADOPTIVE MOTHER: And, of course, er, *it's all the greater, the risk,* the older the child is. And the thought of this also *really* worried my husband too. And we were very glad that the first thing we were told was "You don't choose it yourselves anyway, but we do that for you." So you've got the feeling somehow: Well, that it's . . . how can I explain . . .
ADOPTIVE FATHER: Fate.
ADOPTIVE MOTHER: fate.
ADOPTIVE FATHER: Right, right, it's sort of . . .
ADOPTIVE MOTHER: Or, as if to say *that's the way it's meant to be:* this is the child you should love!

This construction of "that's the way it's meant to be" again illustrates the interpretive suction that emanates from the "normal case" of the constitution of family. Especially adoption applicants who wish to elimi-nate the commodity character of the adoption offer design their emerging family history along the lines of the natural and socially institutionalized development of the constitution of family. In the previous example the freedom of choice is replaced by the action imperative "This is the child you should love!" The "model of fate" is linked with a belief in a scope of autonomous action when constructing adoptive family reality.

Establishing an Emotional Bond

The examples illustrating the problems associated with the act of choosing the child have already indicated the dimensions that rank as qualitative yardsticks for the prospective relationship between adoptive parents and the adopted child: "rapport," "experiencing a liking for the child," "taking to" a child. This third dimension of strain is the key aspect: The indeterminacy of the child together with the possibly incorrect choice become such a burden against the background of the uncertainty of emotionality. The fears that have existed throughout the entire adoption planning phase about the ability to love a strange child are heightened once again during the phase between the notification or specification of the adoption offer and the first face-to-face encounter. Due to their general significance, these fears are also worth dealing with in greater detail to discover more about the "normal case."

The prospect of the artificial status passage for adoption applicants triggers fears that not only illuminate the case of adoption, but also mirror the biological constitution of family. The experience of prospective adoptive parents is structured via a comparison with the normal case. "Can I love someone else's child?" This anxious question before taking in the child signals the extent to which the adoption applicants feel that the missing principle of filiation will jeopardize one of the constitutive qualities of a family, the emotional bond.[10] How much family is typified as involving emotional attachment only becomes clear when an affective bond experienced as a norm is threatened.[11] As long as the principle of filiation is guaranteed, the emotional bond appears to be subject to a certain automatism with no further reflection. It takes the absence of the principle to trigger the question whether both of the qualities experienced as constitutive for a family, kinship and love, have to be conjoint or whether the constitution of family as emotional attachment is also possible in the case of the socially constructed adoptive family. To judge by the respondents in our sample, the majority of individuals who entertain such hopes in the reduced significance of the principle of filiation have themselves previously regarded the principle of filiation as a norm of family constitution in their own biographical design.

The narrative interviews reflect the search for appropriate verbal means of expressing the emotional quality that is constitutive for a family but extremely difficult to describe. Apart from words such as "love," "affection," and "liking each other," expressions are often used that try to define the vague relational norm more precisely. Some adoptive parents, for example, turn to the language of physics to symbolize the force they hope will bind them with the adopted child. There are hopes, for example, for a "vital spark" when they see the child. Sometimes the envisaged "contact" is expressed in the form of a "wire" or "antenna."

ADOPTIVE MOTHER: And then we will see whether . . . whether there is, er, some kind of antenna.

The invisible but powerful force of electricity is referred to in order to metaphorically depict the desired emotional bond, whose existence cannot be automatically assumed due to the missing principle of filiation. The search for orientation in the language of physics illustrates the kind of legitimatory pressure the adoptive parents subject themselves to or are subjected to by others when they try to maintain their conformity towards the general norm of family relations despite the deviation from the principle of filiation. The phenomenon of stress in expectation of a strange child, therefore, reveals the normative potential of the biological constitution of family, which is experienced as just as valid for the future relationship between adoptive parents and the adopted child but not as just as "naturally" guaranteed.

The First Face-to-Face Encounter

Making the Child One's Own

Those prospective adoptive parents who make their way to the infant's or children's home, to the home of the foster mother, or in the case of clinic adoptions, to the maternity ward of the hospital, following the notification and specification of the adoption offer, have already taken a preliminary decision in favor of potential family membership. The degree of certainty about cooptation may differ substantially from case to case. In one case the prospective adoptive parents may go along to see the child in the certain anticipation of their parenthood, whereas in another case they may simply feel that the possibility of adopting the child in question cannot be completely ruled out.

The child's substitute guardians in the homes and other settings generally appear to take the varying degree of expectative certainty into account by playing a reserved role in the construction of family when the potential parents come along to see the child for the first time. Their assigned "midwife" function in this construction of social birth comprises the physical presentation of the child selected in the bureaucratic process of allocation. The act of displaying the child is generally accompanied by a turn of phrase that does not anticipate the constitution of family: "There she is." This situational phraseology reflects the clarity of the communicative framework. The children's nurses in the home would appear to make empathy contributions by refraining from presenting the child by the name chosen by the birth parents. The indexical form of expression covers up the other origin of the child, and nothing obstructs the hopes of many adoptive parents of experiencing the identity of the child by the name they choose.

"Here he is"—these words create a fragment of reality. From this moment on the socially constructed constitution of family is autonomously realizable for the prospective adoptive parents, just as the biological constitution of family is part of the autonomy of action of potential parents. The difference between the natural and the artificial constitution of family, however, is again reflected in the function of the speech act. In all probability midwives place the child in its mother's arms a few seconds or minutes after it is born, and say "Here she is." In this case language merely concretizes what all persons present regard as self-evident without verbal confirmation. Familial attachment in the case of the adoptive family, on the other hand, is enabled only by the very gesture of presenting the child and by its linguistic symbolization.

Whereas the presentation of the child does not generally anticipate the act of choice by the prospective adoptive parents but preserves the potential for making the child one's own, another practice intervenes more fundamentally in the process of family constitution. Using the words "That's your child," kinship is occasionally heteronomously assigned in the case of young babies. Cooptation in these cases is characterized by an inevitability closely related to the predestination of parenthood in the case of birth.

One adoptive mother described the reaction of the children's nurse as follows:

ADOPTIVE MOTHER: And then she suddenly took hold of this bundle and pushed it into my arms and said "Right, that's your child!"

Regardless of how this practice of handing over the child may have developed—as a misinterpretation of the expectancy structure of the prospective adoptive parents, as an evocation of a sense of belonging, or the like—it seems doubtful whether it facilitates the decision-making process or makes it more difficult through the over-hasty ascription of kinship. The prospective adoptive parents appear to have an interest in making their choice of a child autonomously. Later on in the example begun above, the adoptive mother stated that she was completely overpowered, indeed shocked, by this practice; she wanted to "look at the child first." In the interview passage her husband adds:

ADOPTIVE FATHER: The decision wasn't yet taken; it can only be taken when you've seen the child. The agency says "Right, that's your child!" but in the end it's our decision after we've seen it: shall we take it or not?

Whereas the prospective adoptive parents in this case criticize the fact that their decision-making freedom is excluded from the adoption procedure in an exaggeratedly simple reduction of problems, the conception of the prospective adopted child generally reflects the complexity of the decision-making situation. The greater the distance from the normal case, which is primarily measurable along the dimension of age, the larger the number of factors that must be taken into account when arranging the first face-to-face encounter. One reason why the complexity of the decision-making situation grows with the increasing age of the child is that the child's various character "molds" increase the risk of rejection: The child's previous socialization may have produced a different personality to that which the prospective parents feel is best suited for familial attachment. In the end the growing distance from the stage of the tiny and helpless being generally reduces the chances that the child will trigger spontaneous affection. What is more, as the child grows older it has to be treated as a subject rather than as the object of the adoption decision, and becomes a person with its own ability to assess the situation. The influence on the course of the first encounter of both problematic aspects connected with the factor of age—the assumed higher or lower probability of selection and the greater object or subject role of the child—will now be illustrated by specific examples.

Ignoring the extreme equation of young baby = your child, it becomes clear that the presentation of a baby is oriented towards overcoming the feeling of strangeness much faster than the presentation of the older child. In its inability to initiate the course of action the baby becomes the object of a physical transfer: It is placed in the arms of the prospective adoptive mother. This repeatedly described ritual simulates a mother-child relationship and tests its realization. The prospective adoptive parents make the strange child their own by taking physical possession of it. First the mother and then the father are given the opportunity to "feel" whether this could become their child.

The physical transfer of the young baby as a quite "obtrusive" form of establishing contact probably reflects the everyday theory assumption that physical contact increases the already high probability of a decision favoring adoption, an assumption confirmed by the narrative descriptions of the further course of events. Holding the baby indicates to the person that he or she could be the one on whom the baby could rely in its helplessness.

The framework for making the child one's own in the case of an older child is arranged in such a way that the process of decision-making by the prospective parents is not made more difficult by telling the child beforehand that these are its potential adoptive parents, and thus triggering the hopes and fears of the child itself. Describing the first encounter with a five-year-old girl the adoptive mother says:

ADOPTIVE MOTHER: The social worker then took us around the home. But the child didn't know that the visit was meant for her, of course not.

In the following example of a four-year-old child with a varied socialization history a strategy designed to disguise the interest in the child was worked out between the prospective adoptive parents and a psychologist familiar with this particular child. In the recapitulation of this project by the adoptive father it is interesting to note how the then-prospective parents view the encounter, which does not comply with the framework of normal family constitution, with a certain role distance as the "first inspection of the child."

ADOPTIVE FATHER: And then we agreed that during the first visit in the home we . . . where we first [laughing] had to take a first look at the child, . . .
INTERVIEWER: Hm . . .
ADOPTIVE FATHER: necessarily, whether we want to or not, the first inspection of the child, er. . . .
INTERVIEWER: Hm . . .
ADOPTIVE FATHER: We should take a look at all the children, because we hadn't yet said whether we wanted to have the child or not, that was still undecided. . . .

Even in this example, aimed at keeping a distance, the prospective mother wants to "feel" the child. This establishment of closer contact, an act that is taken for granted in the case of the first encounter with a baby, is only accomplished in this case within the framework of the strategic concept "we should take a look at all the children." Any fixation of attention on the actual object of interest would have narrowed the scope for decision-making, because in a vague interpretation of the situation the child may have elicited a response that could have then made any reversal an additional detrimental factor for the already damaged child.

ADOPTIVE MOTHER: The first time Susanne, even though I only held her just for fun, just like [I held] all the other children, I held them all, romped around with them and things like that, well Susanne didn't want to. She resisted.

In this case physical contact disguised as the equal treatment of all children is the only means of achieving a noncommittal simulation of the mother–child relationship. As the test fails because of the child's own ability to act, making the child one's own is still a long way off. The following sections take a closer look at the varying courses of development during this process of making the child one's own.

From the Immediate Affection Aroused by a Baby to the Reserved Response to an Older Child

The Affective Potential of a Baby. The apprehensive concern that the choice of a strange child might signify nonconformity with the normal pattern of familial attachment, and the doubts about the plan to save the parental role in the biographical design, often disappear when the prospective adoptive parents see the child, especially if the child is a young baby. Although members of society may not be familiar with the situation of expecting a strange child under the aspect of possible parenthood, the mere physical presence of the newborn child is often able to make the interaction situation seem familiar despite its unusual moments. A first glance at the child often enables prospective adoptive parents to gain the footing they need for the accomplishment of the status passage.

The following examples underline how the child's physical presence can immediately dispel initial fears. Following the recapitulation of the tension during the phase preceding the first face-to-face contact, the encounter with a three-month-old child is described as follows:

ADOPTIVE MOTHER: It [the tension] all vanished very fast when we saw the child.

Another adoptive mother, who had suffered agonizing doubts about her own ability to love a strange child, summed up her experiences on seeing the four-month-old child as follows:

ADOPTIVE MOTHER: It was . . . *for me it was like a tiny miracle*. This . . . this *fear*, it was *completely* gone.

What explanation is there for the power of the infant to induce adults within such a short space of time to take on the role of parents? The fundamental willingness to adopt a child that has evolved during the nerve-racking application procedure is undoubtedly a major explanatory factor. Yet how is it possible for adults to dismiss their rationally founded misgivings towards coopting a child so quickly that their fixation on problems of matching persons without a genealogical bond vanishes into thin air and their scepticism towards the child as a stranger is forgotten? If the burden of the comparison with the normal case of family constitution is able to suddenly disappear at the sight of the child, the infant must possess an affective potential of which the actors were unaware up until that time. In the eyes of the applicants this sudden change comes as a surprise, and is sometimes even described as "the tiny miracle."

The question of the power that emanates from the infant is particularly significant in view of the fact that familial attachment is created here without the principle of filiation. The question, however, has a much more general significance. In view of the "instinctual reduction" of human beings anthropologists have repeatedly tried to discover what could be regarded as the basis of the institutionalization of family and what guarantees a mother's affection for her child. In search of the prerequisites for living together as a family Gehlen, for example, referred to the "protective and caring reaction" ("Schutz- und Pflegereaktion")[12] that the tiny being "in need of help"[13] triggers in adults. This minimum of instinctual endowment, which Gehlen ranks as an anthropological constant, by no means appears to be restricted to "one's own" child. The "initial helplessness of man" also described by Freud as the "primary source of all moral motives" ("Urquelle aller moralischen Motive")[14] also seems to overwhelm many adoption applicants when they notice a rising affection at the sight of the young infant and sense a certainty in their parental role.

A few text examples show that the deviant case of family constitution is particularly well-suited to clarify the baby's contribution towards initiating a parent–child relationship. The recapitulation of motherly feelings at the sight of a child just a few days after it was born, for example, shows how a sense of attachment can be triggered beyond the "blood ties":

ADOPTIVE MOTHER: I could have melted away when I saw her lie . . .
ADOPTIVE FATHER: Yes.
ADOPTIVE MOTHER: lying there. Such a *sweet thing* and such a, no really! Small, of course, and *crumpled*.

The appeal of the miniature version of a human being is also reflected in the description of the situation by one adoptive mother, who—in line with the preparation by the adoption counselor—had prepared herself for possible "resistance" at the sight of the child and who then expressed her relief:

ADOPTIVE MOTHER: She was so cute, so small and tiny.

The "great and beautiful moment" does not always trigger the emotional response that corresponds to certainty that "this is my child" in all 25 cases of infant adoption (Table 33). Sometimes the prospective parents see the "very sorry-looking version" of a human being or the "poor little mite.'' Yet even the sorry sight and helplessness of the little creature does, sooner or later, stimulate something inside the prospective adoptive parents that enables the status passage. There are undoubtedly cases in which very young infants and not just handicapped children are rejected; this study did not investigate this aspect. In the majority of cases in which babies are adopted, however, the following hypothesis probably applies: The greater the passivity and helplessness of the child, or the greater the child's missing autonomy of action, the greater the ability of applicants to take on the parental role. The mere physical presence of the extremely small and helpless being simulates a parent–child relationship that approximates the normal case of family constitution and—according to Gehlen— stirs the instinctual residues inside human beings.

The Affective Potential of a Toddler. The toddler would appear to shape interaction with its possible adoptive parents by actively utilizing its action resources to document its need for parents. The three examples in the survey demonstrate how the one to two-year-old child makes use of its physical, speaking, and body language abilities during the first encounter to indicate its affection to the adults.

Prospective adoptive parents do not make the toddler their own by physically taking possession of the child as in the case of a baby. As shown by the example of a girl aged one and three-quarter years, a toddler is able to play an active part in this process:

ADOPTIVE MOTHER: The first time we visited her, well, that was a wonderful feeling. She ran straight up to me, flew into my arms and sat next to me for two hours. She didn't budge. . . .

The child's attempt to establish contact, probably influenced in this case by deprivation experiences (nine months in a home), is apparently interpreted by the prospective adoptive mother as a sign of affection specifically intended for her. The woman in this case, inwardly willing to assume the role of mother, probably interprets the scene as an indication of the hopes pinned on her by the child and of her chances of giving the child a feeling of security. She does not appear to belittle the significance of the child's action by classifying the search for close contact as an act that would probably be repeated towards every potential mother. The child's attention gives her ''such a wonderful feeling.'' In her eyes the relevance of the scene would seem to lie in the fact that she has been chosen on account of her uniqueness, not because of her personal type.[15] This interpretation of the situation, which ignores a number of aspects of reality, enables her to establish the reciprocity of the act of choice between mother and child and to construct attachment.

In the case of a one-and-a-half-year-old girl the already acquired action resources are also utilized in such a way as to be interpreted by the prospective adoptive parents as denoting affection, presumably affection for them alone.

ADOPTIVE MOTHER: She was incredibly friendly. We had no trouble at all taking her along with us. She laughed and was friendly and just came along.

Both the child's active communicative signals—friendliness and laughter— and the lack of any resistance—caused no trouble, just came along—favor the constitution of family in the assumption of reciprocal interaction. The action resources the child has already developed thus seem to be proportionately related to its active involvement in the process of family constitution. Together with the stlll-existing cuteness of the one-and-a-half-year-old girl ("blonde and blue-eyed," "a perfect child"), this potential of apparent confirmation of parental plans is able to shore up cooptation.

Whereas in this case the applicants would have preferred a somewhat older child, the next case is a particularly clear example of an infant who is still young but whose action resources are more fully developed. Both the child's age and the color of its skin failed to come up to the expectations of the adoption applicants. Aware of the limited number of children available for adoption and the prospect pointed out by the adoption counselor of a long waiting period if they turned down this offer, these applicants (members of the lower middle class) decided to lower their expectations in order to ensure the parental role in their biographical design.

After outlining the preliminary history of the visit to the child's foster mother, the prospective adoptive father invites his wife to elucidate the first encounter with the child by asking, "Do you want to say something on this aspect too?" His narrative remains as it were in the "forecourt" of events, whereas he leaves it up to his wife to enter the "inner sanctum." In all probability, organizing the narrative in this way is not coincidental. In the overwhelming majority of cases in which the first encounter with the child is described, the couple organizes narration in such a way that the adoptive mother recapitulates the encounter with the child first. Despite extreme differences in the constellations of narrative development by the narrating couple—varying degrees of narrative activity on the part of the man and the woman, topic-specific narrative activity on the part of the man and the woman—women almost always hold a narrative monopoly when it comes to outlining the first encounter. The woman's dominant role in narration relating to this event probably reflects the mother's self-typification as the person primarily responsible for the child. In the case of the dark-skinned child the frame of the role-typical narrative structure is set by the adoptive father's turn allocation to his wife, that is, by his typification of the mother as the person primarily involved in this event. Invited by her husband to take over the narrative the adoptive mother requires a short moment of planning before reconstructing the event:

ADOPTIVE MOTHER: Well, and, er, the child was in the, in the playpen, stretched up its arms and said straight away "Mommy," saw us from a long way off and immediately shouted "Mommy." Well, and then I held her, and then she wouldn't let go, clung to me and kept on saying "Mommy, Mommy." And kept on laughing and was incredibly friendly. . . .

In this case the same forms of expression are used by the child as in the previous cases—the search for close physical contact, friendliness, and laughter—only this time the verbal symbolization of the relationship hoped for by the child and the assignment of the role of "Mommy" give the decision-making situation, which was initially kept open, a particularly dramatic turn. The child, who had been neglected and treated cruelly by its birth mother and had been placed in the meantime in the care of an overburdened foster mother, creates facts by actively influencing the situation. It is not clear to what extent the prospective adoptive parents regard the form of address "Mommy" as a categorical classification. The interpretation of this speech act as a special expectation in their direction, however, was probably compounded by the fact that the foster mother emphasized the uniqueness of this occurrence ("She'd not experienced that before with the child").

The relevance frame for the decision by the prospective adoptive parents is redefined if the decision is no longer taken from the perspective of the person who chooses, but of the person who has already been chosen by the child. The rejection of a mother role assigned by the child is likely to clash much more markedly with the applicant's internalized norms of motherly action than the rejection of just an official adoption offer itself. As the adoptive mother accepts the ascription as the child's "Mommy," the construction of a family with a toddler would also appear to be based on a reciprocal act of choice in this case too. The uniformity of the child's contribution in the three examples covered by the sample, however, cannot hide the fact that there are presumably also cases of a cooptation of a reluctant child.

Whereas the tininess and helplessness of the baby triggers affection without questioning cooptation as one-sided act on the part of the applicants, the toddler creates the fiction of a bilaterally initiated parent–child relationship via the means of expression it has just acquired. To judge by the examples in our sample the infant is still at a developmental stage in which it can signal its need for parents in an active and passive form without this developmental stage contradicting the self-evidence of its need for help. The older child finds it more difficult to appeal to adults in such a way that its already achieved character mold is congruent with the need for the formative influence of parents.

The Reserved Response Triggered by the Older Child. The immediate "that could be my child" vision is presumably a rare occurrence in the case of the first encounter with an older child. The child's development is too advanced to be able to activate the potential of the small child, the cute child, the helpless child, or the affectionate child. The four to six-year-old child with its generally problematic biography has long since lost this power of parent recruitment. This is indicated by the interviews with those adoptive parents, who admit that they experienced scepticism or even shock when they first saw the child. Even if the adoption applicants chose to have "a somewhat older child," the cornerstones of the normal case of family constitution would also appear to have a more or less unconscious orientation function. Above all, the inability to exert a formative influence on the child at the start of its socialization forms the frame of interpretation within which a feeling of sadness and dismay develop at the sight of the child at an "advanced" stage of development.

Of the 37 adopted children covered by the interview sample, nine were taken in between the ages of three and six (Table 33). For the purposes of describing the structure of experiences during the first face-to-face encounter with the child available for adoption, two cases in which the adoptive mothers were already familiar with the children because of their work in the children's home are excluded. Two examples in which the foster child status was initially chosen are also omitted. In a further case, a five-and-a-half-year-old girl was taken into the adoptive family in a serious emergency situation without a prior "inspection" of the child—this was one of the few cases of a pronounced child-centered orientation on the part of the adoptive parents. The remaining four examples of the placement of older children, all of them girls between the ages of four and a half and six, round off the range of possible beginnings of the history of the relationship between adoptive parents and the child.

A common aspect in all cases was the desire for a younger child, albeit not necessarily for a baby. The original expectations with respect to the constitution of a family or the extension of a family had already been lowered by the time the applicants set off to see the child. Under the influence of a scarce "supply" situation and the reduced chances of relatively old applicants (during the first encounter with the child the adoptive mothes were aged between 35 and 42), a willingness to compromise had already developed following the specification of the adoption offer, because—especially for the women involved—a meaningful structuring of life was at stake.

In order to present a range of cases that is as extensive as possible, we will begin by singling out a pair of contrasting examples to show the extreme types of parental conception of a child and the implications of this conception for the evaluation of the specific child in each case. In a second approach of comparative analysis and with reference to the parallelism of two examples, there will be a shift in the focus of attention towards the older child who is deprived in its socializational chances. The intention is to work out how prospective adoptive parents respond to the child who has been dragged into a whirlpool of parental allocation and how, after the first few moments, the offer of family constitution is subjected to a depressing interim appraisal.

First of all, let us turn to the polar types of the parental conception of the child. The instrumentalization of the older child can also unfold against the background of very differingly specified expectations of the child. One couple (case A) with a 14-year-old biological son was looking for a "gentle" girl for the prolongation of family life ("so that mother has got someone again"). The expectations are solely developed within the frame of sex-specific stereotypification:

ADOPTIVE MOTHER: We always wanted a really gentle girl.
ADOPTIVE FATHER: Yes, we thought to ourselves, a girl should be gentle and
    well-behaved and . . . always really nice.

A few years after the sudden loss of a daughter (at primary school age) another couple (case B), which also has a teenage daughter of its own, hopes to be able to again fill the gap "following a period of absolute *numbness* and of absolute . . . petrification." The mother clings to the model of the birth daughter much more intensely than the father.

ADOPTIVE MOTHER: of course, I, er, said what I wanted, I wanted something
    nimble again and something very affectionate and something very lively . . .
    a kind of wishful thinking . . .
INTERVIEWER: Hm . . .
ADOPTIVE MOTHER: although I fully realized that it was no more than wishful
    thinking.

Just as the prospective adoptive mother in case A works on the assumption of a vague uniformity of all girls, her everyday theory assessment of the factor of age reflects a minimizing underrating of the child's former socialization phases. As a working mother (in the position of a lower-level salaried employee) she would like "a somewhat older child who brings along a certain amount of independence."[16] The prospective adoptive mother in case B, on the other hand, feels that the extent of the already completed socialization might jeopardize her model:

ADOPTIVE MOTHER: And then, however, I expressed the desire . . . to adopt a
    somewhat younger child, in the hope of being able to mold its character.

INTERVIEWER: Hm . . .
ADOPTIVE MOTHER: My, my . . .
ADOPTIVE FATHER: Not a baby, right, not a baby.
ADOPTIVE MOTHER: with the idea of being able to fit it into a mold. . . .

The scene of the first encounter—with a five-year-old girl in each case—can only be properly understood against the background of specified expectations. Whereas the applicants in case A find a child in the care of a foster mother "wide-eyed and like all children are at that age," the adoptive mother in case B faces the collapse of her "illusions":

ADOPTIVE MOTHER: And then the social worker took us around the home. But the child didn't know that we'd come to see her, of course not.
INTERVIEWER: Hm . . .
ADOPTIVE MOTHER: And then both my husband and my daughter, they said quite spontaneously "She's cute, we'll take her." She was playing in the corner, lost in a world of her own, sucking her thumb and seemed somehow . . . somehow isolated, to be honest quite cute, and it was *tremendously* difficult for me. It was a bitter blow because it was a completely different child, . . .
INTERVIEWER: Hm, yes . . .
ADOPTIVE MOTHER: and I left feeling pretty much in despair.

In order to illustrate the contrastive patterns of orientation at the sight of the child I would like to refer to the shift of emphasis in socialization described by Lüscher from a social history perspective.[17] Lüscher points out the fact that there is a shift in everyday knowledge from the aspects of care to those of personality development. These two poles can be illustrated by referring to the two examples, which differ in terms of class membership and in particular according to their educational levels. In case A the adoptive parents organize their experience of their first encounter with the prospective daughter according to the criteria of clothing, getting dirty, and getting changed:

ADOPTIVE MOTHER: First of all, there was a whole horde [to see?] One more cheeky than the other.
ADOPTIVE FATHER: But we should have been warned, er, we should have been warned, shouldn't we? Because our child had to be . . .
ADOPTIVE MOTHER: Changed.
ADOPTIVE FATHER: changed first and cleaned up [laughter].
ADOPTIVE MOTHER: [Laughter.]
ADOPTIVE FATHER: And that's the way things have stayed, right? [Laughter.] Yes, at any rate, er, along she came and, er, wide-eyed and like all children are at that age and . . . dressed in the most ridiculous clothes, I felt anyway.
ADOPTIVE MOTHER: She was . . . she was . . . nicely dressed.
ADOPTIVE FATHER: Yes, nice [laughter] . . .
ADOPTIVE MOTHER: [Laughter.]
ADOPTIVE FATHER: in quotation marks, I'd say. . . .
ADOPTIVE MOTHER: No, a wine-red velvet dress [and?] black stockings. . . . [They were probably white to start off with?] [Laughter.]

In this example the adoption applicants view the child, as it were, as a member of the category "children," inspect it under the aspect of care and appearance, and show no sign of empathy work in their narrative. The child is described as an object without any statement on the relational level. By way of contrast, the prospective mother in case B (upper middle class) primarily interprets the scene of the first encounter under personality aspects: She makes an effort to take on the role of the child in order to grasp the child's communicative situation ("somehow isolated"). Yet although she tries to assess the child in accordance with the child's own parameters, even taking into account appealing infant relics ("sucking her thumb," "quite cute"), the negative classification of its social identity as "a completely different child" predominates. As the idea of a continuation of the model of her own lost birth child as a means of establishing familial continuity breaks down she is driven to "despair": "I didn't find my ideal." The strangeness of the other personality causes a crisis in her own biographical design, because the gap between the vision of "my" child and reality seems unbridgeable.

Even though the expectations vis-à-vis the child are not always so clearly specified as in this case with a clear family history background, the outward appearance, facial expressions, and gestures of the older child can trigger shock and despair, because they are experienced as a violation of vague conceptions of normality. In the following example of a four-year-old girl with a long "institutional" history, ideas of adequacy about the child's physical appearance and clothing form the frame of interpretation within which the beginning of the history of the child–parent relationship is described.

ADOPTIVE MOTHER: We came along to the home . . . and then, then we looked at each other: which one is it? It had to be a girl, and half of the children were girls or . . . roughly half. So there weren't many left. There were six or seven. We both looked at each other and said "Good God, surely not her!" [Laughter.] Let's hope that. . . . Well, it was her, of course, and through her glasses, . . . well, she looked over the rims of her spectacles in a strange way because she couldn't look through them.

INTERVIEWER: Hm . . .

ADOPTIVE MOTHER: And she had strands of hair in her face, well [laughing] it looked a real sight, and then she had, she was somehow psychologically disturbed, kept on doing this.

INTERVIEWER: Yes.

ADOPTIVE MOTHER: She got tensed up, she had sort of half a hunchback.

INTERVIEWER: Yes.

ADOPTIVE FATHER: And then she had . . . sloppy terry towelling trousers, which were really pulled up high,

ADOPTIVE MOTHER: In her backside somehow.

ADOPTIVE FATHER: [Laughing] Well, jammed in, and then an old undershirt was hanging out, dear oh dear!

ADOPTIVE MOTHER: And then she pushed her lower . . . she kept on pushing her lower jaw forward because she was nervous.
ADOPTIVE FATHER: And I thought to myself "Good lord, good lord."
ADOPTIVE MOTHER: [We thought?] see, there is a hunchback. It was terrible.
ADOPTIVE FATHER: And then we said "Good God, it can't be true!" And, er, er. . . .
ADOPTIVE MOTHER: It was chaotic.

Poor eyesight, a hunchback, a protruding lower jaw—an accumulation of handicaps that trigger the immediate defensive response of the prospective adoptive parents: "Good God, it can't be true!" The retrospective association by the adoptive mother of the hunchback with tension and of the protruding lower jaw with unsureness indicates that the visiting routine in the home ("of course, someone or other walks through the home all the time") represents stress for the child, regardless of how much she knows about adoption plans. The four-year-old child, whose relationship to parents (and foster parents) broke down twice, would appear to suffer from tension as an object of inspection. This tenseness counteracts any impression of cuteness in the eye of the beholder and rules out the possibility of spontaneous affection. Whereas the baby relinquished for adoption by its birth parents is able to appeal to adults unburdened by memory, the older child has stored up the memory of its sad history and relates the new situation of being treated like an object to former experiences. By coping with the situation in such a way the child loses its parent recruitment potential, and the adoption applicants withdraw into a reserved stance.

The following narrative also confirms the intensity with which the first moments of the encounter with a six-year-old child are experienced as a violation of concepts of normality[18] and—at least on the part of the prospective[18] adoptive father—trigger an attempt to flee from the situation. Neither the child's physical attributes nor her mental development seem to come up to expectations. The adoptive mother describes the visit to the foster family:

ADOPTIVE MOTHER: And then we turned up there, and then several children came up to us, among them a *small, titchy* child, we thought, yes, we looked around, where a six-year-old *child* could be, but we couldn't find any six-year-old child. And we found out afterwards that the *small, pale and titchy* girl who came creeping up to us, that she was the *six-year-old*. And she wasn't particularly pretty, stood there with an *absolutely lopsided mouth, tongue like this,* hanging out, she *really didn't* look good. My husband said "She's mad!" Good God, no, [laughing] it was awful! He said she's a Mongoloid child. . . .

As in the preceding example the adoptive mother in this case also recalls that she "really didn't look good," a sight intensified by the child's nervous tension in the inspection situation. Whereas the child in the first example can at most sense the significance of the situation, the adoptive mother in this case is convinced that the foster mother told the child "Some people are coming along who want to be your parents." The child is already familiar with this situation of a possible allocation of parents.

ADOPTIVE MOTHER: As she'd *already* gone through the same thing two months before, where people turned up and didn't get her, she was incredibly tensed up.
INTERVIEWER: Hm . . .
ADOPTIVE MOTHER: Which explains the lopsided mouth with the tongue hanging out and . . . wasn't a pretty sight. . . .

These two examples clearly indicate that the beginning of the adoption history at least is a stressful phase for the four to six-year-old child. If the child has been informed about or senses the significance of the situation, this presumably creates a context of mutually intensifying tension on the part of the prospective parents and the child, something that does not exactly contribute towards improving the aesthetic impression of the first encounter. Whereas the prospective adoptive parents are worried about gaining access to the parental role during their inspection of the child, the child itself is tensed up because of the test situation. In the development of its capacity to act independently the child has become a "subject" to such an extent that it is able to experience itself as the "object" of parent recruitment. The open or semiopen awareness context on the part of the child placed later on in life creates a further distancing element to the normal case, because the lack of the principle of filiation is complemented by the mutual awareness of this fact. As opposed to the child born into the family or the adopted child placed at an early age, the older child brings its knowledge of its history into the family.[19] The allocation of parents becomes a precarious act against the background of neglect, cruelty, and rejection by others. The child's physical reactions to the situation of the first encounter as well as the shrinking back of the prospective adoptive parents give an idea of what is at stake for the actors in this context.

Differences in the Intensity and Rhythm of Emotional Interaction by the Prospective Adoptive Parents

Up to now the first encounter between the prospective adoptive parents and the child selected for adoption by the adoption agency was primarily described under the aspect of how the child with its age-specific potential of parent recruitment influences interaction, and how the prospective adoptive parents respond to the child. The analysis of the narrative accounts of the two girls placed later on in life already indicated that the child's presentation of self only triggers affection or rejection via a number of other factors. The beginning of the relationship's history could only be understood against the background of the differently specified expectations, which in their turn are rooted in class-specific variance of socialization norms and in varying family histories.

Our attention now turns to confirming the social structuring of interaction during the first encounter via reference to a number of other examples. A comparison between the various patterns of maternal behavior, followed by a look at the contrast between maternal and paternal behavior at the moment of status passage (or shortly beforehand), will show that even such an intimate event as the first encounter with a child selectable as "our" child cannot be viewed as purely idiosyncratic behavior but in many ways reflects social norms.

Motherhood Fixation and Motherly Feelings. The prospective adoptive mothers are certain of their role as mothers-to-be to a differing degree. If women have already given birth to a child they are generally able to experience the first encounter with the child with greater role distance than those who are at long last close to fulfilling a central biographical goal after a long period of suffering under marital infertility. Their competence of maternal action enables them to approach the potential adopted child with emotional composure. One mother, for example, is pleased that the baby is "ready to be picked up"; another welcomes the child's similarity with the birth child. There are no cases of emotional overexuberance in the sense of exaggerated conformity to the mother role. The familiarity with the various segments of the role of mother and the certainty of being able to experience oneself as a "genuine" and authentic mother in line with the normal case prevent any compulsive conformity to a mother image presumed to be normal.

Even if adoption serves the purpose of constituting a family, and the first encounter with the child is generally experienced as the "great and beautiful moment," the uncertainty connected with the status passage is not as a rule reflected in precipitate attempts to move closer to the norm of profound motherly feelings. The prospective adoptive mothers assume that motherly feelings towards the child in the absence of a filiative bond will automatically develop in the foreseeable future; "liking" the child and finding it "cute" suffice to begin with as an emotional foundation. Two of the extreme examples in the sample, however, serve to illustrate how some women internalize the mother role as a compulsion to such an extent that they abandon themselves to fantasies of biological motherhood on seeing the child.

One adoptive mother explains how the sight of the child gives her the feeling that she has achieved her goal following a period of unsuccessful attempts at the status passage and following a pregnancy and subsequent miscarriage contrary to all gynecological predictions.

ADOPTIVE MOTHER: And then they showed us Niklas, and I must admit . . . that I was extremely lucky. The little lad wasn't good-looking, not at all, . . .
ADOPTIVE FATHER: [Laughing] Hm, no, he wasn't.
ADOPTIVE MOTHER: but when I held him in my a . . . in my . . . when I picked him up, I really had the feeling—it sounds a bit crazy—but I had the feeling "that's the one." He . . . I reckon he I would taken him even if his nose was on the back of his head. I . . . that's the way I explain to him today, that I've got the feeling "Boy, that's *our* child, the one you gave birth to."

The following example also indicates attempts at a biological normalization following the first encounter:

ADOPTIVE MOTHER: And then for the first time, for the very first time, we saw our daughter through the glass screen, and that was . . .
ADOPTIVE FATHER: Hm . . .
ADOPTIVE MOTHER: a feeling you just can't describe.
ADOPTIVE FATHER: Yes, it was incredible, wasn't it?
ADOPTIVE MOTHER: It might, I don't know, I shall never [laughing] be able to say objectively, as I shall never in all probability have children of my own, but, er, it must be a similar feeling when you give birth to a child and after all the strain the child is placed on your belly and you look at the child together with your husband.

In this example there is no fantasizing equation of adoption and birth. Nevertheless, the reference to the event of a birth delivery to interpret her own deviating situation is not coincidental. The couple was informed about the possibility of a clinic adoption a few weeks before the child was born. Just before the scheduled date of birth the adoptive mother unexpectedly had to undergo a gynecological operation, which triggered fantasies of pregnancy and birth delivery. She describes her stay in the hospital:

ADOPTIVE MOTHER: And then I drove all the doctors mad because we're were getting a child and then . . . normally I should have been put in a bed in the gynecological department, . . .
INTERVIEWER: Hm . . .
ADOPTIVE MOTHER: There was an empty bed. And a mother had a stillbirth or something like that, and then they asked me "Would it be perhaps . . . would you mind if we put you in the maternity ward and move the woman who lost her child to another ward? She probably finds it difficult . . . among all the babies.
INTERVIEWER: Hm . . .
ADOPTIVE MOTHER: Well, it was a funny feeling, lying there in the maternity ward of the hospital.
INTERVIEWER: [Laughter.]
ADOPTIVE MOTHER: I had an incision, like a Caesarian section, [laughing], I somehow find it's as if I really had a child myself, isn't it? There I was lying between all the mothers with their labor pains and the all the equipment. . . .

This woman's reference to her experience of what she calls an "adoptive pregnancy" following the notification of the adoption offer and the birth fantasies of the adoptive mother in the first example point to a motherhood fixation that can only be understood as an expression of the indispensability and nonoptional nature of the mother role and thus entails an element of compulsion. The narrative interviews do not allow a clear interpretation of the extent to which the women surveyed regard the birth of a child as a contribution expected of them by their marital partner or as a means of safeguarding and enriching marriage. One thing, however, is certain: These two women, both with a relatively low educational level, do not view occupational activity as a means of structuring the meaning of their lives. Instead, the biological mother role is so firmly anchored in their biographical design that their ego identities are inextricably linked with the achievement of birth. Even after the medical confirmation of the improbability of a biological birth and the prospect of an adoption they are unable to find the role flexibility needed to dissociate themselves from the biological aspect of the mother role and accept the differentness of the alternative constitution of family. The relative inability to reorganize action plans up until the first encounter with the child yet again documents the power of social norms relating to the female "normal biography"[20] and the relative powerlessness of certain women to resist pressures to conform. If they have no other resources of self-respect or respect vis-à-vis others, especially in the occupational field, they may succumb to the temptation of regarding adoption as the cure to childlessness and of evading the cognitive appreciation of their special status passage. The profound motherly feelings that are assumed to exist in the case of biological mothers allow them to move level with the normal case of family constitution. Indeed, in one of the two cases outlined here the normal case is even transcended as the adoptive mother contrasts the immediacy of the emotional bond she forms with the child with the phenomenon of delayed emotional response sometimes observed in the case of biological mothers shortly after birth.

The fixation on motherly feelings, albeit not on biological motherhood, is also discernible in a number of other interviews in which the women classify the first signs of emotionality just a short while after the first encounter with the child as proof that the correct choice has been made. The search for confirmation of one's own ability to give love to a strange child is primarily connected with the norms of family relationships internalized by the woman herself; this is compounded, however, by the adoption procedure itself. Just as a number of adoption applicants turn to the language of physics to try to symbolize their desired relationship to the child, a number of interviews show that the adoption counselor introduces the idea of "resistance" as a decision-making criterion. Referring to the counselor, one adoptive mother says:

ADOPTIVE MOTHER: By the way that is very well explained by the adoption counselor: "If you notice the least bit of resistance when you see the child," she told everyone, "then please say so, then the whole thing is pointless."

To judge by the interviews, the theory of resistance appears to intensify the tension during the pre-encounter and encounter phases, because the women anticipate the possibility of resistance and thus—in the awareness of a scarcity of children available for adoption—the failure of their adoption plans. This explains their relief on discovering the first signs of an affirmation of emotionality after just a few days. One adoptive mother describes her experience of affective certainty when she tried to feed a strange child and not the child she was planning to adopt:

ADOPTIVE MOTHER: And then I took another child out of its bed. It looked just the same, just as small, they all look very much alike, babies. I took it in my arms and fed it. That was after already feeding our child at least four or five times. And I noticed there and then "No, that's not your child, that a different one." I really sensed it. I'd somehow already got used to our child and sensed somehow . . . when I held our child in my arms I felt more than when I held a different child.

Although the adoptive mother physically senses the force of attachment to the child, this interpretation of the beginning of the adoption history is not marked by the kind of biological normalization that characterized the previous two examples. Sensing one's "own" child is the result of an interactive process that also enables the relational structure valid in the normal case without the filiative bond. The fact that adoptive mothers focus so much on themselves and their own feelings shows how difficult it is to present their "deviant" family constitution as acceptable to themselves and to others. When emulating the mother role they regard as normal, the adoptive mothers primarily focus on the aspect of emotionality as the yardstick for the correctness of their cooptation decision. This, however, throws very little light on anthropologically constant elements of the mother role. It simply touches on the bourgeois type of mother–child relationship,[21] as it has gradually evolved in our society since the beginning of industrialization. The narrative interviews with adoptive parents underline the binding nature of this model of the mother–child relationship with its "cultivation of expressivity."[22] The cultural contributions in structuring the mother–child relationship become particularly clear in the deviant case. The type of the socially constructed family is thus able to reduce statements on the nature of blood ties to society-specific interpretations of filiation and uncover the element of everyday knowledge behind the contributions of nature.

The Differing Rhythm of Emotional Interaction of Men and Women.
The bourgeois model of the mother–child relationship evolved as a result
of general processes of change in society, processes that at the same time
altered the role of the father. The emotional bond between a mother and
her child and the fact that the father "becomes invisible"[23] in the family
are two sides of one and the same process. Although the functional
differentiation of the workplace and the family, of occupational activity
and family life,[24] reinforced the expressive specialization of the mother
role, this could only take place as a result of a polarization of the sex
roles.[25] The longer periods of absence by the father from the family
produced a situation in which his instrumental role elements[26] often observed in the intercultural comparison increased. At the same time the
distance increased to the mother role, which was viewed as complemen-
tary and in which the emotional structuring of relationships was much
more firmly anchored in the role definition. Moves in today's society
towards overcoming role polarity—for example, by splitting male and
female involvement in productive and reproductive tasks—are primarily
innovative efforts limited to the "upper academic middle class."[27] The
motivational histories of the adoptive parents, however, already show that
adoptive parents are not characterized by a dissociation from traditional
patterns of the marital division of labor. A look at the event of the first
encounter between adoptive parents and the child, a small segment of
adoptive family reality, demonstrates how the conventional male and
female role orientation predominant in our society leads to differing
rhythms of emotional interaction between the adoptive father and mother
on the one hand and the child on the other. The socially constructed family
can be expected to show with particular clarity the differences that are
also visible in the case of a birth.

The male partner generally takes on the father role less quickly and less
spontaneously than the female partner the mother role. As a rule he keeps
a scrutinizing distance to the child before being able to accept it emotionally. Of course, there are cases (as in our study) in which the husband
takes the initiative to seek adoption and is highly moved when retrospectively reconstructing the moment of arrival in the children's home: "We're
going to be given a child!" There is also the case in which the adoptive
father is the first to recall the "overwhelming feeling" of holding the child
in his arms, and the enthusiasm of the adoptive father who wants to wrap
the child up straight away, whereas his wife—something she finds inexplicable—is panic-stricken on seeing the child and tries to avoid the decision.
As for all the other narrative descriptions of the first encounter, insofar as
the varying pace of sex-specific emotional interaction with the child was
mentioned (in roughly a quarter of all cases), it is fair to claim that the

husband took longer to establish an emotional bond. The main differences of role access can be interpreted in such a way that on seeing the child the husband has to explore the parental role first and gradually "grasp" the role with his eyes and hands, whereas all the wife needs to do is actualize the role with which she is already familiar thanks to anticipatory socialization.

The differences in role access are documented in the typifications used to classify the child in familiar categories. The adoptive mother is sometimes able within just a few minutes to effect the transformation from the general category of "the strange child" to the category "the child for me." The centrality of the mother role in her biographical design, possibly shored up by the residual instincts reinforced at the sight of the child, triggers her ability to accept the small child in its human differentness. The prospective adoptive father, on the other hand, frequently approaches the little creature more gropingly by initially referring to the familiar parameters of a respectable physical appearance and noting its deficiencies. Here are two examples of male descriptions of the child:

ADOPTIVE FATHER: Well, women feel a bit differently about the whole thing than a man. . . . Somehow it was like a little monkey lying there. He had red hair, a snub nose and really deep-set, er . . .
ADOPTIVE MOTHER: circles under his eyes.
ADOPTIVE FATHER: circles under his eyes. [Clears his throat.] He wasn't good-looking. . . . *Well* "take it slowly, wait and see what the mother says," right. . . . He had just a little ruff and at the back here [points to the back of his head] and then we saw these uneven parts . . .
INTERVIEWER: Hm . . .
ADOPTIVE FATHER: I thought to myself "Christ, what's he got? Doesn't he . . . his head look strange, Christ, is that normal?" Well, you . . . well I . . . you often see things perhaps a bit more, er, critically as a man. . . .

These examples of how prospective adoptive fathers come to terms with the situation contrasts with the spontaneous affection shown by the adoptive mothers towards the child.

ADOPTIVE FATHER: Well, you were *completely* . . . *immediately* took a spontaneous, er, liking to Martin. In *my* case it took a bit longer.

The narrators interpret their own reservedness within the frame of a concept of male normality (women feel different about the whole thing; men see things more critically), which affords a certain legitimacy at the moment when their female partners take an emotionality lead. The critical detachment often so highly rated in our society makes it impossible for the adoptive fathers (as shown in the examples) to overlook the similarity with a little monkey in any emotional overexuberance. Even if the adoptive mother is able to draw up different criteria for the newborn child than the aesthetic appearance, this evaluation of the child does not cause the husband to doubt his sense of realism.

Whereas some adoptive fathers are initially displeased by the child's outward appearance ("I didn't find it wonderful"), this is soon followed by the first steps towards establishing familiarity. The physical contact with the young baby plays a key role in the acquisition of the father role.

ADOPTIVE FATHER: We visited him every day, and I, well, . . . by holding him in my arms and trying to play with him, I also put aside my inhibitions, er, it was only then that I really established a proper relationship with him. . . . I never held a child in my arms before, which . . . which was such a *fresh* arrival, he was just two-and-a-half months old at the time.

A number of narratives indicate that the roundabout way in which the adoptive father gains access to the little child via the steps of "looking inside" and feeling it eventually leads to the same point of experiencing familial attachment that many women reach immediately after seeing the child for the first time.

ADOPTIVE FATHER: But . . . it was really good that we were able to get ready *for the event,* . . .
INTERVIEWER: Hm . . .
ADOPTIVE MOTHER: Hm . . .
ADOPTIVE FATHER: that we could play with the child; since—I must admit—it takes time to develop, in my case at any rate, the . . . my affection gradually grew. It wasn't so . . . so direct: *Right, that's our son,* but I had to have a look inside him first . . .
INTERVIEWER: Hm . . .
ADOPTIVE FATHER: and the—the—discover his habits.

The difference in the rhythm of emotional interaction of men and women reflects the difference in the "biographically determined situations"[28]: establishing an emotional relationship with the child in a different temporal structure the husband is able to incorporate into his role what was not "within his reach"[29] up to that time due to the dominance of typically male orientations. Just as he is not generally the "driving force" of the decision to adopt but merely goes along with his wife's plan, he is initially faced by greater difficulties of role acceptance and concretization. The adoptive mother, on the other hand, "spontaneously" actualizes something that corresponds to her own concept of the normality of the female role. In a woman's case the process of role-making[30] as the individual handling of socially dominant norms of motherliness is already so anticipatively advanced that no more than a small step is needed to actualize the plan of action. For a man, on the other hand, role design and its actualization coincide to a greater extent; he designs the role by already actualizing it via "looking inside" the child, physical contact, playing, and feeding, which means that his status passage is much more abrupt.

However, once adoptive fathers and mothers reach a similar point of emotional affection, as described in many of the examples, the orienting power of familial norms with their emphasis on "personal" emotional relationships becomes visible. It is eventually also effective where the missing principle of filiation and the hitherto relatively peripheral significance of the father role in the male role set produced a situation in which the prospective child could only initially be typified from an emotional distance as the strange child.

From the Immediate Acceptance of the Child to the Momentum of Emotional Involvement

Most of the narratives suggest that adoptive parents already accepted the as-yet-unknown child as their own during the first encounter and thus actualized their residual autonomy as parents-to-be as soon as they were able. This "right from the start" feeling probably develops integrative power in the case of many interaction histories, since it symbolizes the shortest possible path to family attachment in the absence of the principle of filiation. The readiness to take on the parental role, the potential of parent recruitment on the part of the child, the scarcity of available adoption offers, and the interest of the "supplier" in a prompt confirmation of the bureaucratic preselection—all these factors interact when the cooptation decision is taken at the earliest possible opportunity. A brief process of mutual communication between the adoptive couple—"a kind of dialogue you have to conduct with yourself"—forms the basis for the highly consequential decision to take the child.

This study does not show what takes place inside of adoption applicants if they reject a child. A few examples, however, do cast some light on a gray area between rejection and acceptance: How do adoption applicants come to terms with the threat of an unsuccessful cooptation? Which norms are set for one's own action if, despite an initially undesired cooptation, the child is nevertheless not rejected? The threatening failure of cooptation is the moment when, despite all the instrumentalization of the child, the initially latent potential of parental care is able to surface. The case of the impending failure of cooptation gives a particularly informative insight into the deeper layers of parental affection, layers that are not so clearly discernible in the case of the fascination with a newborn child.

The most impressive example of a blocked withdrawal after seeing the child for the first time is described in the narration of a couple that applied for an adopted child to prevent their birth child growing up as an only child. When the time arrived to take a look at the six-month-old girl, the adoptive father started out on the premise of absolute decision-making autonomy.

ADOPTIVE FATHER: And when the whole thing really got going I still presumed that we could take a look at a child in the children's home and if we don't hit it off straight away, I thought "Then you'll just have to reject it."

This lead-in to the adoption story already indicates the threat of rejection during the subsequent chain of events:

ADOPTIVE FATHER: And then we went along to this home, both of us, and took a look at this child . . . and I was . . . to be honest . . . *when I saw the child . . . when I had this first encounter with the child, was not taken with the child at all. I didn't really want . . .*
ADOPTIVE MOTHER: [Laughter.]
ADOPTIVE FATHER: *to adopt it.*
ADOPTIVE MOTHER: You were pretty upset, I'd . . . I'd say.

The adoptive mother then takes over the description of the details of the first encounter:

ADOPTIVE MOTHER: It was a *poor little mite*. Had a really bad cold, from birth onwards, these chronic . . .
INTERVIEWER: Hm . . .
ADOPTIVE MOTHER: er, [nasal?] infections, a kind of . . . wheezing. She had a very strange mouth anyway, her mouth was hanging down somehow. . . . Well, this *totally* stuffed up nose, her mouth *automatically* hanging down, you see. And this little thing *also* tried to smile.
INTERVIEWER: Hm . . .
ADOPTIVE MOTHER: It had such small eyes, which to top it all were also *watering*.
INTERVIEWER: Really.
ADOPTIVE MOTHER: Well, a *really poor little mite*.

The adoptive father tries to influence the outcome of the first encounter by asking his wife to refrain from adoption in this case.

ADOPTIVE MOTHER: And in the *doorway* of the home you already said "No, please do me a favor, . . .
INTERVIEWER: Hm . . .
ADOPTIVE MOTHER: I just can't, no, it's impossible." I was afraid he might reject it. I would have wanted it straight away.

And then the turning point:

ADOPTIVE FATHER: And after we saw the child and got back home we realized *all at once* that we would adopt this child.
INTERVIEWER: Hm . . .
ADOPTIVE FATHER: Not for *rational* reasons, somehow.
INTERVIEWER: Hm . . .
ADOPTIVE MOTHER: Hm . . .

ADOPTIVE FATHER: We just *couldn't* resist the child. It was a force which just could not resist and—that was already . . .
INTERVIEWER: Hm . . .
ADOPTIVE FATHER: the chain of this, after this . . .
INTERVIEWER: After this single, er . . .
ADOPTIVE FATHER: single, er, encounter. I really must admit . . .
INTERVIEWER: Hm . . .
ADOPTIVE FATHER: it was . . .
ADOPTIVE MOTHER: Was not a decision, that wasn't *due.*
INTERVIEWER: Hm . . .
ADOPTIVE FATHER: an experience which I never thought would be possible.

The narrator makes a second attempt to reconstruct what took place inside him so many years ago:

ADOPTIVE FATHER: I said "We can't leave X lying there. She's adopted. There's *absolutely nothing* to think over.
INTERVIEWER: Hm . . .
ADOPTIVE MOTHER: No question about it.
ADOPTIVE FATHER: Right, and not because of any, er, well, . . . social considerations or . . .
INTERVIEWER: Hm . . .
ADOPTIVE FATHER: that you just can't leave this poor child lying in a home . . .
INTERVIEWER: Hm, hm . . .
ADOPTIVE FATHER: lying in a home.
INTERVIEWER: Hm . . .
ADOPTIVE FATHER: And . . . really *instinctively* you just struck up some kind of relationship to this child and you just *couldn't* leave it.

This emotional entanglement resulting from the first step of establishing contact with the child is unique among the narratives. As a phenomenon the fact that the applicants felt unable to resist the little child and tied to the child against their original plan of action is probably not easily accessible to sociological analysis, especially since the persons concerned themselves explicitly rule out the relevance of possible inferences that could be made regarding the nature of this bond—"rational reasons," "social considerations." All that remains is the residual category of the "really instinctive relationship," which serves to make the willingness to take on the parental role seem automatic: Beyond the more or less subconscious expectations vis-à-vis the adoptable child the decisive factor is, in the final analysis, simply the fact that a child who needs parental care should have parents.

The cognitive management of a possible failure of cooptation is more transparent in the example of the adoptive mother who clings to her ideal of the deceased birth daughter and despairs on seeing the discrepancy between this ideal and the child available for adoption. In an arduous process of mentally weighing up the pros and the cons she realizes the exceptional quality of the child "on offer":

ADOPTIVE MOTHER: I also thought to myself, a child is not some commodity . . .
INTERVIEWER: Hm . . .
ADOPTIVE MOTHER: which you can take away and bring back, or say "I don't
like it."

She agrees to a second encounter with the child, influenced by the fact
that her husband and her older daughter find the child "cute." She
experiences the child as "very trusting," "extremely sociable," and "very
communicative." Finally, the family situation is simulated by letting the
child stay with the prospective adoptive parents for a weekend. The child
responds to the attempted familial integration by asking whether she can
stay for good. The adoptive mother also emphasizes the moral constraints
of action that, following the weekend visit, make cooptation unavoidable:

ADOPTIVE MOTHER: We took this decision because we simply said "It's
impossible to send her back," isn't it?
INTERVIEWER: Hm . . .
ADOPTIVE MOTHER: I mean that's *inhumane,* although it was still a struggle for
me, I didn't find my ideal, . . .
INTERVIEWER: Hm . . .
ADOPTIVE MOTHER: of course, and, er, we said to ourselves "It's inhumane to
bring the child back . . .
INTERVIEWER: Hm . . .
ADOPTIVE MOTHER: or reject it, that's impossible," right?

Although this story of emotional entanglement reveals a greater share of
autonomous action than the first example, reference is also made in this
case to the momentum of interaction with the child, beginning with the
rejection of the equation "child = commodity" up to the confirmation of
constraints of action. The personal internalized norms of humane behavior
make it impossible for the prospective adoptive parents to beat a retreat,
especially after encouraging the child's own hopes of finding parents by
asking it to stay for the weekend with the intention of clarifying their own
decision. In this case, too, it looks as if the "fallow" potential of parental
activity finally surfaces after the applicants have indicated their readiness
to take on the parental role. The fact that there is such a disparity between
the actual child to be adopted and the idealized child documents just how
much role flexibility many adoption applicants can develop beyond the
originally planned instrumentalization of the child. What is more, the
decision to take in the child is the humane continuation of one's own
application at the stage where the strange child was initially degraded by
highly specified expectations concerning the role of substitute for a birth
child.

Finally, emotional entanglement in the fundamental willingness to take
on the parental role will be illustrated with reference to an example

presenting the counterpole to the rapid construction of family in the case of the young baby. The reaction of the child to the adoption plan produces such a complex decision-making situation that the status passage can only be accomplished several months after the first encounter with the child. The phase preceding the constitution of family reveals the multitude of possible levels involved in the social construction of family. The following aspects are included in the inception of this family: the deprivation-ridden early history of the four-year-old child, its ambivalence towards possible parents, the strategies pursued by the child's substitute guardians, and finally, the significance of the time and effort invested in a taxing application procedure and the hope that a successful procedural outcome will make it all worthwhile.

The interaction history begins with the first commentary of the prospective adoptive parents on the child they are offered: "Good God, it can't be true." Against the background of an application procedure that had already taken a whole year, the couple lacks the "courage" to say no after just one face-to-face encounter. Although they feel really "mixed-up" after this first encounter they want to show their "good will" and venture a second attempt. Whereas the couple initially feels that it is too early to say no, they almost feel that it is too late following the second visit to the children's home:

ADOPTIVE MOTHER: The second time, we came along a kind of pergola, and walked towards this little residential unit. . . .
ADOPTIVE FATHER: And the whole group was outside playing in the garden.
ADOPTIVE MOTHER: Yes, and suddenly some of the children in the group who remembered us from the first visit started shouting "Katja, Katja," like that, and "Your new mother and father are coming," didn't they?

After conjecturing about what might have taken place in the meantime in the home and how the passing on of information by the staff was possibly intended to ensure the success of the adoption ("Be nice, otherwise they might not take you"), the applicants sum up:

ADOPTIVE MOTHER: Well, just imagine: we were already singled out as [future?] . . .
ADOPTIVE FATHER: And then we were in this lousy situation.
ADOPTIVE MOTHER: Right.
ADOPTIVE FATHER: The decision to back out was already made much . . . much more difficult. . . .

After three or four more visits the prospective adoptive parents experienced a child who evaded their attempts to establish contact, but who cried because she felt abandoned and enthused about "her parents" as soon as there was no longer an immediate danger of parental affection. After a long series of unsuccessful attempts to establish contact in different ways, the prospective parents are able to take the child home. The simulation of a family situation is described as follows:

ADOPTIVE MOTHER: The first time at our place [the decision?] matured as we suddenly saw her here, . . .
INTERVIEWER: Hm . . .
ADOPTIVE MOTHER: how she was acting.

Renewed setbacks followed. The child whose emotional attention was now divided, and who had already been disappointed twice by parents or foster parents, was told off by the staff of the children's home. After the enforced return to the home after a weekend visit (home regulations!), the adoptive parents finally managed to keep the child at home following a weekend visit. There is an element of emotional inextricability when the adoptive parents interpret the will of the child as a fateful signal:

ADOPTIVE FATHER: As she didn't want to go back to the home, we said . . .
ADOPTIVE MOTHER: Yes, it would have been terrible.
ADOPTIVE FATHER: "if she's already that far then we'll *give it a try,* then we'll *accept* it."

In the final analysis, the cooptation decision in the two earlier examples was embedded in the fatefulness of the union itself ("It was somehow just as fateful as if you've got your child lying in the cradle"). The initially assumed freedom of choice thus gradually disappears in the perspective of the actors, and the adoptive family constitutes itself with an automaticity very much resembling the way in which the birth of a child creates a fait accompli. In all three cases the fundamental willingness to adopt already entails a potential of emotional entanglement: Once the parental role is within reach, the momentum of the orientation to a child finally induces the prospective adoptive parents to relinquish their own expectations, irrespective of whether they are highly specified or orientated to patterns of normality. The only aspect that ultimately counts is the complementarity between parents able to give affection and a child who needs that affection. As in the normal case of family constitution, the parental role is finally taken on regardless of the qualities of the child—a result that the actors themselves are only able to interpret by referring to fateful guidance.

Whereas all the adoption examples act as a compass for the normal case, under a variety of aspects the cases of impending failure of adoption are particularly indicative with regard to normative structures of the parental role. Only a discussion of the cases that involve a problematic access to the parental role is able to uncover the complex of responsible and child-centered orientations often concealed beneath the instrumentalization of the child for one's own biographical design. In these cases the motivational history underlying the adoption procedure alone cannot provide an adequate explanation for the decision to choose a certain child. The child itself evokes a commitment to parental behavior inside the applicants (Helene Deutsch calls this "altruistic feelings") of which the applicants themselves were previously unaware. As an unanticipated determinant factor, the child's need for parental care enables a constitution of family that can only be interpreted as the outcome of the interaction history.

Notes

1. Cf. the remarks on the sequential order of status passages in Barney Glaser and Anselm Strauss, Status Passage. London 1971, pp. 34ff.
2. Schuetz and Luckmann (1974), p. 51.
3. Cf. the concept of conditional relevance that Harvey Sacks and his colleagues designed in the context of conversational analysis: Harvey Sacks, Gail Jefferson, and Emmanuel Schegloff, "A Simplest Systematics for the Organization of Turn-Taking for Conversation," in Language, vol. 50, 1974, pp. 696–735.
4. Cf. the concept of "status placement" in William Goode, "Illegitimacy, Anomie and Cultural Penetration," in William Goode, ed., Readings on the Family and Society. Englewood Cliffs, New Jersey 1964, p. 41.
5. Cf. the remarks on the change in professional ideas on adoption practices in the United States in Sorosky, Baran, and Pannor (1979), pp. 20ff. There was a development from withholding information on the birth parents to withholding information on socially degrading data to disclosing all—positive as well as negative—information.
6. Tyrell (1979), p. 42.
7. Cf. Tyrell (1978), e.g., p. 625.
8. Cf. Tyrell (1981), pp. 422 ff.
9. Cf. Tyrell (1981), pp. 421f; Friedhelm Neidhardt, "Strukturbedingungen und Probleme familialer Sozialisation," in Dieter Claessens and Petra Milhoffer, eds., Familiensoziologie—Ein Reader als Einführung. Frankfurt 1973, pp. 206ff.
10. Cf. Roland Eckert, "Geschlechtsrollen im Wandel gesellschaftlicher Arbeitsteilung," in R. Eckert, ed., Geschlechtsrollen und Arbeitsteilung—Mann und Frau in soziologischer Sicht. Munich 1979, p. 241.
11. The idea of the modern family as an "intimate group," as formulated, for example, by René König, is confirmed under the conditions of a social construction; see König (1969), p. 237; Tyrell (1979), pp. 32ff.
12. Arnold Gehlen, Urmensch und Spätkultur. Bonn 1956, p. 50.
13. Gehlen (1956), p. 50.
14. Quoted according to Tyrell (1978), p. 631.
15. Cf. the concepts of personal type and course-of-action type in Schuetz (1971), pp. 18ff.
16. This attitude is probably typical for a whole number of cases observed with reference to the supplementary survey. Members of the lower middle class or lower class express their willingness to also adopt an older child more frequently to a significant degree; in many cases, however, they fail to realize

their adoption plan, even though the adoption agency has an interest in placing older children. It can only be assumed that the inadequate range of socializational knowledge becomes clear during the course of the assessment procedure and that the adoption procedure is terminated because of the risk of overtaxing these prospective adopters.

17. Cf. Kurt Lüscher, "Die Entwicklung der Rolle des Kindes," in Klaus Hurrelmann, ed., Sozialisation und Lebenslauf. Reinbek 1976, pp. 139ff.
18. The relevance criteria mentioned in the narratives at first sight of the child in this and in the preceding example indicate that the idea of normal form typification elaborated by Cicourel and intended in particular for the field of verbal interaction can also be applied in this situation. See Aaron V. Cicourel, Cognitive Sociology: Language and Meaning in Social Interaction. Harmondsworth, Middlesex 1973, p. 35.
19. Cf. the remarks on the development of personal identity and in particular the significance of awareness in the process of the physiological evolution of the body in Thomas Luckmann, "Personal Identity as an Evolutionary and Historical Problem," in H. Aschoff, M. von Cranach, and R. Lepenies, eds., Human Ethology; Claims and Limits of a New Discipline. Cambridge 1979, pp. 56–74.
20. Cf. the title of the book by René Levy, Lebenslauf als Statusbiographie—Die weibliche Normalbiographie in makrosoziologischer Perspektive. Stuttgart 1977.
21. Cf. the differentiated analysis of this type of family in Tyrell (1981), pp. 423ff.
22. Eckert (1979), p. 241.
23. Cf. the characterization of this development in Alexander Mitscherlich, Auf dem Weg zur vaterlosen Gesellschaft. Munich 1965.
24. Cf. Tyrell (1981), p. 423.
25. Cf. Eckert (1979), pp. 24ff.
26. Morris Zelditch examined the hypothesis of the instrumental elements of the male and the expressive elements of female role formulated by Parsons in an intercultural comparison: Morris Zelditch, "Role Differentiation in the Nuclear Family: A Comparative Study," in Talcott Parsons and Robert F. Bales, eds., Family, Socialisation and Interaction Process. Glencoe, Illinois 1960 (first ed. 1955), pp. 307–352. See also the assessment of this Parsonian conceptual combination in Barbara Zahlmann-Willenbacher, "Kritik des funktionalistischen Konzepts geschlechtypischer Arbeitsteilung," in Eckert (1979), pp. 66–69. For more information on the historical relativization of Parsons' sex role theory see also Eckert (1979), p. 241.
27. Tyrell (1979), p. 60. Eckert (1979, p. 256) suspects that the "de-differentiation" of sex roles is particularly common in social groups with enhanced "chances of the articulation of self." The presentation of a changed parent–child symbiosis due to a more intense emotional involvement of fathers right from the beginning of family life is described in Yvonne Schuetze, "Zur Veränderung im Eltern-Kind-Verhältnis seit der Nachkriegszeit," in Rosemarie Nave-Herz, ed., Wandel und Kontinuität der Familie in der Bundesrepublik Deutschland. Stuttgart 1988, pp. 109–112.
28. My reference here is to a concept elaborated by Alfred Schuetz (1971, pp. 9f) in which he tries to illustrate the respective definition of the situation in its history as a sedimentation of past experiences. The varying biographically determined situations of males and females are very clearly reflected in the works of Daniel Stern. In both the laboratory situation and in natural commu-

nication situations Stern discovered that women were more willing to react to the schema of the little child than men: Daniel Stern, The First Relationship—Infant and Mother. Cambridge, Mass. 1980 (first printed 1977), p. 28. One of the few studies that tried to discover the extent of emotional affection shown by fathers is Ross D. Parke, Fathers. Cambridge, Mass. 1981, pp. 27ff.

29. Cf. Schuetz (1971), pp. 11ff.
30. In my opinion, the emphasis placed by this concept—which originates from the field of symbolic interactionism—on the action scope of the individual does not do justice to the differences between maternal role anticipations and maternal action at the beginning of the interaction history; cf. the concept in, for example, Ralph H. Turner, "Role-Taking: Process Versus Conformity," in Arnold M. Rose, ed., Human Behavior and Social Processes. London 1962, p. 22.

4

The Constitution of the Adoptive Family: Emotionality and Awareness

The history of interaction between adoptive parents and the adopted child is marked by a number of structural specificities that even persist in areas of shared everyday life apparently organized in accordance with the same rules as the parent–child relationship in a biologically constituted family. In the interests of an analytical differentiation of the structural features characteristic of families in general and adoptive families in particular, this chapter separates elements that closely overlap during the course of family life. I will begin with the evaluation of narrative accounts containing statements on emotional bonding, because this aspect is a particular focal point for adoptive parents at the start of their family history, as already shown by the descriptions of the first encounter with the child. This is followed by a clarification of how the knowledge of the differentness of one's own mode of family constitution is handled in various interaction relationships. Finally, the insights gained with respect to the significance of emotionality and knowledge serve to outline the structural demands made on the adoptive family when overcoming its specific problems.

From Strangeness to Familiarity: Emotional Normalization

The Moment of Emotional Normalization in Narrative Accounts

Irrespective of whether adoptive parents found it easy to form an affective bond with their adopted child, as in the case of the young baby, or whether they had to work their way through a long period of strangeness, as in the case of the older child, at some point almost every interview arrives at a key statement on the quality of the relationship: "And then I (very quickly/gradually) developed an intense relationship with the child."

This development of emotionality, which adoptive parents feel has resulted from the constant contact with the child, signifies the attainment of conformity with a central norm of family life. The structure of the narrative interviews, however, reveals that this statement on emotional bonding is not the final presentation of the relational quality. It is followed by a further key statement that reveals how adoptive parents organize their experiences in relation to the normal case. In the majority of narrative interviews the following sentiment is expressed: "It is like a child of our own."

As the majority of adoptive parents[1]—without any interviewer guid-ance—arrive at this turning point when recapitulating their adoption his-tories, it is fair to assume that this event represents a highly relevant experience. The explanation for this presentation marked by a sense of satisfied certainty is probably rooted in the fact that the second key statement means moving level with the normal case. Within its own frame of reference the special status of adoption would not appear to allow statements to be made on the relational quality without the risk of misunderstanding. To judge by the uniform strategy of management pur-sued by adoptive parents, the deviant case would appear to require an evaluation of experiences framed[2] by the clear yardstick of the normal case. With the statement, "It is like a child of our own," the adoptive parents indicate achieved normality to themselves and to others.

The newly accomplished relational level can be interpreted as the result of a process in which the idea of the differentness of one's own constitution of family is slightly annulled by the intensive emotions triggered by day-to-day experiences with the adopted child. At the beginning of adoptive family life parents seem to be primarily concerned with coming to terms with their own alternative constitution of family, with the exception of a few cases marked by motherhood fixation. As time goes by the shared interaction would appear to gradually phase out the separate preadoption history of parents and child. This enables a relational structure in which emotions are able to assert an independent existence alongside the aware-ness of the adopted "stranger."[3]

Regardless of the variance in the rhythm of emotional bonding almost every narrative reaches the point at which adoptive parents no longer typify the child as the adopted child but accept it as their child. The emotional distance between the adoptive parents and the child caused by their concentration on the adoptive status would seem to be gradually replaced by emotional identification. I would like to call this turning point in symbolic interaction with the child—the turning point from adopted child to child—the moment of emotional normalization. The relational quality achieved at this stage can be presumed to lead to a substantial degree of congruence between "normal" family and adoptive family structures.[4]

This assumption, however, should be cautiously modified. The fact that almost all adoptive parents express the achieved relational quality in verbally synonymous evaluations in their narratives would suggest that they feel that there is a need to articulate this emotionally experienced equation of the adopted child with a child of their own. Both the experience of involuntary childlessness and of adoption as a second-best solution, as well as the anticipation of the discrepancy between a biological and an adopted child in the value rating of others, probably explain why the quality of the relationship finds its expression with such regularity in the interviews. Even though there are no interviews with birth parents by way of comparison, I propose the thesis that the need to articulate emotional bonding is experienced much more intensely in adoptive than in "normal" families. The assumed congruence of parental emotions, therefore, should be cautiously extended as follows: The degree of reflective management of the experience of emotionality probably leaves its marks in everyday interaction and thus introduces a qualitative difference into the reality of adoptive family life.

This difference is taken up as a topic in some of the narrative interviews; not, however, as the agonizing experience of uncertainty compelling adoptive parents to repeatedly reassure themselves that they have moved level with the normal case of the constitution of family. The interviews show that the greater degree of reflective management of the situation is accompanied by a growing sensitization to the fact that the adopted child is an enrichment. In one interview we find the following:

ADOPTIVE FATHER: And what you . . . can also fundamentally say . . . is that, that . . . such children . . . are experienced much *more consciously* . . . by us, too, than the, the . . . the ones you have yourself. That's the way it is, that's the most natural thing in the world and, er, then to take this step, right, let's go and fetch a child, and we don't know what we're going to get. . . . [The uncertainty is] gone completely, but instead there's the, er, *the joy* about the child and the looking forward to the child, that's tremendous, because, of course, we now really wanted it that way. . . .

The following text example points in the same direction of a strong feeling of joy, but focuses on the affection shown by the child rather than on the ability of the adoptive parents to give love to the child:

ADOPTIVE MOTHER: But I—afterwards you—that's the way I felt anyway, *so* grateful when this strange (in quotation marks) child shows you its affection. Strictly speaking, undeservedly, and that's really a tremendous feeling. I don't know whether, er, parents with children of their own experience that *so* consciously, that . . .

INTERVIEWER: Hm . . .

ADOPTIVE MOTHER: this is a small personality, someone who gives you *affection* and . . . who shows you trust.

ADOPTIVE FATHER: It's not as if you're automatically *entitled* to that, is it. OK, in the case of birth parents. . . .

ADOPTIVE MOTHER: Sort of, sort of in advance. I don't know whether other parents also experience that so consciously.

ADOPTIVE FATHER: Right, and in the case of birth parents I always get the impression that they . . . it's automatic . . . that's the way they expect it: after all, this is my child. . . .

Whereas these two examples overtake the normal case with respect to the quality of the parent–child relationship, most adoptive parents are content to remain with the equation "like a child of our own." Moving beyond the mere evaluation of its content, it is worth taking a closer look at this key statement and its positioning in the interview to illuminate a characteristic feature of the research instrument employed, the narrative interview. The fact that almost all adoptive parents steer towards this evaluation with a kind of automatism was interpreted as an indication of the fact that attaining parity with the normal case represents the fulfillment of a norm regarded as constitutive for family life. The position of the corresponding statement in the interviews will probably be able to dispel doubts that the statement is simply a calculated presentation of events and that the phrase "like a child of our own" is just a concession to societal guidelines. This key statement does not crop up just anywhere in the interview: it is the respectively consistent continuation of a narrative recapitulation in which the taking in of the child, its initial behavior, and the fast or slow overcoming of the feeling of strangeness, is articulated. In the recapitulation of events it is generally positioned exactly where the relational quality described breaks through in the factual interaction history.

The orientation of the narrator to the chronological order of events detected in narrations[5] is also maintained without exception throughout the narrative interviews. If adoptive family life got off to a good start, for example, the narrators may steer the narrative towards the key statement of relational quality after just a few orienting remarks (perhaps on the same page of the transcripts as the reference to taking in the child at home). In another case, on the other hand, the lengthy history of the problems involved in organizing adoptive family life also has to be worked through in the interview before a breakthrough to a new relational quality can be narrated (perhaps 30 pages later). If a parallelism between the events experienced and the events recapitulated can be generally shown in the interviews, it seems fair to assume that, after examining the concomitant variables,[6] narrative constraints guarantee the validity of the research instrument and the accuracy of the narrative content.

The following subsections set out to discover how the possibilities and limitations of overcoming strangeness vary depending on the age at which the child was taken into the family. Consequently, clearly differing trajectories of emotional normalization are reflected in narration.

Emotional Normalization When Adopting a Baby. "I've grown so fond of the child so quickly"—this thought was commonly expressed during the 21 interviews with parents who adopted a child younger than seven months. For the adoptive parents it needs no further explanation. The fact that it is a privilege to be able to take in a young baby is reflected in the parental experiences. The emotional bond can evolve as a matter of course, unburdened by the difficulties of a longer "prehistory" and as if the process had unfolded "automatically":

ADOPTIVE MOTHER: He was simply so tiny and so in need of help that you
    automatically direct your affection towards the child, and that happens . . .
    immediately, you see. . . .

As the process of emotional bonding to the young baby is felt to develop a momentum of its own, there are generally no lengthy reflections on how the bond came into being. The achieved quality of the parent–child relationship is regarded as normal and is not analyzed from a reflective distance. The declining preoccupation with one's own special family status is viewed by some adoptive parents as evidence that everyday family life can now be taken for granted ("I don't think about it at all any more"). The fact that the child is now unquestionably accepted as belonging to the family or—in the words of Alfred Schuetz—that a new "natural attitude"[7] has developed, would appear to indicate that the child's strangeness no longer poses a problem for the adoptive parents.

The baby's physical dependence in itself leads to a tremendous density of interaction between the adoptive parents and the child. This produces a situation in which the child, at a stage in life during which it is extremely dependent and in need of parental care, becomes the little being who seems familiar to the adoptive parents. The child's physical growth and its first efforts to communicate bear the traces of their parental influence. Several recent studies in developmental psychology have tried to identify the individual aspects of the process of the emerging parent–child relationship to discover aspects of which the actors themselves are unaware. These investigations detected a wide-ranging repertoire of interactive behavior that a baby only a few months old can initiate and sustain.[8] Its smile, the movement of its eyes, hands, and feet, the way it moves its head, and, finally, its first prevocal sounds—all these means of expressions form the bonding contribution of the child to which the parents "automatically" react ("infant-elicited behavior"[9]). The rapid fascination for the young baby is probably connected with the fact that the child unfolds its communicative abilities and radiates the charm of a small partner in parental care.[10]

Opportunities to shape socialization somewhere near the zero stage of personality development apparently soon induce the adoptive parents of very young babies to class the principle of filiation as irrelevant for emotional bonding. Here is one of the few examples in which the establishment of the emotional bond is again recapitulated in reflective distance:

ADOPTIVE FATHER: What is it that really sets up, er, builds up the relationship? I'm not sure if it is really established because the child has been, er, borne for nine months. Isn't it *rather* established because, er, when it's still very young you have to feed it six times a day, put on its diapers and care for it and . . . play with it and observe its reactions to . . . to your own, er, remarks and aura. . . . I feel that this, er, this is much more important than bearing the child for nine months during pregnancy. . . .

According to the narrative interviews, pregnancy and birth are not essential as binding experiences if the adoptive parents can utilize the plasticity of the child in its most formative developmental phase,[11] and if they are able to superimpose social familiarity on biological strangeness.[12] The turning point from adopted child to child is then reached, a point that is expressed in almost every interview concerning a very young adopted child. Here is just one example:

ADOPTIVE FATHER: There's just no other feeling any more, just . . .
ADOPTIVE MOTHER: No, it's really your own child, and that's that.
ADOPTIVE FATHER: it's your own child, that's the way you see it.
ADOPTIVE MOTHER: It's your *own* child, and that's that, it's, er, you forget it now and again, that it's adopted, it's incredible just how much you forget.

Achieving parity with the normal case is emotionally felt, but even such an experienced certainty still has to be described in a way that underlines the logical problem associated with a comparison. Adoptive parents without biological children can only set their comparison in relation to emotions they assume to exist in the case of biological parents. This means that there's still a risk that even the experienced certainty of emotional normality could appear inadequate in terms of the (assumed) emotionality lead of biological parents. The following example is representative of the few narrative interviews that articulated the problem of this unbridgeable experiential deficiency:

ADOPTIVE FATHER: I *can* only speak from my own experience, you see, well, for *me* it's, as I said, er, a child just like any other child, just like, er, my *own*

child, which my wife might have given birth to, you see, it's, well, it's the *same* feeling, you see.
INTERVIEWER: Hm . . .
ADOPTIVE FATHER: I mean, I can only speak with reference to the situation of the *adopted* child, since I've never experienced what it might have been like if my wife had had a child herself.

As in the remaining examples the significance of the experience lag is undermined by once again emphasizing the certainty of the emotional bond. Individual narratives also show how even those parents for whom the logical problem of a comparison with the normal case does not exist— parents of both an adopted child and a biological child[13]—attempt to grasp the quality of the emotional relationship. Here is an operationalization attempt:

ADOPTIVE FATHER: Well, for me there's no such difference between an adopted child and a biological child. . . . For one thing, you don't sit around . . .
ADOPTIVE MOTHER: Right.
ADOPTIVE FATHER: the whole day and dissect your feelings, . . .
INTERVIEWER: Hm . . .
ADOPTIVE FATHER: but you've got everyday experiences, you play with the child, we play with a train set or I play football with him, . . .
INTERVIEWER: Yes.
ADOPTIVE FATHER: and I can't imagine that I'd play football any *differently* with a child of my own . . .
INTERVIEWER: Hm . . .
ADOPTIVE FATHER: than with this lad here [laughter]. It's not as if you're constantly watching the children when they sit there, is it, asking yourself do you prefer that one to that one or something like that [laughter].
INTERVIEWER: Hm . . .
ADOPTIVE FATHER: It's not like that, and looking back on the years . . . I can't say that in Lars' case . . . I didn't have such a good inner relationship as with Katrin just because of the fact he was adopted and Katrin wasn't.

This couple in particular, however, experienced that the rapidly achieved "natural attitude"[14] in the emotional bond with the adopted child is only valid for the case in which the common relational history begins somewhere near zero level in the development of the child's personality. As opposed to the cases in which a transition from strangeness to familiarity is possible within just a few days, we will now examine those cases in which longer and crisis-ridden trajectories can develop if the adopted child brings its early history to bear in adoptive family life.

Emotional Normalization When Adopting a Toddler. Studies in the field of psychoanalysis and developmental psychology[15] as well as sociological socialization research[16] have repeatedly stressed the significance of steady interactive relations during early childhood and suggested that the development of the "healthy personality"[17] is limited in cases where there is a frequent change of reference persons. With regard to adoption the conclusion was drawn that the child should be placed at as early an age as possible, because the child would not suffer from the accompanying discontinuity so much during the first few months after birth as the older child who has perhaps experienced several changes of guardians.[18] In many cases the first six months of the child's life were defined as the rough dividing line between the more or less dramatically experienced hiatuses on the part of the child, because it was claimed that up to this stage the child is not yet in the "vulnerable phase,"[19] a phase in which its advanced cognitive development[20] allows it to be consciously aware and—as the symptoms show—suffer more intensely as a result of the separation from reference persons.[21]

The plasticity of the child during its first few months is the source from which parents, biological or adoptive, can derive the experience of belonging together as a family. This plasticity, however, can also become the source of a long and persistent burden if adoptive parents, as successors to several other socializing agents, adopt an older child or toddler. The beginning of adoptive family life may then be marked by confrontation with the child's previous formative influences. These character "molds" may play such a dominant role that the adoptive parents find it extremely difficult to overcome their preoccupation with a sense of artificial family construction. In the following section reference is made to three narratives dealing with children aged 12 months, 18 months, and 21 months. Prior to adoption all three children were looked after by their biological mothers. The reasons why these mothers, who lived alone, were unable to take proper care of their children is the subject of conjecture rather than of definitive reliable information for the adoptive parents. In two cases custody for the child was taken away from the mother because of neglect and cruelty; the children were handed over to foster families and remained there for several months while the mother decided whether to relinquish the child for adoption or not. In the third case the 18-month-old child would have been sent to a home if the mother had not opted for adoption, because the mother's relatives and friends had declared that they were no longer willing to take care of the child.

At the beginning of adoption placement the children had reached a developmental stage at which they were apparently—as indicated by the narrative reconstructions of the first encounter with the child (see "The Affective Potential of a Toddler" in Chapter 3)—to play an active part in shaping the relationship with their potential adoptive parents. By calling the prospective adoptive mother "Mommy," by looking for physical contact (sitting on her lap or rushing into her arms), and by giving a clear signal that they want to go along with the adoptive parents, they actively influenced the decision by the applicants to adopt. The child's utilization of its action resources in this way can have a favorable or unfavorable influence on the constitution of family.

Not the adoption age as such, but the quality of the child's experiences prior to adoption determines whether or not the beginning of family life is experienced as a crisis. Whereas the 21-month-old child who was adopted from a home was well-adjusted "right from the very first moment" ("lovable and well-behaved"), much to the adoptive mother's surprise, the 12-month-old child was seized by anxiety and confusion following a renewed move to new surroundings and relationships, the seventh move of this kind in its life. Between the initial care of its biological mother and the withdrawal of the mother's custody the child had "changed reference persons five times" within the circle of relatives and friends before finally being handed over to a foster mother. The fact that the child's response to the change was a virtually nonstop bout of crying suggests that it probably interpreted the new situation as yet another "unreliable" one.

ADOPTIVE MOTHER: You just can't imagine what it was like, I don't know, I think many people who . . . have no children or . . . who haven't experienced the situation cannot imagine what *she* had to suffer.

INTERVIEWER: Yes.

ADOPTIVE MOTHER: For in the beginning she had fever, nightmares and . . . she cried terribly. It's difficult to imagine but she would sit in her stroller till 11 P.M., and when we wanted to put her, er, to bed or when we tried to get her to sleep she would start to cry, to *writhe,* she didn't want to be touched, especially not by my husband, then she would cry even more. And, er, when she really got worked up during the course of hours . . .

INTERVIEWER: Hm . . .

ADOPTIVE MOTHER: and that lasted about two hours, then she would calm down, exhausted. As soon as she had regained her strength she would start again.

INTERVIEWER: Hm . . .

ADOPTIVE MOTHER: We took turns during the night for weeks on end, for about three weeks, wasn't it?

The tremendous and overpowering strain of the beginning of the adoption history, which is reflected as a powerful experience of suffering right at the beginning and recapitulated repeatedly during the course of the interview, contrasts strikingly with the narratives relating to the children adopted when they were babies. Just a few months after the first three months or six months of the child's life the damage suffered by the child can be so substantial as to make adoptive family life an excessive physical and mental strain. This is also something the adoption counselor decides when he or she allocates the child who is not desired by other applicants to a married couple in the lower segment of the lower middle class. The degree of (under)privilegedness during the placement phase (see Index of the Degree of Privilegedness) correlates with the degree of criticality of the beginning of family life. The adoptive mother sums up:

ADOPTIVE MOTHER: Either you can cope with the situation or you have to take valium or something else afterwards.

Such a strain is an obstacle to any emotional normalization. It is impossible for a sense of familiarity to develop as long as the physically exhausted adoptive parents are faced by such an excessive strain of interpretation work:

ADOPTIVE FATHER: Of course, we asked ourselves "What's the reason? What's the matter? What's going on, what can we *do*? What can we do?"

Many passages in the narratives reveal that the adoptive parents try to understand the child's screaming ("screamed, not just cried," "screamed without tears") by speculating about its preadoption history ("something must have happened," fear of men, fear of dogs, scars all over its body). As long as so much effort has to be invested in reconstructing the child's unknown yet still influential past in order to determine its identity, the adopted child cannot be transformed into the "child." The statement on the current emotional bond ("We've grown so fond of the little one") is made after two hours of interviewing and points towards a relational quality that was only achieved several months after the child was taken in.

The child taken in at the age of 18 months also caused an "enormous nervous strain" (and stomach trouble). As she had not spent more than a few weeks with her various reference persons she tried to relate to everybody and was unable to keep an emotional distance.[22] This was a signal to the adoptive parents that she did not feel exclusively tied to them. Due to the child's physical mobility and curiosity[23] the child was in a developmental phase in which the stress[24] usually connected with the transition to the role of parents is magnified ("We looked like death warmed up"). After about six months the adoptive parents sensed that the child felt she belonged to them. Finally, in this narrative too the recapitulation of the mutually reinforcing bond between parents and child leads to the (second) key statement on relational quality:

ADOPTIVE MOTHER: In the meantime, we no longer have the feeling that it's an adopted child. In our case it's as if it were a child of our own.

The third example in this toddler category extends the range of possibilities by presenting the case of a child who although already 21 months old, experienced a smooth start to family life ("We were a proper family right from the very start"). The significance of the example within the framework of this study, however, is that it underlines the impermanence of

emotional normalization once it has been achieved. The emotionally experienced equation of adopted child and child can be threatened in later
phases of family life. Strains may occur that necessitate a change in
symbolic interaction with the child. The struggle to establish the normality
of one's family, an aspect to be dealt with a little later on, may once again
move the special status of the adoptive family sharply into focus. In the
case considered here a complicated interplay can be observed of feelings
of inferiority on the part of the adoptive mother, acts of discrimination she
experiences in interaction outside of the family, and the longing of the
adopted child, now 10, to be like all other children.

ADOPTIVE MOTHER: What I tend to *believe* is that she thinks about it again and
again, that it never settles down inside her, so to speak. . . . That she is also
a completely normal child too, a completely normal human being.

In the wake of her cognitive development this adopted child is able to
more clearly comprehend her own special status and hurl her deep distress
at the rejection by the birth mother at the adoptive mother. The once-
achieved normality of the emotional bond in the eyes of the adoptive
mother thus disappears. The new crisis-laden relationship requires an act
of reinterpretation,[25] during which the long repressed special status reasserts its significance. The child is once again experienced to a certain
extent as an adopted child, an experience compounded by the fact that the
adopted child experiences herself as such.

This example borders on the cases of limited emotional normalization to
be dealt with later on, even though it does not belong to that category due
to the intensity of the emotional attachment. The adoption history of the
now ten-year-old child is so important within the framework of our sample,
with its predominance of children who are still young, because it reveals
the temporal relativity of those statements through which the adoptive
parents document the achieved normality of the relationship for themselves and for others. As long as such statements are made with reference
to a child who is still young (up to about six years old), they ignore the
part of adoptive family reality in which the adopted child codefines family
normality via its own reflective management of its adoptive status and thus
casts doubt upon the equation of its own status with the normal case. In
such a case the trajectory of emotional normalization may suddenly begin
to fall after having remained at a high level for a long time.

Emotional Normalization When Adopting an Older Child. The strains
accompanying the establishment of an emotional bond between adoptive
parents and a toddler seem relatively insignificant in comparison with the
tension of a "late" construction of family, that is, a construction of family
without the common experience of the child's early history. After taking

in an older child adoptive parents may not have the impression of being an authentic family for several years due to the missing experience of emotional attachment.

The following statement was frequently made by parents in the interviews relating to the older child when referring to the beginning of adoptive family life: "It already had a little personality of its own." With all its previous molds this little personality symbolizes the strange worlds from which it comes: the world of the birth parents who first cared for the child, and perhaps the world of the foster mother or of the children's home.

With just one exception all six adoption histories covered in this category indicate that the world of the birth mother (the birth parents) had determined the child's biography for a relatively long time (one to five years). These children spent the phase of establishing basic trust or mistrust,[26] a fundamental phase in the development of a child's personality, in the care of the birth mother or birth parents,[27] even though they were perhaps exposed to a regular change of reference persons. Three of the six children also experienced the possibilities and limitations of autonomy in the sphere of influence of the birth mother or birth parents; that is, they developed their advanced physical, affective, and cognitive abilities and the fundamental control of their own feelings[28] in the milieu of the family of origin.

In the case of two five-year-old children, life in the adoptive family followed immediately after life in the family of origin, although parental care in the latter context was interrupted in both cases by stays in the children's home or in a hospital (for treatment due to cruelty). Another child moved from its birth mother to a foster mother at the age of three. Confronted by considerable bureaucratic difficulties the foster mother finally adopted the child, and thus helped it overcome the feeling of being torn between its family of origin and the foster family. Two other children were taken away from their mothers at the age of one year following signs of serious neglect or cruelty. Whereas in one case a series of stays in various homes was repeatedly interrupted by stays in the family of origin up until adoption at the age of five, the other child experienced a varied history of bureaucratic allocation between the children's home and the foster home. There was only one case in which the influence of the birth mother was limited to just a few months; this was continued in brief episodes during the child's stay in the children's home, episodes that—in the view of the adoptive parents—led to a renewed experience of abandonment for the child (the last time the birth mother took care of the child she brought it back two or three days later than agreed, "screaming, highly feverish and completely dirty").[29]

In order to outline the experience of strangeness associated with the adoption of an older child I will deal with four of the six adoption histories, which illuminate the beginning of adoptive family life with children aged three to five. Two interviews are not included in the examination of this aspect, because the narrative presentations hardly relate to the development of an emotional bond between the adoptive parents and the adopted child. Whereas one of the two interviews omitted here focuses on the behavior and abnormal behavior of the adopted child, the other concentrates on the question—completely oriented to the interests of the adopted child—of when the child is able to distance itself from the strains of the first seven years of its life (longer status as foster child) and able to identify with its new adoptive status.

The narratives show that the older child may be experienced in its entirety as "the stranger." The initial strangeness can range from physical strangeness to strangeness of outward appearance, strangeness of language, strangeness of cognitive reactions to events of everyday life, and strangeness of family conception. The strangeness caused by the child's behavioral symptoms (aggressivity, fear of abandonment, somnambulism, wetting, nail-biting, and so on) are disregarded here. If the unit of adoptive parents and child is to be constituted as a family, the persons concerned must cope with all dimensions of the experience of strangeness, with all its various implications for the ego-identity of the adoptive parents and the child.

The narrative descriptions of the initial physical strangeness by three adoptive mothers reveal the extent to which the suffering caused by this experience of strangeness is caused by the fact that the relationship with the adopted child is compared with an assumed norm of parental emotionality. All three mothers adopted a girl aged between four-and-a-half and five. Here is one example.

ADOPTIVE MOTHER: It was still just too difficult for me to constantly look after the child, to touch her, to wash her and all these things.
INTERVIEWER: Hm . . .
ADOPTIVE MOTHER: In the beginning I found this *very* difficult, any kind of physical contact.

It is obvious that the adoptive mother's experience of resistance to any kind of physical contact does not result from the fact that she is unable to look after a child. Rather, the discrepancy between her differing experiences with regard to physical contact with the adopted child and her biological daughters probably makes her feel that the new relationship is deficient. In this case, a further factor explaining the adoptive mother's initial inability to handle the physical experiences of mothering is the fact that the frame of reference was the relationship with her own deceased biological daughter. This increased the already existing strangeness of the adopted child.

The adoptive mother's initial experience of resistance against any kind of physical contact can be regarded as an example of how, in the words of Mary Douglas, the social and physical bodily experiences mutually reinforce one another.[30] The adoptive mother cannot limit her involvement to the physical bodily experience of a children's nurse as long as the social norm of the mother–child bond is determinant for her action. If, like Goffman, one assumes that a person's skin can be regarded as "the purest form of egocentric territoriality,"[31] a threat to the territory of motherly action can be expected to continue until the idealized model of the deceased biological daughter ceases to be the frame of reference.

Another adoptive mother recognizes a discrepancy between her feelings for the five-and-a-half-year-old adopted girl and her previous experiences with her biological daughter on the one hand and her son adopted at an early age on the other. She has particular problems with the aspect of physical contact. Finally, the adoptive mother in the third case under review in this category, who cannot fall back by way of comparison on previous experiences, relates to the norms of the mother–child bond when emphasizing the deficiencies of the relationship with the adopted child during the early stages of the adoption history.

ADOPTIVE MOTHER: She was a little strange to me . . . and I could not accept her physically . . . not in the sense of, er, fully accepting her, you understand, somehow . . .
INTERVIEWER: Hm . . .
ADOPTIVE MOTHER: it was, well . . . all guided by intellect. . . . Of course, I embraced her and kissed her and so on . . . but there was no spontaneity, you see, somehow it was a case of controlled action. . . .

Even though in this case the first approximations to the norm of the mother–child bond could be observed at the level of visible behavior (fulfilling the norm of embracing and kissing the child), the adoptive mother feels only too well that she falls short of complying with the norm as long as her behavior is not spontaneous. This passage documents the pressure of emotional expectations on adoptive parents, who feel that they can only then define the relationship as normal when bodily contact with the child is no longer guided by their intellect. Strangeness is probably experienced as such a burden because the norm of emotionality,[32] which has become fully accepted only during the course of this century, serves as the yardstick for a successful parent–child relationship. Adoptive mothers at the beginning of the 20th century were probably spared the experience of suffering caused by the physical strangeness of the (in many cases) older adopted child,[33] because the desired goal of providing a legal heir was much less concerned with the more subtle relational aspects than the conception of family realized via adoption today.

The strangeness of outward appearance is perhaps the easiest to overcome. The lack of an attractive appearance described in detail in the case of two of the three girls when they were taken into the family was offset by attempts on the part of the adoptive parents to shape the child "in their image":

ADOPTIVE FATHER: Well, an emotional relationship cannot develop, of course, in just one day.
ADOPTIVE MOTHER: No, that's true, so we started changing her outward appearance first, to make the child look the way, in our image, the way we wanted her to look. . . .

The following narrative passage illustrates which requisites may prove helpful for the acculturation of the child's physical appearance:

ADOPTIVE FATHER: In order to identify with the child it all starts, for example, . . .
INTERVIEWER: Hm . . .
ADOPTIVE FATHER: we started by . . . throwing away the child's national health insurance glasses and buying her a proper pair . . .
INTERVIEWER: Hm . . .
ADOPTIVE FATHER: which suited her a bit better. We then changed her haircut, . . .
ADOPTIVE MOTHER: Yes.
ADOPTIVE FATHER: didn't we, and her clothes, you just have to. . . .
ADOPTIVE MOTHER: Yes, she had to start by smelling as if she comes from our stable. . . .

A great deal of time and effort is required to overcome the cultural strangeness that remains after every possible step has been taken to rearrange the "personal facade"[34] and superimpose the strange molding of the child's personality to such an extent as to enable a common adoptive family world. The strangeness of language as a barrier between adoptive parents and the child is extremely difficult to overcome. The child's language as a sedimentation of the strange worlds preceding adoption[35] is only able to adapt slowly to the pattern of speech expected in middle-class families. Even though the child's vocabulary is described as "meager" or even as a "catastrophe,"[36] it is not so much the retardation of the child's language that is experienced as a burden to everyday life as the different way the child uses language in everyday interaction. The adopted child, for example, may use a part of its meager vocabulary intended to "let off steam" in a monotonous way in order to defend itself in line with the previously experienced language context. With reference to a five-year-old girl whose character was marked by the aftereffects of cruelty, for example, we find the following:

ADOPTIVE MOTHER: That was what I found particularly difficult to cope with, you see.
INTERVIEWER: Hm . . .
ADOPTIVE MOTHER: Well, the child was full of swearwords and . . . and they kept on being used all the time, and that was something we just weren't *used to*.

Whereas the adoptive mother in this case found it "particularly difficult to cope" with the relational structure created by the child's language, some adoptive parents are also irritated by the strangeness of cognitive reactions in everyday life.[37] Here are just a few examples: an almost five-year-old girl does not know that goods in stores have to be bought and cannot simply be taken away; a five-year-old boy embraces the saleswoman because he thinks she gave him a present; a five-year-old girl "is unable to name one in three meals served"; or—to refer to a less serious example with a class-specific background—one child bursts out laughing on seeing the adoptive mother dressed in a tennis outfit. All these situations prove embarrassing in everyday family life and repeatedly make the child appear as a stranger.

Finally, there is the problem of the strangeness of family conception. A prerequisite for the constitution of family is that all members can grow into their roles. The child taken into the family at a later stage, however, has to undergo a process of desocialization before becoming familiar with the value orientations of its new family. If a five-year-old girl is directly transferred from her family of origin to the adoptive family, it is hardly surprising that she relates her previous concept of a mother to the adoptive mother believing, for example, that she has to fight for survival.

Such a clash between different family worlds means that adoptive parents are permanently confronted by the task of interpreting the strange behavior of the adopted child and deciphering the largely unknown early history of the child in order to grasp its relevance for the child's action in specific situations. Here is an example of the interpretation work invested by the adoptive parents, work that begins in the phase of initial strangeness and seeks to construct reciprocity.

ADOPTIVE MOTHER: To begin with, I felt sorry for the child because she was so rejected, and it wasn't as if, as if I really liked her . . . like a child of one's own.
ADOPTIVE FATHER: Somehow she was like a little magpie.
INTERVIEWER: Hm . . .
ADOPTIVE MOTHER: Of course, she became aggressive very quickly. And then we also gradually went through a process of learning, particularly in my case as I had to take care of her all the time. First of all, I had to learn why the child behaved the way she did, and after a while I discovered that after she came to live with us she still believed that she had her back against the wall and had to *fight* for things which were *automatic*, . . .

INTERVIEWER: Hm . . .

ADOPTIVE MOTHER: for things that she *was* given without discussion, since she still thought she had to fight to get them . . .

INTERVIEWER: Hm . . .

ADOPTIVE MOTHER: by *screaming* and [being] *very loud* and aggressive and stomping her feet and things like that, you see?

INTERVIEWER: Hm . . .

ADOPTIVE MOTHER: And that's something I had to learn first, why she reacted the way she did, because I thought she still felt as if she was in a hostile world.

The interpretation work invested by adoptive parents in their own comprehension of the situation corresponds to a considerable amount of account work[38] vis-à-vis the child in order to accomplish the family world that other children are able to construct in continuity from the first day of their lives onwards. In other words, a child at the age of five is shown by parental affection and its explanation how to develop a trust in interactive relationships that is established during the first few months of the child's life in the case of other children. The following is an example of parental account work through which the adoptive mother tries to reorganize the adoptive child's conception of family. This passage is preceded by the description of how the adoptive child once cried the whole night through, a night during which the child was very reserved towards its adoptive parents and made it extremely difficult for them to discover the reasons for its suffering.

ADOPTIVE MOTHER: The next morning I then explained to her how life is in a family. I said "You can wake us up anytime, go along to Daddy or to me, you can wake up Katrin. If anything hurts and you can't sleep, don't forget, I'm always there."

Two of the three narrative interviews dealt with here show how the five-year-old child is able to gradually understand the willingness of the adoptive parents to show affection and how the child then "overflows with thankfulness." Although both adoptive mothers do not feel that this exuberant gratitude is really appropriate ("Of course, that's too much as well," "it really made me feel embarrassed"), probably because the emphatically expressed gratitude also reveals the discrepancy between the adoptive family situation and the fact that family care should be something a child should be able to take for granted, they nevertheless let themselves be emotionally moved. This is one of the little experiences that help overcome strangeness.

The narratives concerning late adoptions in particular indicate the extent to which the trajectory of emotional normalization does more than simply reflect the quality of the relationship between the adoptive parents and the child. It also reveals a process of self-communication, especially on the part of the adoptive mother, which determines the quality of the relationship. It may take years before motherly emotions for the child are recognized as such in everyday interaction, because attention initially focuses on coming to terms with other more immediate problems. The narrative passages relating to a late start to family life illustrate that in many cases emotionality is grasped retrospectively rather than in the ongoing interaction process.

One adoptive mother, for example, infers from the sadness she feels when her adopted daughter has to stay in hospital that the emotional bond has developed more intensely than she had assumed. The fact that her daughter also shows a more intense attachment to her than she expected reinforces the new feeling of belonging together. Another adoptive mother observes with relief that she now defends the child more vigorously against people outside of the family or that she has greater sympathy for the child when it is ill or has been injured than at the beginning of adoptive family life.

These examples point towards a process of interpretation in which the adoptive mother infers a general change in the quality of the relationship from an apparent change in a single relational component. This "documentary method of interpretation"[39] means recognizing[40] how emotional normalization is guided by motherly self-communication.[41] It may take months or years before an adoptive mother is able to appreciate that she has achieved parity with the normal case. The fact that she bases self-communication on indicators shows her need for self-reassurance following a long phase of the experience of strangeness.

In all three narratives this indicator-based certainty leads on to the key statement on achieved relational quality (for example, "today I no longer have the feeling that she's really an adopted child").

The pace of the transition from a purely rationally guided relationship with the adopted child or one based on pity to an emotional bond, however, varies from case to case. In the case of the five-and-a-half-year-old girl, who continued to suffer for many years from the aftereffects of being cruelly treated by her birth mother, for example, it was not until three years after the child was taken into the family that the adoptive mother noticed that she also no longer felt any "emotional" difference between her feelings for her biological daughter and the son she adopted at an early age on the one hand, and her adopted daughter on the other.

The following narrative passage relating to a boy adopted at the age of three exemplifies the hard-earned yet highly rewarding experience of emotional normalization. Following a quite detailed recapitulation of the problematic history of the adopted child—beginning with his vehemently expressed rejection of the adoptive mother and moving on to his fears of abandonment, somnambulism accompanied by persecution mania, signs of injured self-esteem, and deep-rooted deprivation caused by its relinquishment by the birth mother—the interview arrives at the turning point from the adopted child to "our child." This point of transformation is recapitulated duet-style.

ADOPTIVE FATHER: Yes, he's like a child of our own,
ADOPTIVE MOTHER: Yes, hm . . .
ADOPTIVE FATHER: I, I see . . . I reckon I, er, feel no difference.
INTERVIEWER: Hm, hm . . .
ADOPTIVE MOTHER: No, it *fades away* very noticeably.
ADOPTIVE FATHER: It fades away after a while.
INTERVIEWER: Hm, Hm . . .
ADOPTIVE MOTHER: Doesn't it, the feeling, it . . . that it isn't your own child, you see?
INTERVIEWER: Hm . . .
ADOPTIVE MOTHER: That, er, disappears somehow over the years. . . . You're *aware* of it, but it fades away.
ADOPTIVE FATHER: It fades away, the feeling.
ADOPTIVE MOTHER: Especially *the feeling,* you see.

This jointly recapitulated key statement contrasts markedly with the previous lengthy presentation of the problem. Whereas the narrative constraints are initially oriented towards reconstructing the history of suffering of the in many respects deprived child, and emphasizing its implications for the emotional bonding, the adoptive parents suddenly become aware of the one-sidedness of their presentation ("One shouldn't just talk about difficulties"). This organization of narrative activity to balance strains and gratifications could be viewed as a characteristic feature of the narrative interview. In accordance with the narrative volume it focuses on the recapitulation of events rather than on the description of a given state of affairs. As in this study no inferences can be made from the narrative volume to content relevance, the characteristic feature of the narrative interview indicated here does not allow conclusions to be drawn about, for example, its limited usefulness. It merely becomes clear that situational descriptions, in this case of the achieved relational quality, should be given particular attention in data analysis, because they seem to be hidden behind the flow of communication concerning other events (see the gradual layering of statements preceding the key statement of the emotional quality in the "duet" above).

It is now worth taking a look at the processes of experiencing and overcoming strangeness in the adoptive family with an eye to the basic conditions underlying the constitution of family. The difficulties involved when constructing familial reality in the absence of the principle of filiation and without a shared socializational history in early childhood suggest that the conditions for the "healthy" personality as described, for example, in Erikson's model of psychosocial development[42] also exist as preconditions for the healthy family in terms of emotional attachment. Such a model would have to be interpreted in two directions. Not only the child has to experience certain interactive contributions, but the parents must be able to make these contributions in order to realize familiarity.[43] Not only does the child need further behavioral guidance, but the parents need to be able to convey this behavioral guidance to the child in order to be able to classify the child's extended action range in their orientational knowledge and experience this as relatively predictable. The greater the number of preadoption developmental stages, the greater the discrepancy between the systems of relevance of the adoptive parents and the adopted child and the greater the long-term threat that emotional normalization as a differentiated interactive contribution will not be achieved.

Limited Emotional Normalization in the Narrative Accounts

One reason why some adoptive parents feel they do not satisfy their own norm of a parent–child relationship may be the fact that the realization of this norm is still very much an ongoing process. For example, a child who had been living with the family for only three weeks at the time of interview (six months old at the time of placement) is primarily experienced as a strain, because its eating problems throw the well-adjusted everyday family life with the first adopted child into disorder ("I sometimes think to myself, Christ, what a great time we had before he came along"). In this case there were already noticeable signs of the child's problems coping with the change of parental substitutes after the first six months of the child's life; the adoptive mother, for example, puts the child's increased spitting out back to its "adjustment" to the new situation.[44] In the case of a child placed for adoption at the age of six, on the other hand, there were so many layers of experiences of deprivation that at the time of the interview, one year after the child was taken into the family, emotional normalization seems no more than a distant goal. This child, who was taken away from its birth mother at the age of two because of neglect, lived with a very old foster mother for four years, a period only briefly interrupted by a renewed attempt by the birth mother to take care of her child. The child experiences the late allocation of its new parents as an arbitrary act,[45] which—in realization of an intense oedipal relationship to the adoptive father—it cannot accept with respect to the adoptive mother ("That's not the way I thought it would be, I certainly didn't want a mother like that"). As opposed to the histories of an early adoption, motherly attention does not focus on the aspect of the ability of the adoptive parents to love the child but on the question of when the child will be able to accept the parents.

The narrative interview presents an accumulation of conflicting attempts at normalization. Whereas the adoptive mother emphasizes that she does all she can to compensate for the child's developmental deficiency and enable behavior appropriate to the child's age, the child—in constant rebellion against the adoptive mother—fights to obtain "nice" parents who grant it everything it wants. The child's instability, which is rooted in its experience of being neglected by the birth mother and in its envy of other children ("belly children"), drives the adoption mother to the verge of exhaustion.

ADOPTIVE MOTHER: She gets into an *incredibly violent temper,* from one moment to the next; one minute she's *lovable* and settled *and then* she'll explode and start shouting at you, you see, she's an hourly, half-hourly shower, hot, cold, hot, cold, hot, cold. That's the way it goes all the time, you see?
INTERVIEWER: Hm . . .
ADOPTIVE MOTHER: And I reckon she's got such *incredible* ups and downs inside which she just can't harmonize [laughter].
INTERVIEWER: Hm, hm . . .
ADOPTIVE MOTHER: And I reckon I *must try* to *get rid of* all these difficulties, to help her . . .
INTERVIEWER: Hm, hm . . .
ADOPTIVE MOTHER: because that is *terrible, no one can stand* that, constantly living with this alternating hot and cold, can they?

The behavioral alternation between hot and cold is a symbol of the as-yet-unachieved predictability of the child's behavior. The requirements for emotional normalization, therefore, do not exist. Whereas the two cases considered so far show that the norm of the relational quality has not yet been fulfilled, two other examples point towards the relativity of the intensity of the emotional bond once it has been achieved. The dynamics of family constitution can trigger a momentum that leads away from the achieved emotional equilibrium. The adoption history of a girl taken in at the age of six months is a case of emotional normality that no longer exists to a full extent. Although the emotional bond developed with varying intensity during the ten years of adoption, the child drifted to a growing degree into the role of the stranger, surrounded by the birth children of the adoptive parents, surrounded by persons who resemble each other but not the adopted child. This produced a process of mutual definition, in which the child characterizes herself "as a different type" and this differentness is reinforced by the adoptive parents and the birth children. In her restlessness and "instability" the child is in constant need of motherly affection. However, whereas the adoptive mother arduously establishes emotional closeness, the polarization from the birth children is intensified. They act independently and do not burden the mother by taking up her time. The vicious circle between an unstable sense of self-esteem, "nerve-racking" attempts to establish contact, the repeated experience of rejection, the feelings of inferiority, and so on, is in full swing.

The following text passage reflects the intensity of emotional entanglements within the family. Whereas the adoptive mother tries not to present the child as a stranger, she at the same time again emphasizes the child's differentness.

ADOPTIVE MOTHER: I really do like her, I . . . I *am* fond of her . . .
INTERVIEWER: Hm . . .
ADOPTIVE MOTHER: the way she is.
INTERVIEWER: Hm . . .
ADOPTIVE MOTHER: I could never say that she is a stranger in our family . . .
INTERVIEWER: Hm . . .
ADOPTIVE MOTHER: or anything like that, what with her being so different. . . .

The polarization between birth child and adopted child would also appear to have produced a moderation of the previously achieved emotional normality in the following adoption case. A young boy admitted to a children's home at the age of two with serious health problems is taken into the family two years later after the woman who later became his adoptive mother developed "a hot line" to this child while working in the home. Looking back on the situation, even the adoptive mother herself describes the development of the emotional bond as a mystery:

ADOPTIVE MOTHER: I just don't know why I took to the little lad. He often causes me [laughing] so much trouble and gives me so many headaches. We're constantly at loggerheads.

Other passages in this narrative interview indicate that this woman, who was still waiting for a child of her own at that time, was fascinated by the child's "small and cute" attributes. The narrative as a whole is pervaded with sadness at the fact that this "smallness" and "cuteness" has vanished and that the child turned out to be a hectic and aggressive "rascal" who is not accepted by others.[46] The adoptive mother herself suspects that the emotional turnabout is connected with the pregnancy that began soon after the child was adopted. Tormented by a strong sense of guilt, she admits that the "emotional relationship to Jörg is not the same" as to her birth child. In this case the only solution is to withdraw into a kind of private normalization, coming to terms with one's own limitations. This approach, however, is clearly experienced as unable to satisfy the self-set norm of emotional bonding. The following passage could perhaps be described as a prototype of limited emotional normalization:

ADOPTIVE MOTHER: With all children you adopt, whether a foster child or an adopted child, who are a bit older, you *have* to assume that the sweet and cute side will disappear at some stage and that, er, there will always be difficulties. I also believe that when, er, I've reached a stage now when I say I accept this feeling inside me that I don't shout out "hooray, that's my son" or something like that, but . . . that I simply . . . *notice* the feeling inside me and that I have to *simply accept* it

Although both examples of a no longer existing emotional normality relate to families with an adopted child and birth children, one should not jump to conclusions and infer that the "mixed" family is more susceptible to relational problems. It seems fair to assume that the juxtaposition of adopted children and birth children in the various interaction relationships (adoptive parents–adopted child/birth child, adopted child–birth child) triggers polarizations and thus creates an increased awareness of the aspect of differentness. Conversely, "purely" adoptive families probably possess their conflict potential if, as can be seen in the case of the adoption histories relating to young children, the adoptive parents try to suppress the special status created by adoption and banish the awareness of the problem of differentness to such an extent that they fail to do justice to the adopted child's interest in cognitive and emotional management of its other genealogical origin.

Living with the Artificial Status Passage: Structuring the Awareness Context

Even if the experience of emotionality enables the adoptive family to achieve parity with the normal case at a constitutive stage, a number of problems associated with the differentness of the adoptive family status remain. These problems threaten to upset the balance of respective degrees of normality. The structural specificity of this type of family not only requires its interpretive management by the adoptive parents themselves with regard to their own persons and their identity as parents, but also raises the problem of how to deal with the relevance of their deviation from the norm in the context of social interaction. Considerations frequently revolve around the questions: Who is to be informed about the artificiality of the status passage? How great an insight should be afforded to others, including the adopted child itself? When should the special status be discussed and how should the subject be broached?

The preoccupation of adoptive families with information policy questions is connected with the fact that, in line with all the available "rules of membership categorization" (Harvey Sacks)[47] in our society, the social unit of parents and child is interpreted as a family in expectancy of a normal, biological family (the case of colored children is disregarded here).

In a country such as the Federal Republic of Germany, in which only about 0.7 percent of all children are adopted by nonrelatives, the existence of a common biological bond is generally taken for granted in the social unit of parents and child. In other words, to refer to a term used by Goffman, the adoptive family is categorized "within the primary framework"[48] of family. In many situations the problem facing the adoptive parents, therefore, of how to impart information boils down to the following question: Should I or should I not participate in the pretense of a "natural" family?

In accordance with the expression employed by Barney Glaser and Anselm Strauss I would like to term the management of this disclosure of knowledge via a potentially threatening piece of information as structuring of the awareness context.[49] In my view this concept, which was initially developed for the analysis of observations on dying patients (centering on the problem of whether to tell patients that they are going to die or whether to keep this a secret), is well suited for the purpose of analyzing the interactive articulation of one's own special status by a group that deviates from the normal case. Depending on the type of interaction partner I would like to examine the aspect of structuring the awareness context at three levels: the management of knowledge disclosure by adoptive parents (1) to interaction partners outside of the nuclear family, (2) to the adopted child, and (3) to the adoptive parents themselves—that is, the degree to which the adoptive parents make themselves aware of their special status. In addition, attention will focus on how the adopted child itself structures its own awareness context.

Structuring the Awareness Context towards Interaction Partners Outside of the Nuclear Family

The interviews provide a number of indications of a shifting trend of preference from the closed to the open awareness context. If the interviews are arranged in the order of the calendar year in which the child was taken into the adoptive family's home, we discover evidence of increasing efforts to come to terms with one's own special status and to make it readily acceptable to others by informing them of the true nature of the status passage. In historical terms, this process appears to have reached the stage at which this information is disclosed to persons who play a significant part in the family's everyday life (referred to henceforth as "the significant others"). Prospective grandparents and other relatives are informed about the plan. The significance of the notification of friends is also clearly detectable. In cases where neighbors are included in the open awareness context, however, reference is frequently made to certain pressures to do so resulting from the fact that the growing visibility in the case of the biological status passage necessitates a clarifying explanation of the circumstances of the artificial access to the parental role.

Whereas the prevention of an incorrect typification as a "natural" family would at least seem to be gradually becoming the maxim for interaction in communication with significant others, interaction with casual acquaintances or strangers is still experienced as a dilemma. The problems associated with another person's increasing degree of anonymity are connected with the fact that the construction of reciprocity is experienced as precarious. Casual contacts are defined as those that remain peripheral to one's own biographical management. The question, "What was your pregnancy like?" asked by another mother when looking into the child's stroller, for example, requires more than just the exposure of a deception—this itself could lead to embarrassment on both sides. Instead, to ensure a recognition of the equal status of the adoptive mother–child relationship, a more extensive involvement in the adoption history is essential, beginning with the decision to adopt prompted by childlessness right through to the successful establishment of emotionality. Confused by the harmlessly meant question, the adoptive mother will presume that the doubts she once harbored herself during a certain phase of the adoption history with regard to the overcoming of strangeness are also harbored by the other mother. These doubts would trigger a devaluation of the mother–child relationship, which the adoptive mother herself regards as being of equal status. She will fear that the other woman, in her limited role-taking capacity, would interpret an open declaration of the adoptive status as the adoptive mother's dissociation from her child. Taking into account the meta-perspective, therefore, the price for such honesty would be a sense of guilt towards the child.

The dilemma associated with the incomplete construction of reciprocity is addressed in many of the interviews, especially in cases where the child was taken into the family relatively recently. The problem is resolved, for example, as follows:

ADOPTIVE MOTHER: Of course, I didn't want to make a big issue out of the fact that it was our adopted child in front of a complete stranger.

The structuring of the awareness context reflects the anticipation of the adoptive parents with respect to their social normality classification. The practice of a closed awareness context is rooted in the assumption that recognition as a normal family is ruled out in the case of the open awareness context. Consequently, the only possible strategy of constructing normality is to participate in the pretense of normality. This strategy of normalization, of acting as if the family were a natural family—in short, the "as-if normalization"—is not, however, suited for a construction of reciprocity of perspectives with regard to adoption; the role-taking ability of others cannot be extended by structuring a closed awareness context.

The link between the structuring of the awareness context and the normality classification by others finds its expression in the case of the open awareness context in the fact that the empathy practiced by significant others forms the foundation for an extension of the open awareness context. At the same time, the communication of special status gives others a greater opportunity to construct reciprocities marked by the corresponding normality classification. In contrast to the "as-if normalization" I would like to call this strategy of normality construction, characterized by a clearly articulated differentiation of one's own type of family, as the "own-type normalization." The more this "own-type normalization" asserts itself, the less frequently adoptive parents will be confronted in the long term by the dilemma of truth-pretense, because they themselves will be helping to change the conditions for the social placement of adoptive families.

This study not only reveals that the "as-if normalization" and "own-type normalization" are chosen depending on the assumed normality classification. It also provides several indications that members of the lower class and of the lower middle class may be subjected to many more acts of discrimination than, for example, members of the upper middle class. Such a tendency would fit in with the picture that emerged in connection with class-specific adoption application ratios (see "The Traces of Social Status during Adoption Placement" in Chapter 2). If, as shown in the studies by Lee Rainwater (1959, 1960), the self-esteem of the lower-class female is very strongly linked with the realization of a pregnancy, it is conceivable that the reservations towards an alternative constitution of family in this social stratum are more persistent than, for example, in the upper middle class with its extended opportunities of self-realization.[50]

Irrespective of the exact nature of the objective conditions for a derogatory treatment of the adoptive status, the experience of discriminating probably results from a bilateral process of acts of discrimination by others on the one hand, and self-discrimination on the other. The two narratives from the lower class and the lower middle class, for example, the interviews that articulate the prejudice of others most, indicate that the adoptive mothers have not successfully come to terms with the feelings of inferiority they associate with their special status. It is not clear how far the experience of degradation is based on ascription by others or on projections. During the course of a self-fulfilling prophecy the closed awareness context may repeatedly turn out to be desirable. On the other hand, adoptive parents belonging to the middle and upper middle class emphasize without exception the lack of acts of discrimination by others. This leads to the assumption that they are able to draw from other interaction resources (social status, self-esteem) if they take the offensive by supporting their alternative constitution of family via an "own-type normalization."

Occasionally, their problem is not so much social degradation as elevation. An inadequate construction of reciprocity, for example, can also find its expression in the fact that adoption is transfigured by others as a "noble deed." The narrative passages repeatedly reflect the irritation of adoptive parents when faced by such an assumed motivation. It not only ignores the significance of parent-centered motives in the adoption history but also implies an attitude of self-sacrifice that does not comply with the parental experience of reciprocal bonding and emotionality as an enrichment of everyday life. Despite the fundamental opening of the awareness context with respect to the adoptive status in these cases, this opening is generally not effected to such an extent that personal motives and the intimacy of the relationship with the adopted child are included in communication with "less familiar others." Here too, therefore, the open awareness context is characterized by elements of closure.

Structuring the Awareness Context towards the Adopted Child

In order to construct normality within the family, adoptive parents have to decide how much importance should be attached to the child's awareness of its own origins. As opposed to the externally-oriented structuring of the awareness context, the problems here are located at a deeper psychological level. The key question for adoptive parents in this respect is how much relevance the birth parents should have in the child's life once the adoptive parents have replaced them by assuming "de facto parenthood."

In reference to König's concept of the "biological-social duality" (biologisch-soziale Doppelnatur) of family, I would like to characterize the adoptive family as a social-type family with double parenthood: social parenthood and—as is always the case in the background of family reality—biological parenthood. This structural peculiarity involves the conflict over real, authentic parenthood. The tension between the one set of parents and the other set of parents cannot be eliminated by a single act on the part of the adoptive parents. The solution to this problem accompanies the entire history of the adoptive family, irrespective of whether mention is made of the birth parents or not. Each of these two initial management possibilities triggers a chain of further decisions, the course of which cannot be determined by the adoptive parents alone but which is also shaped by the careful and persistent, unsuspecting or suspicious activity of the adopted child. This section will attempt to analyze the basic structural features of how this chain of action with its accompanying situational coercion evolves vis-à-vis the adopted child in both the closed and open awareness contexts. To begin with, reference will not be made to specific text examples.

If adoptive parents try to avoid rivalry over the issue of double parenthood by withholding information on the birth parents, they must accept that the adopted child will grow up a victim of a deception. In line with what this society takes for granted, it will classify itself as a birth child within the adoptive family and build up its ego-identity in an unbroken trust in that family bond. In order to keep the awareness context closed, constant efforts will be needed to ward off the danger that third parties who are aware of the "secret" might disclose this information to the child. Furthermore, like any other child who assumes that it is living together with its birth parents, the adopted child may occasionally trigger interaction sequences touching upon the subject of its birth and early childhood.[51] The adoptive parents will be obliged to take further deceptive action in order to maintain the initiated self-deception of the adopted child. This reproduction of the facade of normal family, which may have to be repeated on numerous occasions, may help confirm the position of adoptive parents in their sole parenthood. However, their efforts to negate the existence of the birth parents will undermine the foundation of their relationship with the adopted child. The price of this nonexistence of the birth parents is a breach of confidence towards the child. In the meantime, there is sufficient evidence indicating that this breach of confidence at the point of genealogical self-orientation, with all the concomitants required to safeguard the deception, is not of purely peripheral significance to the development of the identity of the adopted child.[52]

Whereas the closed awareness context with regard to the adopted child is to be understood as an "as-if normalization" strategy, the open awareness context cannot be generally equated with an "own-type normalization." The latter approach means that the adoptive parents truthfully no longer lay claim to sole parenthood; via the disclosure of the adopted child's other origin they provide the child with the opportunity of a continuous biographical orientation. However, the danger of a breach of confidence is still present. The initial disclosure may trigger complicated interaction sequences, during which the adopted child will generally demand more precise information on its other origin. The adoptive parents for their part will constantly have to reassess in each case how much information to divulge to "personalize" the birth parents. The opening of the awareness context can develop a highly unpredictable and dynamic momentum, because the child may initiate questions that again leave the adoptive parents facing the dilemma of how to answer them both truthfully and in a way conducive to the consolidation of the adoptive family bond. A variety of efforts to solve this problem can be observed between the interaction cornerstones of the desired relationship with the adopted child, the satisfaction of one's own needs, and the fulfillment of the demands— which are difficult to anticipate—on the child's identity formation. These efforts can lead to a further opening of the awareness context, to its continued closure, to its misleading further opening, and so on. The step towards the disclosure of the key biographical statement of the child's other origin still leaves the adoptive parents confronted by the problem of whether they should continue to claim sole authentic parenthood and exclude the subject of origin from future communication with the adopted child, with the accompanying risk of a breach of confidence, or whether they should build up a relationship of trust that also encompasses the existence of the birth parents, with the risk that the birth parents may "penetrate" deep into the reality of adoptive family life. Each further "prising open" of the awareness context means that the adoptive parents concede their own limitations as sole parents and acknowledge the relevance of the birth parents. It represents a step on the way towards constructing normality under the aspect of double parenthood—that is, towards an "own-type normalization."

The Significance of the Awareness of Origin from the Point of View of the Adoptive Parents. The policy of keeping the artificial status passage a secret would appear to have declined in proportion to the growing extent to which adoption has become a socially acceptable means of solving the problem of involuntary childlessness. Whereas there was still clear preference for the closed awareness context in two cases in which children were placed before 1970—in both cases the adoptive mothers were more or less obliged to tell their children that they were adopted[53] and were not really able to cope with this step—the interviews dealing with the adoption of younger children all reveal a tendency towards disclosing the adoptive status. The generally practiced openness towards the adopted child presented in this section, however, may not be typical for the situation in the Federal Republic of Germany as a whole, because most of the interview partners with young children adopted during the 1970s belonged to the discussion circle for adoptive parents. The proclaimed maxim of this circle was to inform the children about their adoptive status at an early stage with the aim of enabling them to grow up in the natural acceptance of the knowledge of their own origin.

Opening the awareness context towards the adopted child means accepting that knowledge of origin is relevant for the child. Which criteria are available to adoptive parents to determine relevance, however, when they try to solve a familial information problem for which there are virtually no institutionalized guidelines? A great deal would suggest that during the first few decades of this century the strategy of nondisclosure had the character of an institutionalized model, which was also supported in the field of social work.[54] If, as indicated by the narrative interviews in this study, the orientational power of this model has diminished this is not only due to the changed advisory practices of social work institutions. During the course of placement procedure, for example, the Hamburg adoption agency already recommends informing the child of the fact of adoption at an early age. Rather, the generally observable trend in Western society towards the realization of intimacy,[55] openness, and reciprocity[56] within the familial context, would appear to counteract the practice of a closed awareness context. For this reason our attention when analyzing the narrative passages concerned with the planning and implementation of disclosure work focuses on the following aspect: How do adoptive parents try to align the fact of double parenthood with their norms of establishing a relationship? Or, to put it another way, how do they try to determine the relevance of the knowledge of own origin against the background of the desired relational quality?

The significance of the knowledge of own origin is not generally explicated by adoptive parents in the interviews. It does not surface, for example, in the form of everyday theory explanations during the presentation of the disclosure work. This aspect is considered by the adoptive parents in terms of its practical side. Insofar as the opening of the awareness context takes place without external intervention, every communication towards the child relating to its origin can be interpreted as an event during which the adoptive parents rate the knowledge of the other genealogical origin as somehow relevant for the child. During the interviews the presented acts of disclosure, both those planned and those recapitulated, are very often associated with a pragmatic motive that enables a better circumscription of the uncertain relevance of the knowledge of own origin. In one case, for example, we find the following:

ADOPTIVE MOTHER: And as for the subject of adoption, *we felt it was important that she didn't find out about it in a roundabout way.*

Not in a roundabout way—this explanation lays bare a deeper level of grounding for parental action. The fact that adoptive parents wish to retain control over who opens the awareness context would indicate that they view the fact-of-adoption message as a piece of information for the child with possibly existential significance. They are thus keen to autonomously steer the course of communication that reveals the fact that they are not the birth parents. Via the envisaged monopolization of the right of initial disclosure, the parents intend creating a situation in which they exercise de facto parenthood by making themselves available to the child as interactants in the case of a potentially threatening piece of information. They create, as it were, the precondition for the fact that the content level[57] of the communication of the message is in their opinion anchored in the appropriate relationship structure and a breach of confidence avoided.

To judge by the interviews, adoptive parents quite often deduce that the aspect of origin is relevant for the adopted child from the experiences made by other adoptive parents who adopted a child ten or twenty years previously and let the children grow up in a closed awareness context. The descriptions of the incorrectness of this approach, with their key statement on the shock the child suffered and its embitterment about the breach of confidence on finding out about its adoptive status, are a pointer for the adoptive parents on the advisability of disclosing double parenthood for the sake of the child. In the following narrative passage the adoptive parents refer to the past experience of another couple:

ADOPTIVE FATHER: This friend then told you about . . .
ADOPTIVE MOTHER: That's right.
ADOPTIVE FATHER: that she is an adoptee herself and has got a brother, too.
    . . . He was told at a very late age, 14, or round about that age, he was going through puberty, already had plenty of problems, then he found out or was told about it somehow, and he was *absolutely distraught*; the way she explained it, it took a *long time* before he again built up a fairly reasonable relationship with his adoptive parents, and I feel that that was quite an experience at that time, or where people said "Look, that's what happens if you don't do it."

The accumulation of reference to examples of mistakes made by others in the past suggests that adoptive parents today dissociate themselves from the formerly practiced structuring of the awareness context, especially in the light of the observed consequences. Yet until a new institutionalized model exists for the management of double parenthood, the adoptive parents continue to derive the identity needs of their child with respect to its genealogical origin from the incorrect practices of others and to take these into account when constituting their own parent–child relationship.

The pragmatic motive of avoiding a breach of confidence is replaced in individual cases by more fundamental specifications of relevance for the disclosure of knowledge of origin, for example, "It's the child's right [to know]." Against the background of an emerging reorientation in the disclosure practice this argument could be interpreted as a further step towards the acceptance of an open approach to the question of the child's other origin. Formulated as the child's "fundamental right" to be informed about its origin, such a conception would probably reinforce the process of institutionalization, especially if it is based on knowledge about identity development. In the phraseology of Berger and Luckmann, the fundamental right version could be viewed as an indicator of a level of legitimation transcending explanatory schemes that are directly related to concrete action.[58] Its points of reference for the scheme of action may be able to promote the normative acceptance of the open awareness context.

Following this preliminary conceptional clarification we will take a brief look at the means of imparting the knowledge of origin before concentrating on the recapitulated chain of events surrounding the other origin in the narrative interviews. During the planning phase of the initial disclosure as well as during each further stage of communication on this point, the adoptive parents find themselves confronted by the following major problem: How can we communicate a potentially threatening piece of information in as "natural" a way as possible? Some parents hope that they will be able to pass on the information to the child as if it were "a matter of course," since they assume that the often-cited shock suffered by a child after having been told about its other origin is basically due to mistakes made by the adoptive parents—for example, by disclosing the information too late or much too dramatically. The interviews, however, show a number of examples in which the adoptive mothers in particular regard themselves as the possible obstacle to the realization of a "natural" communication situation. One adoptive mother, for example, describes her feelings in view of the disclosure situation she expects during the course of the next two years or so:

ADOPTIVE MOTHER: Sometimes I'm pretty worried, you see, what is likely . . . what is likely [to happen?]. . . . And let's hope that I stay natural and don't show any fear and so on, you see, [laughing] you get really tensed up in advance.

The struggle to ensure the naturalness of the communication situation, a struggle that becomes apparent in many of the interviews, can be interpreted as an attempt to frame the missing normality of the constitution of family in such a way for the child as if it represents normality.[59] The fact that this assumes the character of a paradoxical injunction demanding specific behavior[60] ("Be natural!") indicates the continuing sadness at the fact that the child is not a birth child. It also makes it clear that the normality of the information the parents wish to convey to the child is not properly anchored in the parental experience of normality. As the examples on the planned natural communication situation show, even an already successfully established emotional relationship would not appear to be able to overcome the sadness at the fact that the child is not a birth child.[61]

The natural communication situation is also set in relation to the developmental stage the adopted child has reached. When making the difficult decision of when the child is "ready" to be informed about its adoptive status, the adoptive parents quite often act in accordance with the maxim that the child is probably able to cope with the information when it addresses the problem itself. The following narrative passage can be viewed as representative of a number of other examples in this respect, illustrating how adoptive parents hope that the child will initiate the first opening of the awareness context.

ADOPTIVE MOTHER: Well, what we're hoping for is that we can tell her as early as possible, when the first questions come: "Was I in your belly too?" or something like that. . . . I should imagine that that's how it will happen, don't you think so, let's hope it's that easy, . . .
ADOPTIVE FATHER: Yes.
ADOPTIVE MOTHER: but only as far as they can understand it at that age, you see. . . .
ADOPTIVE FATHER: Or as far as they ask, you see.

The principle of initiation by the child as a safeguard for its sufficient cognitive capacity can—as shown by several narratives—also be applied to every further opening of the awareness context. With reference to an already effected impartation of information, for example, we find the following:

ADOPTIVE FATHER: We follow a very simple principle. We answer every question . . .
INTERVIEWER: Hm . . .
ADOPTIVE FATHER: which the child asks, but nothing more than is asked.
INTERVIEWER: Hm . . .
ADOPTIVE FATHER: It's not as if a single question is regarded as a spark which sets the whole story rolling. That would undoubtedly be wrong, . . .
INTERVIEWER: Hm . . .
ADOPTIVE FATHER: because the child would not be able to cope with that.

Although the autonomous asking of the question by the child gives adoptive parents a certainty of orientation, it also raises the problem that the child sets the "conditional relevances"[62] itself and the adoptive parents are maneuvered into the position of reacting parties. In this position they must not only be prepared to respond at short notice to the next initiation of disclosure by the child and to realize the planned natural communication situation, but they must also take the risk of having to modify their disclosure plan and venture the first step towards articulating double parenthood themselves if they wait in vain for the child to make the first move.[63]

The Biological Disclosure

The gradual opening of the awareness context often begins with a question usually asked by the child at the age of three: "Was I in your belly too?" Leaving aside the dramatic exceptions, the child generally accepts the negative reply, "It just wasn't possible, you were in another woman's belly," with composure—much to the relief of the adoptive mother. The child then carries on with whatever it was doing before. This recurrent pattern in interviews was recapitulated in particular detail by one adoptive mother who still includes the sadness associated with this disclosure in her description many years after the event. Against this background she conveys the emotional tension of that one moment in her detailed account of the scene.

ADOPTIVE MOTHER: And if I'm really honest, when I told my daughter I felt *tremendously* sad about the fact that she wasn't my own child, because she said to me . . .
INTERVIEWER: Hm . . .
ADOPTIVE MOTHER: the whole thing was *really* strange, I intended telling her right from the start, I'd more or less thought about what to say for *three years* and that really helped. If I hadn't, I would have told her a downright lie. I'll never forget the situation, it was a Sunday morning. I was drying my feet after taking a shower, she was three at the time and sitting in the corner on the washing basket, and the fact that I stood there in the nude must have prompted her. She suddenly asked "Was I in your belly too?" I would have loved to have said "yes," [laughing], it would have been so easy, wouldn't it. I said "no." She asked "Why not?" Then I said "That was another woman, I couldn't have you in my belly," or something like that and "I see," OK that was the first time.
INTERVIEWER: Hm . . .
ADOPTIVE MOTHER: That's the funny thing when you discover it's not all that important to children. . . .

In some cases, the adoptive mother explains this unruffled response to the disclosure by pointing out that during this stage in its development the child is unable to judge how normal or abnormal this fact is. One adoptive mother, for example, says of her four-year-old adopted daughter:

ADOPTIVE MOTHER: I don't think that it is, er, clear to her that she is a, that she belongs to a minority of children who grow up somewhere other than in, than . . .
INTERVIEWER: Hm . . .
ADOPTIVE MOTHER: with her birth mother.

The following example also shows how normal the disclosure is for a young child, who cannot as yet comprehend the links between family and the principle of filiation. The child initiated the opening of the awareness context itself during the pregnancy of the adoptive mother. The fact that she did not seem disturbed about having been in the belly of another woman whereas another child of the family was growing in the mother's belly, is explained by the adoptive mother as follows:

ADOPTIVE MOTHER: Yes, she, she found the idea quite *natural*. In the child's mind every family may consist of the children born by different women. She, she doesn't have any idea of what a normal family is at that age, . . .

INTERVIEWER: Hm . . .

ADOPTIVE MOTHER: at the age of two or two-and-a-half, does she? It could, therefore, . . .

INTERVIEWER: Hm . . .

ADOPTIVE MOTHER: quite well be normal for children born by different women to live in one family.

To judge by the experiences outlined in many cases, it seems relatively easy to establish a natural communication situation providing the still-young child views the disclosure as "natural" and as long as the way in which the adoptive parents communicate this information (facial expression, gestures, tone of voice) does not arouse suspicion on the part of the child. The history of one mother, who allowed herself to be carried away by birth fantasies during her first encounter with the child, shows that this is not always possible and that the suddenness of the child's interest can ruin the planned ease of communication. This mother begins her recapitulation of events surrounding the disclosure with the words:

ADOPTIVE MOTHER: And then came the biggest problem for me, er, telling my child the truth. . . .

Prompted by the pregnancy of a friend of the mother, the child addresses the subject earlier than expected. This time, the opening of the awareness context does not begin with a question, but with the assertion "Mom, I was in your belly too." The mother's negation of the assertion by referring to the "belly of another woman" caused the child to burst out in tears and claim that what the mother said just was not true.

There is one more case that deviates from the pattern of the natural communication situation. It also illustrates that it is not unimportant to the child whose belly it was in. The "gentle" opening of the awareness context planned by the adoptive parents to avoid a breach of confidence, the frustration of these plans, and the sense of deprivation experienced by the child, are reflected in the following interview extract:

ADOPTIVE FATHER: So we always stuck to the following principle: If we don't want our child to grow up living a lie we'll have to tell her the truth right from the start, . . .

INTERVIEWER: Hm . . .

ADOPTIVE FATHER: and . . . we didn't want to lie.

INTERVIEWER: Hm . . .
ADOPTIVE FATHER: For various reasons, therefore, we decided that, that's no
    good, that won't work, at some stage she will feel cheated, and then there
    will be real trouble.
INTERVIEWER: Hm . . .
ADOPTIVE FATHER: We wanted to confront her with truth gently right from the
    start. That wasn't as easy as we thought, as our son [the older son], who
    often felt, er, cornered by her . . . once said in a defensive position "Ha, ha.
    And I was in Mommy's belly and you weren't."
INTERVIEWER: Hm . . .
ADOPTIVE MOTHER: Well, not quite that bad.
ADOPTIVE FATHER: She *cried* out . . .
ADOPTIVE MOTHER: But there was something in her tone of voice.
ADOPTIVE FATHER: didn't she, she *cried* out . . . *terrible!*
ADOPTIVE MOTHER: She said "No," that. . . .
ADOPTIVE FATHER: [Worked up] Well, I never thought it possible that such . . .
    a two-year-old girl in such . . .
ADOPTIVE MOTHER: No, she was three at the time, but. . . .
ADOPTIVE FATHER: or between two or three, she *wasn't* three by then. She was
    so . . .
ADOPTIVE MOTHER: Hm, I don't know?
ADOPTIVE FATHER: small, that such a thing could be . . . so *significant* . . .
    important to such a young girl, . . .
INTERVIEWER: Hm, hm . . .
ADOPTIVE FATHER: that was something I just couldn't imagine.

The crying out of the child after her older brother had played his
psychological trump card must be seen against the background of the fact
that, contrary to all medical predictions, the adoptive mother had become
pregnant. The adopted child had witnessed and "experienced" the whole
course of this pregnancy:

ADOPTIVE FATHER: She also acted through the pregnancy with her doll. She
    pretended to breast-feed the doll and so on, didn't she?
ADOPTIVE MOTHER: She was really *direct,* with her whole femininity. *She also*
    fed a child, *really,* er, *intensively.*

The adoptive parents feel that the intensity of her reaction is due to the
fact that she was particularly vulnerable to her brother's remarks as a
result of her intensive involvement in the mother's pregnancy:

ADOPTIVE MOTHER: And I feel that it was then [during pregnancy] that a deep
    relationship to these natural events, you see . . .
INTERVIEWER: Hm . . .
ADOPTIVE MOTHER: already *showed* itself and that she therefore realized that
    she wasn't in my belly, you see, . . .
INTERVIEWER: Hm . . .
ADOPTIVE MOTHER: that what she had experienced in the case of her [younger]
    brother and what she . . .
INTERVIEWER: Hm . . .

ADOPTIVE MOTHER: had probably taken for granted in her own case, you
    see, . . .
INTERVIEWER: Hm . . .
ADOPTIVE MOTHER: that all that wasn't true, for her that was, I feel, a feeling
    of having been really cheated out of something.

The reaction to the existence of another belly ranges between the
extremes of feeling cheated or merely acknowledging an uninteresting fact.
The exact nature of this reaction depends on the concept of family already
developed by the child itself. If the child has already begun to incorporate
the aspect of growing up with its birth parents within its concept of a
"normal" family there will be a risk of a sense of deprivation as soon as it
discovers that it does not share this normality. If, on the other hand, it
cannot yet appreciate the difference between Mommy's belly and the belly
of another woman, the news of another origin will be treated as a relatively
uninteresting[64] fact and the child will maintain its natural attitude.

The Social Disclosure

Whereas the contours of the planned and practiced biological disclosure
of origin become pretty clear during the interviews, the subsequent opening of the awareness context is not so clearly depicted. In one third of the
cases under review one reason for this may be that in view of the adopted
child's young age, information of this kind can only be provided from a
planning stage perspective. Nevertheless, it already becomes clear at this
stage that the "belly of another woman" is easier to address in the
interview as a planned topic of the adoptive parent–child relationship than
information on the social background and motives of the actual birth
mother.

Many accounts briefly relate to the act of the relinquishment of the child
for adoption, which both in the planned and practiced mode of communication is presented to the child as an incontrovertible necessity: "She
couldn't keep you." After focusing for a moment on the birth mother as
the person forced to take this course of action for reasons that are not
explicitly named, the new parents proceed to the message,[65] "We wanted
to take care of you. And that's how you became our child," thus trying to
restabilize the child's orientation. This line of lovingly taking the child into
the adoptive family is presented in detail in many accounts, for example,
in connection with the desire repeatedly expressed by the child to discover
its story. This story, however, generally begins with the handing over of
the child, which often locationally and temporally relates to the children's
home in which the child first stayed. Although this reconstruction of
events may be suited for the young child, it is not unquestionably appro-

priate during the further course of the child's cognitive development to enable the child's self-orientation between "the other woman" and its adoptive parents. Whether there was a further opening of the awareness context, how this took place, who initiated it, which facts were disclosed, and which kept secret: all these aspects could not be reconstructed on the basis of the interviews in our sample, not even those with parents of older children.

Of course, the desire to ensure anonymity must be taken into account when pointing towards the gaps in the interviews. However, it also seems reasonable to assume that the step from the abstract "belly of another woman" to the specific person is not articulated as a topic for the adoptive parent–child relationship because the personalization of the other mother is perceived by the adoptive parents as a threat to their own parenthood. The further opening of the awareness context observable in some interviews, therefore, will be examined to establish the extent to which the assumed tendency can be confirmed or must be modified.

As demonstrated by a few examples, once the awareness context has been opened it can soon develop its own momentum and lead to a further opening via questions initiated by the child's inquisitiveness. The fact that the child dwells on its knowledge of the "other woman" is indicated by the question asked by the four-year-old child: "What does the woman do now whose belly I was in?" When the child is five or six, this may be followed by questions that reveal a new level of cognitive understanding of the family context and pose new problems to the adoptive parents: "Where is my mother?" or "Who is my mother?" and, finally, the tormenting question for the child, "Why?"

The "my mother" terminology often introduced by the child itself clashes with the language generally used by the adoptive parents, which draws the distinction between "the other woman" and "the mother" in order to avoid confusion over double parenthood. There are only a few examples of cases in which adoptive parents take up the ascription of maternal quality to "the other woman" as a signal to revise their own terminology.

ADOPTIVE MOTHER: She corrected me as a five-year-old, as I always, daft as one is, always said "the other woman" [laughter]. One day, I can still see her standing in the kitchen, she says to me "I've got a real mother." I first felt as if I'd been knocked on the head with a hammer, and I said "Why, am I a false one?" And then she looked at me and started grinning in an underhand way and said "No, not like the one in Hansel and Gretel."

The cases in which the customary terminological practice of adoptive parents is obstinately defended are more frequent, for example:

ADOPTIVE FATHER: We then avoided, er, talking about two mothers.
ADOPTIVE MOTHER: But all the effort was in vain. She still refers to, er, the one mother and the other mother and . . . well, *she* drew up her own picture of this mother right from the start, didn't she.

In another interview the six- or seven-year-old child is cited as having said the following:

ADOPTED CHILD: I don't mind you saying they are, that is the woman who had you in her belly, or the man, but for me they are parents.

The suffering involved in coming to terms with double parenthood is illustrated in the following case of a ten-year-old girl:

ADOPTIVE MOTHER: Things came to a head last year. . . . Suddenly . . . she became aggressive and drifted into a phase of defiance, well, we just didn't know what to do. She stood in front of me with clenched fists and shouted at me "I hate you!" . . . until she finally burst out "I've got two [sets of] parents."

These remarks shed light on the current stage in the development of the opening of the awareness context. The opening of the context is generally ventured with regard to the biological fact. In many cases, the role of the other woman or other man is reduced to that of child-bearer or progenitor. Although they are thus acknowledged as the starting point of adoptive history and as persons with a biological parental quality related to some stage in the past, they are not accepted in their ongoing significance for the identity formation of the adopted child. Many adoptive parents appear to believe that the disclosure of genealogical origin will help avoid the feared breach of confidence. However, they seem less prepared for the fact that this genealogical attachment is also accompanied throughout life by an effective social relational quality ("For me the other woman is my mother"). The danger that the child will feel injured also looms, therefore, wherever—in line with the terminological pattern—the awareness context has only been biologically opened.

The rigid insistence of certain adoptive parents on a carefully selected use of language and the equally obstinate dissociation of the child from kinship-neutral terminology makes one thing clear: The child-bearer and the progenitor acquire a different degree of relevance to that planned by the adoptive parents. The congruence of relevance systems is eliminated when, following the clarification of biological origin, adoptive parents hope that they will be ascribed exclusive parenthood, whereas the child itself is in the process of sharing out this ascription of parental quality. The opening of the awareness context with regard to genealogical origin signifies a first step towards an "own-type normalization." However, adoptive parents again slip into the problem of "as-if normalization" if they fail to come to terms with the problem of permanent double parenthood. The retention of terminological practice beyond the infancy stage can thus be regarded as an indication of the threat to their parenthood experienced by adoptive parents; this serves to corroborate the hypothesis mentioned earlier: As the "personalization" of the other parents harbors risks, efforts are made to avert the risks by not articulating this as a topic at all.

The widespread differentiation between the mother and the other woman can also be interpreted as representing a closure of the child's awareness context with regard to the parental quality of child-bearer and progenitor. As shown earlier by the possible responses by the child to terminological practice, the structuring of the awareness context may be limited to one particular phase in the life of the adoptive family. For the child is able to open the awareness context itself: A surging interest in its birth parents will initiate discussion on the subject of dual parenthood and, assuming that they are able to empathize,[66] steer the adoptive parents towards a changed concept of the other woman. During the following I will refer to five accounts relating to children who are already somewhat older (than seven), in which there are signs that, with one exception, the subject of the other parents has been jointly addressed by both the adoptive mother and the child during later childhood (after seven years).

Irrespective of the differences between the constellations of opening the awareness context to be discussed here, they all have one thing in common: How the birth parents are personalized depends on the quality of the relationship achieved between the adoptive parents and the child. If the point of emotional normalization has already been reached, the few examples of a further opening of the awareness context appear to indicate that adoptive mothers are able to initiate the discussion about birth parents from the child's perspective and assess its acceptability for the child.[67] If adoptive parents and the child, however, are still going through the phase of laboriously establishing clear mutual expectations and mutual acceptance, the personalization of the other parents can assume the character of degradation and—complementarily—self-upgrading.

The network of factors that can influence the further opening of the awareness context can be considered as follows. As the achieved quality of the adoptive parent–child relationship differs depending on how old the child was when it was taken into the family, it is also dependent on all those events that caused the early or late relinquishment of the child for adoption. The delaying of this step over a longer period by the birth mother, perhaps the withdrawal of the right of custody, especially without parental consent, are all factors that may have not just triggered a problematic development of the child's personality and thus prestructured a strained adoptive parent–child relationship. They may also create an image of the birth parents in the minds of the adoptive parents that, like a delayed reaction to neglect or cruelty, causes further strain for the adoptive child. This may happen when the parents who have been banished from the child's memory reemerge. The adopted child placed at an early age, on the other hand, would appear to be privileged in two senses. Apart from the relatively rapid achievement of emotional normality, there is a better chance of personalizing the birth mother as a good mother. Her decision to relinquish the child for adoption can be presented as a deed in the child's interest. The following five case examples illustrate how adoptive mothers realize the construction of reality with respect to the birth parents. The cases are arranged along on a line depending on whether the adoptive mother bases her presentation of the birth parents on factual information, conjecture, suspicion, or on nothing more than imagination.

The first account recapitulates the history of a child who was adopted a few days after birth. This case differs from all others in that the adoptive mother was a fleeting acquaintance of the birth mother and had a pretty exact idea of why the birth mother felt forced to relinquish her child for adoption. After the adopted daughter began to show greater interest in her origin at the age of six or seven, the adoptive mother introduced the same facts into communication with the child that had helped the adoptive mother herself understand the reasons for the action of the birth mother. She summarized the content of the recurrent discussions on this subject as follows:

ADOPTIVE MOTHER: She knew that the mother was good. She had decided to let the child live and that she . . . well, that she be handed over to grow up in a normal or proper home, to somebody who'd take good care of her.
INTERVIEWER: Hm . . .
ADOPTIVE MOTHER: She herself had three, that was the third, . . .
INTERVIEWER: Hm . . .
ADOPTIVE MOTHER: and her parents, I could tell her that already, were in the middle of getting a divorce, and she found out that she was expecting a child, and he said "It's not mine." And that must have bowled her over and she didn't want the child any more. But she said, she wanted to make sure that you are sent somewhere, and that was good and proper. . . .

I would like to refer to this opening of the awareness context as the truthful construction of acceptability for the child. The birth mother is described as a person faced by considerable difficulties during pregnancy. Despite all the pressures of circumstance explaining the birth mother's action, the reconstruction of this person for the child still contains, in the final analysis, a willful decision: She didn't want to keep the child. Falling back on the action motives anchored in the original family constellation, the adoptive mother can venture to present this final act by the birth mother without triggering a lack of understanding on the part of the adoptive child; the fact that the birth mother did not want the child is offset by the fact that she wanted the child to be properly taken care of ("that you are sent somewhere"). The remarks made by the adopted child while watching a TV film dealing with the fate of a number of children sent to children's homes by their mothers makes it clear that the child has accepted the image of the good mother: "But my mother would not have done that."

The next example relates to a boy who was taken into the adoptive family home at the age of three and who had previously lived in a children's home for two years following neglectful treatment by his mother. As opposed to the previous case, a mutual emotional bond proved difficult to establish, because the child—disoriented by the repeated change of reference persons—initially rejected the adoptive mother. Deeply rooted fears and intense aggressions led to a situation that was experienced as crisis-laden by the adoptive parents during the early stages of family life. The situation only improved after a definite sense of familial attachment developed.

The opening of the awareness context began shortly after the child had been taken into the adoptive family. The boy already indicated at the age of six that he would like to see his birth mother, saying that he would like to get to know his "proper" mother. After a certain waning of interest in his own origins, the crucial question of "Why?" again surfaced at the age of nine.

ADOPTIVE MOTHER: Well, it was *really bad* just under a year ago, and I don't
    know the reason, I even asked the teacher. He was *tremendously* preoccu-
    pied with the problem. *Again and again* he asked, er, "why couldn't she
    take me?" Not *who,* but "*why* did she give me away?" That was a . . .
INTERVIEWER: Hm . . .
ADOPTIVE MOTHER: pretty—*every* evening in bed. . . .

The young boy with an at least vague idea of contraception or abortion, then penetrates to a deeper level than the motives (whys) of the birth mother's decision to have him adopted. He raises the question as to why he came into existence. With recourse to the boy's own world of experience, the adoptive mother tries to make him understand how he perhaps came into the world. The preceding section of the interview continues as follows:

ADOPTIVE MOTHER: And "she could have—today you don't need to have
    children if you don't want them."
INTERVIEWER: Hm . . .
ADOPTIVE MOTHER: "And why did she want to have the child at all if she
    couldn't bring it up?" This question came *again and again,* every evening
    for weeks on end.

INTERVIEWER: Hm . . .
ADOPTIVE MOTHER: And then I said "Now listen"—I know of cases[68]—"take a look, for example, at this and that girl in the children's home. She wasn't much older, and she just couldn't cope with the situation. She, er, lived with her boyfriend and then, er, they didn't think about the consequences." OK, things were . . . alright then, but next evening the question came again.

In order to strengthen the boy's self-esteem,[69] which was damaged by the thought of having been given away for adoption by his birth parents, the adoptive mother constructs the image of a birth mother who "definitely loved you." However, as she is aware of the birth mother's repeated neglect of her child and sees this as the key to his fears, during the interview itself she relativizes the version of the loving mother she constructed to calm down her adopted son:

ADOPTIVE MOTHER: I told him again and again: "Now listen, . . . they definitely loved you too, but she just *could not* . . .
INTERVIEWER: Hm . . .
ADOPTIVE MOTHER: manage. She had to earn money," and, er . . .
INTERVIEWER: Hm . . .
ADOPTIVE MOTHER: I mean, that's not quite right, but, er, you try . . .
INTERVIEWER: Hm . . .
ADOPTIVE MOTHER: you try to see it a bit . . .
INTERVIEWER: Hm . . .
ADOPTIVE MOTHER: more positively.
INTERVIEWER: Hm . . .
ADOPTIVE MOTHER: And "She, er, just could not keep you."

In this case, the opening of the awareness context and its simultaneous closure (circumstances of relinquishment) are marked by considerable empathy contributions on the part of the adoptive mother, who—due to the lack of transparency concerning the true motives—resorts to conjecture and extenuating interpretations in order to help the adopted child understand the action taken by his birth mother. This well-meaning and amended construction of acceptability, however, leaves the birth mother as a shadowy figure, because the concrete description of the mother is limited by the degree of conjecture involved.

The adoptive mother's version of the birth mother's decision to have the child adopted culminates in the statement "She just could not keep you," because the pressures of circumstance most readily excuse the action of a birth mother whose chain of motives are not transparent. Whereas the adopted son, now ten, seems "content" with this "there-was-no-alternative" presentation, the adoptive mother expects new phases of unrest and inquisitiveness, as "he just can't come to terms with the idea that he was given away."

The third example, a child from a children's home placed between the ages of one and two years, involves a number of elements of disclosure already dealt with. The child itself opened the awareness context with regard to the parental quality "of the other woman" at the age of six ("So she's my mother too"). A phase of growing restlessness about the double parenthood set in when the child was nine ("It all came to a head last year"). The adoptive mother responds to the questions initiated by the child in an attempt at a well-meaning and amended construction of acceptability, which ran along the following lines with respect to the birth mother (who "abandoned" the child):

ADOPTIVE MOTHER: I *never* told her, for example, that her mother didn't want her, but explained to her that her mother didn't have a place for her to live. She didn't know what to do with her. "And she was probably in dire need when she . . .
INTERVIEWER: Hm . . .
ADOPTIVE MOTHER: took you to the children's home." I never stirred her up.
    . . .

Yet again there is reference to the pressures of circumstance that forced the birth mother to relinquish the child, accompanied by an aspect of suffering that points towards a bond between the birth mother and her child (dire need rather than not wanting the child). The amended presentation of the birth father assumes the form of a false opening of the awareness context, embedded in conjecture.

ADOPTIVE MOTHER: "And let's try and understand your father, who . . . didn't take care of your Mommy. Maybe he didn't know that you were born."
INTERVIEWER: Yes.
ADOPTIVE MOTHER: He certainly did know, for he has to pay, he *had* to pay. But that's the way I explained it to her. . . .

This distorted opening of the awareness context would appear to result from the fact that in the adoptive mother's version the birth father is a key figure explaining the distress of the birth mother, because he did not marry her. In another part of the interview this adoptive mother indicates that the illegitimacy of a birth is associated with feelings of guilt and shame in her everyday world orientation ("We assume that that is why the mother abandoned the child [no longer visited the child in the home] because she may have been ashamed of being pregnant again"). After triggering a similar perspective concerning the problematic role of the birth father, the adoptive mother is confronted by the daughter's tremendous aggressions against the birth father ("She indirectly called him a scoundrel because he didn't marry her mother"), her outbursts even extending to fantasizing about his punishment (she would like to "give him a proper clip round the ears").[70] Against this background the amended presentation of the birth father develops in the form of a rectification of the already initiated opening of the awareness context.

Whereas the acceptability of the birth father for the child continues to remain doubtful, a certain understanding for the birth mother develops via the presentation of the "act in the child's interest":

ADOPTIVE MOTHER: "And that's something we must also remember in your Mommy's favor. She said [in the children's home] "When parents come who would like to have a child then please ask them to take *you*."
INTERVIEWER: Hm . . .
ADOPTIVE MOTHER: And that was something she understood very well, and she also understood her mother better. And she, and since then she has never really had aggressive feelings towards her mother. . . .

The fact that the child is able to "settle down" inside following this version of the birth mother shows—as in the first example—that the child experiences the possibility of identifying with the good part of the birth mother as a relief. At the same time opening the awareness context in this way implies a certain legitimation of the role of the adoptive parents during a phase in family life at which they do not unequivocally possess such legitimation in the eyes of the adopted child (considerable aggression following the discovery of double parenthood, "I hate you"). The legitimation of the substitute parents derived from the good intentions of the birth mother acts like a link in the "adoption triangle" (consisting of the adopted child, the adoptive parents, and the birth parents), and enables the daughter to reconcile herself to the secondary placement.

The start to adoptive family life in the fourth case history was extremely difficult for both the adoptive parents and the child. The child, who had suffered great deprivation, was first adopted at the age of six and experienced the late allocation to its adoptive parents as an arbitrary act. The following opening of the awareness context must be seen against this background of divided feelings and rebelliousness on the part of the child and the still-outstanding "acceptance" by the adoptive parents. The point of emotional normalization is still a long way off when the psychologically exhausted adoptive mother first mentions the child's dark family history in an effort to make the child aware through this contrast with the past of her present privileged position. The child is told about this period of neglect, which preceded an officially enforced committal to a children's home at the age of two, as follows:

ADOPTIVE MOTHER: She was already with us for three months, yes, a good three months. And, er, we told her: Now look, we want to tell you what things *were* like when you were younger, and, er, we thought to ourselves we want to help you out of the situation, but you have to do your bit too, no *ifs and buts*. Then we told her that she had been neglected, got nothing to eat, had no diapers changed. . . .

Following this truthful construction of inacceptability the child works her way through to a conception of her own family past, which is reflected in the suggested dissociation from the birth parents:

ADOPTIVE MOTHER: And in autumn she said "My parents were not *at all* nice." I said "what do you mean?" "Well, you may say they are, that is the woman who had me in her belly or, or the man, but to me they are parents, and they were not *at all* nice not to take care of me. They could have at least done that!"

Finally, the child's question as to why she was rejected by her birth parents is answered by the adoptive mother herself, who takes into account the child's weaknesses and instability:

ADOPTIVE MOTHER: And three months later she said "Didn't they want to *have* me *at all?* They wanted to *have* me really, why did they do that?" I said "You just can't say." I just told her that she often says herself "That's boring. I can't be bothered," forget about anything repetitive, and putting on diapers, feeding the child and things like that *are repetitive.* I said "Christ, you know how *you* always feel. You don't *like* clearing things away, there are things you don't like doing, which you find boring. Your . . . the woman felt the *same* way. She didn't want to put on diapers *all the time,* that's not the way she thought things would be. She imagined a cute little baby, *looked forward* to the baby, but after *changing diapers* for *fourteen days, day in, day out,* and *always* feeding the baby, she was *fed up,* couldn't be bothered any more." And, er, well, she found it a little easier to imagine the situation. . . .

This opening of the awareness context on the basis of suspicions tries to secure an understanding of the inadequate motherly care (the action of "the other woman") via the construction of similarity between the mother and child. In this case, coming to terms with double parenthood can be seen as an attempt by the adoptive mother to ensure her own acceptance against the background of the failure of the birth parents. This account was given only one year after the child was taken into the adoptive family. It is, therefore, impossible to say whether this cognitive orientation towards darkness and brightness in her life will enhance the child's ability to accept her substitute parents, or whether the initiated identification with the negative traits of the birth parents[71] will leave this child uprooted in her efforts to establish a parent–child relationship based on trust. At the moment, the adoptive mother also notices "tremendous inner variations of temperature."

Although adopted children generally focus on their birth mothers, the final example clearly shows the importance in this respect of the father as the origin of life. The boy in this case knew his birth mother personally; she had neglected him and left him on his own in the mother-and-child home; however, she did visit him occasionally during his stay in the home and also got in touch with him when he was already living in a foster family. Her last visits were characterized by threats to take the son away from the foster family, if need be by force. The feeling of inner conflict within the child, of being torn between the birth mother and the foster family, dragged on for many years (Adoptive mother: "The boy paid the price for it almost four years") until adoption was eventually finalized. In his restlessness with regard to the questionable acceptability of his birth mother ("Is she odd?") the boy realizes at the age of eight or so that he must also have a father. In an act of role-taking for her child the adoptive mother opens the awareness context by truthfully explaining:

ADOPTIVE MOTHER: I'll tell you what though, Peter, your father, he . . . we don't know who he is. But he must have been a great kind of person; after all, you are a great little man, and I'm sure you take after him. . . .

This fantasized construction of acceptability[72] has a soothing effect: the "somehow valuable" father boosts the child's self-esteem, for which he is no longer dependent on the birth mother. The preceding interview extract continues:

ADOPTIVE MOTHER: And that really did him good, for he now has the feeling that he may well be a fantastic person by birth, without having to relate to his mother. . . .

These case histories reveal how important it is for the development of the adopted child's identity that the child also "accepts" itself—regardless of the quality of relationships in the adoptive family—as the child of the birth parents. As shown by these examples, both the truthful, the well-meaning (amended), and the fantasized construction of acceptability[73] can lead the child towards the point of identification with its origins. Nonetheless, the approach chosen by the adoptive parents to personalize the other parents is not irrelevant to the child. Because the truthful construction of acceptability is most conducive to a concrete reconstruction of the birth parents, priority should be given to this approach in this context, providing a number of requirements have been met. Of course, extreme phenomena, such as neglect or even cruelty against the child, would, taken at their face value, only seem suited to induce a child's negative identification with its birth parents.

However, if the adoption agency is able to subordinate its often predominantly middle-class value orientation[74] in favor of an open-minded approach to the other sociostructural conditions affecting the decision to relinquish the child for adoption, and if the agency is able to convey to the adoptive parents the extent of objective strain and subjective suffering experienced by the birth mothers when relinquishing their children,[75] there is a chance that greater background knowledge could trigger greater understanding and thus initiate the truthful construction of acceptability. What adoptive parents often label "terrible circumstances" in their accounts when referring to the birth parents may well be a manifestation of a situation of social need, which members of the middle class all too readily view in isolation from its origins and tend to regard as an expression of individual incompetence. The accumulation of experiences of deprivation discovered in a further study on birth mothers[76] should—conveyed via the social bureaucracy—enter into the perspective of the adoptive parents. This would prevent them from speaking of the bond between the birth mother and the child in a well-meaning and amending, supposedly counterfactual, manner, and would allow this important message to be conveyed as the truth.[77]

An opening of the awareness context that falls back on deeper social causal factors must, of course, be carefully coordinated with the cognitive and emotional development of the child. Regardless of when the final step in the reconstruction of the birth parents can be handled by the child in the opinion of the adoptive parents, it would be useful if the adoptive parents themselves were provided with more detailed background information. The description of the life of the mother and child during the few hours between the announcement on the phone, "We have a child for you," and the first encounter with the child, for example, is hardly likely to satisfy this need. The lack of information on the other origin and the child's early history occasionally criticized in the narrative accounts is not simply an economical shortening of procedure—this would only then be justified if the social bureaucracy could assume the possibility of an "as-if normalization."[78] It also comprises a false basis for the management of double parenthood: By economizing on background information the adoption agency encourages the vague reconstruction of the birth parents and, without realizing it, creates the potential for damage to the identity of the child,[79] which sees itself severed from its origins.

The Significance of the Awareness of Origin from the Point of View of the Adopted Child. Following the initiation by the adopted child to disclose more information about its origin, the relevance of the knowledge of origin, which was initially perhaps vaguely assumed by the adoptive parents, becomes a certainty. The fact that the clarification of genealogical origin is of key significance to the child's identity formation, however, is not only reflected in questions. The desire for a concretization of the other mother or parents may even make the child or "adoptee"[80] want to visit its closest blood relatives. Alongside the few short narrative passages dealing with the event feared (rarely accepted) at some time in the future, alongside occasional references to planned or realized attempts to block (rarely encourage) this event, and, finally, alongside the hope that a bond triggered in such a way will have no more than a limited significance for the child, there is only one example in this study of a reunion[81] with the birth mother prompted by the adoptive mother. This, however, is also the only adoption history that already covers the adolescent phase. The following narrative passage reflects how the adoptive mother suspects the growing restlessness of her daughter about the lack of clarity regarding the definition of her own identity and how she feels that her suspicions are confirmed by the child's behavior:

ADOPTIVE MOTHER: I mean, she had . . . I noticed that that she wasn't indifferent to the fact for quite some time, when she was 13 . . . that was when she was confirmed . . . she picked out the verse "And shall I wander in the valley of darkness." Oh dear, oh dear, I thought to myself, that must mean something. And during the confirmation [the recent adoption of a child by an aunt was being discussed at the time] Petra said to me "She [the aunt] shouldn't start thinking that that's so easy. It's a stupid feeling if you have to start wondering about where you come from," or something like that. I said "I know." That really caused her a lot of worry. She then said "What do you know about it?" I said "To begin with, I can imagine what it's like, and, second, I drew my conclusions from your, er, confirmation citation," and then she said "Ah well, I've got over that now."

INTERVIEWER: Hm . . .

ADOPTIVE MOTHER: She said "and that's all over" or something like that. And then she, oh yes, and then I said to her "Your mother's in the telephone directory, and if you want to"—she was twelve or so—"if you want to, I can help you," and then she said "No, no, I'll do that on my own." And as I was aware of how long my daughter takes to get around to doing certain things, I knew that that would take a long time, and it took another two years, and then she started. . . .

The reunion itself is recapitulated by the adoptive mother in reference to its significant outcome:

ADOPTIVE MOTHER: She came back and said "Thank God that I'm not there . . . that you're my mother."

As shown by the more recent literature on adoption, the phenomena exposed by this example can be analyzed from a more general perspective. To supplement the information gathered in this study on the structuring of the awareness context with respect to the adopted child, I would therefore like to briefly incorporate the cognitive and emotional management of the problem of double parenthood by adolescents as described in this literature. I would like to propound three theses demarcating the nature of the adolescent's management of special status associated with the task of self-identification.

Thesis no. 1: Adolescent adoptees are generally keen on a concretization of their idea of the birth mother or birth parents in order to discover their identity via the knowledge of their own origin.

The sentence in the afore-mentioned narrative passage, "It's a stupid feeling if you have to start wondering about where you come from," brings a problem into focus that only started to draw greater interest following the work by Erik H. Erikson. Sensitized to the hardships facing the child or adolescent who feels different[82] because of genealogical problems— Erikson himself only discovered at a very late stage in life that the man he thought was his father was not his father at all[83]—he developed his theory of the identity crisis that has to be overcome at three levels: the psychobiological, the psychosocial, and the psychohistorical level. Whereas in his concept of the psychohistorical side of identity Erikson even related to historical time, "the historical moment,"[84] other researchers have approached this aspect under the specific aspect of genealogical history and tried to render it fruitful for the discovery of identity in adoption.[85]

In the last case example cited, the adoptive mother helps the daughter handle her psychohistorical identity work.[86] She not only drops the hint on how to find the birth mother (telephone directory) but also draws up a genealogical tree for her daughter dating back into the 19th century, whose power of orientation during the period of inner conflict is often mentioned in the narrative interview.

The desire for a concretization of the image of the birth mother or birth parents becomes particularly clear in the supplementary survey of older adoptees: "During their lives all interviewees had more or less given serious thought to their special status and their birth parents."[87] Of the 19 adoptees, 12 actively tried to find out more about the birth parents, and a reunion took place in five cases.[88]

The desire for a clarification of genealogical origin is reflected in a particularly drastic way in a multitude of studies on North American adoption practices. The extreme denial of the significance of knowledge of own origin (the "sealed record," the adopted child's birth certificate sealed for all time[89]) created a conflict potential that, as if in a "natural" experiment, exposed the relevance of knowledge of own origin.[90] Adoptees fought against all legal barriers to try to find their birth parents; they took legal action to be allowed to look at their birth certificates; they joined together to form a movement that tried to make it a basic right of adoptees to know about their origin.[91] The clarification of genealogical origin has become a manifesto whose realization has already produced commendable organizational structures: adoptees and birth parents are provided with practical information on how to find each other.[92]

The significance of genealogical search for the identity is reflected in numerous adoptee documents.[93] A particularly instructive study is the autobiographical account by Betty Jean Lifton, who—after being psychiatrically categorized as neurotic—was only then able to resolve the problem of "the two egos" after she found her birth mother.[94] The response to her book by adoptees shows that her story can be regarded as an exemplary accomplishment of the "psychohistorical dimension of identity."

Following this presentation of a number of facts surrounding the search for one's roots, let us again turn to the more general significance of the phenomena observed in adoption. An examination of literature on this subject has shown that the surge of interest in blood relatives during adolescence is a step towards a clarification of identity, for which genealogical origin is clearly a highly significant factor. Our society may try to play down the significance of kinship ties[95] without, however, being able to infer from the limited current relevance of certain relatives for the realization of the biographical design that the genealogical line does not have a guiding function for the grounding of ego-identity. As long as the transparency of "descent" is given there may be no awareness of its power of orientation. The confrontation of the adoptee with an unknown genealogy draws attention to the attachment to the line of descent that also exists in but may not be realized by the biologically constituted family. The suffering caused by the childlessness in marriage, especially the suffering of the prospective adoptive mothers, finds its equivalent in the suffering of adolescent adoptees. The validity of the principle of filiation breaks through in two phases: one documents the suffering caused by missing consanguinity, the other the suffering caused by the broken line of descent. Both aspects symbolize an anthropologically significant phenomenon, which remains hidden in the "normal case" of the biologically constituted family. Once again, this confirms the indicator function of the deviant case.

Thesis no. 2: Adolescent adoptees search for the knowledge of their own origin regardless of the relational quality achieved with their adoptive parents.

The attempt to establish an anthropological grounding of the interest in kinship already suggests that any linking of curiosity with a problematic adoptive parent–child relationship is oversimplified. In the last example cited, the empathy contributions by the adoptive mother in themselves indicate a firm emotional bond. A study by Petra Speck also shows that adolescent adoptees are not prompted to search for their "better" parents by any deficits in the adoptive parent–child relationship. She confirms that in the majority of cases the initiation of active steps to find birth parents generally occurred in adoptive families in which the quality of the adoptive parent–child relationship could be described as "very good to average." In the group of adoptees who remain "bogged down" in the mental preoccupation with the birth parents, on the other hand, there would appear to be quite a few cases in which "the problems with the [adoptive]

198 The Adopted Child

parents cover up the problems with genealogical origin and reduce interest in this subject.''[96]

The absence shown here of a link between genealogical interest and the quality of the adoptive parent–child relationship does not yet appear to have been adequately realized by adoptive parents. The anxious question ''What have we done wrong?'' asked by the adoptive parents when the adopted child expresses its curiosity about its origin is already anticipatorily hinted at in an interview relating to a baby in our study. The adoptive parents in this case express their doubts about the meaningfulness for the child of painful examinations to determine paternity:

ADOPTIVE FATHER: Yes, even though we're not interested in having it done. This paternity procedure, from our point of view, I don't know whether it's going to make his happiness complete when he's, say, 21 or 18, the fact that he knows who his father is. No, I reckon that something must have gone wrong here [in the adoptive family] if it's that important to him. . . .

It would be beneficial to the management of double parenthood if the interest shown by adoptees in their origin were not to be burdened by the interpretation of this act as a failure of the adoptive parent–child relationship, a failure that is interpreted in retrospect as a devaluation of the relational history.

Thesis no. 3: The relational quality achieved between adolescent adoptees and their adoptive parents does not generally suffer—in the long term at least—as a result of the search for origin.

Through its knowledge of own origin the adoptee is able to accept the adoptive parents at a more mature level. The search for the birth mother or birth parents can be coped with psychologically in the biographical recapitulation as a mere episode. Knowledge of one's origin or, in more concrete terms, seeing and touching the person(s) with whom the adoptee has a genealogical bond, removes the ''nimbus'' of the ''other parents'' and redefines them as parental interaction partners with limited significance.

The conflicts of the adolescent adoptee associated with the search for its birth parents, its sense of guilt towards the adoptive parents,[97] and its uncertainty about the outcome of the project, can lead to a short-term distancing from the adoptive parents. The sadness of the adoptive parents at the adopted child's genealogical interest has repeatedly contributed towards inducing the adoptee to carry out its search for birth parents without the knowledge of the adoptive parents.[98] Mirror-inverted to the cover-up tendencies of the adoptive parents, the adopted child has also established a closed awareness context vis-à-vis his or her adoptive parents in order to cope with the confrontation with the principle of filiation and to realize the "own-type normalization." In the meantime, many adoption studies have shown that the search for birth parents does not produce rivals to the adoptive parents. In fact, after the tension of the first encounter between the birth parent(s) and the adopted child has been dispelled, the birth parents provide the adoptee with the certainty of orientation it needs to discover its true identity. This in turn enables the adopted child to accept its adoptive parents more unreservedly as parents.[99] This certainty of orientation is not only provided by the birth parents via discussion with the birth child and giving it an insight into their life history and the motives for their decision to relinquish the child for adoption. To be seen and touched—it may sound like magic—would also appear to represent a finalization of the search for origin.[100]

Many adoptees were themselves surprised to discover that the birth mother or birth parents did not become the significant future interaction partners they had initially expected.[101] Just as a large number of adoptive parents reduce the parental quality of the birth parents to the role of child-bearer and progenitor, many adoptees would also appear to be content with this part of the parental personality[102] once the step has been taken from the abstract notion of "the belly of another woman" to the actual person. In retrospect it is then possible to classify the search for birth parents as an episode,[103] whose biographical relevance consists of having clarified the question of origin.

The three theses explicated here are able to provide relief for adoptive parents in their management of the problem of double parenthood. The acceptance of the "naturalness" of the search for birth parents can relieve adoptive parents of the (assumed) need to repress the child's interest and thus exclude a subject of key significance for the child from communication. A realization of the fact that the child's interest is not dependent on the relational quality achieved between the adoptive parents and the adopted child can prevent them from rating themselves as failures in their parental role when the child is preoccupied with and takes steps to see its "other parents." Finally, the realization that the search for birth parents does not pose a threat to their parental quality can give them the imperturbability enabling them to allow the child to "go its own way" in its endeavor to discover its identity. What is now needed in the light of all the numerous adoption studies published during recent years is an opening of the awareness context by adoption placement agencies as well as by adoptive parents in order to ensure that the organization of the status passage to parenthood is organized as a status passage to double parenthood right from the very start.

Structuring the Awareness Context towards Oneself

Finally, the structuring of the awareness context will be examined at a third level, the level at which the adoptive parents interact with themselves. The cognitive management of one's own differentness is linked with, albeit not fully determined by, the structure of emotional experience developed between the adoptive parents and the child. The following presents a number of the interplay variants between emotions and cognition, beginning with successful emotional normalization and then moving on to limited emotional normalization.

The experience of emotional bonding can mean that achieving parity with the normal case is not limited to the emotional quality of the adoptive parent–child relationship, but is followed by a negation of other differences to the normal case of family constitution. Adoptive parents can also close the awareness context with regard to their own persons.[104] The host of statements such as "the child is like a child of our own" or "I'm no longer even aware of the fact that it's an adopted child" makes it difficult to determine whether these remarks merely reflect the newly developed sense of a familial attachment or a closure of the awareness context with regard to oneself. For the sake of clarity, the following will exemplify the tendency towards the closure of the awareness context in this respect by relating solely to those statements that reflect a minimizing of the biological difference.

In five of the 30 narrations it could be observed that the adoptive mothers almost practiced a demythologization of pregnancy and childbearing. These women, for example, all of whom had not given birth to children themselves and who experienced a fast emotional bond to the still-young infant, all too eagerly refer to descriptions given by birth mothers negating the significance of pregnancy and childbearing experiences. In one case, for example:

ADOPTIVE MOTHER: And friends, who . . . who all . . . who have their own children, have told me that the relationship between a mother and her child is not necessarily—a *birth* mother—is not necessarily *immediately* there and "That's growing inside me, and what comes out is the greatest experience on earth and pregnancy and giving birth to a child is the most beautiful thing, well that's something you can do without," some say.

The minimization of the biological difference visible here[105]—cautiously presented in citations of what others have said—can be interpreted as the attempt to also move level with the normal case in terms of the relevance of biological processes and to normalize the social motherhood of the period before the child was taken into the adoptive family's home. This mode of management constructs an equivalence with regard to the normal case at the emotional and the biological level. The closed awareness context towards oneself is the "as-if normalization" extended into one's own theoretical management of family.

In the interviews there are only isolated instances in which the awareness context can be emphatically kept open towards oneself even in cases of successful emotional normalization. In the extreme case one's own special familial status may be coped with in such a way as to make the normal case uninteresting as a model:

ADOPTIVE FATHER: The relationship between the parents and the children is, of course, probably a different one than between parents and their own children. I should imagine this could be objectively confirmed. We, at any rate, er, thought about this quite often and realized that it's an advantage to have a child where you don't always look for the characteristics of one or the other parent.

ADOPTIVE MOTHER: And abilities, am I right?

ADOPTIVE FATHER: Abilities.

ADOPTIVE MOTHER: Or dispositions. Right from the start, therefore, you have a certain, er, distance to the child, not emotional but mental distance. The fact that it's a completely different person than you are yourself, you understand? And that helps develop a relationship with the child on a much freer basis.

INTERVIEWER: Hm . . .

ADOPTIVE FATHER: We thought about what it would be like if it was our own child, didn't we? Always thinking he's got his father's this or the child has got his mother's that, you know what I mean?

INTERVIEWER: Hm . . .

ADOPTIVE FATHER: All this looking for what's there, you see?

INTERVIEWER: Hm . . .

ADOPTIVE FATHER: There's none of that. There's no, er, what you often think of, a possessiveness . . .

ADOPTIVE MOTHER: Yes.

ADOPTIVE FATHER: one's own child, my flesh and blood or something like that, er, such a feeling is also probably, tends to get in the way of a relationship based on true partnership.

Even if this interpretation of the "preferability" of adoptive family life must also be rated as just as much a rationalization as the already considered tendency towards a nihilation of pregnancy and birth, there is nevertheless a need to clarify why the repression work amounts to a minimization of the biological difference in the one case and a maximization of this difference in the other. The comparison between the two modes of management would suggest that reference could be made here to a number of hypotheses put forward in earlier sections of this study* to

*"The Traces of Social Status during Adoption Placement" in Chapter 2 and "Structuring the Awareness Context towards Interaction Partners Outside of the Nuclear Family" in Chapter 4.

clarify the difference, the hypothesis of the greater power of orientation of
pregnancy and birth in the lower social strata, the hypothesis of the greater
deprivation triggered by childlessness,[106] and the hypothesized link between interaction resources and strategies of normalization. There were
already indications that members of the higher social strata back their
alternative constitution of family more offensively and with an emphatic
distance to the model of normality (see "Structuring the Awareness
Context towards Interaction Partners Outside of the Nuclear Family"
earlier in the chapter). Whereas with one exception the tendency to
minimize the biological difference could be observed in the narrative
interviews rendered by members of the lower middle class and the lower
class, the narrative passage containing the presentation of the superiority
of the special status of the adoptive parents is rendered by members of the
upper middle class. In the latter case both the adoptive mother and the
adoptive father are able to fall back on respected occupational activities
and other symbols of success when they free themselves from the fixation
on the normal family case. The congruence with the normal case at the
level of relational emotionality is not utilized to achieve parity with the
dominant family model, but to stress the exceptional quality of one's own
family model. Via their "mental distance" the adoptive parents in this
case practice the "own-type normalization" towards themselves.

Whereas the means of structuring the awareness context dealt with so
far were each accompanied by a successful emotional bond, cases in which
emotional attachment can no longer unquestioningly be assumed to exist
only permit one mode of structuring: open, or to be more precise, an
exaggeratedly open awareness context. This denotes a situation in which,
as reflected in two narrative interviews, the permanent typification of the
child as a stranger and as problematic itself represents a further step
towards preventing emotional normalization. The awareness of the differentness of the adoptive family situation can become so extreme that the
resultant construction of reality itself has a denormalizing effect.

*The Interdependence of the Structuring of the Awareness Contexts
towards the Various Interaction Partners*

The strategies of normalization towards the various interaction partners,
which have been discussed separately so far, can merge into an overall
strategy in individual cases. The consistency of this structuring of the
various awareness contexts will depend on the answer to the crucial
question of how the classification of the normality of the special family
status by other members of society is anticipated. Those who participate
in the pretense of normality because they are unable to imagine that others

will classify the alternative constitution of family as normal, will work towards structuring the awareness of adoptive family reality towards others, towards the adopted child, and toward themselves "within the primary framework." Those who are willing to openly typify themselves as different in the belief that only this form of self-typification will be able to do justice to the structural peculiarity of the adoptive family will introduce this conviction of the legitimacy of differentiation into communication with the child, with others, and with themselves. What is more, those who demonstrate this preference will also feel that the realization of normality is possible even following a transformation of the framework. The internal consistency of the overall strategy can be illustrated with reference to the data of the following two contrasting examples.

The first interview was conducted with a lower-class couple, which took in a child aged seven months (eight years old at the time of the interview) because of involuntary childlessness. Referring to the awareness context towards interaction partners outside of the family the adoptive mother states that, although everyone knows about the adoption in the village where the grandmother lives a few hundred kilometers outside of Hamburg:

ADOPTIVE MOTHER: No one knows it here.
INTERVIEWER: Hm . . .
ADOPTIVE MOTHER: After all, he was three years old when we moved here.
INTERVIEWER: Hm . . .
ADOPTIVE MOTHER: And why . . . why should we tell people, hm?
INTERVIEWER: Hm . . .
ADOPTIVE MOTHER: That's nobody's business.

Explaining the disclosure of the fact of adoption to the adopted child the adoptive mother says:

ADOPTIVE MOTHER: And we told Dieter at that time . . .
ADOPTIVE FATHER: Before he started school.
ADOPTIVE MOTHER: before he started school, the people at the welfare office advised us to, didn't they, . . .
INTERVIEWER: Hm . . .
ADOPTIVE MOTHER: that, er, that it's better for us to . . . to tell him as parents than if he were to find out by some *silly* coincidence from someone else.
INTERVIEWER: Yes, hm . . .
ADOPTIVE MOTHER: And we already told him when he was five.
INTERVIEWER: Hm . . .
ADOPTIVE FATHER: That's right.
ADOPTIVE MOTHER: And he's grown up with that knowledge, but . . . it doesn't *interest* him, does it?

The closed awareness context towards others and the opening of the awareness context initiated towards the child by the welfare institution, the significance of which has so far been neutralized by the boy's outward disinterest, is accompanied by a tendency on the part of the adoptive parents to close the awareness context towards themselves. The adoptive mother emphasizes the fact of achieving parity with the normal case in terms of emotionality and that—in her opinion—a pregnancy is not superior to adoption in this respect. She backs up her claim of the limited significance of biological processes by referring to a hearsay case of a cesarian birth following which it took a year and a half before the birth mother could develop any relationship with the child.

As opposed to this example, which is perhaps the closest to a pure version of an overall strategy of "as-if normalization," the following case history represents a counterpole. For genetic reasons a couple from the middle middle class decided not to have a child of their own and, with pronounced child-centered orientations, they initially adopted a healthy child and then a handicapped child two years later.

The awareness context towards others is open. The first adopted child was told at the age of two years and three months, when the second child was adopted, that it came from a children's home. It repeatedly asked to be told about the story of how it was taken into the family. The further opening of the awareness context is planned with the intention of helping the children understand the action of the birth parents. This adoptive mother is the only woman to express her conviction that it is "definitely best" for a child if it is able to stay with its birth mother. In comparison with the other cases in this study she reveals an astonishing degree of empathy with birth mothers ("I can imagine that it's endlessly bitter to bear a child for nine months and not to be able to keep it afterwards"). Both the adoptive mother and the adoptive father want to bring up their children in such a way that they can develop autonomous personalities, who—in the event of an interest in the birth parents—will be able to make use of all available possibilities to get in touch with them. The openness of the adoptive parents towards others and towards the children is supplemented by their efforts to construct an open awareness context towards themselves. First of all, here is the example of the adoptive father, who changes from the subject of establishing an emotional bond to the aspect of cognitive management:

ADOPTIVE FATHER: As long as the child's not there you're preoccupied with this problem [with the question of whether an emotional bond will develop], but once the child is there . . .
INTERVIEWER: Yes . . .
ADOPTIVE MOTHER: Yes.
ADOPTIVE FATHER: and you establish contact with the child, then it disappears without trace.

ADOPTIVE MOTHER: Hm . . .

ADOPTIVE FATHER: And then you've got, I'd say, exactly the same feeling as, er, parents have towards their *own* children, you see?

INTERVIEWER: Hm . . .

ADOPTIVE FATHER: And, er, you mustn't . . . shouldn't fool yourself that it *is* your own child. Some do, and then have trouble dropping the idea afterwards.

The attempt discernible in this case to avoid structuring the awareness context towards oneself under the false guidance of the experience of emotional normalization becomes even more apparent in the narrative contribution of the adoptive mother. This woman, who presents a detailed description in another part of the interview of her emotional response to the experience of the child's affection, outlines the difficulties she has in coming to terms with the special adoptive status once she has got used to an everyday routine of familial attachment. In the following narrative passage she establishes a link between the early opening of the awareness context towards the child and the structuring of the awareness context towards herself. In the light of her observations of the two-and-a-half-year-old adopted child, which already showed a keen interest in its story at such an early age, she formulates recommendations on how to cope with the special adoptive family situation, against the background of her own personal experience.

ADOPTIVE MOTHER: Maybe it [my experience] should be a *really important* lesson to other parents, well . . .

INTERVIEWER: Hm . . .

ADOPTIVE MOTHER: a lot more was going on at the age of two and a half than I thought possible, you see, . . .

INTERVIEWER: Hm . . .

ADOPTIVE MOTHER: because the question is asked again and again: When should you deal with the subject [of disclosing the fact of adoption]?

INTERVIEWER: Hm . . .

ADOPTIVE MOTHER: Well, I'd almost go so far as saying, *for oneself too,* from the very first day onwards.

INTERVIEWER: Hm . . .

ADOPTIVE MOTHER: Even if the child doesn't understand *at all,* just to lose one's inhibitions about talking about it. *I noticed myself,* if you don't make any mention of the subject for *weeks* on end it *takes* a little *nudge* to take it up again.

INTERVIEWER: Hm . . .

ADOPTIVE FATHER: To become aware of the situation; then you tend to forget.

ADOPTIVE MOTHER: Right, no, I'm aware of it myself, that's . . .

ADOPTIVE FATHER: Right. But to talk about it?

ADOPTIVE MOTHER: not the problem, but to try and talk about it uninhibitedly.

The struggle, with oneself too, for the natural communication situation underlines the identity work invested by a mother who wishes to cope with the special family status in accordance with the "substitute mother concept."[107] Her attempts to realize "own-type normalization" stand out as a clear contrast to the strategies of normalization pursued by those mothers who feel that they can only derive confirmation of the value frame of the adoptive family in approximation to the biological role of mother.

The two categories of "as-if normalization" and "own-type normalization" enable a rough classification of interviews along an imagined continuum. As-if normalization would appear to be more frequent in the case of adoptions carried out some time ago than in more recent cases (1975 to 1978). The lower and lower middle class would seem to practice as-if normalization more frequently than the middle and upper class. If we were to progress in a kind of cohort analysis beyond the sample under review in this book, we would probably confirm that the relationship between the special case and the normal case in this society and in this century has been primarily regulated via as-if normalization. A gradual shift towards own-type normalization can be expected in the future, during the course of which the courage to differentiate and the experience of an achieved construction of normality are mutually reinforced.[108]

Emotionality and Awareness: The Preference for the Open Awareness Context

Although the emphasis of the previous analysis has been on the description of the emotional and cognitive management of the adoptive status, individual consequences for adoption practices have already been deduced from these observations. The preference for the open awareness context or—to put it another way—for own-type normalization supported here, can be expounded as follows in thesis form.

1. The suffering of involuntary childlessness, the painstaking dependence on bureaucratic authorities when setting up a family, the experience of the child's potential with regard to parent recruitment, and finally, the development of emotional attachment, are all background factors explaining why adoptive parents frequently allow themselves to be drawn towards an "as-if normalization" (above all, if a young, healthy, and white-skinned infant is being adopted). The power of orientation of the biologically rooted family originally planned in the biographical design retains its power of orientation in the case of the bureaucratically constructed family. Although there is a generally discernible trend over time towards a greater openness of the awareness context, quite a large number of individual cases still indicate that the special family status of the adoptive family is classified as deficient in comparison with the normal case and that the articulation of this specific status is avoided.

The approximation to the as-if normalization would above all seem able to assert itself relatively unproblematically and satisfactorily for the adoptive parents during the early phase of the family cycle,[109] early infancy.

2. In accordance with an extension of cognitive abilities when the child starts going to school, the adopted child will probably decode the knowledge of the "belly of another woman" in such a way that the realization of motherly quality will lead to a growing interest in a more concrete description of that person. The child will present the topic of double parenthood as a task for its family and hope for empathy and communication. For the adopted child or the adoptee, the degree to which the family is viewed as satisfactory will decisively depend on the extent to which the family enables it to cope with identity formation along "own-type normalization" lines.

3. If, when weighing up interests, priority is given to the well-being of the child, adoptive parents should avoid a simulation of the biological family rather than allow the adopted child to pay the price for their pretense of familial normality. The declared principle of adoption placement work, the best interests of the child, should be translated into practice by the adoptive parents. They should abandon "as-if normalization" in the realization that the special status of the family is a fact that cannot be simply ignored. The adoptive parents should also remain open to the management of double parenthood. This step towards opening the awareness context with regard to others, the adopted child, and oneself should be taken right from the very start, because a start to adoptive family life against a background of as-if normalization may prove difficult to reverse in later stages of the family cycle,[110] especially as it neglects the cognitive and emotional management of one's own marital infertility.[111] As shown by the examples of a clearly practiced own-type normalization in this study, it is questionable whether the open awareness context reduces the degree of satisfaction associated with adoptive family life by the adoptive parents. In his book *Shared Fate,* David Kirk already pointed out that the pattern of "acknowledgement-of-difference" is not only accompanied by greater degrees of empathy and communicative abilities,[112] but also by parental satisfaction with the adoptive situation.[113] Even though this may initially be associated with sadness, particularly on the part of the adoptive mothers, the persevering dissociation from the normal family case would signify the realization of an alternative family model. This would correspond to a generally observable trend in our society towards a greater orientation to the child's own personality and needs.[114] Furthermore, it would contribute towards changing a social institution. The imposition of the biologically constituted family in its model character would be fundamentally questioned if adoptive parents were to offensively stand up for adoption as the best solution for substitute upbring-

ing from the perspective of its own normality. They would set role-taking processes in motion that could then lead in the long term to an enhanced societal acceptance of the normality pattern developed within the adoptive family context.

Notes

1. This key statement is only missing in three of the 30 interviews. Various reasons may explain this fact. In one of the cases, for example, the adoptive relationship in question had in the meantime lasted 18 years (the child was taken in just a few days after birth). This probably made any articulation of the achieved extent of emotional bonding superfluous. Four other cases are dealt with later on in this chapter as examples of limited emotional normalization, one of them only with respect to the second adopted child. Altogether, therefore, a total of 24 interviews contain one or both of the two key statements. Five cases in which the children were mainly adopted after the age of one contain only the first key statement ("We and the little one have become so close"), whereas 19 cases contain explicit equations with a birth child, e.g., "It's like a child of our own," "I sometimes forget that it's not our own child," "I don't notice any difference to a child of our own," or "To me it's our child just like in every other family."

2. Erving Goffman, Frame Analysis: An Essay on the Organization of Experience. Cambridge, Mass. 1974, pp. 21ff.

3. The aspect of emotional quality, which is not dealt with all that often in literature on adoption, is considered, for example, in a "theory of bonding" by David Kirk (1981), pp. 39–54. Tizard and Rees carried out a rating of the emotional climate by classifying the behavior of the adoptive mothers of four-year-old children and that of birth mothers who were again allowed to take care of their in the meantime four-year-old children after the latter had stayed in children's homes for some time. They reached the conclusion that the adoptive mothers expressed significantly more positive feelings: Barbara Tizard and Judith Rees, "The Effect of Early Institutional Rearing on the Behavior Problems and Affectional Relationship of Four-Year-Old Children," in Journal of Child Psychology and Psychiatry, vol. 16, 1975, pp. 61–73.

4. Cf. the discussion of congruence in Wolfgang Huth, Adoption und Familiendynamik. Frankfurt 1983, p. 14.

5. Labov and Waletzky (1967) were the first to point out this fact; see in addition, Fritz Schuetze (1976), p. 7; Jochen Rehbein, "Sequentielles Erzählen—Erzählstrukturen von Immigranten bei Sozialberatungen in England," in Konrad Ehlich, ed., Erzählen im Alltag. Frankfurt 1980, pp. 66ff.

6. This examination of variables, which is generally not presented in the text, includes the clarification of the context in which a remark was made, for example, checking the aspect of the organization of turn-taking by narrators or the schemata of the presentation of events; see Werner Kallmeyer and Fritz Schütze (1976) and (1977); for details of the consideration of such an examination procedure in research, see Joachim Matthes, "Religion als Thema komparativer Sozialforschung—Erfahrungen mit einem Forschungsprojekt zum religiösen Wandel in einer Entwicklungsgesellschaft (Singapore)," in Soziale Welt, vol. 34, no. 1, 1983, p. 14.

7. Alfred Portmann characterizes this phase as the prolongation of the fetal period ("extrauterines Frühjahr"): Alfred Schuetz and Thomas Luckmann (1974), p. 4: the term describes the things which are taken for granted in the everyday life-world and which are "unproblematic until further notice."
8. Cf. Daniel Stern (1980), pp. 33–49; Rudolph Schaffer, Mothering. Cambridge, Mass. 1980 (first printed 1977), pp. 34–39, 61–77.
9. Stern (1980), p. 24.
10. Cf. the role of the mother as the "senior partner" in Schaffer (1980), p. 77.
11. Alfred Portmann, Die Biologie und das neue Bild vom Menschen. Bern 1942, p. 21. See also Berger and Luckmann (1967), pp. 66, 220.
12. Margaret Ward sums up her findings on "bonding" as follows: "Fortunately for adoptive families, a matter so important to the healthy development, even survival, of the child as the attachment to the parents is not dependent solely on biological factors." Margaret Ward, "Parental Bonding in Older-Child Adoptions," in Child Welfare, vol. 60, no. 1, 1981, pp. 24–34.
13. With regard to the following example the logical problem would at most be the fact that a comparison between the adopted son and the birth son is not possible.
14. Schuetz and Luckmann (1974), p. 4.
15. The following are just some of the influential studies dealing with the aspect of mother-child separation: René Spitz, The First Year of Life. New York 1965; J. Bowlby, Attachment, vol. 1: Attachment and Loss. New York 1969; vol. 2: Separation, Anxiety and Anger. New York 1973; Erik Erikson, Identity and the Life Cycle. New York 1959. See also the overview of literature in Kagan, Kearsley, and Zelazo (1980), pp. 133–174. See in addition, on the question of the restitutability of early damage, C. Rathbun, L. DiVirgilio, and S. Waldfogel, "The Restitutive Process in Children Following Radical Separation from Family and Culture," in American Journal of Orthopsychiatry, vol. 28, 1959, pp. 408–415; Betty Margaret Flint, The Child and the Institution, A Study of Deprivation and Recovery. Toronto 1966, pp. 30ff; Betty Margaret Flint, New Hope for Deprived Children. Toronto 1978, pp. 29, 77ff.
16. Once again, just a few examples: Dieter Claessens, Familie und Wertsystem. Berlin 1967, pp. 73ff; Friedhelm Neidhardt, ed., Frühkindliche Sozialisation. Stuttgart 1975; Friedhelm Neidhardt, "Strukturbedingungen und Probleme familialer Sozialisation," in Dieter Claessens and Petra Milhoffer, eds., Familiensoziologie—Ein Reader als Einführung. Frankfurt 1973, pp. 205–215.
17. Cf. the term in Erikson (1959), pp. 52–94.
18. Goldstein, Freud, and Solnit developed a number of guidelines for adoption placement, taking the problem of the experience of discontinuity as their point of departure: cf. Joseph Goldstein, Anna Freud, and Albert J. Solnit, Beyond the Best Interest of the Child. New York 1973, pp. 31ff. See also Horst Meester, "Psychiatrische Probleme der Adoption," in U. U. Peters, ed., Kindlers Psychologie des 20. Jahrhunderts, vol. 10. Zürich 1980, pp. 270f; Jean Seglow, Mia Kellner Pringle, and Peter Wedge, Growing Up Adopted. Windsor National Foundation for Educational Research in England and Wales, 1972, pp. 74ff.
19. Schaffer (1980, p. 99) refers to the "vulnerable age" that begins after the seventh month.
20. Via his theory of cognitive development Jean Piaget helped clarify the changed behavior of the roughly eight-month-old child when the mother disappears.

He posits this phase as the beginning of the awareness of object permanence and interprets the child's behavior in the absence of its mother as a response to the inwardly represented object "mother"; cf. the synoptical presentation of Piaget's theory of development in Jean H. Flavell, Cognitive Development. Englewood Cliffs, New Jersey 1977, pp. 52–56.

21. A list of the symptoms frequently observed in child care following a disruption of continuity, subdivided according to the child's age, can be found in Goldstein, Freud, and Solnit (1973), pp. 32ff.

22. For information on this behavioral problem often associated with children's home histories, see, for example, Tizard and Rees (1975).

23. Cf. the stage of autonomy in Erikson (1959), pp. 65–74.

24. Cf. E. E. LeMasters, "Parenthood as Crisis," in Marvin B. Sussman, ed., Sourcebook in Marriage and the Family. Boston 1963, pp. 194–198; Karol Szemkus, "Geburt des ersten Kindes und Übernahme der Elternrolle," in Hans Braun and Ute Leitner, eds., Problem Familie—Familienprobleme. Frankfurt 1976, pp. 51–61.

25. On the change from the natural attitude to its being "brought into question" cf. Schuetz and Luckmann (1974), p. 11.

26. Cf. Erikson (1959), pp. 55–65.

27. The percentage share of children born in wedlock is greater among the children placed for adoption at an older age than among those placed at a younger age (Tables 22 and 36); see, for example, Seglow, Kellner-Pringle, and Wedge (1972) for a discussion of this aspect.

28. Cf. Erikson (1959), pp. 68ff.

29. The fact that the misguidances during the child's early history produce an accumulation of problems in the adoptive family that correlate with the factor of increasing age is outlined in Wolfgang Huth, "Psychische Störungen bei Adoptivkindern—Eine Übersicht über den Stand der klinischen Forschung," in Zeitschrift für klinische Psychologie und Psychotherapie, vol. 26, no. 34, 1978, p. 264. ("In the case of adoptive children the age of placement is more than just a piece of information on how old the child was when it was taken in by its future adoptive parents. It is almost always associated with far-reaching changes in the child's life. . . . The age of placement, therefore, is an indicator of a complex of developmental circumstances, whose adverse implications become more serious as the child grows older." Translation, M.B.)

30. Cf. Mary Douglas, Natural Symbols. Explorations in Cosmology. London 1970, p. 65.

31. Goffman (1971), p. 38.

32. Cf. the analysis by Tyrell, which takes a detailed look at the norm of emotionality in the bourgeois type of mother–child relationship: Hartmann Tyrell, "Soziologische Überlegungen zur Struktur des bürgerlichen Typus der Mutter-Kind-Beziehung," in Joachim Matthes, ed., Lebenswelt und soziale Probleme, Verhandlungen des 20. Deutschen Soziologentages in Bremen, 1980. Frankfurt 1981, pp. 417–428. Other ways of integrating the adopted child apart from by establishing an emotional bond are described by Kirk with reference to ancient Greece and Rome; he pays particular attention to the functions of religious rituals. See David Kirk, Integrating the Stranger: A Problem in Modern Adoption But Not in Ancient Greece and Rome, paper prepared for the International Conference on Adoption, Athens 1987, pp. 5–9.

33. The stipulations on adoption specified in the German Civil Code of 1896 were still geared to older children, indeed children who had already reached the age of majority; cf. Napp-Peters (1978), p. 29.
34. Goffman (1959), pp. 21ff.
35. On the problem of language in the context of the experience of strangeness, cf. Alfred Schuetz, "The Stranger," in Alfred Schuetz, Collected Papers, vol. 2. The Hague 1972, p. 101.
36. On the problem of backwardness of language see, e.g., Flint (1978), p. 80.
37. On the obstacles facing children adopted at an older age when coping with new experiences, see, e.g., Flint (1978), pp. 87f.
38. I use this term here as employed by the ethnomethodologists: by using an account a world is accomplished. Cf. the overview article by Elmar Weingarten and Fritz Sack, "Ethnomethodologie. Die methodische Konstruktion der Realität," in Elmar Weingarten, Fritz Sack, and Jim Schenkhein, eds., Ethnomethodologie. Beiträge zu einer Soziologie des Alltagshandelns. Frankfurt 1976, pp. 7–27. This account work can be understood along the lines of Anselm Strauss' "identity work," namely in the sense of an identity of child and family yet to be created; see Anselm Strauss, Shizuko Fagerhaugh, Barbara Suczek, and Carolyn Wiener (1985), pp. 129–150.
39. The method elaborated by Karl Mannheim is respected as a method of the everyday world actor as well as of the social scientists in interpretive sociology; cf. Harold Garfinkel (1967), pp. 76–103; Thomas P. Wilson, "Conceptions of Interaction and Forms of Sociological Explanation," in American Sociological Review, 1970, pp. 700f.
40. This recognizing is a "proposition" as in the sense used by Garfinkel (1967, pp. 76ff). It is not a description based on the method of literal observation. By taking an actual appearance as "the document of normalization" normalization is itself accomplished.
41. Cf. Blumer's remarks on the interaction of the actor with himself when he "indicates" the things to which he attributes meaning: Blumer (1969), p. 5.
42. Cf. Erikson (1959), pp. 50–100.
43. Cf., for example, the thesis put forward by Luescher (1976, p. 144) that the "intimate social interaction" is also significant for the parents when establishing reciprocal relationships.
44. Cf. spitting out as a typical symptom at this age resulting from the experience of discontinuity in Goldstein, Freud, and Solnit (1973), p. 32.
45. Whereas this case tells of how the child wanted parents, other studies describe the ambivalence if not fear of the older child with regard to adoption. See Robert Borgman, "Antecedents and Consequences of Parental Rights Termination for Abused and Neglected Children," in Child Welfare, vol. 60, no. 6, 1981, p. 397.
46. The behavioral problems mentioned in this narrative interview, such as restlessness, aggressiveness, and poor concentration, are often primarily confirmed in the relevant literature in the cases of male adopted children. See, e.g., Michael Bohman, Adopted Children and Their Families: A Follow-Up Study of Adopted Children, Their Background, Environment and Adjustment. Stockholm 1970; Seglow, Kellner-Pringle, and Wedge (1972), pp. 59–61; Benson Jaffee and David Fanshel, How They Fared in Adoption: A Follow-Up Study. New York 1970; Ralph Maurer, Remi J. Cadoret, and Colleen Cain, "Cluster Analysis of Childhood Temperament Data on Adoptees," in Ameri-

can Journal of Orthopsychiatry, vol. 50, no. 3, 1980, p. 532; Bryan W. Lindholm and John Touliators, "Psychological Adjustment of Adopted and Non-Adopted Children," in Psychological Reports, vol. 46, 1980, p. 310.

47. Harvey Sacks, "On the Analyzability of Stories by Children," in John J. Gumperz and Dell Hymes, eds., Directions in Sociolinguistics. New York 1972, pp. 332ff.

48. Goffman (1974), pp. 21ff.

49. Glaser and Strauss (1965), pp. 9–13.

50. As the interviews as a whole make little reference to the prejudice of others, this aspect—which is undoubtedly an important one for the constructionn of adoptive family reality—will not be dealt with in further detail here. A detailed analysis of the prejudices that exist among relatives and within the community above and beyond any openly expressed approval towards adoption is presented in Kirk (1964), pp. 17–35.

51. By way of illustration I would like to fall back on an example referred to in the dissertations by Petra Speck and Annegret Liebke. A man who was not informed about his adoptive status until he was 23 tells how he often asked when younger why there were no childhood photographs. The adoptive parents answered that they were all lost in the war.

52. Here are just two of the numerous studies and articles dealing with the problems of incomplete disclosure of the fact of adoption: Benson Jaffee, "Adoption Outcome: A Two-Generation View," in Child Welfare, vol. 53, 1974, pp. 211–224; Benson Jaffee and David Fanshel, How They Fared in Adoption. New York 1970, pp. 13–18.

53. In one case there was a risk that a third party might inform the child of its adoptive status; in the other case the welfare social worker urgently advised the parents to tell the child the truth before it started school.

54. An informative overview of the changes in the ideas of social welfare institutions in this respect in the United States can be found in Sorosky, Baran, and Pannor (1979), pp. 17–22. David Kirk (1964, p. 37) pointed out in 1964 that American adoption placement encouraged adoptive parents to inform their children of the fact of adoption and that this had been part of the professional practice in child placement for at least the two preceding decades. See also Schechter (1970), p. 367. As regards the situation in the Federal Republic of Germany reference is made here to the narrative interviews with 19 young adoptees conducted to supplement the studies presented here. These interviews indicate that roughly half of the persons interviewed were not informed or only informed by chance about their adoptive status (after inquiries by others, their own discovery of adoption documents, etc.); see Petra Speck, Die Erfahrungsstrukturen Adoptierter—Der Adoptierte zwischen leiblichen Eltern und Adoptiveltern, unpublished thesis, Hamburg 1981, p. 61; see also Annegret Liebke, Die Erfahrungsstrukturen Adoptierter—Der Aufbau der Beziehung zwischen Adoptierten und Adoptiveltern, unpublished thesis, Hamburg 1981, pp. 104ff.

55. On the trend towards intimacy already observed for some time see, above all, René König, Materialien zur Soziologie der Familie. Bern 1946. See also René König, "Soziologie der Familie," in R. König, ed., Handbuch der empirischen Sozialforschung, vol. II. Stuttgart 1969, p. 237; Hartmann Tyrell, "Familie und gesellschaftliche Differenzierung," in Helge Pross, ed., Familie—wohin? Reinbek 1979, pp. 32, 34.

56. One of the very few studies that have attempted to also tackle the aspect of constructing reciprocity empirically is Klaus Mollenhauer, ed., "Soziale Bedingungen familialer Kommunikation," in Materialien zum Zweiten Familienbericht der Bundesregierung, Munich 1975. See also Wolfgang Beicht, Helmer Isecke, Gisela Krings-Huber, and Klaus Mollenhauer, "Familiale Kommunikationsstrukturen—Zwischenbericht einer Untersuchung," in Klaus Hurrelmann, ed., Sozialisation und Lebenslauf. Reinbek 1976, pp. 104–126.

57. Cf. the concepts of "content and relationship level of communication" in Watzlawick, Beavin, and Jackson (1968), pp. 51–54.

58. Cf. Berger and Luckmann (1972), p. 112.

59. In his characterization of primary frames Goffman (1974, pp. 48ff) refers to the category of "make-believe."

60. Cf. this term in Watzlawik, Beavin, and Jackson (1968), p. 199.

61. The problem facing many adoptive parents of having to work their way through their own emotions in connection with marital infertility is dealt with, for example, by Sorosky, Baran, and Pannor (1979), p. 113.

62. This term from the field of conversational analysis denotes that a specific type of action (question by the child) should be followed by a further act of a corresponding type (answer by the parents); cf. the literature overview in Kallmeyer and Schütze (1976), p. 15.

63. Cf. the problem that adoptive parents and the children wait for each other to make the first move, in Kirk (1981), p. 47.

64. The world familiar to the child remains the familiar world even after the revelation of its other origin. A parallel presents itself to Garfinkel's concept of the uninteresting reflexivity of accounts, by which the members of society assure the world taken for granted as taken for granted. These accounts are not therefore examined in terms of their reflexive character; cf. Harold Garfinkel, Studies in Ethnomethodology. Englewood Cliffs, New Jersey 1967, pp. 7–9.

65. The fact, for example, that in many narratives the child wants to hear the story of "how she/he came to us" again and again indicates just how important this message is.

66. In his studies, David Kirk paid considerable attention to the capacity for empathy of adoptive mothers. He discovered a correlation between "empathy" and "acknowledgement-of-difference," whereas adoptive mothers who try to reject the difference between a biological and an adoptive family only scored low on his empathy index. See Kirk (1981), pp. 46, 157.

67. It should be pointed out, however, that there is a host of examples in the relevant literature in which adoptive mothers, especially after having achieved emotionality, advocate the "as-if normalization" and block the communication relating to the other parents; cf. Sorosky, Baran, and Pannor (1979); Kirk (1981); Betty Lifton, Lost and Found—The Adoption Experience. New York 1979; Martin (1980).

68. Both the adoptive mother and the child are familiar with the children's home.

69. Therapeutic treatment the boy is undergoing because of concentration difficulties revealed a pessimistic basic attitude. The tests involving drawing revealed repeated breaks, which were interpreted as being connected with the discontinuity in this biography.

70. The possible problems facing adopted girls when looking for a partner resulting from a negative identification with the birth father are mentioned in Sorosky, Baran, and Pannor (1979), p. 105.

71. Cf. the problems of identification with the negatively viewed birth parents in Nathan M. Simon and Audrey G. Senturia, "Adoption and Psychiatric Illness," in American Journal of Psychiatry, 1966, pp. 858–868.
72. A similar case is described in Sorosky, Baran, and Pannor (1979), p. 85. The authors consider the constellation of unknown birth parents as a model of identification (p. 91).
73. See also in connection with this aspect the discussion on the information strategies of adoption agencies in Sorosky, Baran, and Pannor (1979), pp. 17–31; Betty Lifton (1979, pp. 26f) accusatorily describes the modifications of the facts practiced by adoptive parents.
74. The chapter in this book on the process of adoption placement is referred to as evidence for this bias. See in addition, Kirk (1981), e.g., pp. 88ff; Napp-Peters (1978), e.g., pp. 88–94; Jasinsky (1980), section 7.2; Martin (1980), pp. 82ff.
75. Cf. Christine Swientek, "Ich habe mein Kind fortgegeben"—Die dunkle Seite der Adoption. Reinbek 1982; Sorosky, Baran, and Pannor (1979), pp. 32–61.
76. Cf. Witt (1982).
77. Cf. Swientek (1982), pp. 74–90; Swientek (1986), pp. 304–329; see also the concept of "psychological amputation" that Sorosky, Baran, and Pannor (1979, p. 43) formulated with regard to the unsolvable bond between birth mother and child reflected in many documents of birth mothers.
78. Kirk (1981, pp. 71–83) speaks of a "Gresham's Law" in adoption: the good currency "acknowledgement-of-difference" is replaced by the bad currency "rejection-of-difference," not only by the adoptive parents but also by the agency. On the predominance of the orientation to the natural parental role among professional adoption agencies, see Hesseler (1980), pp. 240–244. The consequences associated with the realization of the significance of knowing about one's genealogical origin are set forth in United Nations: "Declaration on Social and Legal Principles Relating to the Protection and Welfare of Children with Special Reference to Foster Placement and Adoption Nationally and Internationally," Dec. 1986.
79. This includes the notion of adopted children "being chosen" sometimes passed on by the adoption agencies, a notion that can be found in older advisory brochures and books for adoptive parents and that is also mentioned in a number of the narrative interviews. For a discussion of the distortions of reality this triggers for the adopted child, see Lifton (1979), pp. 21ff.
80. Jean Paton pointed out that adoptees are always regarded as adopted children and are not assigned the proper adult status by society; on the influence of her research see Sorosky, Baran, and Pannor (1979), p. 24.
81. The American term "reunion" encapsulates the true significance of this encounter much better than any term in the German language. The corresponding German expression "Wiedervereinigung" is a poor choice because of the political connotation of "reunification."
82. Erik H. Erikson, Life History and the Historical Moment. New York 1975, p. 27.
83. Erikson (1975), p. 27.
84. Erikson (1975), p. 20.
85. Sorosky, Baran, and Pannor (1979), p. xiv.
86. Anselm Strauss uses the concept of identity work to characterize a type of emotional work; Anselm Strauss, Shizuko Fagerhaugh, Barbara Suczek, and Carolyn Wiener (1985), pp. 132, 138–139.

87. Speck (1981), p. 101.
88. Speck (1981), p. 102.
89. Cf. Sorosky, Baran, and Pannor (1979), p. 1.
90. The legal differences in adoption practices in the United States and in the Federal Republic of Germany were dealt with in Christa Hoffmann-Riem, preface to the German version of The Adoption Triangle (Sorosky, Baran, and Pannor, 1979); Sorosky, Baran, and Pannor, Adoption—Zueinander kommen—miteinander leben, Eltern und Kinder erzähler. Reinbek 1982, pp. 10f.
91. Cf. Sorosky, Baran, and Pannor (1979), pp. 17–31.
92. Cf., above all, Jayne Askin and Bob Oskam, Search—A Handbook for Adoptees and Birth Parents. New York 1982. See also the entire book by Betty Jean Lifton (1979) and Kirk (1981), pp. 124ff; Sorosky, Baran, and Pannor (1979), Appendix.
93. Cf. the rundown in Sorosky, Baran, and Pannor (1979), pp. 23ff.
94. Cf. Betty Jean Lifton, Twice Born: Memoirs of an Adopted Daughter. New York 1975.
95. Cf. the discussion on the reduction of kinship ties to the nuclear family in König (1969), pp. 210ff; Marvin B. Sussman, "The Isolated Nuclear Family: Fact or Fiction?" in Marvin B. Sussman, ed., Sourcebook in Marriage and the Family. Boston 1963, pp. 48–53.
96. Speck (1981), p. 104. A different connection between searching and the quality of adoptive family life is assumed by Carole R. Smith, Adoption and Fostering: Why and How. London 1984, p. 145. This "pathological model," however, is rejected by Erica Haimes and Noel Timms, Adoption, Identity and Social Policy: The Search for Distant Relatives. Aldershot, Hants 1985, pp. 75–77.
97. Cf. the examples in Sorosky, Baran, and Pannor (1979), pp. 155ff; a detailed description can be found in the autobiography by Betty Jean Lifton (1975).
98. Cf. the examples in Sorosky, Baran, and Pannor (1979), pp. 139ff; Speck (1981), p. 109; Lifton (1979), pp. 78ff.
99. Commenting on this aspect, Sorosky, Baran, and Pannor (1979, p. 195) write: "One feeling, however, was shared in some measure by all adoptive parents: they feared losing the love of their adopted child to the birth parent. Not only was this fear unfounded, but if one statement can be made unequivocally, it is that a primary benefit of the reunion experience is the strengthening of the adoptive family relationship."
100. Cf. the examples in Sorosky, Baran, and Pannor (1979), pp. 155ff.
101. Cf. Lifton (1979), pp. 100ff. Sorosky, Baran, and Pannor (1979, p. 171) refer to the many examples of the "one-contact" reunions in their study.
102. In determining what constitutes kinship, David Schneider differentiates betwen the two poles "common biogenetic substance" and "diffuse enduring solidarity." David Schneider, American Kinship: A Cultural Account. Chicago 1980 (first printed 1968), p. 65. In the terminology used by Schneider, therefore, the for many adoptees surprising "reunion experience" is reduced to the common biogenetic substance.
103. Cf. the useful concept for life history analysis in Schuetze (1981), pp. 77–79.
104. Cf. the consideration of repression and forgetting as mechanisms of "rejection-of-difference" in Kirk (1964), p. 63.
105. Cf. the repression of the experience of sterility in Kirk (1964), p. 72; Helene Deutsch listed what, from a psychoanalytical perspective, adoptive mothers affected by childlessness miss by not experiencing conception, pregnancy,

birth, and breast-feeding. At the same time Deutsch (1945, pp. 393ff) feels that adoptive mothers are fully able to fulfill motherly love.

106. David Kirk (1964, pp. 76–81) elucidated most exactly the relationship between deprivation and the tendency towards "rejection-of-difference."

107. Kirk (1964), pp. 44, 50. See also the application of Kirk's concepts to the situation of the foster mother in Jürgen Blandow, Rollendiskrepanzen in der Pflegefamilie—Analyse einer sozialpädagogischen Institution. Munich 1972, pp. 55ff.

108. Cf. the predictions in Kirk (1964), p. 68.

109. Cf. the connection between family cycle and "coping patterns" in Kirk (1964), p. 89.

110. Cf. Kirk (1964), p. 89. In our study several examples were given for the fact that adoptive mothers learn to adjust to the communication initiated by the child.

111. On the connection between deprivation caused by infertility and the tendency towards "rejection-of-difference" see Kirk (1964), pp. 75–81, 90.

112. Kirk's variable is "capacity for communication about natural parents"; Kirk (1964), p. 94.

113. Cf. Kirk (1964), pp. 90f, 94.

114. Cf. Luescher (1976), pp. 139ff.

5

A Number of Special Aspects of the Construction of Biography and Identity in the Adoptive Family

The adoptive child's biographical discontinuity confronts adoptive parents with the question of how much importance should be attached to the past, to the adoptive family's "prehistory," when structuring the shared present. Of the host of problems that emerge in this context I will single out the following special aspects: (1) the symbolic structuring of the turning point between the prehistory and the period of shared family life (giving the child a name), (2) the reconstruction of the past to illuminate the child's present problems, and (3) the construction of resemblance in accordance with the significance of shared family life (similarity between adoptive parents and child) or in accordance with the power of the adoptive family's prehistory (similarity between birth parents and the child).

The Child's Name

One of the first ways parents actualize their parental role following the birth of the child is the choice of the child's first name. Giving the child a name is so important because parents thus ascribe a personal identity to the child[1] against the background of possibly vague hopes and expectations. At the same time, this act of ascription is a means of self-definition for the parents.[2] The, as a rule, life-long identifiability via the name throws light upon the naming persons[3]; the act of choosing the name refers back to them and to their albeit highly rudimentary biographical design for the child. The name is a "thread of continuity"[4] that (to retain the metaphor used by Lindesmith and Strauss) leads back to the point of origin.

Against this background of a double biographical definition of child and parents by the name, we will take a look at how adoptive parents react to the fact that the child has already been given a name by the birth parents. First of all, a few comments on the circumstances under which the aspect of the child's name is apparently articulated in the narrative interview. Unlike, for example, the development of an emotional adoptive parent–child bond, the retention or changing of the first name are not events that are expressed in each story. The fact that the first name is nevertheless significant can be inferred from the two constellations in which reference to the name to made. The changing of the child's name is either mentioned more or less casually together with the presentation of other events, or is explicitly articulated as a separate topic in cases in which this act was faced by obstacles. Both constellations will initially be considered with reference to children placed at an early age (up to about the age of one year).

In a number of examples the impression that the subject was articulated casually is gained from the fact that the alteration of the child's name simply represents one aspect in a long chain of bureaucratic procedures.

ADOPTIVE MOTHER: And then we went to see the lawyer . . . and made the official application to adopt the child [after the adoption care period] . . . and to change its first name.

Here is another example:

ADOPTIVE FATHER: But once you've reached the stage where you've got the birth certificate—with the family name and the proper first name—that's the procedure. . . .

With reference to a Third World child placed via Terre des Hommes, the adoptive father describes the act of name-changing as follows:

ADOPTIVE FATHER: Yes and then all the usual papers and paperwork came along, to begin with the adoption agreement through the lawyer, that it's our child, the changing of its name. . . .

Casual reference can also be made to the act of changing the child's first name by recapitulating a scene before the child was taken into the family, at a time when the child still had its former name. The adoptive parents in the following passage, for example, describe the cold way the child and the foster mother said goodbye to each other:

ADOPTIVE MOTHER: And the foster mother, she, er, said: "Bye," er . . .
ADOPTIVE FATHER: Ilona.
ADOPTIVE MOTHER: Ilona.
ADOPTIVE FATHER: That's her real name, you see.
ADOPTIVE MOTHER: And, er, there was no sign of emotions at all, was there?

Bearing these examples in mind, I would like to venture the thesis that the changing of the first name of the child placed at an early age is not articulated as a separate topic, because it is regarded as an act that can be taken for granted by the adoptive parents. This view contrasts with the new adoption law, which makes provisions that the guardianship court can change the first name "if there are serious grounds (to do so) in the best interests of the child" (section 1757, paragraph 2). The explicit articulation of the subject of the desired, modified, or impeded changing of the child's name by the adoptive parents is almost always related to problems caused by this regulation. Whereas only one couple refrains from changing the name, three interviews relating to more recent judicial practice reveal a compromise solution: The adoptive parents continue to call the child by its original first name and fight in court for the right to add the name they have chosen as a second name behind the name chosen by the birth parents. To justify their efforts they refer to exactly the same identity-related argument used in the commentary to the government regulation. The line of argument in the latter is that, regardless of the child's age, its name should only be changed if there are "serious grounds,"[5] because the name already belongs "to the most important means of orientation for the child" in early childhood. The adoptive parents for their part point towards the new de facto situation. As shown by the following example of a child taken into the family at the age of three months, the argument designed to protect the child's identity can then cease to be meaningful.

ADOPTIVE FATHER: And he was *already* in our family for almost a year, and everyone knew him *only* by the name of Sven, you see. And you can just imagine the situation, telling everyone who comes to visit us "Wait, don't say Sven any more, he's called Mark now," you see. And that's how we explained it to the judge, and he said "OK, for heaven's sake . . . let's add the name Sven."

As in the case of the previously considered cases in which this aspect was casually mentioned (or in which there was a resigned dissociation from the plan to change the name), the two other examples of a combination of the old and the new first names illustrate that adoptive parents are keen to erase the child's prehistory and symbolically reinforce the start of a new era in "our family." They set in motion the same process of double biographical definition of parents and child for their family as birth parents; the beginning is replaced by the new start and is marked by a significant "rite de passage."[6] The orientational power of this parental naming of the child would appear to assert its significance to such an extent that the fact that the "thread of continuity" that links the child to its origin is cut is not reflected in the interviews, not even in cases where adoptive parents pursue the strategy of own-type normalization. In two instances the adoptive parents ask themselves what induced them to change the child's name, and settle for explanations such as "we already knew so many (children) with that name," "that's a dog's name," and "a matter of taste." The name is apparently regarded as an alterable tag, but not as a pointer to a relationship that could have any significance following the "cut" between the child's prehistory and the shared history of adoptive family life. Beginning life as an adoptive family with a young child would appear to almost indisputably include the parental ascription of a new "identity peg."[7]

The clarity—discernible in the text of the interviews—with which the child's prehistory is dematerialized or was intended to be dematerialized in 17 cases of infant adoption (two cases are not clear with respect to their connection with the new adoption law) would suggest that there is a similar tendency for the nine other narrative interviews in which there is no reference to the aspect of changing the child's name. A critical threshold, on the other hand, would appear to exist for adoptive parents if the child's self-identity has also started to evolve via its name in addition to the externally ascribed personal identity. In two interviews dealing with the adoption of children aged between one and two years, the changing or retention of the first name was not articulated as a topic. The interviews relating to children adopted at a later age (older than three) indicate that there was no changing of names in these cases. In this context, the same statement applies as in the case of the adopted babies, namely that action that is taken for granted is not explicitly articulated as a topic of the narrative interview—the only difference being that it is taken for granted in these cases that the name should not be changed. With one exception, the changing of the child's name is not considered if the adoptive parents already knew the child before the adoption care period, if the child had the status of a foster child before adoption, or if the child was already five or six years old when taken into the family. The fact that one adoptive mother refers to the impossibility of altering the child's name in the case of a child taken in at the age of five and a half is triggered by the minor problem that the adoptive mother and the child had the same first names.

ADOPTIVE MOTHER: The strange and funny thing was that she's got my first name . . . and we can't change that, you see. I mean, you just can't do that with a five-and-a-half-year-old child. It's too late, that was our opinion anyway. You just can't completely remold the child. The name is about the only thing she really had left, you see. . . .

Whereas this adoptive mother wishes to sustain a minimum of biographical continuity with the familiar first name, a different adoptive mother still works on the realization of a biographical design of her own for her five-year-old adopted child through the act of name-giving. She cautiously refers to an experiment she would have interrupted at any time if her husband's misgivings had been confirmed. As her two birth daughters, one of which had died, had similar foreign-sounding names, she wanted to "align" the name of the adopted child accordingly. By consistently calling the child by this new name it accepted the name and, in connection with this fact, the motherly ascription of identity for the sake of maintaining familial continuity ("that's what your sisters are called"). The almost magic power[8] of parental naming becomes particularly clear in this example, in which it asserts its significance with the risk of identity damage.

Although by altering the child's first name adoptive parents define themselves and their child and thus give outsiders a signal of belonging together as a family, the family name is even more important. It is an instrument for others to categorize the family, as well as, especially in the case of the child placed at an older age, an instrument of self-categorization as a family member. The period up until the child actually bears the shared family name is marked by a series of strains. As long as adopted children bear their original family name—this applies up until the period of adoption care is over (roughly one year)—adoptive parents must decide from one situation to the next when to use the officially valid name and when to present the child with the adoptive family name. Visiting the pediatrician, for example, can be experienced as a conflict-laden event if the child's health insurance certificate still bears the old name and the adoptive mother has to worry in a full waiting room whether the child and the adoptive mother will (as previously agreed on with the doctor's assistants) be called by the same family name. Not only is the risk of a misinterpretation of the mother–child relationship at stake, an aspect already considered in connection with structuring of the awareness context towards others, but also the fear that the child's original family name will become publicly known.

If the child starts school during the period of adoption care or foster care, this is experienced as an extremely threatening event. There is a tremendous concern about maintaining anonymity and about the possible threat to the child caused by the discriminating acts of others. Despite numerous parental interventions, the bureaucratic channels occasionally appear to be so entangled in their routine that they primarily classify the attempts to obtain a common family name as a procedural problem that requires time to be "processed," as shown by two examples. The bureaucrats fail to realize, however, that the adopted child placed at an older age, already faced by the arduous work of developing a bond with its new family, experiences its exclusion from the common family name as confirmation of its familial strangeness.

The following interview passage illustrates how the child's feeling of being torn between the family of origin and the adoptive family is reflected in the validity of two family names. The adoptive mother makes this observation in the interview in an effort to justify her approach to the name problem in the case of her younger adopted child. During the adoption care period, the mother used her own family name to register the child for in-patient treatment in hospital. A senior nurse kicked up a tremendous fuss about this later on ("she shouted as if I'd stolen the child"). With reference to the significance of the family name for the older adopted child, whose relinquishment for adoption dragged on for many years, the adoptive mother says:

ADOPTIVE MOTHER: I've known for a long time now how much our Peter suffered mainly from the fact that he had a different name wherever he went. I didn't expect that originally. But children are terribly sensitive. If everyone in the family has got the name then that's the name they want too. First of all, I couldn't see the problem and I told our Peter "Well, you've got a different family name." And when we went to see the doctor and handed in the health insurance certificate or were somewhere else he was always called by the other name, and I was called by a different name. And I always noticed just how much he suffered when I was in the school. When he started school I had to register him with reservations under our name. I changed it later on. But he went through such difficult phases at school, he'd suddenly jump up during lessons and shout "My name's not Sander! My name's not Sander!" And then he'd say his other name: "My name's Schrader!" That's how much he suffered.

The following example of a girl who was five years old at the time of the interview shows how the ascription of the family name is experienced by the adopted child itself as a turning point and as a symbol of unquestionably belonging together as a family. It is a flashback to the child's celebration of its "rite de passage:"

ADOPTIVE MOTHER: Well, a really touching occasion was also when, it's something you'd find almost difficult to believe, that that was so important for her, in spring . . . when she got her name. . . . Well, a written notification came that Katja is adopted, etc. . . . You just can't imagine what that already meant in the child's mind. . . . She already realized the significance of adoption, that this was another . . . another seal of approval for the situation, er, when . . . when I told her "Listen, Katja, look. In this letter, it's from the authority . . . and it says there you're our daughter, and your name is now Katja Schäfer, . . .
INTERVIEWER: Hm . . .
ADOPTIVE MOTHER: and, er, well, OK, now . . . we're now parents and child once and for all." And she was so happy, and jumped for joy, and then she came afterwards, got out of the car here, and started dancing around the courtyard, and kept on shouting "My name's Katja Schäfer, my name's Katja Schäfer."

The Reconstruction of the Past

The Reconstruction Work by the Adoptive Parents

Adoptive family life begins without knowing the beginning of the child's biography. However, as the unknown past influences the present family situation by the child's experiential structures, this family type is particularly useful to clarify the significance of the past for the constitution of the present.[9] Its structure may help demonstrate how members of society "decipher . . . the past which exists in the present."[10] This means that the fundamental problem considered by Mead of restating the past as conditioning for the future can be observed with particular clarity in the everyday world of the adoptive family, because the generally unknown past triggers intensive reconstruction work. In the case of adoption interpretative access to the past can only be gained on the basis of sparse empirical relics, whereas biological parents are usually able to construct their history of interpretation of the child's action on the basis of shared experiences right from the very beginning of the child's life. They refer to this as a background yardstick for the ongoing process of understanding. Familiarity with the entire biographical history probably makes it easier to decipher the meaning of a great deal of the child's action than does being cut off from the biological start to the child's life. First of all, the need for an interpretation of the unknown past will be dealt with from the perspective of the adoptive parents before briefly presenting the child's reconstruction work.

The interviews show that adoptive parents typically wish to find out more about the child's past when confronted by an immediate problem. The adoptive parents' own history with the child is the focal point of experiential recapitulation. The child's prehistory becomes significant in an effort to solve concrete problems relating to understanding and orientational certainty rather than with the aim of a more general determination of identity. The unknown past generally becomes a point of reference wherever the present would remain a mystery without recourse to the child's past experiential strata. This mysteriousness in turn represents an element of strangeness in the adoptive parent–child relationship.

The following examples will try to illustrate how adoptive parents set about reconstructing the biography of their child within the framework of attempts to solve specific problems. The cases are arranged in such a way that the unknown past becomes more and more extensive, enabling an examination of how the focus of parental reconstruction work in the child's subsequent developmental stages shifts as the lack of knowledge becomes greater. I will begin with the decoding of a beginning of the child's biography at a phase in which, strictly speaking, reference cannot yet be made to a child's experience: the embryonic stage.

In one example of a clinic adoption it is the physical state of the child that serves as the key to solving the mystery of the nine-month pregnancy of the newborn child. To begin with, the adoptive mother viewed this as less disquieting than the pediatrician.

ADOPTIVE MOTHER: He looked like—like a premature birth. He looked—and then he had such *really* blotchy skin, and he was so—he was a bit odd, I must honestly admit, only . . . *that's just the . . . the impression,* er, which . . . a really superficial impression which you get, and I started . . . despite everything proudly telling the pediatrician that this is the second child, and somehow . . .
INTERVIEWER: Hm . . .
ADOPTIVE MOTHER: yes, and he examined him and said, he looks so tiny, whether I couldn't give him back?
ADOPTIVE FATHER:[Ironically] Well, what do you say to that? Great, isn't it? What a thing for a pediatrician to say!

After outlining the pediatrician's comments the adoptive parents begin with the reconstruction work in their interview. The adoptive mother, who is actively involved in a discussion group of adoptive parents, comes up with the following explanation:

ADOPTIVE MOTHER: Well, what I always say is these women don't want the children. You just don't know what they've gone through. Have they had an abortion? She [the birth mother] undoubtedly didn't live like a pregnant woman should in the restaurant in which she worked, perhaps . . . didn't get enough vitamins and, you see, undoubtedly ate there . . .
INTERVIEWER: Yes, a bit of alcohol and what have you, right.
ADOPTIVE MOTHER: and drunk alcohol there, who knows, because . . . she was basically not interested in the child, and, er, they always say that things like that have an effect on the children, on newborn children.

The construction of a causal connection selected here works on the basis of a typification of birth mothers. In the opinion of a woman who has been involuntarily childless for many years they are typified as women who suddenly discover that they are unintentionally pregnant. The predominant motive during pregnancy is disinterest towards the child, which can manifest itself in an attempted abortion. Against the background of this design of a typical motive for birth mothers in general, the adoptive mother then sets out to prove the rule by referring to the particular case of the birth mother of her child. Around the relic she has been told about, "work in a small restaurant," she reconstructs the way of life and, in particular, the eating habits of the pregnant birth mother (the subject of alcohol was introduced in a case of false interviewer guidance). By twice using the adverb "undoubtedly" to reinforce her assumption that this birth mother's way of life was not organized in a manner conducive to a healthy pregnancy—in accordance with the typical construction of the course of action "of these women"—the adoptive mother then fills in the narrative by turning to conjecture (perhaps no vitamins). The generally asserted disinterest of the birth mothers is then confirmed for the specific case ("she was basically not interested in the child"). Finally, the causal chain comes full circle when the child's problematic physical state is presented as the result of the birth mother's motives and way of living. As discernible in the other interviews, the grounding for this typification in an assumed complex cause–effect relationship takes place by referring to a medical or psychological authority ("they always say"). This lends credibility to the reconstruction work of the adoptive mother in this case.

After the adoptive mother has established a link between the (in her eyes) typical motherly behavior and the child's embryonic development—a link that has only minimal grounding in available relics of the past (information on the birth mother's place of work)—the constructed typification of the anonymous woman moves into a different light after the adoptive father recapitulates an event mentioned in the adoption records. During pregnancy the birth mother had an accident at work and decided not to receive any medicinal treatment so as not to damage the child in her womb. The adoptive father rates this act in the interests of the child as follows:

ADOPTIVE FATHER: That's *really fantastic,* that is.
ADOPTIVE MOTHER: Hm . . .
INTERVIEWER: Hm . . .
ADOPTIVE FATHER: I was really impressed by that.
ADOPTIVE MOTHER: Hm . . .
ADOPTIVE FATHER: I said "Look, she was pretty reasonable after all in the end."

This narrative passage shows how the typification constructed by the adoptive mother is able to assert its relevance despite a "trace" of the actual behavior of the birth mother in the adoption records. What prompts the adoptive mother to interpret the past along such counterfactual and, more or less, utterly fictitious lines? It seems fair to assume that this constructed typification possesses greater explanatory power for the problematic nature of adoptive family life than the more realistic construction of a birth mother who is also good. It illuminates the genesis of a problem that the adoptive parents had to overcome when taking in a "tiny" baby just a few days after its birth. The reference to a constructed causal chain makes the problem comprehensible at a commonsense level. It takes the cognition of the genesis of a given problem, no matter how speculatively it has been acquired, to be able to "determine" what the problem really is.

Cicourel's remarks on the "determination" of the meaning of language could be applied to this phenomenon: The current "sense of occurrence" of the physical state of the child can only be determined via its retrospective interpretation.[11]

The next example of a child placed at the age of one year also illustrates how the management of ongoing problems in the adoptive family is repeatedly organized through reconstruction of the unknown beginning of the child's biographical history. The adoptive parents in this case concentrate on the socializational history rather than on the embryonic period. Following a sudden status passage to parenthood, adoptive family life begins with the almost never-ending crying of the child, with nightmares and a rearing up of the child on being touched or—to use the phrase often used in the interview—with "panic-like fear."

ADOPTIVE MOTHER: You just can't imagine what it was like . . . what she went through.
INTERVIEWER: Yes.
ADOPTIVE MOTHER: She had fever to begin with, nightmares. . . . It was *terrible* the way she cried. She, you just can't imagine, sat here in her cot until 11 o'clock, and when we wanted to, er, take her to bed or when we wanted to try and make her sleep at all that's when she started, she *reared up,* didn't let herself be touched at all, especially not by my husband, then she cried even more.

In their attempts to understand the child's fears the adoptive parents can only fall back on the sparse information provided and filtered by the adoption counselor on the child's prehistory. Together with information on the frequent change of reference-persons, the parents are also aware of a legal fact: the birth mother was deprived of the custody of the child because of child abuse when the child was six months old. Even though the chain of events that induced the youth welfare office to take action against the birth mother was not made known to the adoptive parents, they globally attribute the fears repeatedly shown by the child to the events that took place during the first six months of its life (a period followed by six months in a foster home):

ADOPTIVE FATHER: That's when . . . during . . . this period she probably suffered these—these terrible experiences, which she still dreams about today.

This vague "abuse-triggers-fear" typology construction is the guideline for subsequent parental reconstruction work, which tries to explain the genesis of specific types of fear. The adoptive parents discover certain relics of the past on the child's body, which the applicants were not told about during an adoption procedure characterized by extremely sparce information. They try their best to decipher two scars, find out how they were inflicted, and view them as a key for an understanding of their child's fears. This not only enables them to grasp the child's initial fear of big animals, but also helps them understand the suffering the child must have experienced during repeated blood tests carried out to determine paternity during the adoption care period. This connection is perceived as follows:

ADOPTIVE FATHER: And we don't know anything definite about the other wound, nobody told us anything about that.
ADOPTIVE MOTHER: Only that it was clipped.
ADOPTIVE FATHER: All we know is that she received medical treatment, . . .
ADOPTIVE MOTHER: Right, right.
ADOPTIVE FATHER: and that's where she probably got the idea that people in white coats automatically mean pain.
INTERVIEWER: Yes, I see.
ADOPTIVE FATHER: In this case that had a really negative effect, of course, because in the meantime we've had to take her along to three blood tests, you see.
ADOPTIVE MOTHER: There's that as well, the paternity suit, which is currently in progress.

Finally, the reconstruction of the child's early experiences prompted by the pressure of immediate problems will be illustrated by a final example that the adoptive father articulates as proof of the fact that the child has still not achieved a "psychological consolidation" one year after being in the adoptive family.

ADOPTIVE FATHER: In the beginning she had a panic-like fear of young men, . . .
INTERVIEWER: Hm . . .
ADOPTIVE FATHER: including myself, . . .
INTERVIEWER: Hm . . .
ADOPTIVE FATHER: a certain size, certain appearance, certain hair color.
ADOPTIVE MOTHER: Hm . . .
ADOPTIVE FATHER: We presume that she had some obviously bad experiences. My friend was here yesterday. And, er, he's got roughly my build. . . .

Following very cautious attempts by this friend to move closer to the child—not too close—the child expressed her wish that he should come to the edge of the bed. The scene that followed also demands an interpretation of the child's prehistory:

ADOPTIVE FATHER: He then went into her room, and she immediately started crying like mad from one second to the next . . . as if a memory has suddenly surfaced.

This network of problems and references to problems illustrates how much interpretational work is triggered by a family life in which the beginning of the child's socialization remains a missing link. The remark by the adoptive father, "We knew very little, and we had to figure out the rest ourselves whether we wanted to or not," again reflects the need for reconstruction work. The child's early biography must, no matter how speculatively, be brought into the adoptive family situation in order to make the present interpretable. A current problem has to be comprehended as the product of a layering of past experiences, because the problem can only be tackled with the help of the retrospective "sense of occurrence." Structuring the present through reference to the past must— albeit with the help of conjecture—be clarified to allow the present and the future to assume more distinct contours.

Although the adoptive parents in the previous example had to grope in the dark to figure out the child's early biography, they reached the stage just a few months after taking in the child when the successful emotional normalization made the past seem less significant. The following example illustrates how these efforts to discover the child's unknown past can remain significant if adoptive family life began without any knowledge of a six-year preadoption biography and if there is still no unquestionable mutual familiarity between the parents and the child one year after the child was taken in.

The common daily routine of this adoptive family is determined by the child's tremendous restlessness and brief periods of relaxed playing and communication, which recurrently come to an abrupt end in the form of unpredictable outbursts of anger and an unbridled display of dominant behavior. The child's outbursts, especially against the adoptive mother, signal the rejection of the parents allocated at such a late stage ("I didn't want a mother like that"). They conceal the child's sadness and hurt feelings at having been relinquished by the birth mother ("she's really, really angry that she couldn't grow up with this woman"). I would like to describe the child's suffering at such motherly neglect as elementary deprivation. Although the data in this study do not permit a generalization of the phenomenon for adoptive children—there are only isolated cases of such intense feelings of being hurt ("he simply can't cope with the fact that he was given away")—I am nevertheless convinced that this is a key to understanding the "psychological disorders" of adoptive children described in the literature on this subject.[12] The envy at the other children who live with their birth mothers ("the belly children"), idealization of the birth parents, susceptibility to disappointment with respect to the adoptive parents, lack of self-esteem ("she finds herself ugly"), and the child's compensation in its striving for dominance—all these phenomena accumulate in the previous case, but also exist in a less pronounced form in the other narrative interviews.[13]

We will now examine whether, in view of such a complexity of problems, the past can be familiarized with the help of parental reconstruction work.

First of all, a glance at the information available to adoptive parents for their appraisal of the child's prehistory. The custody of the child was withdrawn from the birth mother due to child neglect when the child was two years old. Around this time the birth father was in prison. The child was put into the care of a very old foster mother. The fate of this child is not only marked by the lack of parental affection but also by failure on the part of the bureaucratic institutions (not in Hamburg) responsible for mapping out the child's development. In the wake of administrative reforms the child was simply forgotten; the file was lost and never turned up again. By chance the child was then discovered in the care of the foster mother years later when a social worker checked the foster homes and families to see how many children were available for adoption. Full of embitterment, the adoptive mother looks back on the socializational chances ruined by the social administration ("I get annoyed again and again at the fact that that could happen"). There is also a clear note of embitterment when the adoptive mother describes the information she was given on the first two years of the child's life as "absolutely nothing":

ADOPTIVE MOTHER: We know *absolutely nothing* about her, at any rate what, what we *really* know is our daughter was born on January 4, 1971; after three days she was given a vaccination against tuberculosis, you know, this TBC injection . . .
INTERVIEWER: In the hospital.
ADOPTIVE MOTHER: which most still get, you see, and then we know that she had a serious bronchitis at the age of one. . . .

This "real" knowledge is followed in the narrative passage by conjecture revolving round the possibility of "simple living conditions" and the "withdrawal of custody." The presentation by the adoptive mother in this way gives the impression that, in line with information documented in the child's records (vaccination card), the social administration described the beginning of the child's biography in such a way that events generally classified as of secondary importance (TBC vaccination) become the paramount document of the child's existence. Even though the birth parents are still alive (consent to relinquishment for adoption), and even though other aspects could have been recapitulated, the adoption agency hands over a six-year-old child without providing information on her history. Cut off in this way from the child's previous experiences the adoptive parents begin reconstruction work that tries to gain access to the child's early biography by referring to possible events, possible motives of the birth mother, and possible living conditions. This approach, however, is unable to provide the explanatory power of a problem genesis. There is a partial linking of the present and the past, for example, when the child's current fear of starvation is linked with former neglect in this respect. The entire deprivational history of the child, however, cannot be "figured out" to such an extent that current problems become comprehensible as the product of a development. In all probability, adoptive parents are fundamentally overtaxed if they are expected to retrospectively analyze problem complexes such as "envy at belly children." Even though therapeutic help should be provided in each such case of placement of older children, the value of a careful briefing of the parents by the adoption counselor on the child's past should not be underrated. The beginning of adoptive family life with a six-year-old child should be designed as the continuation of a past that has a crucial significance for the present rather than just as the beginning of a shared history.

In this example the adoptive mother tried to compensate for the information deficit left by the adoption agency by frequently visiting the child's foster mother ("because I tried to get as much information as possible about our daughter"). She then partly interprets her observations as an indication of the genesis of new or the reinforcement of old problems during the foster period (retardation), and partly construes continuities between the difficulties arising in the adoptive family and those in the foster family (already the feeling of being neglected and the striving for dominance in the foster family situation). Yet in view of the host of problems, only partial aspects can be illuminated in this way. Despite all her reconstruction efforts the adoptive mother still continues to attribute the current strain of the beginning of adoptive family life to general misguidance during the first six years of the child's life, regardless of whether they were caused by the birth parents, foster mother, or social administration. The missing specificity in the linkage of present and past is probably partly to blame for the fact that emotional normalization has not yet been achieved.

There are numerous other examples illustrating how adoptive parents focus on current problems in their attempt to structure the child's unknown biography in order to create a means of understanding the child's behavior. The contrast between the normal case and the deviant case of the constitution of family allows a number of fundamental statements to be made on how the past is incorporated into the present in each case. Each family type assumes clearer contours thanks to the contrastive comparison.

1. A comparison between the extent of the interpretative appraisal of the past by the adoptive family and the retrospective interpretation of current problems in the biologically constituted family shows that the possibility of referring to the experienced, cognitively accessible past represents a reduction of complexity in comparison with the reliance on speculative conjecture about a possible past. Although the experi-

enced past is also interpreted and its relevance for current courses of action redefined by birth parents, this interpretation work has a different substratum. Even if psychological occurrences are not unambiguously comprehensible on the basis of parental observations, the temporal, spatial, and person-related framework of the course of the child's development provides a reliable point of reference for parental interpretation work in the biologically constituted family. The insight into the extent and intensity of reconstruction work in the absence of knowledge concerning early childhood makes it clear just how relieving the knowledge the biologically constituted family has about its own history can be. This knowledge possesses a power of orientation that is not generally reflected upon by members of society. The known past is integrated into the present and guides the interpretation of the "sense of occurrence" in the ongoing parent–child relationship.

2. The child's prehistory, which cannot be unquestionably integrated into the present of the adoptive family, is viewed in its entirety as the sad period, as shown by the narrative interviews. Irrespective of whether the adoptive parents retrospectively seek the clarification of a specific problem and are thus fixated on the problem's possible genesis, or whether the adoption agency presented the child's prehistory as almost completely deficient,[14] the construction of the no more than dark and gloomy past is probably a simplification. Without wishing to play down the suffering experienced by these children because of a lack of affection, my presumption is that the one-sided black-and-white portrayal of the past and present is also reinforced by legitimatory efforts on the part of the adoptive family (as well as on the part of the social administration). When remarks in the interviews, such as the one that the birth mother had refrained from medicinal treatment during pregnancy for the sake of the child, are extremely rare,[15] this probably points to a case of "historiography" through which the picture of the dark past makes the adoptive family situation seem even brighter, but which is an obstacle to coming to terms with double parenthood. The shared experiential frame of the biologically constituted family, on the other hand, probably produces a situation in which the child's previous biography as a period of parental involvement does not have to be fundamentally rejected. The continuity of past and present probably enables the family to safeguard its identity in the present through an identification with the past.

3. In individual cases the construction of the dark beginning of the child's biography can become so significant that it devalues the influence of the shared adoptive family history on the development of the child's personality and is subordinated to the influence of irreversible early misguidance. Even after more than ten years after taking the child into the family, adoptive parents may, for example, single out the experience of deprivation in the children's home during the first six months

of the child's life as a cause of irreparable damage to the child. Another example illustrates how adoptive parents capitulate in the face of the birth parents' influence on the child during its first two years ("they ruined him," "I also doubt whether he'll ever be able to make up for the deficits"), even though they had shared family life for 5 years. Confronted by a host of difficulties when trying to cope with an unstable emotional normalization, adoptive parents may tend to feel that their responsibility for the child's biography is restricted by the power of the dark past. The prehistory may be blamed for the fact that the shared present fails to come up to parental expectations of normality.

By way of contrast, birth parents have a more clearly delineated responsibility thanks to the shared history. Their opportunities to shape the child's socialization right from the very start form a basis for their present and future responsibility for the child. The comparison with the "deviant" case of the constitution of family shows how the parent–child relationship based on consanguineous ties is also socially constituted: The shared common genealogy becomes a common social history, and the previous parental responsibility represents a binding factor for the present and future.

The Reconstruction Work by the Adopted Child

The adopted child also has to come to terms with the hiatus in its life and the associated complex time structure of adoptive family life. The significance of the prehistory and the shared family history varies depending on the varying developmental phases. The adopted child placed at an early stage in life initially fades out—in an open awareness context—"the time before" and concentrates completely on the beginning of adoptive family life. During the phase of intense emotional bonding with the adoptive parents, all that matters is that the parents "wanted to have" and "took in" the child. As early as the age of two-and-a-half years, a child can "sit there attentively" and ask, "Mommy, tell me more," when listening to the story of how it was taken into the adoptive family.

This ritual of telling the child how it came to be adopted, a ritual often referred to in the interviews, reflects the uncertainty of a child who has understood that its connection with the adoptive parents was not determined by nature but by an act of selection. Just as the adoptive parents try to understand a current problem by means of reconstruction work, the adopted child seeks reassurance of its sense of belonging to the family by asking to be told "its story" in times of slight or more serious restlessness. The two-and-a-half-year-old child who asked to be told more, for example, surprised its adoptive mother by vehemently expressing its rejection of the fate of children in children's homes. Referring to a child who shared the same room as his sister in a home and was still there months later, the young child says "Don't want a children's home, don't want like Olaf." The child's desire for a renewed symbolic reinforcement of its family membership is reflected very clearly in the following two examples, in which doubts had arisen (for different reasons) about the fact that the child belonged to the family. In the one case the adopted child kept on asking to be told her history up until the age of seven after her brother—beginning with "ha, ha"—had opened the awareness context and played out his superiority as someone who was in mommy's belly.

ADOPTIVE FATHER: From then on we spoke to her about her story again and again . . . and how everything came about and how we so wanted to have her and how she came to us. . . . That always made her feel *calm,* and she enjoyed hearing it again every time, how everything happened.

The second example relates to a child placed at the age of three, who keeps on asking to hear his story following repeated changes of persons of reference and initial confusion about the newly allocated mother.

ADOPTIVE MOTHER: And gradually he felt at home, didn't he. And then I started, he was at most three and a half, he wanted—he *really* enjoys listening to stories, still does today—when I told him *his* story in story form.
INTERVIEWER: Hm, hm . . .
ADOPTIVE MOTHER: He wanted to hear it again and again, something like . . . well that his mother had no time for him and, er, that he was in a home because of that and one day we said, er, we said "Right, er, we want to have him," you see, . . .
INTERVIEWER: Hm . . .
ADOPTIVE MOTHER: and, er, that that was why he came along to us. Well, he listened to this like a story, his story.

This text passage is a striking illustration of how story-telling lends the complicated life history the lucidity of a factual story. Whereas the child was initially content to hear the rudimentary data about his prehistory, he then insists on a concretization of his story, above all of how everything began. Other case histories also show that the sensitive aspect of the child's reconstruction work is its preoccupation with the relinquishment by the birth mother. For some adopted children the feeling of being hurt by the motherly rejection is aggravated by the fact that they know about their shared history with the birth mother. The children placed at an older age in this study spent at least nine months with the birth mother, and two children spent almost five years. As a rule children in general are unlikely to suffer to such an extent from the lack of memory[16] as adopted children who have lost their awareness of the significant shared period with the birth parents. Referring to a child placed at an older age who had heard about her neglect by her birth parents and tried to somehow understand the background, one adoptive mother says:

ADOPTIVE MOTHER: She always says "That's a *funny* thing that I don't know *anything at all* about that. I can't remember a thing. But I experienced it. Why don't I know anything about it?"

Not only the thoughts of the forgotten past can represent a strain for the adopted child. The remembered past can also cause problems, not just because of the lasting suffering of the experiences recalled. The following passage shows how the feeling of being cut off from the shared family history can finally induce the child to rewrite her five-year prehistory and what sort of complications this can produce.

ADOPTIVE MOTHER: She didn't talk about her home . . . *not at all.*
INTERVIEWER: Hm . . .
ADOPTIVE MOTHER: And then she . . . after about one and a half years, she began more often to . . . no, it, er, all began when she got everything mixed up, chronologically, that she talked about something and we realized that wasn't here with us. That must have been before our time. That must have been an experience she had before.
INTERVIEWER: Hm . . .
ADOPTIVE MOTHER: And then I was always in the situation, when *no one* else was there, when I was alone with her or only Lars [the younger adopted child] was there, who can't control it anyway, then I said nothing. And then when she said it was at our place, . . .
INTERVIEWER: Hm . . .
ADOPTIVE MOTHER: then I left things as they were. But in Katrin's case [the older birth child] who really pays attention, who always *follows up* things, I always . . . I was always in the situation, well . . . on the one hand, of not wanting to hurt Erika, on the other hand, Katrin, who was right, you see. . . . And then I talked about this a few times with Eri, with Katrin, and said "You've got to be a bit careful. It's all a bit mixed up, and she *would feel a lot better,* I said, I don't know whether it's true, at any rate (did I put it that way?) "she would prefer it if she'd experienced it all with us."

Whereas this example of arduous but in the end successful emotional normalization following the adoption of a five-and-a-half-year-old child shows how the child extends the shared present into her past, the reverse case was also observed. The child can superimpose an idealized past with the birth parents on the shared present. The child fantasizes in line with the model of the "family romance"[17] about her former parents, whereas the mutual bonding in the adoptive family fails to live up to parental expectations of normality.

ADOPTIVE MOTHER: And then he got older, and started fantasizing about where he was [with his parents?]. In the Tyrol region we were taken up in a chairlift, there were red ones and blue ones. "I was here before with my mother! My

mother sat in the red one and I sat in the blue one," you see, and "My
mother, she's *rich* and my old father." "My old father and my old mother,"
they were the richest people, you see. They had a *car* and a *house,* you see?
ADOPTIVE FATHER: "And I was in England already, too, with my mother."
ADOPTIVE MOTHER: In England! Oh!
ADOPTIVE FATHER: That's what he said, when he was down in the harbor,
when we were down in the harbor.

Regardless of how the adopted child begins its reconstruction work the
relationship of conflict between the prehistory and the shared family
history already triggers questions of a child's search for identity at an
early developmental stage. The structuring of the relationship between the
past and the present in this special adoptive family situation also reflects
the structuring of the child's feeling of self. The statements already made
on the child's interest in its origins (see "The Significance of the Awareness of Origin from the Point of View of the Adopted Child" in Chapter 4)
can be redefined in a time-structural analysis. The restlessness of the
adoptee about its unclarified genealogical roots reflects the overpowerful
significance of the unknown past for the current search for identity. The
declining extent of inner and outer conflict following the reunion, on the
other hand, reflects how the power of orientation of the known past enables
a current biographical definition of self; in the future, this past then has
only diminished significance.

The Construction of Resemblance

The cultural interpretation of (consanguineal) kinship as bindingness[18]
can be further reinforced experientially by the construction of mutual
resemblance by family members and by other persons who perceive lines
of similarity between various family members. Although nature more or
less makes its unalterable contributions in this respect, statements on
resemblance are not as a rule simply descriptions, but typifications with a
certain binding potential. Whether through the similarity of physical appearance, habits, or personality traits, the construction of resemblance
allows persons to move closer together or be moved closer together. There
are, of course, alternatives to this kind of reinforced relationship between
persons already linked by kinship ties. For the adoptive family the question
arises how, in the absence of "common biogenetic identity,"[19] new identities can be created between adoptive parents and child and how the idea
of the biogenetic identity of the adopted child with its birth parents can
penetrate into everyday adoptive family life.

The fact that resemblance is articulated as a topic without any interviewer guidance in half of the interviews indicates that tracing lines of

similarity represents a focus of adoptive-parental activity. Resemblance can be between the adopted child and an adoptive parent, between the adopted child and a birth parent, between the adoptive mother and the birth mother, between the adopted child and the birth child, or finally, between adopted children themselves.

The following section tries to show how varying constructions of resemblance reflect mutuality or separateness in the adoptive family. The narrative passages can only give an impression of which interpretative contributions are associated with the ascription of the child to the adoptive parents or to the birth parents. Due to the variety of contexts in which constructions of resemblance are narrated, it is impossible to say why they are missing in other interviews. To outline these lines of similarity I shall begin with those examples that reflect the contributions of adoptive parents towards producing congruence within the adoptive family and then clarify how the idea of the biogenetic identity of the child with its birth parents is reflected in constructions of resemblance and reinforces a sense of proximity or remoteness in the adoptive family.

When seeking similarities between themselves and the child or between children, adoptive parents would appear to utilize all the constructions of resemblance also available to biological parents. The following text examples relate to the resemblance of physical appearance, behavior, and personality. First of all, let us turn to the aspect of physical appearance. The background knowledge of the biogenetic identity of parents and child often leads to situations in which the same specific rules of membership categorization are applied to adoptive families as in the normal case of the constitution of family. The child is defined as the image of one or the other parent. A characteristic feature of the interviews is that the physical resemblance knowingly or unsuspectingly assumed by others is not only referred to by the adoptive parents, but also confirmed as their image of family reality. In the following case, for example, the adoptive parents describe their experiences with the ascription of biological similarity (in a closed awareness context):

ADOPTIVE FATHER: Well, people, er, others often say today "Well, that's . . . he looks so much like you!"
ADOPTIVE MOTHER: Yes, Carsten, like my husband was when he was younger.
ADOPTIVE FATHER: Or, er, it only happened once during the whole seven years, er, someone was surprised about the fact that they both have such brown eyes. According to the Mendelian principles it's impossible for our children to have such dark brown eyes.

This section of narrative text continues with longer passages on the so-called family resemblance, which is not only confirmed between the adoptive father and the son but also between the two adopted children.

There are cases in which the insinuation of an "indiscretion" by one of the parents is smilingly tolerated because it underlines the physical resemblance of the adopted child and one of the parents. This illustrates how the ascription of similarity by others fits in with the concept some adoptive parents have of belonging together as a family. The first example is of an assumed biological paternity of the adoptive father. In this case the satisfaction at the construction of resemblance by others is clearly framed by the strategy of as-if normalization.

ADOPTIVE MOTHER: Well, whether you believe it or not: when he was young, a baby, seven or eight months old, a friend said to me, just before the christening, she said "You can hold it against me or not," she said, "the boy really does look like your husband."
INTERVIEWER: [Laughs] Is that right?
ADOPTIVE MOTHER: She's not the only friend who said that.
ADOPTIVE FATHER: Yes, a lot did, who didn't know it.
ADOPTIVE MOTHER: They didn't know that he isn't our own child.
INTERVIEWER: Hm . . .
ADOPTIVE MOTHER: "Well, he does look like his father."

Just how strong the desire for the "normal" biological association between parents and child can become is underlined by the jokes made about a child taken into the family at the age of five. Once again, the classic idea of an indiscretion by the husband is the main line of argument, although, as the adoptive mother points out, the argumentation is inconsistent.

ADOPTIVE MOTHER: The child was foisted on us somehow by everybody.
ADOPTIVE FATHER: Yes, jokes were made again and again, weren't they?
INTERVIEWER: [Laughs]
ADOPTIVE MOTHER: And then there's the . . .
ADOPTIVE FATHER: The resemblance, you see.
ADOPTIVE MOTHER: Then there's this resemblance, she fits *completely* into our family in terms of the way she looks.
INTERVIEWER: I see.
ADOPTIVE MOTHER: The only thing is she looks like *me*. So it can't be an indiscretion by my husband.
ADOPTIVE FATHER: [Laughs]
ADOPTIVE MOTHER: That's somehow, somehow the wrong line of argument [laughs].

The constructions of physical resemblance represent activities through which the adoptive parents try to give themselves the impression that nature was somehow in league with the artificial construction of family. It's as if nature itself has, as it were, belatedly provided the missing natural legitimation of belonging together as a family. The approximation to the normal case is welcomed without feeling that there is any need to explain the relevance of physical resemblance. The following passage illustrates the discrepancy between apparent relevance of physical resemblance (reaching back to the decision to adopt this child) and claimed irrelevance.

ADOPTIVE MOTHER: Yes, it all passed by very quickly [the tension before the first encounter with the child] when we saw the child and, er, we never really talked about it, we just took it for granted, er, she looked and still looks *today* very much like our son. . . .

INTERVIEWER: Hm . . .

ADOPTIVE MOTHER: it was baffling. We had a photo of him when he was about the same age, and *everyone* who saw the photo, said "Well, that's incredible" [laughter] . . .

INTERVIEWER: [Laughter]

ADOPTIVE MOTHER: you see. The resemblance, that was . . . really baffling and today too, er, she looks very much like and, of course, when she wears his clothes, . . .

INTERVIEWER: Hm . . .

ADOPTIVE MOTHER: it's a bit of an optical illusion, but, but a lot of people, er: "Well, she looks more and more like her brother" [laughter].

INTERVIEWER: [Laughter]

ADOPTIVE MOTHER: I mean that's not important for us. . . . It's strange, er, how things develop sometimes. . . . She's now just as blonde as he is and has such big eyes, in fact bigger eyes than he has, much to our delight and to *my* delight too [smiling] brown eyes [laughter]. That really fits in, of course [laughing], er, but, as I said, that has never really been important. . . .

The extremely detailed nature of the remarks on physical resemblance clearly show how the ideal of biogenetic identity continues to have an effect, even though the adoptive parents do not allow themselves to acknowledge its significance for their alternative constitution of family.

Alongside the orientation to nature and its legitimatory support in enabling a sense of belonging together as a family there are a few examples of preoccupation with socially constructed resemblance. The interactional history of adoptive parents and the child can lead to similarities in outward behavior patterns. As a result, the adoptive parents can see themselves reflected in the child's behavior. Especially in the absence of biogenetic identity, the experience that the child in its plasticity represents a copy of one's self would appear to be a particularly rewarding experience for adoptive parents. The joy at rediscovering oneself in the child can relate to seemingly trivial everyday activities, such as the story of the "looking glass effect"[20] in the bath:

ADOPTIVE FATHER: Adopted children also, also take on—character traits or take on personality traits, you see, . . .

INTERVIEWER: Hm . . .

ADOPTIVE FATHER: because—sometimes you can see yourself.

INTERVIEWER: Hm . . .

ADOPTIVE FATHER: The funniest thing is always when . . . when we have a bath together, Uta and me. When she washes herself she uses the washcloth the same way that I do, you see.

ADOPTIVE MOTHER: [Pleased] Yes [laughter].

ADOPTIVE FATHER: You—you start somewhere, either at the top or at the bottom, and then . . . she looks like this and then . . . like you do yourself, you know [pleased] you *see* yourself again.

A third type of construction of resemblance designed to create a sense of belonging together in the adoptive family is the similarity of "personality" or "character."[21] It is not clear whether the remarks made by the adoptive parents on this aspect relate to biologically or socially constituted phenomena. The decisive aspect is the "looking glass effect," which apparently touches on a deeply rooted parental desire to rediscover themselves in the child. At the same time individual text passages show how significant this mirroring of one's own personality in the child is for the process of understanding the child.

ADOPTIVE MOTHER: *Karsten tends to take after me* . . . I mean, he loves his father and everything, . . .

INTERVIEWER: Hm . . .

ADOPTIVE MOTHER: but you know [what children are like?].

INTERVIEWER: Hm . . .

ADOPTIVE MOTHER: And Robby tends to be more like my husband because he's got this quiet and stable personality. I am, Karsten is more like me, er, very moody. And we're extremely moody. We're *very intensely happy* and also very intensely grumpy. And . . .

INTERVIEWER: Hm . . .

ADOPTIVE MOTHER: Karsten has to, he's so spontaneous, that's the way he has to be treated.

INTERVIEWER: Hm . . .

ADOPTIVE MOTHER: And I sometimes notice that I go easy on Robby . . .

INTERVIEWER: Hm . . .

ADOPTIVE MOTHER: even though he should also be told off now and again and, and, and given tougher treatment. . . . Sometimes I think over the day, in bed in the evening, if I can't sleep and then I have a bad conscience. That's where I see the difficulties in doing justice to these different characters.

It looks as if both the missing as well as the existing resemblance in adoptive families is constructed in particularly intensive interpretation work and made a subject of reflection in socializational action. In the case just quoted the connection between resemblance and understanding, or resemblance and certainty of socializational action, becomes visible during the course of the management of varying resemblances in everyday adoptive family life.

No matter how resemblance is constructed, whether through the contributions of nature, behavioral habits, or similarity of personality, it becomes clear that the adoptive parent–child relationship is given a special symbolic frame. By construction of resemblance adoptive parents put something into the child that refers back to them. They create an identity of substance that covers up missing biogenetic identity and enables them to experience the child as the continuation of their selves. They thus participate in processes that have been illuminated by psychoanalysis, namely that parents identify their children as part of their selves and are thus able to transcend themselves.[22]

Although a number of interviews suggest that constructions of resemblance eclipse biogenetic strangeness, other interviews show the limits to this "incorporation." Although adoptive parents quite frequently argue in stereotyped form that the environment is more important than hereditary factors, that milieu is more important than chromosomes, there are references to the biogenetic identity of the child with its birth parents in eight of the 30 interviews. Especially when confronted by problems, adoptive parents tend to look back to find their origins. The construction of resemblance with the birth parents then fulfills the function generally assumed by the reconstruction of the past: It serves to clarify the genesis of the problem.

The following text examples begin by giving an impression of how adoptive parents activate the means of resorting to biogenetic identity. This leads on to a description of how the construction of resemblance with birth parents may not only represent an easily available means of interpretation but also a relieving one.

Two types of construction emerge if problems are framed by the ascription of the child to its birth parents, as shown in the text examples. At the point of conflict, the question may surface in a completely unspecified manner about whether the child should not be understood in its psychobiological individuality against the background of its other biogenetic endowment. On the other hand, an attempt may also be made—a mode of approach that is more frequent—to design a specific endowment of the child by referring to ongoing relational problems. Let us turn to the former type of construction first. All that is articulated as a topic here in the very cautious narration by the adoptive father is the fact of differentness. In this case, it was the adoptive father himself who initiated adoption and who expressed great satisfaction at the fact that an emotionally stable relationship had been established with the child. He finally arrives at the insight that the child, despite all the molding by the adoptive family, refers back to another origin. Commenting on the comparison between the adopted child and his two birth children he says:

ADOPTIVE FATHER: In my opinion the information [of the youth welfare office] is inadequate. They should tell you that the child . . . can have very personal traits, which are obviously less familiar than those your own children have. This has nothing to do with rating. There are patterns of behavior, at least that's the way I see it, where our children, our own children, . . .

INTERVIEWER: Hm . . .

ADOPTIVE FATHER: react differently, where Anke and I would also react differently and the reaction, my reaction would be more similar to that of my own children.

INTERVIEWER: Hm . . .

ADOPTIVE FATHER: Maybe it's only my imagination, but I'm pretty certain that there are moments where something like that can happen. . . . For example . . . the activity Anke shows in our family sometimes runs contrary to our own mentality, and that can lead to conflicts. That's something you must be . . . prepared for.

Just as social sciences vacillate between the demand for an exact clarification of genetic influences and the concern about artifacts, this adoptive father vacillates between a certain experiential certainty ("pretty certain") with respect to the differentness of the adopted child and the admission of possible imagination. He considers the possibility that the differentness he experiences as an objective fact could be his own construct. He tends, however, to be more convinced about the certainty of genetic influences ("For example . . . the activity . . .") than that this could be the result of his own interpretation.

As opposed to this general interpretation of the child against the background of its biogenetic endowment, other narrative passages indicate that in the eyes of the adoptive parents the child appears as a definite reflection of its birth parents with regard to certain aspects of its personality structure. This second type of construction can be found, for example, in a narration by adoptive parents who are working hard on the strategy of as-if normalization, who assume that their son is disinterested in his adoptive status, and who attribute his occasional outbursts ("I'm going back to the children's home . . . I know you don't love me anyway") to his hot-headedness. The information contained in the adoption agency files that the birth father is "very irascible" develops its momentum insofar as the son's "terrible hot-headedness" is associated with the birth father in the narrative presentation. The adoptive parents leave the question of genetic predispositions open ("Is it inherited or isn't it inherited?"). The unalterability of the outbursts of bad temper is qualified by the reference to the fact that the adoptive parents "have gradually reduced his violent temper a little"; nevertheless, the association of this trait with the birth father appears in the interview.[23]

In another example, unusually detailed information on the birth mother is cited as the key to understanding the son.

ADOPTIVE MOTHER: And the guardian explained that she [the birth mother] was *very sensitive inside* and, er, well . . .

ADOPTIVE FATHER: Quick-tempered outside.
ADOPTIVE MOTHER: quick-tempered towards others. And my son is very much
    the same in this respect.

As opposed to the two earlier examples, in which the construction of
resemblance is based on at least vaguely known personality traits of one
of the parents, adoptive parents can venture their biogenetic interpretation
without much knowledge about the child's early history. Their interest in
clarifying the roots of a given problem can be so great that the birth mother
is occasionally designed more as a reflection of the child than the child as
representing the continuation of the birth mother. The following construction of resemblance is based solely on the adoptive mother's knowledge
that the birth mother still—despite neglecting her children—lives in her
old environment. She interprets this fact in such a way as to establish a
connection between the birth mother and the child, who refuses to be put
in its place by other children on account of its striving for dominance, a
trait that the adoptive mother finds extremely difficult to accept.

ADOPTIVE MOTHER: The other children don't really *fight against* it, they all
    follow her, because we already took them along with us a couple of times on
    the weekend.
INTERVIEWER: Hm . . .
ADOPTIVE MOTHER: That's the *big question,* whether the children follow her
    because of the weekends . . . or whether she really has such an aura that you
    forgive her everything. That's my big question whether that's not the *same*
    aura that her mother has. I somehow feel that she is so similar to her mother
    that she also manages to get everybody's support no matter what. . . .

The possibility open to adoptive parents to ascribe certain traits to
biogenetical factors can also be activated by turning the child's double
inheritance, its kinship with mother and father, into double constructions
of resemblance. The following text example illustrates how a phenomenon
that is not limited to adoptive families, the child's inadequate ambitious-
ness at school, can be seen in an even more problematic light if the
adoptive mother discovers biographical parallels. The inheritance is split
into a good and a bad part.

ADOPTIVE MOTHER: Petra is ambitious, just like her mother.
INTERVIEWER: Hm . . .
ADOPTIVE MOTHER: First of all, she had to . . . it wasn't until after her third
    child that she began with her vocational training, . . .
INTERVIEWER: Hm . . .
ADOPTIVE MOTHER: and she pulled her boots up. . . . But sometimes she's got
    her father's character, we sometimes spoke about that. . . .

As a justification for the adoptive mother's insistence on a good school
education against the opposition of her daughter we find the following:

ADOPTIVE MOTHER: "You're so intelligent that it [the secondary school], that you'll manage it," I said. I started thinking sometimes, of course, I said "Your father, he always went a bit further downhill, the next job was a peg lower than the last and so on." I said "Well, maybe he's got a disposition, but" I said, er, "there were also the after-effects of the war in his case, . . .

INTERVIEWER: Hm . . .

ADOPTIVE MOTHER: and the broken marriage." I said "I can well imagine that if you know that you can do something against it."

This example gives an idea of the problems triggered by the fact that the child's biogenetic endowment is very difficult to assess. Whereas the ascription of the child to the birth mother fits in with the educational plans of the adoptive mother, the birth father appears as a threatening model of identification. It is this threatening facet that is thrust into the child's awareness in order to encourage the child ("if you know that . . .") to fight against this part of its supposed inheritance. It is during this process of exposing existing resemblances that these resemblances are vested with their powers of constructing reality.[24]

The availability of the biogenetic interpretation will now be illustrated in a final example. Once again, both parents are considered and rated on the basis of assumed traits, without the interpretational work of the adoptive parents resulting in a double construction of resemblance. The following narrative passage illustrates the extensibility of the scope of interpretation available to adoptive parents when determining the child's inheritance. Their hopes for the child's biogenetic endowment are more likely to shape the construction of lines of association than any reliable data on the personality structure of the birth parents. In the following example the biogenetic ascription of the child results from an interpretational process that begins by dissociating the child from the birth mother as outlined in the adoption records (prostitution, child abuse, delayed relinquishment). The construction of nonresemblance between daughter and birth mother emerges as follows:

ADOPTIVE MOTHER: She has, she is said not to take after her mother in any way, Mrs. Lorenz [the adoption counselor] said . . . not in any way. . . .

ADOPTIVE FATHER: Not even, not even, er, character-wise.

ADOPTIVE MOTHER: The mother was unstable in every way. . . . You can't say that about Nicola, . . .

INTERVIEWER: Hm . . .

ADOPTIVE MOTHER: that she's unstable, in no way.

Whereas there is a clear dissociation from any influence of the vaguely known birth mother on the character endowment of the child, the hopes of the adoptive parents center on the unknown father. The contours of the father, whose only known attribute is the color of his skin, appear during the course of interpretation work that the adoptive parents themselves describe as "theory." The guiding principle for his reconstruction is the search for an explanation of the high intelligence of the two-year-old child, to which the adoptive parents refer full of astonishment several times during the interview.

ADOPTIVE FATHER: Well, we've got this theory, you see.
INTERVIEWER: Hm . . .
ADOPTIVE FATHER: Which runs as follows. . . . Let's presume that she, that the father is a Negro, an African and, er, although we presume, to judge by her intelligence quotient, that it can only be, er, for example, a, er, student . . .
ADOPTIVE MOTHER: But that's just a theory of course.
ADOPTIVE FATHER: that's just an assumption, you see, . . .
ADOPTIVE MOTHER: But . . .
ADOPTIVE FATHER: you can't really say much, even though, the father's hereditary dispositions are clearly dominant.

As opposed to the previously considered examples, this construction of resemblance centers on the child's talent and not on the genesis of a specific problem. The fantasies about the possible origin of this resemblance are part of the efforts by the adoptive parents to arrive at a positive assessment of their family life following a difficult start. The child, who hardly corresponded to the criteria of the "determination of values" of the child during the placement procedure, develops astonishing intelligence values during the course of family life. This raises the question of her favorable biogenetic identity and leads to a theory of her descent and character endowment.

As if in a secondary procedural stage, the construction of resemblance with the birth parents establishes kinship. In addition to its analytical function, this renewed awareness of the kinship with others can result in a legitimation of the relational problems confronting the adoptive family. Just like the missing shared history, the biogenetic ascription of the child to its birth parents can become a focal point in terms of which the adoptive parents gauge the limits to their own influence. This tendency is visible, for example, in the case of a child who experiences itself in a large family of persons with whom she is related as a "different type" and whose differentness is also confirmed by the other members of the family. The following interview passage relates to this aspect:

ADOPTIVE MOTHER: I mean, she is a bit, er, well, how shall I put it, a bit of a *different type,* you see, right from the start, I'd say, and *more spirited* too . . .
ADOPTIVE FATHER: Energetic, yes more spirited, er, more straightforward.
ADOPTIVE MOTHER: and with—a different appetite in every respect, I'd say. . . .
ADOPTIVE FATHER: But she feels strange because of *her nature,* which is really different from our children's nature and different from *our* nature, . . .

INTERVIEWER: Hm . . .

ADOPTIVE FATHER: but she then always feels, of course, confirmed in her *strangeness*.

ADOPTIVE MOTHER: That's what I've been afraid of, for some time now. . . .

After realizing her daughter's differentness, the adoptive mother tries again and again to activate the behavior she feels this child needs. The following account illustrates that this construction of understanding is sometimes a success.

ADOPTIVE MOTHER: And I sometimes . . .

INTERVIEWER: Yes.

ADOPTIVE MOTHER: also under*stood* her, I think.

INTERVIEWER: Hm, hm . . .

ADOPTIVE MOTHER: It was typical, for example, for her to ask [following the opening of the awareness context] sometimes *"What* would you do *if* my, er, these people come?" or something like that, you see.

INTERVIEWER: Hm . . .

ADOPTIVE MOTHER: "And someone comes along," she said sometimes, *"and wants to take me away,"* you see.

INTERVIEWER: Hm . . .

ADOPTIVE MOTHER: *"What* would you do then," see [despairingly]? Well, first of all, crazy as you are sometimes and without understanding, I said "Listen, they can't do that, and we've got something official here with so many stamps on it, they're not allowed to do that," but that didn't help. That just didn't get through to the child. . . . And, *finally, at some stage* I then said "Hey, do you know what? Daddy'll then take a big stick and say "Now go to hell, that's *our* child and we want *her*," etc., you see.

INTERVIEWER: Hm . . .

ADOPTIVE MOTHER: [Pleased] "That's gr-r-reat."

INTERVIEWER: I see, I see.

ADOPTIVE MOTHER: That's *exactly* what she wanted to hear, you see.

Despite the repeatedly successful attempts at communication, the adoptive mother self-critically admits that "in comparison with what this child perhaps needs in the form of an echo" this is probably not enough. The focus then moves to the birth mother, "who has the same mentality" and who "might have been able to do that better." The adoptive mother wonders, for example, whether the birth mother might not have been able to more automatically do justice to the child's needs, whereas the adoptive mother gets through to the child by chance only by contravening her own norms. The following text passage again illustrates the varying initial situations of the adoptive mother and the child.

ADOPTIVE MOTHER: *Once* I really, er, [energetically] *got so annoyed at her,* that I *really shouted* at her, which I don't normally do, you see.

INTERVIEWER: Hm . . .

ADOPTIVE MOTHER: In this respect I'm perhaps a bit *more self-controlled,* you see.

INTERVIEWER: Hm . . .
ADOPTIVE MOTHER: Well, I really *showed* my feelings, you see, . . .
INTERVIEWER: Hm . . .
ADOPTIVE MOTHER: and she stood there, *completely unshaken,* you see. . . .
INTERVIEWER: Hm . . .
ADOPTIVE MOTHER: [Surprised] "Christ, you can really shout." And then *I realized,* you see, . . .
INTERVIEWER: I see.
ADOPTIVE MOTHER: [Pleased] that's it, that's it, *at long last there were sounds,* which *somehow* moved . . .
INTERVIEWER: Yes, yes.
ADOPTIVE MOTHER: in her *direction,* etc., you see.
INTERVIEWER: I see.
ADOPTIVE MOTHER: All my *control* and everything which our children find so pleasant . . .
INTERVIEWER: Yes.
ADOPTIVE MOTHER: and also need, our other ones, you see, . . .
INTERVIEWER: Yes, hm . . .
ADOPTIVE MOTHER: for *her* it was probably always a, a *challenge,* you see.
ADOPTIVE FATHER: It got on her nerves.

In their efforts to analytically understand the no longer unquestionable emotional bond between the child and the family, the adoptive parents often concentrate on the concept of identical mentality.

ADOPTIVE MOTHER: I mean, the fact that she sometimes feels somewhat strange here in our place, for mentality reasons, you see, *we* can't change it, *she* can't change it.
INTERVIEWER: Hm . . .
ADOPTIVE MOTHER: That's *a fact,* and that's that.
INTERVIEWER: Hm . . .
ADOPTIVE MOTHER: And that's probably the way it is in umpteen adoption cases.
INTERVIEWER: Hm . . .
ADOPTIVE MOTHER: I mean who can say whether a child will, er, come into the world, er, into the mentality from which it *originates.*

With the help of this substantialized identity of mentality, the adoptive parents create the framework within which the relational problems of the adoptive family appear to be the result of incompatible biological determinants. An attribution of blame to the adoptive parents or the child is avoided, because a third party—nature or, as specified elsewhere, fate—has its hand in the situation. Although the suffering caused by the inability to fulfill the concept of familial normality still continues, when familial reality is constructed in this way the adoptive parents feel that their ability to influence the situation is limited by biogenetic factors and thus feel relieved to a certain degree of their responsibility.

To conclude this chapter a case history is selected that symbolically reflects how adoptive parents have come to terms with shared parenthood by means of multiple constructions of resemblance. These adoptive parents transcend the fact that nature fails to provide the basis for belonging together as a family by referring to family resemblance(s), resemblance between one of the parents and a child or resemblance between the children. Whereas this reaffirms the socially constructed family there is still room for the birth parents in the image adoptive parents have of their family. In certain situations the adoptive parents see their children as a reflection of the birth parents, as a reflection of their positive and negative personality potential. This integration of the children into constructions of resemblance in orientation to both the family of origin and the adoptive family symbolically conveys that the children have become the children of the adoptive parents yet remain the children of the birth parents. The renewed ascription of kinship is marked by a thank-you to the birth parents who enabled adoptive family life by relinquishing their children for adoption.

Notes

1. Cf. Anselm Strauss, Mirrors and Masks: The Search for Identity. Glencoe, Illinois 1959, p. 15.
2. Lévi-Strauss described the twofold process of the classification of the person named and the self-classification of the naming person; Claude Lévi Strauss, Das wilde Denken. Frankfurt 1968, pp. 211f.
3. Cf. Strauss (1959), p. 13.
4. Alfred R. Lindesmith and Anselm Strauss, Social Psychology. New York 1968, p. 323.
5. Among the "serious grounds in the best interests of the child" the government regulation lists the situation in which the integration of the child into the new family is made more difficult by "foreign names or names that are only common in certain areas," because this would make it "immediately clear that this is not the birth child of the adoptive parents" (Roth-Stielow, 1976, p. 117). This is an example of as-if normalization in the structuring of the institutional framework for adoption.
6. Cf. the consideration of the phenomenon "passing," which individuals initiate themselves by changing their names at a biographical turning point, in Strauss (1959), p. 16. Leisi tried to analyze the phenomenon of renaming a partner by tracing it back to the "rites de passage" observable in almost all cultures; Ernst Leisi, Poor und Sprache. Linguistische Aspekte der Zweierbeziehung. Heidelberg 1978, pp. 24ff.
7. Erving Goffman, Stigma: Notes On the Management of Spoiled Identity. Englewood Cliffs, N.J. 1963, p. 56.
8. Cf. the description of the magic of names as the background of the changing of a person's name in Leisi (1978), pp. 25ff.
9. Phenomenonologically oriented sociology has paid particular attention to the problem of the constitution of the present against the background of the past

and the future. Recently, Luhmann (1980, pp. 23f, 236f) in particular took up the question of time and time horizons. See also Bergmann (1983).

10. Cf. the presentation of the work of George Herbert Mead (Philosophy of the Present) in Hans Joas, G. H. Mead. A Contemporary Re-examination of His Thoughts. Cambridge, England 1985, pp. 173f.

11. Cf. the interpretative procedure of the "retrospective-prospective sense of occurrence" in Cicourel (1973), p. 54.

12. This thesis is undoubtedly one-sided as it neglects the significance of family dynamics in the adoptive family. Huth (1978, p. 269), on the other hand, tries to link the main problems facing adoptive children with the difficulties facing the adoptive family in maintaining a satisfactory familial identity. The remarks made on "Emotionality and Awareness" (Chapter V) could form the background for a comprehensive sociological analysis of "psychological disorders."

13. An overview of the psychological problems of adoptive children dealt with in the relevant literature can be found, for example, in Wolfgang Huth (1978).

14. Attempts by adoption agencies to convey the image of "the good mother," for example, by giving letters written by the birth mother to the child, diary notes, poems, and so on, to the adoptive parents at the end of adoption procedure, have probably not yet become common practice.

15. At most the relinquishment of the child is interpreted as an act in the interests of the child.

16. Piaget assumes that the ability of the child to store memories other than on the basis of "recognition memory" first develops at about the age of between one and a half and two; see Flavell (1977), p. 188.

17. Freud used this term to characterize a phenomenon frequently observed in psychoanalysis that children develop fantasies in their families that they are only adopted or stepchildren and that they are really the children of high-ranking personalities. Helene Deutsch (1945, pp. 476f) outlined which conflicts might induce the adopted child, which actually has two sets of parents, to develop "speculative fantasies" about its birth parents. See also Huth (1982), p. 29.

18. Cf. Tyrell (1978), p. 623.

19. Schneider (1980, p. 23) considers kinship in the family conception in the United States as "biogenetically" defined. He also interprets statements on resemblance (looking like their parents, taking after one or another parent or grandparent) as a sign of "common biological identity" (p. 25).

20. Charles Cooley developed the term "looking glass effect" (Human Nature and the Social Order, [New York, 1922], p. 184) to describe the origin of self via its reflection in others.

21. As this section deals with the subjective interpretation of resemblance, it is worth pointing to the literature in which the "objective" correspondence of personality traits between one or another parent and the child is clarified using various measuring techniques. See the overview in Sandra Scarr, Patricia L. Webber, Richard A. Weinberg, and Michele A. Wittig, "Personality Resemblance Among Adolescents and Their Parents in Biologically Related and Adoptive Families," in Journal of Personality and Social Psychology, vol. 40, no. 5, 1981, pp. 885–898.

22. Reference is made here, for example, to Helene Deutsch (1945, p. 1), who characterizes motherhood as "the wonderful opportunity" for a woman to grasp herself as a link in a long chain of historical development: "In this type

of experience, existence is no longer defined by the personal past; instead, the impersonal past creates for the individual experience a timeless background, a perspective of 'eternity' and "immortality.' "

23. The interviews provide several examples of how the child's lack of self-control becomes a problem for the adoptive parents. Wolfgang Huth (1982, p. 169) views this problem in a wider framework. He takes a look at the fact that in the case of adoptive children, who belong to the surveyed clientele of therapeutic institutions, disturbed social behavior (such as lying, stealing, tantrums, destructiveness, and sexually deviant behavior) prevails over the otherwise dominant neurotic disturbances. He attributes this phenomenon to the fact that, as almost all adoptive children come from problem families, "especially those types of overt behavior are difficult to cope with in adoptive families which appear to correspond with characteristics of the child's origin."

24. Helene Deutsch (1945, p. 397) took a very detailed look at the fear adoptive mothers have of heredity. She describes a number of examples of how motherly fantasies drove the child into heredity ("the curse of heredity"). See also Huth (1982), pp. 168f.

6

Outlook

This study of the everyday world of the adoptive family advocates a reappraisal of the bureaucratic construction of the adoptive family. Concepts such as that of double or shared parenthood, for example, have not yet led to practical social policy consequences. I hope that the findings of this study will help provide access to an institution that likes to conceal its obstetrical role in the artificial construction of family.

The insights gained from the analysis of the adoptive family are probably significant for other forms of artificial construction of family. The adoptive family as the "pure" type of nonconsanguineal family ties develops relevance structures whose validity could be examined with respect to other types of constructed family. The feasibility of family life even if the husband is sterile (artificial insemination of the wife with the semen of an anonymous donor) or the wife (artificial fertilization of a surrogate mother with the semen of the husband) are likely to seem less impressive feats of technological progress if the complications involved in structuring awareness contexts or the child's identity formation are considered.[1] The strains confronting a child when it finds out about its artificial procreation and has to come to terms with its genealogical ties to unknown or known parents outside of the family probably move close to the critical point of ethical justifiability. The problems of a marital relationship in which one of the partners has a constant "superiority" because of a biological relationship with the child should also be carefully considered before involuntarily childless couples entrust their fate to "nature" as defined by technical feasibility.

One of the guiding principles of the evaluation was the attempt to utilize the deviant case of the constitution of family, with its different awareness of familial structures of meaning, as a means of gaining access to the normal case (indicator function). This indirect documentation approach enables a better understanding of a type of family that has asserted its significance as the normal case of family throughout the centuries and will continue to do so in the future. The continuity of living together in a nuclear family, however, would appear to be marked by a tendency towards denormalization. The processes of familial disintegration discernible in society for some time now due, for example, to divorce,[2] indicate that despite the continuing recognition of the family as an institution[3] the norm of relational permanency between marital partners is being eroded.[4] The observation of a growing number of children who experience family life as divorce "orphans" or stepchildren with disrupted kinship structures prompted David Kirk to consider whether the adoptive family and its efforts to overcome its differentness could act as a "compass" for the "mainstream family."[5] He refers to the central abilities (assuming "acknowledgement-of-difference") of "authenticity, empathy, and communication"[6] in the adoptive family to signal orientational values for the overcoming of the complex loyalty demands in families constituted with only partial consanguineal kinship. However, as Kirk also emphasizes, apart from such common foundations of sociality, a number of differences can be assumed between the adoptive family and, for example, a family extended by the remarriage of one of the parents. These differences, rooted to a certain extent in the partially filiative parent–child relationship, could be made identifiable with the help of a number of categories developed by referring to the socially constructed family. The concept of normality with respect to structuring emotional relationships, the shaping of the awareness contexts, and the interpretation work invested in legitimating a sense of belonging together as a family in the absence of biological ties—these are all concepts that could help clarify processes through which married couples in situations with only partial genealogical ties to the child cope with their differentness in comparison with the normal family case. Presumably, one would then discover that the normal case also brings its orientational power to bear in constellations in which the norm according to which parents and their filiative children live together is no longer binding.

In my opinion, the concepts derived from the field of adoption could also prove useful for the analysis of social processes outside of the familial context. In line with a formal sociological approach the theoretical constructs could be applied to social processes in other settings and not just to family types. The utilization of the normal case as a referential frame in the example of adoption is just one aspect of the general phenomenon via which a potentially large number of individuals are categorized as pertaining to social fields marked by missing or insufficient normality.[7] The interpretation of the relationship between one's own differentness and the normal case is a problem confronting a host of discredited and discreditable[8] individuals; for example, the sick, the handicapped, homosexuals, or persons restricted in their scope of societal action by the color of their skin or their sex. The strategies of as-if normalization and own-type normalization exposed in the analysis of the adoptive family probably also exist in other social fields, because the decision has to be made between self-subjection to a superimposed conformity or open dissociation from the normal case.

Not only is it likely that the normalization strategies as such will be identifiable in other fields, but also that the course of development shown in the field of adoption—from as-if normalization to own-type normalization—will also be generalizable. If, for example, homosexuals switch to the strategy of organizing "gay demonstrations" or holding "gay congresses" instead of pursuing the strategy of hiding their differentness, this signals a move from the closed to the open awareness context.

My assumption is that the parallelism of the course of such developments in various subsectors of society results from the comprehensive processes of change described in macrosociological theory concepts, for example, as phenomena of the "postindustrial society."[9] In agreement with Daniel Bell, Alan Gartner and Frank Riessman described the "new values" and the "new movements"[10] discernible during the 1960s as characteristic features of the "service society," emphasizing the new points of orientation such as openness, self-fulfillment,[11] and the dissociation from constraints of conformity. Certain developments in the adoptive family field thus appear to be elements of a more general pattern.[12] Unfortunately, this statement remains vague. Irrespective of how a tendency towards "own-type normalization" in the various social fields is ascertained in a macrotheoretical perspective, the analysis of the movements towards an extended range of normality will probably be able to identify the part played by the communicative realization of a significant process of social change.

Notes

1. Cf. the parallel between adoptive children and children brought into being by artificial insemination in Helen P. Gouldner, Children of the Laboratory. New Brunswick, N.J. 1967, pp. 13–19.
2. Cf., for example, König (1969), pp. 258ff; Tyrell (1979), pp. 20, 60f, 65f; Shorter (1975), pp. 277–279.
3. Cf. Tyrell (1979), p. 65.
4. Cf. Tyrell (1979), p. 61.
5. Kirk (1981), pp. 159–161. The significance of the adoptive family findings to other forms of family is reflected, for example, in the decision of the German

Constitutional Court (January 31, 1989) that makes knowledge of one's own ancestry an integral part of personal rights. The decision followed legal action by a woman who had attained the age of majority, had been recognized by the husband of her mother as his legitimate child, but wanted to insert the name of her biological father in her birth certificate instead of the name of her "apparent father." The court justified its decision by maintaining that in an individual's awareness genetic descent is of key importance to that person's identity formation.

6. Kirk (1981), p. 161.
7. It is not clear how far the concept of normality can be viewed in gradual terms. A fundamental consideration of the implications of the concept of normality can be found in Richard Grathoff, "Über Typik und Normalität im alltäglichen Milieu," in Walter M. Sprondel and Richard Grathoff, eds., Alfred Schvetz und die Idee des Alltags in den Sozialwissenschaften. Stuttgart 1979, pp. 89–107.
8. I fall back here on the conceptual differentiation developed by Goffman (1963, p. 4) to ground the concept of stigma.
9. An influential study in this context is Daniel Bell, The Coming of Post-Industrial Society, A Venture in Social Forecasting. New York 1973.
10. Cf. Alan Gartner and Frank Riessman, The Service Society and the Consumer Vanguard. New York 1974, Chapter IV.
11. Cf. also the study by Yankelovich which is also strongly influenced by Bell: Daniel Yankelovich, New Rules—Searching for Self-Fulfillment in a World Turned Upside Down. Toronto 1982.
12. The more the trend towards an individualization of biographies is reinforced, the more the own-type normalization will probably tend to become easier for individuals with "deviant" life-styles. Reference has been made to such a trend in more recent literature. It describes a weakening of prescribed biographical patterns of normality; there are growing demands on individuals to define their biography via their own decisions, thus extending the range of normality. See Wolfram Fischer and Martin Kohli, "Biographieforschung," in Wolfgang Voges, ed., Methoden der Biographie-und Lebenslaufforschung. Opladen 1987, pp. 40–43, Ulrich Beck, Risikogesellschaft. Auf dem Weg in eine andere Moderne. Frankfurt 1986, pp. 205–219.

Appendix

Theoretical and Methodological Framework of the Adoption Study

Theoretical Background

The artificial construction of family by adoptive parents segregates them from a pattern of normality held in high social esteem due to its interpretation as natural. This assumed naturalness has a firm basis of legitimation; as nature itself shapes and contributes to the constitution of family, the process of social institutionalization remains by and large imperceptible. What nature has created is interpretively extended to imply the naturalness of the institution. This interpretive enhancement to the status of the natural family per se gives the biologically constituted family its normative potential.

Recent family history research reveals that, as in all instances in which aspects of everyday life are taken for granted, the naturalness of this family must, in the final analysis, also be viewed in relative terms. The controversial thesis of the universality of the nuclear family was modified into the thesis of the universality of the mother–child dyad. Yet even this key element in the evolutionary history of the family must be interpreted as a cultural product. As Tyrell emphasized,[1] the contributions of nature neither provide a sufficient explanation for a longer-lasting bond between a woman and the child she has borne nor for the lifelong assignment of the child to its biological mother. Residual instincts and the mother–infant symbiosis triggered by the physical dependence of the newborn child are inadequate explanatory factors for a lifelong bond between a mother and her child determined by the contributions of nature alone. These factors, however, do serve as "almost ideal and highly suggestive points of refer-

255

ence for a massive attribution of meaning . . . and cultural organization of this relationship towards kinship or . . . genealogical unity.''[2]

The suggestive power of the interpretive extension towards the "natural" family can be better grasped by referring to the patterns of understanding biological interrelationships presented in the studies of cultural anthropology.[3] The force of the archaic attribution of meaning to consanguinity is reflected, for example, in the conceptual world of the Trobriands described by Malinowski. Here it is claimed that the mother brings forth her child from her own physical substance and that the siblings have such close ties because they are "built up of the same body.''[4] The concept of the identity of substance, which was extended to include the father at a relatively late stage in terms of evolutionary history,[5] probably represents the beginning of an everyday life theory of legitimation that makes the currently dominant model of the biologically constituted nuclear family seem so natural.

My analysis of the material provided by this adoption study is conducted against this background. With reference to a host of text examples I shall show that the normative potential of the dominant family type also develops its effectuality in adoption. My interest focuses on the constitution of family reality in those cases in which the family does not possess what René König calls "biological–social duality" (biologisch-soziale Doppelnatur).[6] In my interpretation of the data I pursue this interest along two lines of approach: an insight into the beginning and the constant structuring of familial reality without biologically rooted bonds can, as an initial glance at the data suggests, be gained by contrasting it with the pattern of normality. My intention, therefore, is to make use of analytical reference to the "normal" family case to illuminate the "deviant" case. At the same time, I also regard the fact that in adoptive families the naturalness of their own family type cannot be taken for granted as a means of discovering more about the normal case. The naturalness of the biological nuclear family generally assumed in our society is connected with the very fact that things that are taken for granted and constitute normality are unreflected. They remain unnoticed and thus present a barrier for any social researcher seeking to shed light on how the meaning of parenthood and kinship is structured during the constitution of familial reality. The appeal of adoption research, therefore, also lies in its significance for improved access to the normal case. What generally remains unreflected due to the unquestioned normality of the biological constitution of family becomes clear in the deviant case.

The Use of the Narrative Interview and the Composition of the Interviewee Group

Whether fundamental family structures can be exposed or not depends on how much scope research subjects are given to render an autonomous account of their experience. Access to the special familial reality existing beyond what members of society regard as the natural family type cannot be gained by means of prestructured categories elaborated by the social researcher. In my opinion, a study of the adoptive family is a prime example for the application of the methodological considerations developed by "new anthropology."[7] Just as the cultural anthropologist has always been sensitized to the differentness of his research subjects by the drastic change of the cultural background, some sociologists also orient their research activities towards the assumption of a fundamental strangeness between researcher and research subject. They view the construction of a universally shared value system of common values as a simplistic guideline for research activities, which furthermore runs the risk of overlooking the relevance structures of the research subjects themselves.

In this adoption study I have also opted for the characteristic shift of emphasis in interpretive research away from prior theoretical structuring towards field research without premature theoretical orientation. I have adhered to the principle of openness, which states that the theoretical structuring of the research topic must be deferred until the research topic has been structured by the research subjects themselves.[8] Accordingly, I decided to renounce the set of hypotheses desired in other social research conceptions as an instrument for structuring the gathering and analysis of data. I hoped that the procedures of generating hypotheses from data described by Glaser and Strauss to discover "grounded theory"[9] would also function where the relevances of the research subjects are ascertained via the choice of the research instrument of analysis.

Social research that operates in line with the principle of openness requires a type of data that can only be produced if a further principle is observed, the principle of communication.[10] According to this principle, the researcher can, as a rule, only gain access to meaning-structured data if he or she enters into a communicative relationship with the research subject and, in so doing, allows the system of communicative rules observed by the research subjects themselves to remain valid.

In my opinion, the narrative interview as elaborated by Fritz Schütze does justice to both the principle of openness and of communication.[11] I used this instrument, which has been frequently tried and tested during recent years, during a practical empirical research course with students in 1978 to analyze the constitution of adoptive family life from the perspective of adoptive parents. From the knowledge of linguistic schemata of communication (narration, description, and argumentation) and their respective contributions to comprehending reality, Schütze derived the thesis that inference of factual events from verbal presentations is best guaranteed by narrative accounts: "Among verbal representations that refer to but are temporally detached from real action, narratives of one's own experiences have a pre-eminent significance: They are particularly closely linked to this action, since they reconstruct its orientational structures to a considerable degree."[12]

The confidence in the validity of this instrument is based on the knowledge gained in narrative research that the narration of a story has structural features that expose the difference to purely calculated presentations of events—for example, to improve self-presentation[13] or to disguise personal involvement. In the case of the narration of personal experiences one of these formally identifiable structural elements is the presentation of events explicitly relating to the story-actor as the person who acts or suffers.[14] It is a markedly subjective recapitulation of the chain of events, linked to the agent as if to an index ("explicitly indexical"[15]). The degree of narrativity identifiable via reference to the level of indexicalization serves as a yardstick for determining whether the account reflects reality or has been distorted by a calculated presentation of information.[16]

This confidence in narration as a reflection of the factual course of events is also rooted in the often-confirmed fact that the chronology of narratively presented and factual events coincides.[17] This parallelism, initially discovered by Labov and Waletzky,[18] is based on the fact that communicative tasks cannot be solved in an arbitrary manner. The reconstruction of the "structures of world"[19] can only take place in an interactive form, because the narrator has to enable the comprehension of the narration by the listener during the recapitulation of events.[20] The narrator, for example, has to specify the details of his or her account in order to make the connection of events seem plausible to the listener ("constraint of specification of details"[21]); the narrator condenses the account insofar as possible to assume the discernibility to the listener of the recapitulated structures of relevance of factual events ("constraint of condensation")[22]; finally, the narrator fulfills the narrative announcements by reconstructing the entire chain of events in order to satisfy the listener's attentive orientation stimulated by the narrator ("constraint of completion"[23]).

These narrative constraints justify the "assumption of authenticity"[24]; as long as they are effective it can be assumed that the perspectivity valid in the course of factual events will also be maintained in narration.[25] The circumvention or contravention of internal narrative constraints by moving, for example, to a theorizing level of presentation or by trying to hand over the turn to talk to someone else, provides an indication of the existence of problematic passages to which the narrator responds with empirically detectable disguising or legitimating tendencies.[26]

Schütze modeled the narrative interview on everyday storytelling. The idea was to establish a means of gathering data that, by allowing narrative constraints to unfold, would provide the best possible guarantee for the reconstruction and interpretation of past events from the actor's perspective. In order to enable the autonomous presentation of the narrator's experiences in line with his or her own structures of relevance, interview guidance is reduced to a minimum, that is, the pattern of egalitarian turns that can be generally observed in everyday communication[27] is suspended. Instead the interviewer confines his or her activities during most of the interview to "filling in the role of a communicative listener."[28] By merely giving signals that he or she has understood the informant's narration, the interviewer helps ensure that the markedly subjective nature of the reconstruction of events is guaranteed.

Let us now turn to the data-gathering situation when employing the narrative interview. Following initial field inquiries it became clear that reference to official records would not be able to solve the problem of gaining access to adoptive parents. There was reason to fear that reference to addresses obtained from an official authority would revive the feeling of dependence on bureaucratic institutions already suffered by adoptive parents, thus making the study seem like some kind of renewed control. A recapitulation of personal experiences in line with the respective action orientations of the adoptive history only then seemed likely if the research subjects were allowed to personally appreciate the significance of participation in this study, free from the fears of an official investigation. Reference to the lack of information on the experiences of adoptive parents aroused an awareness of being experts in this field. This awareness of their own competence led to two main lines of defining the relevance of personal involvement in the research study. First of all, the reference to the possible social policy implications of an adoption study, and in particular to the placement problems that had become clear in the light of initial research findings, made adoptive parents want to help create more humane adoption practices by discussing their own experiences. Apart from this definition of the interview as an act of solidarity in the interest of future adoptive parents, there was a clear "self-interest" motivation: a scientific analysis was viewed as a means of helping to create a more widespread public empathy for adoptive parents. In my opinion, therefore, the desire to document one's own family normality, expressed several times during the interviews, can be regarded as just as significant a basis for the willingness to communicate experiences as the motivation of role-taking on behalf of future adoptive parents.

In half of the cases (15 interviews) contact with interviewees was established through the discussion circles for adoptive parents organized by government or church-run parental guidance centers. I attended such a discussion circle myself over a period of several months. There was an all too obvious bias in the selected sample in terms of its class recruitment (mainly middle middle class), the privileged position in the placement process connected with class membership, and the adoption of shared everyday theories as a result of numerous discussions in the discussion circle. This seemed acceptable, however, not just for the pragmatic reasons resulting from the limited time schedule allotted to a course of practical empirical research. My investigation of the construction of familial reality without biological roots did not envisage an analytical approach designed to identify the adoptive parents interviewed as persons with this or that attribute[29] and thus enable statistically grounded inferences with respect to a specific universe. The attempt to gain an insight into the strategies of parental perception in the adoptive family suggested giving priority to methods that seek a sociological typification on the basis of typifications articulated by the actors themselves. With an eye to the aspect of theoretical representativeness,[30] the relevance of these typifications can then be assessed for the universe of adoptive parents.

In order to develop the desired sociological typification for a larger number of varying adoption constellations adoptive parents were selected for the second half of the sample in accordance with the criterion of supplementary value[31]: Who has taken in an already older child? Who can look back on a longer adoption history? Who can extend the spectrum of possible adoption cases as a member of the lower class or lower middle class? The adoptive parents chosen for this group pertained to the category of friends or friends of friends of the adoptive parents in the discussion circles.

In addition, I analyzed the list entries for all applicants in the Hamburg adoption agency in 1976. This enabled a comparison between our sample and the universe of successful adoption applicants in 1976 with respect to a limited number of attributes. Our sample is marked by a distortion in favor of the middle middle class. A further discrepancy was intended under theoretical aspects: the second half of the sample was prestructured in such a way as to enable an above-average representation of families with a child who was relatively old (between three and six years of age) when taken in.

In the majority of cases the interviews were carried out by two interviewers; one was responsible for the technical side of the interview (tape recording) while the second interviewer was free to focus his or her attention on maintaining the flow of communication. This arrangement has already become routine, due among other things to the much stronger interrogational character of an interview conducted by just one interviewer.[32] Our study only differed from this practice insofar as the narrative interview was conducted with couples. Although there are reasons to assume that optimum narrative constraints exist in the case of the individual interview, a number of considerations suggested carrying out such a status passage interview with both of the persons involved. One interesting aspect was to discover which narrative sequences are chosen by the adoptive mother and father during a combined recapitulation of their experiences. Although the reconstruction of events surrounding the status passage from a childless couple to a family (or from a one-child to a two-child family) was segmented by two narrators, the individual segments— with the exception of just a few cases—revealed a high degree of narrativity.

The frequency and duration of overlapping in narratives occasionally reflected the tendency towards rivalry (butting in or "hogging" the narrative) between narrators associated with a combined narration by two people. As a rule, however, the narrative account represented a well-ordered activity of the two informants and was possible without any form of verbal interviewer guidance during longer periods of the main interview phase.

The introductory question designed to elicit the initial narration has strategic significance for the success of the narrative interview.[33] Although our interest focused on the adoption history "right from the beginning"— that is, beginning with the motives for the artificial construction of family and their evolution during the course of the marriage—we excluded this question complex from our attempt to solve the problem of initial access, because this complex relates to the central taboo area of marriage. Instead, we began with the second stage of the adoption process, the placement process. At the end of a lengthy introductory lead-in by the interviewer outlining the general orientation for the entire course of narration, the following question was asked: "Can you still remember what it was like when you applied for a child?"[34] The cluster of events surrounding the placement process seemed a good way of solving the problem of how to get the ball rolling, because it enabled the research subjects to decide how much personal engagement and emotional involvement they were willing to show in their narration. It was hoped that this would give couples a sense of a large degree of narrative autonomy. The data evaluation will show that this did not result in an exclusion of the motivational history from narrative accounts.

Objectives and Methods of Data Evaluation

The use of the narrative interview meant that the course of data evaluation was not prestructured, but that the research topic was structured by the adoptive parents themselves. Consequently, the overall objective of the analysis was initially circumscribed in methodological rather than content-related terms. My aim was to order the multitude of recapitulated experiences by seeking a sociological typification as a "construct of the second degree"[35]—in line with the approach forwarded by Alfred Schütz—on the basis of the typifications expressed by the actors themselves. I tried to maintain interpretational clarity through a word-for-word presentation of the accounts by adoptive parents and a rough specification of the modes of communication used.[36] I hope that this method ensures a sufficient control of the theoretical constructions formed on the basis of interview data. I decided not to give a lengthy description of the genesis of each stage of interpretation, in order to present more condensed findings. My own reading of the more than 2,000 transcription pages and my search for systematizing aspects of analysis is presented here only in its final stage of evaluation.

This systematization was not guided by a preplanned orientation towards a specific field of sociological literature. The theoretical and conceptual framework of symbolic interactionism, phenomenology, and in particular, ethnomethodology, proved useful for the interpretation of data structured by meaning. However, reference was also made to concepts stemming from quite different sociological traditions when analyzing the interview texts. During the course of the study it became clear that theory-based sociological studies with or without reference to empirical research provided me with more points of reference for a systematization of data than studies specifically concentrating on adoption.[37] A major exception in this respect are the works of David Kirk, who deserves the credit for giving sociology its first genuinely sociological assessment of this research topic. The convergence of the findings of both his and my studies—obtained via different methods—was a reassuring confirmation of my own approach.

The sociological assessment of the interview texts was guided by a method that neglected the structural specificities of each individual case in favor of a case-transcending presentation of the adoption process. I did not take into consideration the individual case study approach employed successfully in other studies,[38] but entrusted the generation of concepts and abstract statements to the parallel analysis of 30 cases. This principle of a comparative perusal of all the texts could only be accomplished by an increasing segmentation of the narratives. I began by forming rough units corresponding to the chronology of events observed throughout the interviews: motivational history, placement process, first contact, development of the adoptive parent–child relationship. A closer analysis of the text passages relating to respective phases in the adoption history then led to a more detailed breakdown of data with a more pronounced focus on the temporal and causal interconnection of events.

In order to enable a theoretical structuring of the wealth of data that existed despite all attempts at limitation, I fell back upon the case comparison methods developed by Glaser and Strauss.[39] During the parallel analysis of 30 cases the strategy of "maximizing differences"[40] provided an initial means of ordering data by delineating polar types. The analysis of similarly structured cases then enabled a specification of the interpolar range, which in some cases could be plotted as a continuum.

The presentation of findings corresponds to a pattern of increasing differentiation from statements that are initially formulated in a general way. I began by presenting the findings on each individual aspect valid for as many cases as possible, and then further extended the general line by referring to the isolated details of specific cases.

The patterns of adoptive family experience that thus became discernible are not restricted to patterns of presentation. In line with my assumption that the narrative reconstructs the orientation structures of factual events "to a substantial degree,"[41] I view the texts in this study as more than just accounts in the sense of the definition used by ethnomethodologists.[42] I do not regard this study as an insight into cognitive structures whose empirical correspondence is left undecided. Without confidence in the fact that the statements do in fact reflect reality, I would not have dared to occasionally do more than just describe adoptive family experiences by hinting at their social policy implications.

Notes

1. Tyrell (1978), pp. 611–651.
2. Tyrell (1978), p. 619.
3. An instructive application of this approach to American society today, with the same result of an almost mystical union based on consanguineal kinship, can be found in Schneider (1980, e.g., p. 25).
4. Bronislaw Malinowski, Magic, Science and Religion and Other Essays. Garden City, N.Y. 1948, p. 225.
5. Tyrell (1978), pp. 636–640.
6. König (1948), p. 66.
7. Arbeitsgruppe Bielefelder Soziologen (1976), p. 15.
8. Cf. Hoffmann-Riem (1980), pp. 343ff.
9. Glaser and Strauss (1974), p. 1.
10. Hoffmann-Riem (1980), pp. 346ff; for a detailed analysis of this aspect see Schuetze, Meinefeld, Springer, and Weymann (1973), pp. 433–495.
11. Schuetze (1977), pp. 1–62.
12. Schuetze (1977), p. 1.
13. In his analysis of conversational narratives Stempel comes to the conclusion that fictional elements, for example, in the form of embellishments and fabrications, are inserted into the narration in order to realize superordinate action goals (e.g., to improve self-presentation), but that "the core of the narrative is

referentially guaranteed.'' Wolf Dieter Stempel, ''Alltagsfiktion,'' in Konrad Ehlich, ed., Erzählen im Alltag. Frankfurt 1980, p. 392.

14. Cf. Schuetze (1976, p. 7). See especially the fundamental theoretical remarks by Schuetze (1981, pp. 89ff) on the possibilities of analyzing processes of suffering previously neglected by action theory.
15. Schuetze (1976), p. 226; Schuetze (1982), pp. 577f.
16. Cf. Schuetze (1976), pp. 226ff.
17. Cf., for example, Kallmeyer and Schuetze (1977), pp. 189ff; Rehbein (1980); Gühlich (1980), pp. 335–384.
18. Cf. Labov and Waletzky (1967), pp. 12–44..
19. Kallmeyer and Schuetze (1977), p. 224.
20. Cf. Kallmeyer and Schuetze (1977), pp. 168, 187f.
21. Kallmeyer and Schuetze (1977), p. 188.
22. Kallmeyer and Schuetze (1977), p. 188; Schuetze (1977), p. 15.
23. Kallmeyer and Schuetze (1977), p. 188.
24. Matthes (1983), p. 11.
25. Cf. Schuetze (1976), p. 198; a detailed discussion of the effectiveness of these constraints and of the identifiability of intentional or unintentional attempts in the text to steer clear of events the narrator regards as unpleasant can be found in Schuetze (1982), p. 576f.
26. Cf. the consistent employment of this means of control in the dissertation by Riemann, in which the accounts presented by psychiatric patients within the framework of narrative interviews are systematically checked for shifts in the schemata of their description of events. Gerhard Riemann, Das Frenwerden der eigeren Biographie. Narrative Interviews mit Psychiatrischen Patienten. Munich 1987.
27. Sacks (1971), pp. 307–314; Schuetze (1976), p. 9.
28. Schuetze (1977), p. 29.
29. Matthes (1983), p. 16.
30. The method is oriented towards the theoretical sample formation used by Glaser and Strauss (1974), pp. 45ff; see also Schuetze (1978), p. 37.
31. Unfortunately, the principle of ''theoretical sampling'' elaborated by Anselm Strauss could not be applied in the strict sense, because the organizational constraints of academic social research did not permit a continuous coordination between and gradual extension of the data gathered so far and the analytical approach.
32. Cf. Schuetze (1977), p. 46ff.
33. Cf. Schuetze (1977), pp. 17ff.
34. This question was formulated as follows: We would like to start by explaining what our study sets out to achieve. We would like to find out something about how you came to adopt your child and how you experience the way in which a relationship has been established with your child. We hope that our study will be able to help solve some of the questions the new adoption laws still have to solve. It would be a great help if you could tell your story in the way you feel is right and important. We don't want to influence your account too much by asking too many questions ourselves. Perhaps you could begin by telling us something about the adoption placement process when you finally got your child. Can you still remember what it was like when you applied for a child?
35. Schütz, Alfred, Collected Papers, vol. I. The Hague 1971.
36. Because of my concern that cases might be identifiable despite all the efforts

to ensure anonymity, I did not give the transcription extracts case numbers, even though I realize that this makes secondary analysis more difficult.

37. Many of the adoption studies using standardized methods or experimental approaches referred to in the footnotes were of relatively little use to a study on the reality of adoptive family life. The topic is often reduced to such an extent in accordance with the professional stock of variables that the impression is gained of a routinized procedure unable to come to grips with the interconnection between factors. The fixation on intelligence quotients to evaluate early or late placement is an example of how results are produced that are often inexplicable even to the researchers themselves.

38. Cf. Strauss and Glaser (1970), Riemann (1987), Bruno Hildenbrand, Alltag und Krankheit—Ethnographie einer Familie. Stuttgart 1983, Helga Gripp, Problemfeld Ehe—eine Fallanalyse. Stuttgart 1979, Schuetze (1978).

39. Glaser and Strauss (1974), pp. 101–115.

40. Glaser and Strauss (1974), p. 55.

41. Schuetze (1977), p. 1.

42. See for example Garfinkel (1967), e.g., pp. 1–18.

Tables

TABLE 1.
Statistics Federal Republic of Germany: Youth Welfare Office Adoption Placements (including West Berlin), 1950–1986

Year	Total	Adopted by foreigners	Adopted by relatives	Adoptions by nonrelatives in the FRG since 1963[1]
1950[2]	4279	489		
1951[2]	5430	709		
1952[2]	5820	872		
1953[2]	6189	1376		
1954	6523	1840		
1955	8433	2618		
1956	8285	2383		
1957	8396	2628		
1958	7873	2279		
1959	8003	2307		
1960[3]	6416	1649		
1961	7673	1776		
1962	7472	1555		
1963	7608	1557	2169	3882
1964	7684	1380	1928	4376
1965	7748	1226	2058	4464
1966	7481	1219	1984	4278
1967	7249	908	1887	4454
1968	7092	772	1761	4559
1969	7366	743	1952	4671
1970	7165	645	1918	4602
1971	7337	628	2037	4672
1972	7269	590	1848	4831
1973	7745	533	2017	5195
1974	8530	440	2218	5872
1975	9308	414	2540	6354

TABLE 1—Continued

Year	Total	Adopted by foreigners	Adopted by relatives	Adoptions by nonrelatives in the FRG since 1963[1]
1976	9551	373	2564	6614
1977	10074	336	2959	6779
1978	11224	333	3555	7336
1979	9905	339	3867	5701
1980	9298	295	3102	5901
1981	9091	322	3602	5167
1982	9145	256	3968	4921
1983	8801	300	3814	4687
1984	8543	266	4008	4269
1985	7974	247	3871	3856
1986	7875	238	3867	3770

SOURCE: Federal Statistical Office (Wiesbaden), Serie A, Reihe 2: Öffentliche Jugendhilfe; for data after 1982, Fachserie 13, Reihe 6.1.

[1]Own calculations. In order to calculate the percentage share of children adopted by nonrelatives in the total number of minors in the Federal Republic of Germany in 1978, the sum total of adoptions by nonrelatives since 1961 is set in relation to the total number of minors in the population as a whole in 1978 (14,855,400). As the statistics listed by the Federal Statistical Office do not record a figure for adoptions by relatives in 1961 and 1962, a figure of 2,000 such adoptions is assumed for these two years. The sum total of adoptions by nonrelatives then amounts to 90,755. This represents a share of 0.61% of the total number of minors (0.72% if adoptions by foreigners are not subtracted). The share is slightly higher if adoptions placed by institutions other than the youth welfare offices are also taken into account. The number of children placed via Terre des Hommes up until 1980 amounted to 1,650; in addition, a relatively small number of foreign children are selected by the applicants themselves in their native countries.

[2]Excluding West Berlin.

[3]After 1960, including Saarland.

TABLE 2.

Statistics Federal Republic of Germany: Total Number of Minors Registered for Adoption and Assessed Adoption Applicants (as of 31 December of respective review years), 1950–1985

Year	Total number of registered minors (maximum)	Estimate of number of minors registered for adoption by nonrelatives (minimum)[1]	Assessed adoption applicants[2]
1950	3,949[4]		2,434
1951	4,416		3,019
1952	4,159		3,165
1953	4,150		2,917
1954	4,690		2,771
1955	4,624		2,643
1956	5,044		2,882
1957	4,866		2,909
1958	5,026		2,950
1959	4,994		3,074
1960[3]	5,005		3,024
1961	4,957		2,921
1962	4,907		3,345
1963	4,844	2,906	3,828
1964	5,030	3,018	4,257
1965	4,499	2,699	4,455
1966	3,984	2,390	4,512
1967	4,053	2,432	4,861
1968	3,869	2,321	5,224
1969	3,392	2,035	5,345
1970	3,157	2,084	6,009
1971	3,098	2,045	6,537
1972	3,230	2,132	7,632
1973	3,368	2,223	9,211
1974	3,334	2,200	12,210
1975	3,076	2,030	15,674
1976	2,994	1,976	17,909
1977	3,194	2,108	18,817
1978	2,913	1,923	18,884
1979	2,950	1,947	20,014
1980	2,819	1,861	20,282

TABLE 2—Continued

Year	Total number of registered minors (maximum)	Estimate of number of minors registered for adoption by nonrelatives (minimum)[1]	Assessed adoption applicants[2]
1981	2,766	1,826	19,180
1982	1,035[5]		20,746
1983	884		21,249
1984	822		20,003
1985	672		19,726

SOURCE: Federal Statistical Office, Fachserie 13, Reihe 6: Öffentliche Jugendhilfe, 1979; Fachserie 13, Reihe 6.1, 1987.

[1]Own calculations. Between 1963 and 1969 the share of adoptions by nonrelatives in the total number of adoptions fluctuated between 57 and 63% (exception, 1963 with 51%). In order to obtain a rough estimate of the share of adoptions by nonrelatives in the total number of registered children, an estimated figure of 60% of such adoptions was assumed. The share of adoptions by nonrelatives in the total number of adoptions increased during the 1970s; it fluctuated between 64 and 69%. The estimation of the number of children registered for adoption by nonrelatives was therefore based on an average share of 66% for this period. The subtraction of 40 and 34% respectively from the total number of children registered for adoption probably means that the figure for the number of children registered for adoptions by nonrelatives is far too low, since the procedure for adoptions by relatives (e.g., by stepparents) is probably processed much faster and their share on December 31st of respective years in question does not correspond to the annual share.

[2]The number of assessed applicants is probably inflated by the fact that applicants can apply to several adoption agencies for an adoption once they have been granted the adoption care authorization; see also the commentary on this inaccuracy of applicant figures in: Federal Statistical Office, Fachserie 13, Reihe 6: Öffentliche Jugendhilfe, 1979, p. 13. Furthermore, the statistics on assessed applicants do not show the extent to which figures on the assessed adoption applicants also include applications for relative adoptions; this figure, however, is probably very low, since adoption by relatives can generally take place immediately after applicant assessment.

[3]After 1960, including Saarland.

[4]Excluding West Berlin

[5]According to information by the Federal Statistical Office, the sharp decline in the number of minors registered for adoption is connected with readjustments of the youth welfare statistics, following which, for example, children intended for adoption by certain families are no longer listed.

TABLE 3.

Statistics Federal Republic of Germany: Total Number of Children Placed and Registered for Adoption by Nonrelatives and Total Number of Assessed and Successful Applicants,[1] 1963–1981

| Year | PLACED AND REGISTERED CHILDREN (adoption by nonrelatives) | | Successful[4] and assessed applicants |
	Minimum[2]	Maximum[3]	
1963	6,788	8,726	7,710
1964	7,394	9,406	8,635
1965	7,163	8,963	8,919
1966	6,668	8,262	8,790
1967	6,886	8,507	9,315
1968	6,880	8,428	9,783
1969	6,706	8,063	10,016
1970	6,686	7,759	10,611
1971	6,717	7,770	11,209
1972	6,963	8,061	12,463
1973	7,418	8,563	14,406
1974	8,072	9,206	18,082
1975	8,384	9,430	22,028
1976	8,590	9,608	24,523
1977	8,887	9,973	25,596
1978	9,259	10,249	26,220
1979	7,648	8,651	25,715
1980	7,762	8,720	26,183
1981	6,993	7,933	24,347

[1]Combination of Tables 1 and 2.

[2]The minimum figure for each review year is the respective sum total of the children placed in that year and the number of children registered for adoption by nonrelatives calculated on the basis of an assumed proportional share of adoptions by relatives; see Table 2.

[3]The maximum figure for each review year is the respective sum total of the children placed in that year and the total number of children registered for adoption at the end of the same year.

[4]The figure here is the number of children placed in adoptions by nonrelatives, although the number of successful applicants is probably lower because of the placements of sibling pairs in certain cases.

TABLE 4.
Statistics Federal Republic of Germany: Number of Live Births, 1961–1986

| Year | LIVE BIRTHS 1961–1986 | | Children born out of wedlock as percentage of live births |
	Total	Born out of wedlock	
1961	1,012,687	60,269	5.95
1962	1,018,552	56,648	5.56
1963	1,054,123	55,120	5.22
1964	1,065,437	53,131	4.99
1965	1,044,328	48,977	4.69
1966	1,050,345	47,854	4.56
1967	1,019,459	46,964	4.61
1968	969,825	46,209	4.76
1969	903,456	45,498	5.04
1970	810,808	44,280	5.46
1971	778,526	45,263	5.81
1972	701,214	42,410	6.05
1973	635,634	39,839	6.27
1974	626,373	39,277	6.27
1975	600,512	36,774	6.12
1976	602,851	38,251	6.35
1977	582,344	37,649	6.47
1978	576,468	40,141	6.96
1979	581,984	41,504	7.13
1980	620,657	46,923	7.56
1981	624,557	49,363	7.90
1982	621,173	52,750	8.49
1983	594,177	52,442	8.82
1984	584,157	52,998	9.07
1985	586,155	55,070	9.40
1986	625,963	59,808	9.55

SOURCE: Statistical Yearbook of the Federal Republic of Germany, Live Births 1961–1987.

TABLE 5.

Statistics Hamburg: Number of Children Registered for Adoption at the Hamburg Adoption Agency in 1976

Children registered for adoption			
Total on January 1, 1976			76
a) Registrations (Applications)	227		
b) Withdrawn applications	40		
c) Rejected applications	5		
d) Other (placements in foster home, deaths)	20		
Registrations less b–d		162	
Total number of registered children		238	
Total number of child placements		187	
Total in hand on December 31, 1976		51	

SOURCE: Hamburg adoption agency statistics.

TABLE 6.

Statistics Hamburg: Age Structure of the Children Placed by the Hamburg Adoption Agency in 1976

Child's age	Absolute figures	%
0–1 year old	115	61.5
1–2 years old	24	12.8
2–4 years old	32	17.1
4–6 years old	8	4.3
6 years old or older	8	4.3
Total	187	100 %

SOURCE: Hamburg adoption agency statistics.

TABLE 7.
Statistics Hamburg: Applications for Adoption at the Hamburg Adoption Agency in 1976

Total number of applications by January 1, 1976		280
Applications registered	999	
Including:		
Applications by applicants from the Federal Republic of Germany not accepted for further assessment	538	
Applications by applicants from abroad not accepted for further assessment	18	
a) Accepted applicants	443[1]	
b) Applications withdrawn	76	
c) Applications rejected	12	
d) Applications dropped due to external placement	77	
e) Applications withdrawn for other reasons	93	
Accepted applications less b–e		185
Number of adoption applicants granted a child placement in 1976		180
Adoption applications in hand on December 31, 1976		285

SOURCE: Hamburg adoption agency statistics.

[1]This figure does not tally with the figure we obtained on the basis of list entries (357). The number of applications withdrawn is also substantially higher. Some of the applications no longer appear to be considered in the list entries.

TABLE 8.
Statistics Hamburg: The Ratio of Children Registered for Adoption and Adoption Applicants at Hamburg Adoption Agency in 1976

	Absolute	Ratio
Children placed in relation to number of applications accepted	187:465	1:2.5 (40%)
Children placed in relation to total number of applications made	187:1,279	1:7 (15%)

SOURCE: Calculations based on the Hamburg adoption agency statistics.

TABLE 9.
Supplementary Survey: Family Status of Applicants (married couple or single person)

Family status	Absolute	%
Married couple	356	99.7
Single person	1	0.3
Total	357	100%

TABLE 10.

Supplementary Survey: Class Membership of Adoption Applicants on the Basis of Husband's Stated Occupation (total number of applicants 1976)

Class categorization	Absolute	%
Upper class	0	0
Upper middle class	15	4.2
Upper to middle middle class	72	20.2
Middle middle class	71	19.9
Middle to lower middle class	34	9.5
Lower middle class	100	28.0
Lower class	62	17.4
No occupation specified	3	0.8
Total	357	100%

TABLE 11.

Supplementary Survey: Age of Adoption Applicants According to Age of Husband (total number of applicants 1976)

Age	Absolute	%
30–years old and younger	62	17.4
31–35 years old	138	38.6
36–40 years old	117	32.8
41–45 years old	29	8.1
46 years old and above	10	2.8
No age specified	1	0.3
Total	357	100%

TABLE 12.
Supplementary Survey: The Desired Age of the Child

Desired age	APPLICANTS GRANTED ADOPTION CARE BY HAMBURG ADOPTION AGENCY		ALL APPLICANTS	
	Absolute	%	Absolute	%
"Baby"	43	24.2	60	16.9
Up to 6 months old	14	7.9	23	6.4
Up to the age of 1	34	19.1	55	15.4
Subtotal	91	51.2	138	38.7
Up to age of 2	23	12.9	53	14.8
Up to age of 3	17	9.6	35	9.8
Up to age of 4	4	2.2	14	3.9
Up to age of 5	5	2.8	11	3.1
Up to age of 6	3	1.7	5	1.4
Up to and above the age of 6	4	2.2	10	2.8
No age specified	31	17.4	91	25.5
Total	178	100%	357	100%

TABLE 13.
Supplementary Survey: The Desired Sex of the Child

Desired sex	Absolute	%
Girl	39	10.9
Boy	27	7.6
Slight preference for girl	22	6.2
Slight preference for boy	18	5.0
No preference stated	245	68.6
Sibling pair	6	1.7
	357	100%

TABLE 14.
Supplementary Survey: The Desired Age of the Child: Preference "No Baby"

Desired age	APPLICANTS GRANTED ADOPTION CARE BY HAMBURG ADOPTION AGENCY		ALL APPLICANTS	
	Absolute	%	Absolute	%
Preference: Baby	139	78.1	243	68.1
Preference: No baby	8	4.5	23	6.4
No statement	31	17.4	91	25.5
Total	178	100%	357	100%

TABLE 15.
Supplementary Survey: The Fate of the Adoption Applications
(total number of applicants)

Fate of application	Absolute		%	
Adoption care authorization granted	211		59.1	
via Hamburg adoption agency		176		49.3
via external agency		33		9.2
following prior foster child relationship		2		0.6
Application unsuccessful	62		17.4	
application withdrawn		29		8.2
application rejected		9		2.5
"activities discontinued"		24		6.7
Other	84		23.5	
application withdrawn because of pregnancy		23		6.4
no list entry and other		61		17.4
Total	357		100%	

TABLE 16.
Supplementary Survey: Class Membership of Adoption Applicants and the Fate of
Their Applications

Class category	ADOPTION CARE GRANTED IN HAMBRUG OR BY EXTERNAL AGENCY		ADOPTION CARE NOT GRANTED[1]		TOTAL	
	Absolute	%	Absolute	%	Absolute	%
Upper middle class	13	(100)[2]	0	(0)	13	100%
Upper to middle middle class	46	86	7	14	53	100%
Middle middle class	43	82	9	18	52	100%
Middle to lower middle middle class and lower middle class	74	78	27	26	105	100%
Lower class	27	58	19	42	46	100%
Total	207		62		269	

$Chi^2 = 12.95$; degree of freedom $= 4$; $p < 0.02$.
[1]This includes the categories application withdrawn, application rejected, and "activities discontinued."
[2]Percentages of a referential basis lower than 30 are parenthesized.

TABLE 17.
Supplementary Survey: Period of Time from the Application to Adoption Care

Period of time between the adoption application and adoption care	Absolute	%
Up to 3 months	35	19.7
4–6 months	38	21.3
7–9 months	43	24.2
10–12 months	28	15.7
13–18 months	21	11.8
19–24 months	9	5.1
Not specified	4	2.2
Total[1]	178	100%

[1]Number of adoption placements via Hamburg adoption agency including transformation of foster child relationship.

TABLE 18.
Supplementary Survey: The Sex of the Child Placed

Sex of child	Absolute	%
Girl	101	53.7
Boy	85	45.2
No statement	2	1.1
Total[1]	188	100%

[1]Number of children placed by the Hamburg adoption agency, including 10 sibling pairs.

TABLE 19.
Supplementary Survey: The Child's Birth Status

Child's birth status	Absolute	%
Born out of wedlock	127	67.6
Born in wedlock	32	17.0
Officially registered as born in wedlock	17	9.0
No statement	12	6.4
Total	188	100%

TABLE 20.
Supplementary Survey: Desired Age of Child and Child's Age When Adopted

Age when adopted	DESIRED AGE									
	UP TO AGE OF 1		UP TO THE AGE OF 2		UP TO THE AGE OF 3		OLDER THAN 3		NO STATEMENT	
	Absolute	%	Absolute	%	Absolute	%	Absolute	%	Absolute	%
Up to 1 month old	23	25.6	5	(21.8)	2	(11.8)	0	(0)	3	(10.3)
2–6 months old	37	41.2	5	(21.8)	3	(17.6)	0	(0)	6	(20.7)
7–12 months old	13	14.4	3	(13.0)	2	(11.8)	0	(0)	0	(0)
1–2 years old	12	13.3	4	(17.4)	6	(35.2)	2	(11.8)	8	(27.7)
2–4 years old	3	3.3	3	(13.0)	4	(23.4)	9	(52.9)	7	(24.1)
Over 4 years old	2	2.2	3	(13.0)	0	(0)	6	(35.3)	5	(17.2)
Total	90	100%	23	100%	17	100%	17	100%	29	100%

TABLE 21.
Supplementary Survey: Age of Child when Adopted and Age of Adoption Applicant (Husband)

Age of child	AGE OF APPLICANT									
	41 YEARS AND OLDER		36–40 YEARS OLD		31–35 YEARS OLD		21–30 YEARS OLD		Total	
	Absolute	%	Absolute	%	Absolute	%	Absolute	%		
Up to 1 month old	1	(6.3)	7	13.0	17	22.7	8	25.8	33	
2–6 months old	0	(0)	15	27.8	26	34.7	10	32.3	51	
7–12 months old	0	(0)	4	7.4	11	14.7	3	9.7	18	
1–2 years old	6	(37.5)	14	25.9	7	9.3	5	16.1	32	
2–4 years old	5	(31.3)	9	16.7	8	10.7	4	12.9	26	
Over 4 years old	4	(25.0)	5	9.3	6	8.0	1	3.2	16	
Total	16	100%	54	100%	75	100%	31	100%	176	

Chi^2 = 30.95665; degree of freedom = 15; p < 0.01.

TABLE 22.
Supplementary Survey: Birth Status of Child and Age of Child When Adopted

| | BIRTH STATUS | | | | | |
| | BORN OUT OF WEDLOCK | | BORN IN WEDLOCK | | REGISTERED AS BORN IN WEDLOCK | |
Age	Absolute	%	Absolute	%	Absolute	%
Up to 1 month old	27	21.3	3	9.4	3	(17.6)
Older than 1 month and up to the age of 6 months	44	34.6	4	12.5	3	(17.6)
Older than 6 months and up to the age of 1 year	13	10.2	4	12.5	1	(5.9)
Older than 1 and up to the age of 2 years	25	19.7	7	21.8	0	(0)
Older than 2 and up to the age of 4 years	13	10.2	6	18.8	7	(41.2)
Older than 4 years	5	3.9	8	25.0	3	(17.6)
Total	127	100%	32	100%	17	100%	176[1]

Chi^2 = 35.18494; degree of freedom = 10; p = 0.0001.
[1]Total number of children placed (188) less 12 cases with no registration of age.

TABLE 23.
Supplementary Survey: Age of Birth Mother When Child Relinquished

Age of birth mother	Absolute	%
Younger than 16	4	2.2
16–20 years old	38	21.3
21–25 years old	60	33.8
26–30 years old	37	20.8
31–35 years old	12	6.7
36–40 years old	6	3.4
Older than 40	8	4.5
No statement	13	7.3
Total	178	100%

TABLE 24.
Supplementary Survey: Age of Birth Mother and Age of Child When Adopted

Age of birth mother	AGE OF CHILD														
	UP TO 1 MONTH OLD		OLDER THAN 1 MONTH AND UP TO 6 MONTHS OLD		OLDER THAN 6 MONTHS AND UP TO 12 MONTHS OLD		OLDER THAN 1 AND UP TO THE AGE OF 2		OLDER THAN 2 AND UP TO THE AGE OF 4		OLDER THAN 4		TOTAL	
	Absolute	%	Absolute	%	Absolute	%	Absolute	%	Absolute	%	Absolute	%	Absolute	%
Younger than 21	14	32.5	16	37.2	2	4.7	7	16.3	4	9.3	0	0	43	100
21–25 years old	11	16.7	17	25.7	7	10.6	13	19.7	13	19.7	5	7.6	66	100
26–30 years old	6	15.8	10	26.3	7	18.4	6	15.8	6	15.8	3	7.9	38	100
31–35 years old	1	(7.7)	5	(38.4)	1	(7.7)	3	(23.1)	2	(15.4)	1	(7.7)	13	100
Older than 35	1	(6.7)	3	(20.0)	1	(6.7)	3	(20.0)	0	(0)	7	(46.6)	15	100
Total	33		51		18		32		25		16		175	

Chi^2 = 44.97762; degree of freedom = 20; p = 0.0011.

TABLE 25.
Supplementary Survey: Family Status of Birth Mother

Family status of birth mother	Absolute	%
Single	84	47.2
Married	35	19.7
Divorced	39	21.9
Widow	5	2.8
No data	15	8.4
Total	178	100%

TABLE 26.
Supplementary Survey: Number of Birth Mother's Children Other than Child(ren) Relinquished for Adoption

Number of birth mother's other children	Absolute	%	
No child	59	33.1	
1 child, born in wedlock	19	10.7	
2 children, born in wedlock	18	10.1	
3 children, born in wedlock	11	6.2	
More than 3 children, born in wedlock	9	5.1	
			32.1
1 child, born out of wedlock	25	14.0	
2 children, born out of wedlock	6	3.4	
3 children, born out of wedlock	6	3.4	
More than 3 children, born out of wedlock	1	0.6	
			21.4
2 children, born in and out of wedlock	4	2.2	
3 children, born in and out of wedlock	4	2.2	
4 children, born in and out of wedlock	1	0.6	
More than 4 children, born in and out of wedlock	2	1.1	
			6.1
No data	13	7.3	
Total	178	100%	

TABLE 27.
Supplementary Survey: Occupation of Birth Mother

Occupation of birth mother	Absolute	%
Not stated	76	42.6
Housewife	16	9.0
Schoolgirl	9	5.1
Lower-class occupations		
Prostitute	21	11.8
Catering assistant, waitress	11	6.2
Shop assistant, office worker	4	2.2
Blue-collar worker	14	7.9
Occupation with possible completed apprenticeship		
(hairdresser, saleswoman etc.)	14	7.9
Apprentice	3	1.7
		37.7
Lower-middle-class occupations		
Children's nurse, nursery-school teacher, hospital nurse	6	3.4
Secretary	2	1.1
Other lower-middle-class occupations	2	1.1
		5.6
Middle-middle-class occupations	0	0
Upper-middle-class occupations	0	0
Total	178	100%

TABLE 28.

Supplementary Survey: Occupation of Birth Mother and Age of Child when Adopted

	OCCUPATION OF BIRTH MOTHER											
	NOT SPECIFIED OR "HOUSEWIFE"		SCHOOLGIRL, APPRENTICE		PROSTITUTE		JOB WITHOUT COMPLETED APPRENTICESHIP		JOB WITH COMPLETED APPRENTICESHIP		LOWER-MIDDLE-CLASS OCCUPATION	
Age of child	Absolute	%	Absolute	%	Absolute	%	Absolute	%	Absolute	%	Absolute	%
Up to 1 month old	11	12.6	9	(75)	1	(4.8)	3	9.4	3	(21.4)	6	(60)
Older than 1 month and up to 6 months old	28	32.3	3	(25)	6	(28.8)	6	18.8	5	(35.7)	3	(30)
Older than 6 months and up to 12 months old	8	9.2	0	(0)	4	(19.0)	4	12.5	2	(14.3)	0	(0)
Older than 1 and up to the age of 2 years	15	17.2	0	(0)	8	(38.1)	6	18.8	2	(14.3)	1	(10)
Older than 2 and up to the age of 4 years	15	17.2	0	(0)	2	(9.5)	9	28.0	0	(0)	0	(0)
Older than 4 years	10	11.5	0	(0)	0	(0)	4	12.5	2	(14.3)	0	(0)
Total	87	100%	12	100%	21	100%	32	100%	14	100%	10	100%

TABLE 29.
Supplementary Survey: Nationality of Birth Mother

Nationality of birth mother	Absolute	%
German	149	83.7
Migrant workers		
(S.Europe and Turkey)	7	3.9
Other	6	3.4
Not specified	16	9.0
Total	178	100%

TABLE 30.
Supplementary Survey: Data on Birth Father

Data on birth father	Absolute	%
Birth father unknown	100	56.1
Birth father not stated	1	0.6
Occupation probably without completed apprenticeship		
(catering assistant, blue-collar worker)	14	7.9
Occupation possibly with completed apprenticeship		
(gardener)	17	9.6
Lower-middle-class occupation (child care)	8	4.5
Occupation not specified	38	21.3
Total	178	100%

TABLE 31.

Supplementary Survey: Period of Time between the Registration of the Child for Adoption and Adoption Care and the Age of the Child When Adopted

Age of child	PLACEMENT									
	IN THE SAME YEAR		ONE YEAR LATER		TWO YEARS LATER		TOTAL	
	Absolute	%	Absolute	%	Absolute	%	Absolute	%
Up to 1 month old	30	90.9	3	9.1	0	0	33	100
Older than 1 month and up to 6 months old	36	70.6	15	29.4	0	0	51	100
Older than 6 months and up to 12 months old	12	(66.7)	6	(33.3)	0	(0)	18	100
Older than 1 and up to the age of 2 years	19	59.4	11	34.4	2	6.3	32	100
Older than 2 and up to the age of 4 years	15	(57.7)	9	(34.6)	2	(7.7)	26	100
Older than 4 years	6	(37.4)	9	(56.3)	1	(6.3)	16	100
Total	118		53		5		176	

Chi^2 = 32.78224; degree of freedom = 15; p = 0.005.

TALE 32.

Study Sample: Year of Adoption Application

Year	Number
1966–1969	4
1970–1973	8
1974 and 1975	9
1976	6
1977	3
1978	0
	30[1]

[1]Excluded are those cases in which the adopted child was initially a foster child, in which parents asked the agencies to place a child they already knew, or in which placement was via Terre des Hommes.

TABLE 33.

Comparision between Study Sample and Supplementary Survey: Age of Child at the Beginning of Adoption Care for Applicant Year 1976 and in the Study Sample

	AGE OF CHILD AT THE BEGINNING OF ADOPTION CARE			
	APPLICANTS 1976		STUDY SAMPLE	
	Absolute	%	Absolute	%
Up to 10 days old	26	13.8	6	16.1
Older than 10 days and up to 1 month old	7	3.7	0	0
Older than 1 and up to 2 months old	12	6.4	0	0
Older than 2 and up to 4 months old	25	13.3	8	21.6
Older than 4 and up to 6 months old	13	6.9	7	18.9
Older than 6 and up to 9 months old	8	4.2	4	11.0
Older than 9 months and up to the age of 1 year	10	5.3	1	2.7
Older than 1 and up to the age of 2 years	32	17.0	2	5.4
Older than 2 and up to the age of 4 years	27	14.6	2	5.4
Older than 4 and up to the age of 6 years	7	3.7	7	18.9
Older than 6 and up to the age of 8 years	5	2.6	—	—
Older than 8 years	4	2.1	—	—
No age specified	12	6.4	—	—
Total	188	100%	37	100%

TABLE 34.
Comparison between Sample and Supplementary Survey: Class Membership of Supplementary Survey Applicants with Adoption Care Authorization in Hamburg and Class Membership in the Study Sample

	CLASS MEMBERSHIP			
	APPLICANTS 1976		SAMPLE	
	Absolute	%	Absolute	%
Upper class	0	0	0	(0)
Upper middle class	9	5.1	0	(0)
Upper to middle middle class	39	21.9	7	(23)
Middle middle class	38	21.3	16	(54)
Middle to lower middle class (list entry "Kaufmann")	19	10.7	—	—
Lower middle class	49	27.5	6	(20)
Lower class	23	12.9	1	(3)
No specification	1	0.6	0	(0)
Total	178	100%	30	100%

TABLE 35.
Study Sample: Correlation between Class Membership and the Determination of the "Value" of the Child

Class membership of applicant	Number of cases	Mean	Standard deviation
Upper (to middle) middle class	9	−3.66	2.90
Middle middle class	14	−6.5	4.67
Lower middle class	6	−9.16	7.33
Lower class	1	—	—
Other (foster child, parents knew child before, Terre des Hommes)	7	—	—
Total	37		

Annex: Index of the Degree of (Under)Privilegedness	Score

1. Age
   - Clinic adoption — 0
   - Older than 10 days and up to 4 months old — −1
   - Older than 4 and up to 6 months old — −2
   - Older than 6 months and up to the age of 1 year — −3
   - Older than 1 and up to the age of 2 years — −4
   - Older than 2 and up to the age of 3 years — −5
   - Older than 3 years — −6
2. Level of physical development
   - Good — 0
   - Medium — −2
   - Poor — −4
3. Level of mental/psychological development
   - Good — 0
   - Medium — −1
   - Poor — −2

   In accordance with the score for the attributive dimension of age the scores here are weighted in line with the formula $\frac{3 - \text{age}}{3}$. ___ level of mental/psychological development.
4. Color of skin
   - White-skinned — 0
   - Somewhat darker (either father or mother German) — −1
   - Somewhat darker (different race) — −3
   - Dark-skinned = Negroid — −6
5. Background, including the arrangements for the relinquishment of the child for adoption
   - Middle class, voluntary relinquishment — 0
   - Lower class, voluntary relinquishment, and "not specified" — −1
   - Lower class, delayed or compulsory relinquishment — −2

TABLE 36.
Sample: Birth Status of Child and Age of Child When Adopted

	BIRTH STATUS			
Age	Born out of wedlock	Born in wedlock	Officially registered as born in wedlock	No specification	Total
Up to 1 month old	3	1	—	2	6
Older than 1 month and up to 6 months old	8	1	3	3	15
Older than 6 months and up to the age of 1 year	5	—	—	—	5
Older than 1 and up to the age of 2 years	2	—	—	—	2
Older than 2 and up to the age of 4 years	1	1	—	—	2
Older than 4 years	2	3	1	1	7
Total	21	6	4	6	37

Bibliography

Arbeitsgruppe Bielefelder Soziologen (eds.): Alltagswissen, Interaktion und gesellschaftliche Wirklichkeit, 2 vols. Reinbek: Rowohlt, 1973.

Arbeitsgruppe Bielefelder Soziologen: Kommunikative Sozialforschung, Munich: Fink Verlag, 1976.

Askin, Jayne, and Oskam, Bob: Search—A Handbook for Adoptees and Birth Parents. New York: Harper & Row, 1982.

Ayck, Thomas, and Stolten, Inge: Kinderlos aus Verantwortung. Reinbek: Rowohlt, 1978.

Beck, Ulrich: Risikogesellschaft. Auf dem Weg in eine andere Moderne. Frankfurt: Suhrkamp, 1986.

Beicht, Wolfgang, Isecke, Helmer, Krings-Huber, Gisela, and Mollenhauer, Klaus: "Familiale Kommunikationsstrukturen—Zwischenbericht einer Untersuchung," in Klaus Hurrelmann (ed.), Sozialisation und Lebenslauf. Reinbek: Rowohlt, 1976, pp. 104–126.

Bell, Daniel: The Coming of Post-Industrial Society. A Venture in Social Forecasting. New York: Basic Books, 1973.

Berger, Peter L., and Luckmann, Thomas: The Social Construction of Reality. Harmondsworth, Middlesex: Penguin, 1967.

Bergmann, Werner: "Das Problem der Zeit in der Soziologie. Ein Literaturüberblick zum Stand der 'zeitsoziologischen' Theorie und Forschung." Kölner Zeitschrift für Soziologie und Sozialpsychologie, vol. 35, no. 3, 1983, pp. 462–504.

Bericht über Bestrebungen und Leistungen der Jugendhilfe—5. Jugendbericht. Bonn: Bonner Universitäts-Buchdruckerei, 1980.

Blandow, Jürgen: Rollendiskrepanzen in der Pflegefamilie—Analyse einer sozialpädagogischen Institution. Munich: Juventa Verlag, 1972.

Blumer, Herbert: Symbolic Interactionism. Prospective and Method. Englewood Cliffs, New Jersey: Prentice-Hall, 1969, pp. 1–60.

Bohman, Michael: Adopted Children and Their Families: A Follow-Up Study of Adopted Children, Their Background, Environment and Adjustment. Stockholm: Proprius, 1970.

Bonham, Gordon Scott: "Who Adopts: The Relationship of Adoption and Social-Demographic Characteristics of Women." Journal of Marriage and the Family, vol. 39, no. 2, 1977, pp. 295–306.

Borgman, Robert: "Antecedents and Consequences of Parental Rights Termination for Abused and Neglected Children." Child Welfare, vol. 60, no. 6, 1981, pp. 391–404.

Bowlby, J.: Attachment, vol. 1: Attachment and Loss. New York: Basic Books, 1969.

Bowlby, J.: Attachment, vol. 2: Separation, Anxiety and Anger. New York: Basic Books, 1973.

Brusten, Manfred and Hurrelmann, Klaus: Abweichendes Verhalten in der Schule. Munich: Juventa Verlag, 1973.

Bundesminister für Jugend, Familie und Gesundheit (ed.): Zweiter Familienbericht. Bonn: Verlag Deutsches Jugendinstitut, 1975.

Bundesminister Für Jugend, Familie und Gesundheit (ed.): Fuenfter Jugendbericht. Bonn: Universitäts-Buchdruckerei, 1980.

"Chance für kinderlose Ehepaare." Die Welt, no. 240, Oct. 4, 1980.

Chodorow, Nancy: The Reproduction of Mothering, Psychoanalysis and the Sociology of Gender. Berkeley: University of California Press, 1978.

Cicourel, Aaron V.: Cognitive Sociology. Language and Meaning in Social Interaction. London: Coz & Wyman, 1973.

Claessens, Dieter: Familie und Wertsystem. Berlin: Duncker & Humblot, 1967.

Daly, Kerry: "Reshaped Parenthood Identity. The Transition to Adoptive Parenthood." Journal of Contemporary Ethnography, vol. 17, no. 1, 1988, pp. 40–66.

Den Bandt, Marie-Louise: Sex-Role—Socialization and Voluntary Childlessness in the Netherlands. Manuscript for the 17th International Seminar of the Committee on Family Research of the International Sociological Association in Helsinki, 1979.

Deutsch, Helene: The Psychology of Women, vol. 2: Motherhood. New York: Grune & Stratton, 1945.

Douglas, Mary: Natural Symbols. Explorations in Cosmology. London: Barrie & Rockliff, 1970.

Eckert, Roland: "Geschlechtsrollen im Wandel gesellschaftlicher Arbeitsteilung," in Roland Eckert (ed.), Geschlechtsrollen und Arbeitsteilung—Mann und Frau in sozialer Sicht. Munich: Beck Verlag, 1979, pp. 234–275.

Erikson, Erik: Identity and the Life Cycle. New York: International Universities Press, 1959.

Erikson, Erik: Life History and the Historical Moment: Diverse Presentations. New York: Norton, 1975.

Fabe, Marilyn, and Wikler, Norma: Up Against the Clock—Career Women Speak on the Choice to Have Children. New York: Random House, 1979.

Fagerhaugh, Shizuko, and Strauss, Anselm: Politics of Pain Management: Staff–Patient Interaction. Menlo Park: Addison-Wesley, 1977.

Fischer, Wolfram, and Kohli, Martin: "Biographieforschung," in Wolfgang Voges (ed.), Methoden der Biographie- und Lebenslaufforschung. Opladen: Leske & Budrich, 1987, pp. 25–49.

Flavell, Jean H.: Cognitive Development. Englewood Cliffs, New Jersey: Prentice-Hall, 1977.

Flint, Betty Margaret: The Child and the Institution: A Study of Deprivation and Recovery. Toronto: University of Toronto Press, 1966.

Flint, Betty Margaret: New Hope for Deprived Children. Toronto: University of Toronto Press, 1978.

Franck, Barbara: "Männer? Ex und hopp!" Die Zeit, no. 37, September 4, 1981.

Garfinkel, Harold: Studies in Ethnomethodology. Englewood Cliffs, New Jersey: Prentice-Hall, 1967.

Gartner, Alan, and Riessman, Frank: The Service Society and the Consumer Vanguard. New York: Harper & Row, 1974.

Gehlen, Arnold: Urmensch und Spätkultur. Bonn: Athenäum-Verlag, 1956.

Glaser, Barney G., and Strauss, Anselm L.: Awareness of Dying. Chicago: Aldine, 1965.

Glaser, Barney G., and Strauss, Anselm L.: Status Passage. London: Routledge & Paul, 1971.

Glaser, Barney G., and Strauss, Anselm L.: The Discovery of Grounded Theory: Strategies for Qualitative Research. Chicago: Aldine, 1974.

Goffman, Erving: The Presentation of Self in Everyday Life. Garden City, New York: Doubleday, 1959.

Goffman, Erving: Stigma. Notes on the Management of Spoiled Identity. Englewood Cliffs, New Jersey: Prentice-Hall, 1963.

Goffman, Erving: Strategic Interaction. Philadelphia: University of Pennsylvania Press, 1969.

Goffman, Erving: Relations in Public. Microstudies of the Public Order. New York: Basic Books, 1971.

Goffman, Erving: Frame Analysis. An Essay on the Organization of Experience. Cambridge: Harvard University Press, 1974.

Goldstein, Joseph, Freud, Anna, and Solnit, Albert J.: Beyond the Best Interests of the Child. New York: Free Press, 1973.

Goode, William: "Illegitimacy, Anomie, and Cultural Penetration," in William Goode (ed.), Readings on the Family and Society. Englewood Cliffs, New Jersey: Prentice-Hall, 1964, pp. 38–55.

Gouldner, Helen P.: Children of the Laboratory. New Brunswick, New Jersey: Transaction, 1967, pp. 13–19.

Grathoff, Richard: "Über Typik und Normalität im alltäglichen Milieu," in Walter M. Sprondel and Richard Grathoff (eds.), Alfred Schütz und die Idee des Alltags in den Sozialwissenschaften. Stuttgart: Ferdinand Enke, 1979, pp. 89–107.

Gripp, Helga: Problemfeld Ehe—eine Fallanalyse. Stuttgart: Klett-Cotta, 1979.

Grunow, Dieter: Alltagskontakte mit der Verwaltung (vol. 3 of the series) Bürger und Verwaltung. Frankfurt: Campus, 1978.

Gühlich, Elisabeth: Konventionelle Muster und kommunikative Funktion von Alltagserzählungen, in Konrad Ehlich (ed.), Erzählen im Alltag. Frankfurt: Suhrkamp, 1980, pp. 335–384.

Hagemann-White, Carol: Frauenbewegung und Psychoanalyse. Basel: Stroemfeld/Roter Stern, 1979.

Haimes, Erica, and Timms, Noel: Adoption, Identity and Social Policy. The Search for Distant Relatives. Aldershot, Hants.: Gower, 1985.

Hesseler, Michael: "Die Institution der Adoption und die Diskussion einer Sozialisationsperspektive." Soziale Welt, vol. 31, 1980, pp. 230–256.

Hildenbrand, Bruno: Alltag und Krankheit—Ethnographie einer Familie. Stuttgart: Klett-Cotta, 1983.

Hoffmann-Riem, Christa: "Die Sozialforschung einer interpretativen Soziologie—der Datengewinn." Kölner Zeitschrift für Soziologie und Sozialpsychologie, vol. 32, no. 2, 1980, pp. 339–372.

Hoffmann-Riem, Christa: "Die Verarbeitung bedrohter Normalität in der Adoption," in Joachim Matthes (ed.), Lebenswelt und soziale Probleme, Verhandlungen des 20. Deutschen Soziologentages zu Bremen 1980. Frankfurt: Campus, 1981, pp. 369–382.

Hoffmann-Riem, Christa: "Vorwort," in Arthur D. Sorosky, Annette Baran, and Reuben Pannor: Zueinander kommen—miteinander leben. Eltern und Kinder erzählen. Reinbek: Rowohlt, 1982.

Huth, Wolfgang: "Psychische Störungen bei Adoptivkindern—Eine Übersicht über den Stand der klinischen Forschung." Zeitschrift für klinische Psychologie und Psychotherapie, vol. 26, no. 3, 1978, pp. 256–270.

Huth, Wolfgang: Adoption und Familiendynamik. Frankfurt: Fachbuchhandlung für Psychologie, 1983.

Jaffee, Benson: Adoption Outcome: A Two-Generation View. Child Welfare, vol. 53, 1974, pp. 211–224.

Jaffee, Benson, and Fanshel, David: How They Fared in Adoption: A Follow-Up Study. New York: Campus, 1970.

Jasinsky, Michael: Untersuchung zur Bewährung von Adoptionen. Unpublished report of the Hamburger Jugendamt, 1980.

Joas, Hans: G. H. Mead: A Contemporary Re-examination of His Thought. Cambridge, England: Polity Press, 1985.

Kagan, Jerome, Kearsley, Richard B., and Zelazo, Philip R.: Infancy: Its Place in Human Development. Cambridge: Harvard University Press, 1980.

Kallmeyer, Werner, and Schütze, Fritz: Konversationsanalyse. Studium der Linguistik, 1976, no. 1, pp. 1–28.

Kallmeyer, Werner, and Schuetze, Fritz: "Zur Konstitution von Kommunikationsschemata der Sachverhaltsdarstellung," in Dirk Wegner (ed.), Gesprächsanalysen. Hamburg: Helmut Buske Verlag, 1977, pp. 159–274.

Kaufmann, Franz-Xaver: "Familie und Modernität," in: Kurt Lüscher, Franz Schultheis, and Michael Wehrspaun (eds.), Die "postmoderne" Familie. Constance: Universitätsverlag, 1988, pp. 391–415.

Kirk, David: Shared Fate. London: The Free Press, 1964 (rev. ed. 1984).

Kirk, David: Adoptive Kinship: A Modern Institution in Need of Reform. Toronto: Butterworths, 1981.

Kirk, David: Intergrating the Stranger: A Problem in Modern Adoption But Not in Ancient Greece and Rome. Paper prepared for the International Conference on Adoption, Athens, July 6–9, 1987.

Kleining, Gerhard, and Moore, Harriet: "Soziale Selbsteinstufung." Kölner Zeitschrift für Soziologie und Sozialpsychologie, vol. 20, no. 3, 1968, pp. 502–552.

Kleining, Gerhard: "Soziale Mobilität in der Bundesrepublik Deutschland." Kölner Zeitschrift für Soziologie und Sozialpsychologie, vol. 27, no. 1, 1975, pp. 97–121.

König, René: Materialien zur Soziologie der Familie. Bern: Francke, 1946.

König, René: "Familiensoziologie," in René König (ed.), Handbuch der Empirischen Sozialforschung, vol. 2. Stuttgart: Ferdinand Enke Verlag, 1969, pp. 172–305.

Krappmann, Lothar: Soziologische Dimensionen der Identität. Stuttgart: Ernst Klett Verlag, 1973.

Labov, William, and Waletzky, Joshua: "Narrative Analysis: Oral Versions of Personal Experience," in J. H. MacNeish (ed.), Essays on the Verbal and Visual Arts. Proceedings of the 1966 Annual Spring Meeting. Seattle: University of Washington Press, 1967, pp. 12–44.

Leisi, Ernst: Paar und Sprache. Linguistische Aspekte der Zweierbeziehung. Heidelberg: Quelle and Meyer, 1978.

Le Masters, E. E.: "Parenthood as Crisis," in Marvin B. Sussman (ed.), Sourcebook in Marriage and the Family. Boston: Houghton Mifflin, 1963, pp. 194–198.

Levi-Strauss, Claude: Das wilde Denken (Original: La pensée sauvage, 1962). Frankfurt: Luchterhand, 1968.

Levy, René: Der Lebenslauf als Statusbiographie—Die weibliche Normalbiographie in makrosoziologischer Perspektive. Stuttgart: Ferdinand Enke Verlag, 1977.

Liebke, Annegret: Die Erfahrungsstrukturen Adoptierter—Der Aufbau der Beziehung zwischen Adoptierten und Adoptiveltern. Unpublished thesis. University of Hamburg, 1981.

Lifton, Betty Jean: Twice Born—Memoirs of an Adopted Daughter. New York: McGraw-Hill, 1975.

Lifton, Betty Jean: Lost and Found—The Adoption Experience. New York: Dial, 1979.

Lindesmith, Alfred E. and Strauss, Anselm L.: Social Psychology. New York: Holt, Rinehart and Winston, 1968.

Lindholm, Bryan W., and Touliators, John: "Psychological Adjustment of Adopted and Non-Adopted Children." Psychological Reports, vol. 46, 1980, pp. 307–310.

Luckmann, Thomas: "Personal Identity as an Evolutionary and Historical Problem," in H. Aschoff, M. von Cranach, and R. Lepenies (eds.), Human Ethology—Claims and Limits of a New Discipline. Cambridge: Cambridge University Press, 1979, pp. 56–74.

Luescher, Kurt: "Die Entwicklung der Rolle des Kindes," in Klaus Hurrelmann (ed.), Sozialisation und Lebenslauf. Reinbek: Rowohlt, 1976, pp. 129–150.

Luescher, Kurt, Schultheis, Franz and Wehrspaun, Michael (eds.), Die "postmoderne" Familie. Familiale Strategien und Familienpolitik in einer Übergangszeit. Constance: Universitätsverlag, 1988.

Luhmann, Niklas: Legitimation durch Verfahren. Neuwied: Luchterhand, 1969.

Luhmann, Niklas: Gesellschaftsstruktur und Semantik, Studien zur Wissenssoziologie der modernen Gesellschaft, vol. 1. Frankfurt: Suhrkamp, 1980.

Malinowski, Bronislaw: Magic, Science and Religion and Other Essays. Garden City, New York: Doubleday, 1948.

Martin, Cynthia D.: Beating the Adoption Game. La Jolla: Oak Tree Publications, 1980.

Matthes, Joachim (ed.): Lebenswelt und soziale Probleme, Verhandlungen des 20. Deutschen Soziologentages zu Bremen 1980. Frankfurt: Campus, 1981.

Matthes, Joachim: "Religion als Thema komparativer Sozialforschung—Erfahrungen mit einem Forschungsprojekt zum religiösen Wandel in einer Entwicklungsgesellschaft (Singapore). Soziale Welt, vol. 34, no. 1, 1983, pp. 3–24.

Matthes, Joachim, Pfeifenberger, Arno, and Stosberg, Manfred (eds.): Biographie in handlungswissenschaftlicher Perspektive. Nuremberg: Nürnberger Forschungsvereinigung, 1981.

Maurer, Ralph, Cardoret, Remi J., and Cain, Colleen: "Cluster Analysis of Childhood Temperament Data on Adoptees." American Journal of Orthopsychiatry, vol. 50, no. 3, 1980, pp. 522–534.

Mester, Horst: "Psychiatrische Probleme der Adoption," in U. U. Peters (ed.), Kindlers Psychologie des 20. Jahrhunderts, vol. 10. Zurich: Beltz, 1980, pp. 267–273.

Mitscherlich, Alexander: Auf dem Wege zur vaterlosen Gesellschaft. Munich: Piper, 1965.

Mollenhauer, Klaus (ed.): "Soziale Bedingungen familialer Kommunikation," in Materialien zum Zweiten Familienbericht der Bundesregierung. Munich: Deutsches Jugendinstitut Verlag, 1975.

Napp-Peters, Anneke: Adoption. Das alleinstehende Kind und seine Familien, Geschichte, Rechtsprobleme und Vermittlungspraxis. Neuwied: Luchterhand, 1978.

Nave-Herz, Rosemarie (ed.): Wandel und Kontinuität der Familie in der Bundesrepublik Deutschland. Stuttgart: Enke Verlag, 1988.

Neander, Joachim: "Frei, aufgeklärt und emanzipiert eilen die Deutschen dem Aussterben entgegen." Die Welt, no. 76, March 3, 1979.

Neidhardt, Friedhelm: "Strukturbedingungen und Probleme familialer Sozialisation," in Dieter Claessens and Petra Milhoffer (eds.), Familiensoziologie—ein Reader als Einführung. Frankfurt: Athenäum Verlag, 1973, pp. 205–232.

Neidhardt, Friedhelm (ed.): Frühkindliche Sozialisation. Stuttgart: Ferdinand Enke Verlag, 1975.

Neidhardt, Friedhelm: "Systemtheoretische Analysen zur Sozialisationsfähigkeit der Familie," in Friedhelm Neidhardt (ed.), Frühkindliche Sozialisation. Stuttgart: Ferdinand Enke Verlag, 1975, pp. 162–187.

Parke, Ross D.: Fathers. Cambridge: Harvard University Press, 1981.

Portmann, Adolf: Die Biologie und das neue Menschenbild. Bern: Lang, 1972.

Pross, Helge (ed.): Familie—wohin? Reinbek: Rowohlt, 1979.

Rainwater, Lee, Coleman, Richard P., and Handel, Gerald: Workingman's Wife: Her Personality, World and Life Style. New York: Oceana, 1959.

Rainwater, Lee, and Weinstine, Carol K.: And the Poor Get Children. Chicago: Quadrangle, 1960.

Rathbun, C., DiVirgilio, L., and Waldfogel, S.: "The Restitutive Process in Children Following Radical Separation from Family and Culture." American Journal of Orthopsychiatry, vol. 28, 1959, pp. 408–415.

Rehbein, Jochen: "Sequentielles Erzählen—Erzählstrukturen von Immigranten bei Sozialberatungen in England," in Konrad Ehlich (ed.), Erzählen im Alltag. Frankfurt: Suhrkamp, 1980, pp. 64–108.

Richter, Horst-Eberhard: Eltern, Kind und Neurose. Stuttgart: Ernst Klett Verlag, 1967.

Riemann, Gerhard: Stigma, formelle soziale Kontrolle, das Leben mit den anderen—eine empirische Untersuchung zu drei Gegenstandsbereichen des Alltagswissens von Obdachlosen. Unpublished thesis. University of Bielefeld, 1977.

Riemann, Gerhard: "Eine empirische Erfassung von Alltagswissen: Ein Beispiel aus der Obdachlosenforschung," in Hans Georg Soeffner (ed.), Interpretative Verfahren in den Sozial- und Textwissenschaften. Stuttgart: J. B. Metzler, 1979, pp. 127–129.

Riemann, Gerhard: Das Fremdwerden der eigenen Biographie. Narrative Interviews mit psychiatrischen Patienten. Munich: Fink Verlag, 1987.

Roth-Stielow, Klaus: Adoptionsgesetz, Adoptionsvermittlungsgesetz. Stuttgart: Kohlhammer Verlag, 1976.

Sacks, Harvey: "Das Erzählen von Geschichten innerhalb von Unterhaltungen.'' Kölner Zeitschrift für Soziologie und Sozialpsychologie, Sonderheft 15: Zur Soziologie der Sprache, 1971, pp. 307–314.

Sacks, Harvey: "On the Analyzability of Stories by Children," in John J. Gumperz and Dell Hymes (eds.), Directions in Sociolinguistics. New York: Holt, Rinehart and Winston, 1972, pp. 325–345.

Sacks, Harvey, Jefferson, Gail, and Schegloff, Emmanual: "A Simplest Systematics for the Organization of Turn-Taking for Conversation." Language, vol. 50, 1974, pp. 696–735.

Scarr, Sandra, Webber, Patricia L., Weinberg, Richard A., and Wittig, Michele A.: "Personality Resemblance Among Adolescents and Their Parents in Biologically Related and Adoptive Families." Journal of Personality and Social Psychology, vol. 40, no. 5, 1981, pp. 885–898.

Schaffer, Rudolph: Mothering. Cambridge: Harvard University Press, 1980.

Schechter, Marshall D.: "About Adoptive Parents," in E. James Anthony and Therese Benedek (eds.), Parenthood—Its Psychology and Psychopathology. Boston: Little Brown, 1970, pp. 353–371.

Schneider, David M.: American Kinship—A Cultural Account. Chicago: University of Chicago Press, 1980.

Schuetz, Alfred: Collected Papers, vols. I and II. The Hague: Martimus Nijhoff, 1971 and 1972.

Schuetz, Alfred, and Luckmann, Thomas: The Structures of the Life-World. London: Heinemann Educational Books, 1974.

Schuetze, Fritz: "Zur Hervorlockung und Analyse von Erzählungen thematisch relevanter Geschichten im Rahmen soziologischer Feldforschung," in Arbeitsgruppe Bielefelder Soziologen, Kommunikative Sozialforschung. Munich: Fink Verlag, 1976, pp. 159–260.

Schuetze, Fritz: "Zur soziologischen und linguistischen Analyse von Erzählungen. Internationales Jahrbuch für Wissens- und Religionssoziologie, vol. 10, 1976, pp. 7–41.

Schuetze, Fritz: "Die Technik des narrativen Interviews in Interaktionsfeldstudien—dargestellt an einem Projekt zur Erforschung von kommunalen Machtstrukturen," in Arbeitsberichte und Forschungsmaterialien der Fakultät für Soziologie der Universität Bielefeld, 1977, no. 1, pp. 1–62.

Schuetze, Fritz: "Strategische Interaktion im Verwaltungsgericht. Eine soziolinguistische Analyse zum Kommunikationsverlauf im Verfahren zur Anerkennung als Wehrdienstverweigerer," in Winfried Hassemer, Wolfgang Hoffmann-Riem, and Manfred Weiss (eds.), Interaktion vor Gericht. Baden-Baden: Nomos, 1978, pp. 19–100.

Schuetze, Fritz: "Prozess-Strukturen des Lebensablaufs," in Joachim Matthes, Arno Pfeifenberger, and Manfred Stosberg (eds.), Biographie in handlungswissenschaftlicher Perspektive. Nuremberg: Verlag der Nürnberger Forschungsvereinigung, 1981, pp. 67–156.

Schuetze, Fritz: "Narrative Repräsentationen kollektiver Schicksalsbetroffenheit," in Eberhard Lämmert (ed.), Erzählforschung. Stuttgart: J. B. Metzler, 1982, pp. 568–590.

Schuetze, Fritz, Meinefeld, Werner, Springer, Werner, and Weymann, Ansgar: "Grundlagentheoretische Voraussetzungen methodisch kontrollierten Fremdverstehens," in Arbeitsgruppe Bielefelder Soziologen (ed.), Alltagswissen, Interaktion und gesellschaftliche Wirklichkeit, vol. II. Reinbek: Rowohlt, 1973, pp. 433–495.

Schuetze, Yvonne: Innerfamiliale Kommunikation und kindliche Psyche. Berlin: Max Planck Institute, 1978.

Schuetze, Yvonne: "Zur Veränderung im Eltern-Kind-Verhältnis seit der Nachkriegszeit," in Rosemarie Nave-Herz (ed.), Wandel und Kontinuität der Familie in der Bundesrepublik Deutschland. Stuttgart: Enke Verlag, 1988, pp. 95–114.

Seglow, Jean, Kellner-Pringle, Mia, and Wedge, Peter: Growing Up Adopted. Windsor: National Foundation for Educational Research in England and Wales, 1972.

Shawyer, Joss: Death by Adoption. Auckland: Cicada, 1979.

Shorter, Edward: The Making of the Modern Family. New York: Basic Books, 1975.

Simitis, Spiros, Rosenkötter, Lutz, Vogel, Rudolf, Boost-Muss, Barbara, et al.: Kindeswohl. Eine interdisziplinäre Untersuchung über seine Verwirklichung in der vormundschaftsgerichtlichen Praxis. Frankfurt: Suhrkamp, 1979.

Simon, Nathan M., and Senturia, Audrey G.: "Adoption and Psychiatric Illness." American Journal of Psychiatry, 1966, pp. 858–868.

Smith, Carole R.: Adoption and Fostering: Why and How. London: MacMillan, 1984.

Soeffner, Hans-Georg (ed.): Interpretative Verfahren in den Sozial- und Textwissenschaften. Stuttgart: J. B. Metzler, 1979.

Sorosky, Arthur D., Baran, Annette, and Pannor, Reuben: The Adoption Triangle. Garden City, New York: Anchor, 1979.

Speck, Petra: Die Erfahrungsstruktur Adoptierter—Der Adoptierte zwischen leiblichen Eltern und Adoptiveltern. Unpublished thesis. University of Hamburg, 1981.

Spitz, René: The First Year of Life: A Psychoanalytic Study of Normal and Deviant Development of Object Relations. New York: International Universities Press, 1965.

Sprondel, Walter M., and Grathoff, Richard (eds.): Alfred Schuetz und die Idee des Alltags in den Sozialwissenschaften. Stuttgart: Enke Verlag, 1979.

Stempel, Wolf-Dieter: "Alltagsfiktion," in Konrad Ehlich (ed.), Erzählen im Alltag. Frankfurt: Suhrkamp, 1980, pp. 385–402.

Stern, Daniel: The First Relationship—Infant and Mother. Cambridge: Harvard University Press, 1980.

Strauss, Anselm: Mirrors and Masks. The Search for Identity. Glencoe, Illinois: The Free Press, 1959.

Strauss, Anselm: Negotiations—Varieties, Contexts, Processes and Social Order. San Francisco: Jossey-Bass, 1978.

Strauss, Anselm, Fagerhaugh, Shizuko, Suczek, Barbara, and Wiener, Carolyn: Social Organization of Medical Work. Chicago: University of Chicago Press, 1985.

Strauss, Anselm, and Glaser, Barney: Anguish: A Case Study of a Dying Trajectory. San Francisco: Mill Valley, 1970.

Sussman, Marvin B.: "The Isolated Nuclear Family: Fact or Fiction?" in Marvin B. Sussman (ed.), Sourcebook in Marriage and the Family. Boston: Houghton Mifflin, 1963, pp. 48–53.

Swientek, Christine: Ich habe mein Kind fortgegeben—Die dunkle Seite der Adoption. Reinbek: Rowohlt, 1982.

Swientek, Christine: Die "abgebende Mutter" im Adoptionsverfahren. Bielefeld: Kleine Verlag, 1986.

Szemkus, Karol: "Geburt des ersten Kindes und Übernahme der Elternrolle," in Hans Braun and Ute Leitner (eds.), Problem Familie—Familienprobleme. Frankfurt: Campus, 1976, pp. 51–61.

Tizard, Barbara, and Rees, Judith: "The Effect of Early Institutional Rearing on the Behaviour Problems and Affectional Relationship of Four-Year-Old Children." Journal of Child Psychology and Psychiatry, vol. 16, 1975, pp. 61–73.

Turner, Ralph H.: "Role-taking: Process versus Conformity," in Arnold M. Rose (ed.), Human Behavior and Social Process. London: Routledge & Kegan Paul, 1962, pp. 20–40.

Tyrell, Hartmann: Die Familie als "Urinstitution": Neuerliche spekulative Überlegungen zu einer alten Frage. Kölner Zeitschrift für Soziologie und Sozialpsychologie, vol. 30, no. 4, 1978, pp. 611–651.

Tyrell, Hartmann: "Familie und gesellschaftliche Differenzierung," in Helge Pross (ed.), Familie—wohin?, Reinbek: Rowohlt, 1979, pp. 13–77.

Tyrell, Hartmann: "Soziologische Überlegungen zur Struktur des bürgerlichen Typus der Mutter-Kind-Beziehung," in Joachim Matthes (ed.), Lebenswelt und soziale Probleme, Verhandlungen des 20. Deutschen Soziologentages zu Bremen 1980. Frankfurt: Campus, 1981, pp. 417–428.

United Nations: Declaration on Social and Legal Principles Relating to the Protection and Welfare of Children, with Special Reference to Foster Placement and Adoption Nationally and Internationally, Dec. 1986.

Urdze, Andrejs, and Rerrich, Maria S.: Frauenalltag und Kinderwunsch—Motive von Müttern für oder gegen ein zweites Kind. Frankfurt: Campus, 1981.

Wahl, Klaus: "Familienbildung und -beratung in der Bundesrepublik Deutschland," in Schriftenreihe des Bundesministers für Jugend, Familie und Gesundheit, vol. 8. Stuttgart: Kohlhammer, 1975.

Wahl, Klaus, Tüllmann, Greta, Honig, Michael-Sebastian, and Gravenhorst, Lerke: Familien sind anders! Reinbek: Rowohlt, 1980.

Ward, Margaret: "Parental Bonding in Older-Child Adoptions." Child Welfare, vol. 60, no. 1, 1981, pp. 24–34.

Watzlawick, Paul, Beavin, Janet H., and Jackson, Don D.: Pragmatics of Human Communication: A Study of Interactional Patterns, Pathologies and Paradoxes. London: Faber and Faber, 1968.

Weingarten, Elmar, and Sack, Fritz: "Ethnomethodologie. Die methodische Konstruktion der Realität," in Elmar Weingarten, Fritz Sack, and Jim Schenkein (eds.), Ethnomethodologie. Beiträge zu einer Soziologie des Alltagshandeln. Frankfurt: Suhrkamp, 1976, pp. 7–27.

Wilson, Thomas: "Conceptions of Interaction and Forms of Sociological Explanation." American Sociological Review, 1970, pp. 697–710.

Winer, B. J.: Statistical Principles in Experimental Design. New York: McGraw-Hill, 1962.

Witt, Monika: Die Erfahrungsstrukturen von Müttern, die ein Kind zur Adoption freigegeben haben. Unpublished thesis. University of Hamburg, 1982.

Yankelovich, Daniel: New Rules—Searching for Self-Fulfillment in a World Turned Upside Down. Toronto: Bantam, 1982.

Zahlmann-Willenbacher, Barbara: "Kritik des funktionalistischen Konzepts geschlechtstypischer Arbeitsteilung," in Roland Eckert (ed.), Geschlechtsrollen und Arbeitsteilung—Mann und Frau in soziologischer Sicht. Munich: Beck Verlag, 1979, pp. 60–77.

Zelditch, Morris: "Role Differentiation in the Nuclear Family: A Comparative Study," in Talcott Parsons and Robert Bales (eds.), Family, Socialization and Interaction Process. Glencoe, Illinois: The Free Press, 1960, pp. 307–352.

Zimmerman, Don H., and Pollner, Melvin: "The Everyday World as a Phenomenon," in Jack D. Douglas (ed.), Understanding Everyday Life: Toward the Reconstruction of Sociological Knowledge. Chicago: Aldine, 1970, pp. 80–103.

Name Index

Ashoff, M., 145
Askin, J., 215
Ayck, T., 15, 92

Bales, R. F., 145
den Bandt, M., 92
Baran, A., 90, 91, 92, 144, 212, 213, 214, 215
Bar-Hillel, Y., 97, 213
Beavin, J. H., 97, 213
Beck, U., 254
Beicht, W., 213
Bell, D., 254
Berger, P. L., 15, 178, 209, 213
Bergmann, W., 248
Blandow, J., 216
Blumer, H., 94, 211
Bohman, M., 211
Bonham, G. S., 99
Borgman, R., 211
Bowlby, J., 209
Braun, H., 97, 210
Brusten, M., 96

Cadoret, R., 211
Cain, C., 211
Chadorow, N., 14
Cicourel, A. V., 145, 226, 248
Claessens, D., 77, 96, 144, 209
Coleman, R. P., 98
Cooley, C. H., 248
von Cranach, M., 145

Daly, K., 15
Deutsch, H., 14, 15, 16, 144, 215, 216, 248, 249
DiVirgilio, L., 209

Douglas, J. D., 90
Douglas, M., 160, 210

Eckert, R., 144, 145
Ehlich, K., 208, 264
Erikson, E., 209, 210, 211, 214

Fabe, M., 15
Fagerhaugh, S. Y., 95, 211, 214
Fanshel, D., 211, 212
Fischer, W., 254
Flavell, J. H., 210, 248
Flint, B. M., 209, 211
Franck, B., 92
Freud, A., 209, 210, 211
Freud, S., 248

Garfinkel, H., 15, 89, 211, 213, 265
Gartner, A., 254
Gehlen, A., 14, 121, 144
Glaser, B., 43, 93, 94, 95, 160, 170, 208, 211, 212, 213, 247, 254
Goldstein, J., 209, 210, 211
Goode, W., 144
Gouldner, H. P., 253
Grathoff, R., 254
Gravenhorst, L., 14, 98
Gripp, H., 265
Grunow, D., 94, 95, 96, 97, 98, 100
Gumperz, J. J., 212
Gühlich, E., 264

Hagemann-White, C., 15
Haimes, E., 215
Handel, G., 98
Hassemer, W., 93
Hesseler, M., 98, 99, 214
Hildenbrand, B., 265

303